Evolution of a Field:
PERSONAL HISTORIES IN CONFLICT RESOLUTION

Published by DRI Press, an imprint of the Dispute Resolution Institute at Mitchell Hamline School of Law

Dispute Resolution Institute
Mitchell Hamline School of Law
875 Summit Ave, St Paul, MN 55015
Tel. (651) 695-7676
© 2020 DRI Press. All rights reserved.
Printed in the United States of America.
Library of Congress Control Number: **2020918154**
ISBN: 978-1-7349562-0-7

Mitchell Hamline School of Law in Saint Paul, Minnesota has been educating lawyers for more than 100 years and remains committed to innovation in responding to the changing legal market. Mitchell Hamline offers a rich curriculum in advocacy and problem solving. The law school's Dispute Resolution Institute, consistently ranked in the top dispute resolution programs by *U.S. News & World Report*, is committed to advancing the theory and practice of conflict resolution, nationally and internationally, through scholarship and applied practice projects. DRI offers more than 30 dispute resolution courses each year in a variety of domestic and international certificate programs. Established in 2009, DRI Press is the scholarship dissemination arm of the Dispute Resolution Institute which brings significant conflict resolution work to a broad audience. For more information on other DRI Press publications, visit http://open.mitchellhamline.edu/dri_press

Evolution of a Field:
Personal Histories in Conflict Resolution

◆

Edited by
Howard Gadlin &
Nancy A. Welsh

DRI Press
Saint Paul, Minnesota

Table of Contents

Introduction

1. Discovering Our Field in Our Stories 1
   Howard Gadlin and Nancy A. Welsh

Conflict Resolution as (Noble) Craft to End Discord

2. Wabi-Sabi 15
   Peter S. Adler

3. How I Found My Groove 35
   Howard Bellman

Conflict Resolution as Forum for Voice and Connection

4. Mediation and My Life: Moments and Movements 55
   Lela Porter Love

5. What Am I Doing Here? Field Notes on Finding My Way to Mediation 75
   Ian Macduff

6. Born to Mediate 93
   Lucy Moore

7. My Passage to ADR 111
   Geetha Ravindra

8. Crosscurrents 131
   Nancy A. Welsh

Conflict Resolution as Creative Exercise

9. Three to Tango: Reflections of a Mediator 151
   Johnston Barkat

10. A Sort of Career 171
    Chris Honeyman

11. We Can Work It Out 193
    Colin Rule

12. *Bashert*: How I Found Dispute Resolution and It Found Me 211
    Andrea Kupfer Schneider

13. Synchronicity, Paradox, and
    Personal Evolution 231
    Thomas J. Stipanowich

CONFLICT RESOLUTION AS BRIDGE TO A SOCIALLY JUST, DEMOCRATIC, AND INCLUSIVE COMMUNITY

14. The View from the Helicopter 253
    Lisa Blomgren Amsler

15. A Conflict Counter-Story: How a Puerto
    Rican Woman Ended Up in a Field
    Dominated by Anglo Men 275
    Jacqueline N. Font-Guzmán

16. The Accidental Ombudsman 295
    Howard Gadlin

17. A Mediator's Path 317
    David Hoffman

18. Finding Joy Through a Mediation Clinic
    and Asian American Identity 337
    Carol Izumi

19. From the Portal to the Path: Finding the
    "Me" in Mediator 359
    Marvin E. Johnson

20. The Road to Becoming a Neutral:
    Working in the Interest of Human Needs 379
    Homer C. La Rue

21. My Life in Community 401
    Bernie Mayer

22. When Should I Be in the Middle? I've
    Looked at Life from Both Sides Now 421
    Carrie Menkel-Meadow

23. Becoming a Peacemaker 445
    Christopher W. Moore

24. Seeking Justice in the Shadow of the Law 467
    Ellen Waldman

ALTERNATIVE FRAMES FOR *EVOLUTION OF A FIELD* ... 487
    ADR Processes 487
    Career Development 489
    Culture 490
    Gateways to the Field 490
    Generations 491
    Institutional Contexts for Conflict Resolution 492

ABOUT THE EDITORS 495

1

Discovering Our Field in Our Stories

By Howard Gadlin and Nancy A. Welsh

———◆———

It's the people who make a field.

This book draws on the thought-provoking, diverse, delightful, sometimes painful, and ultimately beautiful personal histories of some of the thinkers, inventors, influencers, reformers, disrupters, and transformers who have created—and continue to create—the field of conflict resolution. The authors of the essays in this book play a variety of roles: mediator, facilitator, arbitrator, ombuds, academic, system designer, entrepreneur, leader of public or private conflict resolution organization, researcher, advocate for conflict resolution, critic of conflict resolution. They represent the various waves of people who have populated our field, the founders, the institutionalizers, and the leaders of change.

In his chapter, Peter Adler writes, "Stories are ancient and enduring avenues of human exchange and one of the ways we make discoveries. Stories create hypotheses, explain things, and sometimes connect us to each other and older enduring narratives." And so it is with the histories in this book. The narratives of our contributors allow us to understand the conflict resolution field's real, on-the-ground reason for being, the beating heart underlying its principles. We are not necessarily talking about the principles captured in textbooks or ethics codes; we're thinking of the values, aspirations, and characteristics that have inspired people to become involved with the field, stay with it, and even wrestle with it.

We think this book and its personal histories come at an important time, one when the field of conflict resolution is at an inflection point. Conflict resolution is now a recognized discipline, widely institutionalized in law and graduate schools, often introduced to students as early as elementary school, frequently used to resolve legal and other disputes, and regularly enforced by our courts. The founders of the field, people such as Frank Sander, Margaret Shaw, and Roger Fisher, have left this earthly world behind, and other pioneers have retired or are close to retiring.

A next generation awaits, with many who are eager to shape the field's evolution. Our people and communities face new challenges, new causes for conflict, and new reasons to reach resolution of—or at least manage—those conflicts. Technology is an exciting and ubiquitous part of our lives. So this seems an especially opportune time for people who have played key roles in conflict resolution to reflect upon the experiences, goals, mentors, colleagues, and institutions that have informed their careers and guided their contributions.

The approach of this book is unusual for at least two reasons. First, as many of us who have talked with colleagues know, when neutrals describe their work, they generally begin with the stories that parties tell: what fix the parties are in, how they relate to others around them, what brought them to conflict resolution, and what breakthroughs or interventions led to the resolution of their disputes. Neutrals rarely scrutinize their own lives and influences to probe for the underlying values and meaning they convey. Writing for this book required all the contributors—the neutrals, the entrepreneurs, and the academics—to reflect deeply on these matters. This book's approach is also unusual because although we urged each writer to address some core questions and ideas, we gave them free rein to decide what to say and how to say it. The result is a collection of the principles and aspirations that have *actually* guided people within our field, not those that have been *said* to do so. Twenty-three individuals, each in his or her own voice and own way, have all tried to make sense of who they are, what they do, and how and why they do it.

We are indebted, first and foremost, to our contributors, those who have made this book so much more than just curated CVs. They are accomplished and self-reflective individuals, people open to locating their thinking, actions, and choices in the context of their historical epoch as well as their cultural, social, and even familial context.

We find great variety, insight, and wisdom in these 23 stories, but we also acknowledge that no one collection of essays can really do justice to the rich complexity of the conflict resolution field and the diverse experiences of those in it. We are also indebted to those whose stories are not included. Many whose work we respect, who are extremely accomplished and thoughtful, and who easily meet our criteria for inclusion are not represented in this volume. Some declined to participate, perhaps out of modesty or lack of time. Others, including many people from different generations and different areas of conflict resolution, were simply beyond the scope of what was possible for this one volume.

Developing *Evolution of a Field*

People who work in the world of conflict resolution know that each person's story is a way of presenting herself or himself, emphasizing some things, minimizing others, and even omitting aspects of the story that they feel are unimportant or irrelevant or embarrassing. And we know how important it is to build trust and make people comfortable enough to reveal more than what is in their initial telling.

With this in mind, we asked each author to tell their story in their own words but to consider certain questions about their careers, their practice, and the general field of conflict resolution and address these directly or indirectly.[1] We asked our authors to discuss their personal and professional development in a way that revealed what first attracted them to conflict resolution, what pleasures and satisfactions this focus provided and continues to provide, what values and passions it addresses, and how their lives have been transformed by their profession—or not.

We were quickly reminded of something we should have known from our experiences as mediators: questions can get in the way of the storytelling. We were happy to see that the authors did not allow our questions to structure their stories. Instead they scrutinized their lives and influences to probe for the underlying values and meanings.

We encountered some challenges in finding a publisher (some, both trade and academic, rejected the idea flat out, saying, in essence, "there is no market for autobiography"), but we were pleased to find an enthusiastic partner in DRI Press. In addition to producing a print version of the book, DRI Press will make individual chapters available online, at no cost, through its website, https://open.mitchellhamline.edu/dri_press/. We hope that anyone interested in conflict resolution—teacher, student, would-be neutral, idealist committed to the social good—will download these chapters (with appropriate attribution, of course) and distribute them widely. Working with DRI director and professor of law Sharon Press and DRI staff Debra Berghoff and Kitty Atkins has been a joy. We have also benefitted tremendously from the assistance of our gifted copyeditor,

Louisa Williams. We thank Jonah Fritz for his excellent research assistance, particularly with the endnotes and references for these chapters.

While we are acknowledging important contributions to this book, we thank our spouses—Brenda Hanning (for Howard) and Eric Munck (for Nancy). This book would never have happened without their encouragement, support, advice, and careful proofreading.

Organization of the Book

We have noticed that the cover for *Evolution of a Field* bears some resemblance to a Rorschach test. That's appropriate because there are so many different ways to "see" our field. We discussed organizing this book by subject matter (employment/labor, construction, international affairs, etc.) or by area (mediation, arbitration, ombuds, system design, etc.) but ultimately decided to rely on our authors' voices, their narratives, to determine the book's structure. Principles may anchor a field theoretically, but it's the people who actually bring it to life.

So what did we find most significant in attracting, guiding, and sustaining these people in the field of conflict resolution? Not neutrality or confidentiality or self-determination or efficiency—even though these often show up. The attraction to the conflict resolution field is connected to something much more personal.

Repeatedly, our authors wrote about how their engagement in our field was meaningful for them. Across the chapters, four themes emerged, some explicit, others more implicit, and we followed these in organizing the book. Of course, many of our authors referenced multiple themes, sometimes all of them. Here, though, we locate our authors within the themes that stood out most vividly for us when we read and discussed their chapters.

- *Conflict Resolution as (Noble) Craft to End Discord* —Peter S. Adler, Howard Bellman
- *Conflict Resolution as Forum for Voice and Connection*—Lela Porter Love, Ian Macduff, Lucy Moore, Geetha Ravindra, Nancy A. Welsh
- *Conflict Resolution as Creative Exercise*— Johnston Barkat, Chris Honeyman, Colin Rule, Andrea Kupfer Schneider, Thomas J. Stipanowich
- *Conflict Resolution as Bridge to a Socially Just, Democratic, and Inclusive Community*—Lisa Blomgren Amsler, Jacqueline N. Font-Guzmán, Howard Gadlin, David Hoffman, Carol Izumi, Marvin E. Johnson, Homer C. La Rue, Bernie Mayer, Carrie Menkel-Meadow, Christopher W. Moore, Ellen Waldman

One theme missing from this organizational scheme is the importance of other people. Professors and trainers played key roles for many of our authors in introducing them to the field and particular roles within it. Certain names appeared repeatedly, including Frank Sander, Gary Friedman, Josh Stulberg, Len Riskin, Linda Singer, and Michael Lewis. Many of our authors paid homage to mentors who guided them at crucial personal or career choice points or provided ongoing support throughout stages of their lives. Several authors, we note, commented on the camaraderie, the sense of community they had experienced with fellow professionals and their gratitude for colleagues' willingness to share ideas and resources, even with those who might be competitors for cases, facilitations, trainings, or speaking engagements.

Alternative Frames for *Evolution of a Field*

We considered several perspectives in organizing this book, and because this seems appropriate for a field often labeled as "alternative" and because we think they might be instructive for readers, we include a few here. At the end of the book, we have provided a list of these alternative frames with the chapters that particularly fit within them.

ADR processes. The field of conflict resolution encompasses a diverse variety of processes—i.e., negotiation, mediation, public policy facilitation, arbitration, ombuds, conflict coaching, online dispute resolution, and more. These processes also are used in a wide variety of substantive areas. Our authors vary in their primary focus.

Career development. We think that many people interested in working as professional neutrals or academics or administrators in conflict resolution today will find value in the stories of these individuals, each of whom has built a career around one or more processes.

Culture. As revealed by their narratives, our authors' racial, ethnic, religious, and socioeconomic cultures influenced their identities and their choices as they decided to enter and remain in the field of conflict resolution. Some of our authors were born in foreign lands or were the children of immigrants to the United States, and they write thoughtfully about the complexities of growing up negotiating between two cultures. Those who are members of minority groups who were born in the United States describe a bicultural life shaped partly by racism. Several histories in this book also recount how immersion in a foreign culture changed the authors, made them more curious, more appreciative of ambiguity and paradox, and more appreciative of the need to begin any conflict resolution process by focusing on the people before the problem.

Gateways to the field. Like many people in this relatively young field, almost all our authors were originally educated or grounded in other disciplines: law, psychology, labor-management, social activism, community organizing, even literature. Our contributors write about how they wound up doing the work that they do: the inspirations and roadblocks they encountered; the opportunities they created or discovered; other people who helped them along the way; how they made their choices; how they managed disconnects between their values and career choices; and ultimately how they came to build a career around conflict resolution.

Generations. The autobiographical narratives in this book provide a sort of kaleidoscopic history of the growth of our field from the perspectives of several often-overlapping generations: those who first gained their footing in the world of labor-management; the visionaries who introduced mediation into the community, family, and public policy contexts; the early pioneers who worked to make conflict resolution processes an integral part of the courts and other institutions; the leaders who envisioned and nurtured professional associations; and our new pioneers, who are developing innovative processes to continue the field's evolution.

Institutional contexts for conflict resolution. Conflict resolution processes often exist within institutions. Although these processes can result in outcomes that will influence the institution, more often the reverse is true. Several of our authors focus primarily on this relationship between conflict resolution processes and the institutions that house them, including the courts, the National Institutes of Health, the International Monetary Fund, and corporations.

Why the Field of Conflict Resolution?

Before we close, we return to the inspiring themes that we chose to organize this book.

Many of our authors wrote movingly about how their own history helped explain their focus on providing others with the opportunity to express themselves authentically and personally. These authors also often emphasized the importance of ensuring not just the opportunity to speak but also a forum in which all can be respected and heard. Many authors also wrote about the goal and wonderful gift of enabling human connection on an individual and community level. These two dimensions of what neutrals offer their clients—voice and connection—are also aspects of what the work seems to give to the conflict resolvers themselves. Demographics, though, may play a role: the women more frequently mentioned that what they valued most about doing this work was finding their own voices and helping others do so. The men more frequently referred to the way this work allowed them to engage and connect with others. Our authors of color emphasized the value not just of individual connection but of creating an authentic and inclusive community. All the chapters include direct or indirect acknowledgement of the importance of being part of a profession that is also a community.

Some of our authors were quite humble about their contributions to our field, observing that they felt honored simply to help people bring their disabling conflicts to an end and move on. There is nobility in this apparently straightforward, but actually very difficult, task. Somewhat surprising to us, several of our authors focused on the opportunity that the field of conflict resolution provided to permit them and others—disputing parties, government officials, colleagues, researchers—to indulge their curiosity and be creative in terms of process, solutions, organization-building, and research. Finally, several of our authors described how their work as neutrals complemented their work as activists for social justice, democracy, and inclusion. Indeed, some described the neutral's role as one that had the potential, under certain circumstances, to be more effective and more responsive to individual needs than that of the social activist.

For the authors in this book, as expressed by Howard Bellman, their work is very much "a way of life, not just making a living." The people in this book identify with the goals and aspirations of the field of conflict resolution. They are driven to leave the world better than they found it. What is also striking, though, is that while our authors have retained their idealism, their voices are wise, tempered by experience and acknowledging both the complexity of human beings and institutions and our own inability to know whether our good intentions will translate inevitably into good results. Some, for example, point to all the field's successes in terms of the institutionalization of processes in the courts, in contracts, in private companies, in public agencies—but caution that such successes can invite complacency, routinization, commercialization, and even exploitation.

The next generation cannot and should not just follow. They will need to question, disrupt, improve, and create. They will need to lead.

A Final Note

We began this project just before the world changed. Today, we are bombarded with news of COVID-19 and its spread as well as the challenges of making decisions about the length and extent of quarantining, isolating, and social distancing.

The explosion of the pandemic and the requirements for social isolation have had direct impacts on the field of conflict resolution. Mediators, arbitrators, facilitators, trainers, and educators who once assumed that in-person encounters were an essential aspect of their work (including many contributors to this book who note the value of face-to-face, in-person contact) now find themselves adapting, harnessing the capabilities of new (and sometimes not-so-new) technologies. Online dispute resolution, or ODR, is on everyone's lips, and every feature of every conflict resolution process is being reconceptualized to incorporate technology. This includes learning and creating new ways to connect, to provide voice, to create a sense of community.

During this time, the deaths of George Floyd and so many other African American victims of police brutality also have clearly shown that we have much work to do in addressing racial inequality in every context, including the field of conflict resolution. Some of our authors are leaders in identifying bias in the training, recruiting, mentoring, and selection of neutrals, and they describe their work with major conflict resolution organizations to ensure that these organizations are sufficiently inclusive as well as initiatives to increase the selection of diverse neutrals and open students' eyes to the evidence and aftereffects of racial injustice. Even some core concepts—such as neutrality, confidentiality, and self-determination—are being scrutinized to see whether they inadvertently contribute to the perpetuation of the very social ills with which we are concerned. As some of our authors note, for example, unquestioning loyalty to the concept of neutrality may actually serve the interests of the already privileged—and disserve those who need to be heard and get information to make good decisions.[2]

This has been and probably will continue to be a challenging and exhausting time. At some points during the pandemic, we, like so many others we know, have been tempted to avoid the latest news. But then we turned to the chapter drafts and revisions from our contributors, and we found ourselves energized by the inspiring and ultimately hopeful personal histories contained there. We found reminders that social and political unrest are not new—and that, unfortunately, neither are racism and exclusion.

Don't we often tell the parties in our mediations and the students in our classes that conflict is neither good nor bad but inevitable—and that what actually matters is what we do in response to it?

Our contributors' personal histories underscore this truth. Some authors and their families were scarred by the horrors of the Holocaust. Others and their loved ones endured discrimination and even internment, and still others acknowledge the impact of conflict within their families. Many recall their feelings of alienation and disillusionment in response to the Vietnam War, their consequent participation in student protests, and the pain—but also the determined hopefulness—of the civil rights movement. Even Watergate and its aftermath make an appearance in these pages. These personal essays describe turbulent, troubled times, much like today, and we take heart from knowing that those times molded many of the people who are now stalwarts in the conflict resolution field.

We have felt privileged to read the narratives in this book and to work with their authors. We have been delighted by the alternate passions (jazz, tango, literature, architecture, and more) infusing these chapters. We hope that you, the reader, feel a similar gratitude for the stories here and for the authors who have shared them. Perhaps you will be inspired to do as they have: work to achieve voice, connection, understanding of differences, creative solutions, and ultimately a better world.

Howard Gadlin and Nancy Welsh

October 28, 2020

Notes

[1] We asked our authors to consider the following questions:

ABOUT YOU

History

1) How and when did you become involved with mediation or conflict resolution?
2) Why did you become involved with mediation or conflict resolution? In responding, think beyond the circumstances and consider your own psychological and social makeup, as well as the state of your community, country and the world at that time.

Your Practice/Career

3) Please describe your practice/career. What inspirations and roadblocks did you encounter? How were opportunities created or discovered? How did you make the choices that you made?
4) Did you hope that you would build a career around mediation or conflict resolution?

Reflections on Your Practice

5) Are there types of conflict situations you especially enjoy engaging in? What is it about those cases or about you that attracts you to these types of conflicts?
6) What types of issues or disputants are most challenging for you? Why and how do you handle those?
7) What personal satisfactions have you achieved through doing this work?
8) How do you handle the tension between your own personal beliefs, politics, and values and your role in mediation or conflict resolution?
9) Are there ways in which your role and experience as a mediator/facilitator/neutral has changed the way you conduct yourself in personal relationships? Professional activities? As a political being?

ABOUT YOUR VIEW OF THE PLACE OF MEDIATION AND CONFLICT RESOLUTION

10) What do you see as the limits of mediation or conflict resolution? Are there types of cases or issues you believe ought not be brought to mediation or conflict resolution?
11) Do you see mediation/conflict resolution as a force for social change? Do you see mediation/conflict resolution as having been co-opted by institutions within the larger society?

12) What do you believe/hope should be the agenda for the future use/institutionalization of mediation and conflict resolution?

ABOUT YOUR VIEW OF THE TENETS OF MEDIATION AND CONFLICT RESOLUTION

13) How have your experiences as a mediator/facilitator/neutral changed or influenced your understanding of the core tenets of mediation and conflict resolution – e.g., neutrality, self-determination, procedural fairness, and confidentiality? Do you see these as core tenets? Are there other tenets you believe ought to be given core status?
14) Which of these tenets is the biggest challenge for you to honor? Why?

[2] We realized that we had to revisit the rules of grammar as we thought about how to communicate the diversity of the world in which we live. Earlier this year, *The New York Times* and many other media announced that they would capitalize Black whenever referring to race. There was never any question that this would also be our choice for the book. But what about other color-based racial identifiers? We became aware that White has long been capitalized by hate groups, but we also learned that the National Association of Black Journalists recommended capitalization whenever color was used to describe race. We allowed our authors to make their own choices, but as our default, we chose to follow the lead of the National Association of Black Journalists and capitalize all color-based racial identifiers.

2

Wabi-Sabi

By Peter S. Adler

◆

Gary Snyder, a fine poet and essayist, says, "Good stories are hard to come by, and a good story you can call your

---

Peter S. Adler recently returned to Hawai'i, his home, after serving as president of the Keystone Center for nearly a decade. Adler's specialty is multi-party negotiation and problem-solving. He has worked extensively on water management and resource planning problems and mediates, writes, trains, and teaches in diverse areas of conflict management. He has worked on cases ranging from the siting of a 25-megawatt geothermal energy production facility to the resolution of construction and product-liability claims involving a multimillion-dollar stadium. He has extensive experience in land planning issues, water problems, marine and coastal affairs, and strategic resource management. Prior to his appointment at Keystone, Adler held executive positions with the Hawai'i Justice Foundation, the Hawai'i Supreme Court's Center for Alternative Dispute Resolution (ADR), and the Neighborhood Justice Center. He served as a Peace Corps volunteer in India, an instructor and associate director of the Hawai'i Outward Bound School, and president of the Society of Professionals in Dispute Resolution. He has been awarded the Roberston-Cuninghame Scholar in Residence Fellowship at the University of New England, New South Wales, Australia, a Senior Fellowship at the Western Justice Center, and was a consultant to the US Institute for Environmental Conflict Resolution. Adler has written extensively in the field of mediation and conflict resolution. He is the co-author of *Managing Scientific & Technical Information Environmental Cases* (1999); *Building Trust: 20 Things You Can Do to Help Environmental Stakeholder Groups Talk More Effectively About Science, Culture, Professional Knowledge, and Community Wisdom* (2002); the author of *Beyond Paradise* and *Oxtail Soup* (1993 and 2000) and numerous other articles and monographs. He more recently wrote *Eye of The Storm Leadership* (2008) and *India-40: A Memoir of Death, Sickness, Love, Friendship, Corruption, Political Fanatics, Drugs, Thugs, Psychosis, and Illumination in the US Peace Corps* (2018).

own is an incredible gift." Why? Stories are ancient and enduring avenues of human exchange and one of the ways we make discoveries. Stories create hypotheses, explain things, and sometimes connect us to each other and older enduring narratives.

In the world of conflict management, the right stories, done at the right time with the right people, asked for and spoken in the right way, can crack open a problem and create new possibilities. Science, law, politics, planning, and culture are stories that sometimes harbor larger truths. Many conflicts are built on these. The world is also made of stories with smaller day-to-day truths, and all these stories make the world what it is.

At the most mundane level, I think part of my job is kick-starting and managing often-difficult discussions that enable the telling of old stories and the creation of new ones. I do this case-by-case and project-by-project. Thomas Jefferson reputedly said, "Peace is that brief glorious moment in history when everybody stands around reloading." That's when I do my work.

I think of myself as a "Tertium Quid" specialist, someone who can assist people to negotiate new third stories made up of two or more older conflicting stories that resolve old problems or create new value while they are reloading. I like helping people try to create a story of the future.

How I got this way isn't fully clear in my own mind. I grew up on the south side of Chicago near the steel mills. My parents were immigrants out of the Holocaust. Most of my other family members went into the ovens. A few made it to Palestine. By design, serendipity, and luck, my parents evaded Hitler, came to "Amerika," worked hard, and became doctors, the first in their families to get college-educated.

Growing up, they found that their World War II experiences were always close to the surface and rubbed off.

Nonetheless, Dr. Richard Adler and Dr. Alice Blau made a reasonably good life and wound up with a clean house, two Studebakers, and enough food, clothes, and school supplies for three little boys. I went to a high school on the south side not far from the mills where my father, beyond his general doctoring, practiced industrial medicine, and then to Roosevelt University, which is where some of this narrative begins.

Before and during college, I was convinced life was completely binary. "Binary" wasn't a word I would have used then, but I was fully persuaded that the world was made of dichotomous choices controlled by switches in our brains. In that early world, my switches were always on, and there was a crystal-clear distinction between right and wrong, good and bad, strong and weak, smart and stupid.

This was the tumultuous era of the Vietnam War, which the Vietnamese call "the American War." Life in the United States was churning with politics and full of countercultural caffeine, alive with fresh ideas and every sort of rebellion imaginable. I was part of that turmoil, full of certainties and never confused about how the world worked and where I and everyone else stood in it.

At the time, I thought I was going to be an aquatic biologist. I vaguely envisioned a life working in the cool waters of the Great Lakes and their tributaries with sturgeons, lake trouts, invasive mussels, and lamprey eels. The first disruption came in a strange encounter in a mandatory literature class with a professor named Robert Cosby, who became the first of several mentors.

There is a truth to it: When the student is ready, the teacher appears.

I went to Cosby's class with reluctance. I was far more interested in the comparative lives of carp and bluegills, the inner organs of dissected frogs and fetal pigs, and the way plankton blooms support rapid population explosions of bugs, snakes, birds, and raccoons up the food chain. Poetry was not in my bundle of sureties.

Cosby's main mission in life was to teach undergraduate boneheads something about literature, language, and writing before we were released from college. He did this with passion and precision. He was a decorated World War II veteran and had played a part at the Nuremburg trials but now waxed eloquent on Shakespeare and Emily Dickinson one minute, then veered into split infinitives and the odd and subtle moods of the subjunctive tense.

His specific field was 19th-century writers like Ambrose Bierce, Bret Harte, and Mark Twain, but his love of native writing went hand in hand with his cutthroat knowledge of dangling participles and misplaced adverbs. He was punitive about ending sentences with prepositions and would chastise us with Winston Churchill's purported line, "This is the kind of arrant pedantry up with which I will not put."

I found myself engrossed with Cosby's take on literature, its linkages to history, science, philosophy, and life, and his fierce insistence on applying critical thinking to whatever we were studying. None of this quite fit my assumptions about a "binary" world.

One day, for example, Cosby started a discussion by reading two poems by "Anonymous" that went like this. First, from Beowulf, written about 800-AD.

> So becomes it a youth to quit him well with his father's friends, by fee and gift, that to aid him, aged, in after days, come warriors willing, should war draw nigh, liegemen loyal: by laudd deeds shall an earl have honor in every clan.

A puzzle. The word for puzzle in Spanish is *rompecabeza*, which means "brain-exploder." I had no idea what Beowulf (or Cosby) was saying.

Then this one by some Midwest farmer:

> Carnation milk is the best in the land.
> Here I stand with a can in my hand.
> No tits to pull, no hay to pitch.
> You just punch a hole in the son of a bitch.

More *rompecabezas* ...

Then he asked us to use our noggins and explain how and why these two poems might be similar or different and why they might be anonymous. He asked us to do these baffling exercises all the time. No hands went up. I bent my head low and inspected my shoelaces, which potentially might have needed retying.

"Adler!" he barked.

"Well, sir," I said, "I think both writers were too embarrassed to put their names to them."

People laughed. Cosby snorted. "You're a dolt," he said.

Then he turned to my best friend, Sewell Gelberd, who didn't know if he wanted to be a chemist, accountant, or social worker and gave a long, windy explanation that made no sense at all. Cosby grunted again. "You're an idiot, too—worse than Adler. The right answer," he says, "is they have nothing in common other than being poems, but I could also convince you morons with sound logic that neither of them actually are. So there really are at least two or more answers."

That, and similar exchanges, seemed to trigger the start of a series of pops deep inside my skull.

I've been told that the true sound of critical thinking at work is not "Aha!" but "Huh?" It was one of my first real moments of "Huh," some kind of crunching sound in the world of binaries. "Huh" decoded is another way of saying you are baffled, which can also be a small triumph of curiosity over judgment. This, and other incidents, led me into one of the characteristics I would eventually carry into the world of conflict management. I became nosy. A snoop. A lifter-upper of rocks to look at wiggle worms and a potential wiggle-worm meddler.

Cosby became my adviser. Along the way, when I was weighing after-college options in the Navy and Coast Guard, he said, "Why don't you look into the Peace Corps?"

I said, "Huh ... what's that?"

———◆———

Eighteen months later, in the summer of 1966, I joined 49 other freshly minted college graduates invited to train for a possible Peace Corps assignment to central India. Of the 50 who began training in a Texas border-town called Zapata, only a handful from my group—"The Dirty Dozen," we were called—finished the two-year tour.

Our particular arrangement originated as part of a tough negotiation between Lyndon Johnson and Indira Gandhi. Gandhi wanted excess American wheat at a steep discount. Johnson wanted to get rid of wheat surpluses and create a nicer face for America as the war in Vietnam was accelerating. A bargain was made.

Our training was staged on an old ranch with an abandoned radar site, a windmill, and a horse trough in the desert along the Tex-Mex border. The training ran for three months and required us to build our own village in the scrub and sand. Even as we built our little hovels, the first hints at what was coming emerged.

Language, construction, and culture classes went on all day followed by evenings of tutoring and homework. Camping out in the desert with the other college meatheads, our language and construction teachers, and a bunch of Peace Corps shrinks, I started to get a more detailed sense of India and the potential assignment we might be headed for in Maharashtra State.

The instructors who ran what were called "Value Discussions" had also been early Peace Corps volunteers to India. We called them the "the Culture Vultures." India, the veterans told us, is kaleidoscopic, a land of preposterous and unending contradictions. It is physical, spiritual, ascetic, dirty, sensuous, crass, democratic, dictatorial, rigid, flexible, idealistic, corrupt, ugly, progressive, conservative, and beautiful.

Huh? How could a place on the other side of the planet be all these things?

The head Culture Vulture, a woman named Constance, warned us that in trying to grapple with the mental and cultural dilemmas India presents, we would all take at least one, if not several, predictable paths.

A few of you, she said, will learn to navigate your many dilemmas and thrive on the experience. Some of you will reject the complexity and retreat into the narrowest and most technocratic role you can. You will dig a well, stock a few fish tanks, teach some classes, build a building, and go back to your house and stay inside.

Others of you will pine for home, surround yourself with anything American you can find, and become intolerant of Indians and maybe even abusive. You will listen to the Voice of America all day, order magazines from the United States, and write endless letters home.

Finally, she told us, some of you will go native. You'll dress like Indians, wear *kurtas* and *lungis*, chew betel nut, and spend half your day sitting around smoking a hubbly bubbly full of hash, all in the name of cultural interchange.

That sounded perfectly fine to me, but more interesting was the long, often ponderous and head-scratching discussions about Hinduism. I always assumed there was one big God up there, probably an old Jewish guy with a white beard and a yarmulke sitting on a cloud looking down on us and directing traffic. Not so in India.

Hinduism, we were told, is a vast celestial ocean full of spirit-beings. Some of them are global and perpetual, personified by the big cosmic trifecta of Brahma the creator, Vishnu the stabilizer, and Shiva the destroyer. Others are more granular and particular, devas and devis who are powerful, divine beings below the supreme universal level but moving around above our earthly plane. Then there are those flitting around at ground level, little impish beings, some of them enablers of fresh opportunities, others demons who are sent to annoy us.

Meanwhile, we received extensive training in Marathi, the language we would speak, and in the construction skills and tools we were expected to deploy: blueprints, stone and mortar work, culverts, road sealants, earth-fills, and catchment and runoff calculations for water storage.

At the end of three months and after a humiliating "Night of the Long Knives," when a third of our group was unceremoniously dumped and sent home, we shipped out to New Delhi, from where I was then packed off with my roommate to a small town south of Mumbai and north of Goa called Khed. We then spent two years there killing rats, raising chickens, and building some one- and two-room schools.

My odyssey in India was a fork-in-the road experience—not the only one, but an important one. There were a lot of adventures and dozens of dark moments, but it changed my life and in part, led me to mediation and its many adaptations in ways that I am still puzzling out. I don't think it was culture shock. It was "life shock."

One of those moments happened when I first landed in my assigned village and discovered I was in the middle of serious corruption. Coming from Chicago, I should have known about all this, but I was sheltered and naïve. If you have worked in India or certain other South Asian countries, you know that day-to-day life runs on the reciprocating notion of *baksheesh*, which in its most limited sense means a "tip" for services either solicited or offered.

In India, this is a pleasanter way of describing a broad spectrum of graft, dirty dealing, bribery, extortion, bid-rigging, invoice-padding, insider knowledge, and protection rackets. *Baksheesh* might be overt or subtle, but I found it inspired and occasionally wondrous in its creativity. Here is how I first encountered it.

I am a new, pink-faced 22-year-old Peace Corps volunteer stationed in the boondocks. I am isolated, but I do get regular mail, even if it's slow. One day a little pint-size guy who works for the post office comes to my door in khakis wearing a peaked Nehru cap and starched shorts and says he is collecting contributions for the local chapter of the All-India Postal Workers Cricket Club.

I tell him, "No thanks. I don't play cricket."

The next day my mail stops. I wait. After 10 days of no mail, I go to a trustworthy friend, and he tells me he will look into it. A few days later he comes back and says, "A letter delivery man is going to come to your door and ask for a contribution to the local All-India Postal Workers Cricket

Club. Give him a few rupees. He will keep some and pass more up to his boss, who will pass some onto his higher-up."

Sure enough, he came, I paid, and the next day my mail delivery started again. This was new stuff for me. The crack in my brain opened a little wider.

Another happened when a farmer's bullock cart broke an axle just down the road from where I lived. The shaft splintered, the cart crashed to the ground, a wheel spun off, and vegetables, bags of rice, and large square tins of cooking oil spilled onto the road. One of the man's two majestic Brahma bulls was on his side, moaning. A crowd gathered to stare, me included, lurking at the back, ready to skedaddle if something went bad, which often happens when cows are injured and crowds of Hindus and Muslims coagulate.

The farmer was looking at his bull and crying. Then a policeman arrived but didn't do much. Soon, another officious-looking gent in clean pants and a nylon shirt arrived, examined the bull's leg, and shook his head. Maybe he was a veterinarian or someone experienced with animal injuries. Or some sort of government official. He kept shaking his head and pulling on his mustache.

Meanwhile, the farmer wept uncontrollably, and the animal was in obvious pain. I stared at the bull and thought: *this poor creature needs help.*

But that didn't happen. A small truck appeared, people helped load the farmer's goods in the back, dismantled the remains of the cart, and then drove off. Pushing and shoving, they got the injured animal to the side of the road and left him there. The farmer walked off with his other animal. I stared, a waterfall of emotions cascading through my mind. I thought: *In the United States, we would put a bullet into this animal's head to get him out of his misery.*

Sad but needed. But it's different here, I thought. This is a culture I don't have a grip on.

Later, talking with my friend Tukaram Khedakar, an educated man and yet another mentor, he said I did the right thing not interfering. That fine white bull was the reincarnation of someone from another life and must suffer more before being reborn. Or maybe it was the farmer who must suffer before his own rebirth. Or maybe both of them, plus some of those who were standing around gawking. Regardless, killing a cow in public in a Hindu community would be unthinkable. A riot would ensue.

Then I thought: Maybe it's me who has to suffer. When you are 22 years old, emerging from the bubble of American culture, and going through life shock, maybe that's your job. To learn to navigate through sufferings and find whatever joys are available.

There were many other moments, some ordinary and occurring in slow-motion, others more prominent that still remain in sharp relief. In the end, I came to terms with most of them. I helped build those few little one- and two-room schools in remote cliffhanger villages, helped some entrepreneurial farmers start poultry businesses, killed a lot of rats, introduced the Frisbee to central India, and during the long months of monsoon read a lot of the wonderful books I had missed in high school and college.

Most important in the longer run, I made friends, learned a new language, and absorbed some valuable lessons about the world in some of its more disjunctive, paradoxical, and potentially creative forms.

Maybe it was the worms, bugs, and infections that drilled into my body or the phantasmagoria of Hindu gods and goddesses that my Indian friends kept telling me about. It probably had something to do with the Vietnam War, which was raging a few thousand miles away, plus the suicide and mental breakdowns of some of my Peace Corps comrades. It could have been the strange carrot-colored sunrises, the months of withering heat, the further months of drenching monsoons, the corpses and crabbed beggars in the doorways of buildings in Bombay, and the hypnotic twang of sitars' music.

In 1927 in Japan, Kenji Miyazawa, a man whose life and writings I especially admire, put it this way:

> Yours is the kind of learning
> etched into yourself
> in the blizzards, in the spare free time between work,
> crying—
> which will soon sprout vigorously
> and no one knows how big it will grow.
> That's the beginning of new knowledge.

Miyazawa still speaks to my journey and the peculiar professional world I now inhabit. Those who do this same kind of work know we abide in an often-gauzy netherworld of human affairs, an interstitial trade zone between contending oppositions and powerfully different assertions about what the truth is. That is where we work and where we are occasionally privileged to do something helpful.

―――――◆―――――

After the Peace Corps tour, I went to graduate school and studied sociology. I absorbed a considerable number of ideas about law, conflict, science, stability, change, symbolic interaction, social stratification, and small group behaviors. Much of this came from yet another mentor, Professor Daryl Hobbs. He plunged me into the works of C. Wright Mills, Talcott Parsons, Erving Goffman, and many others.

For a time, I thought the university might be a friendly long-term place for me to land. It wasn't. By the time I finished my PhD, I actually had no idea what I wanted to do, other than being clear that I didn't want to make an academic career. University life felt abstract, remote, and far removed from the kinds of problems I had dealt with on the ground in India. It might be perfectly fine for some people, but my temperament seemed more suited to doing something pragmatic.

That led me to what I thought would be a hiatus, a two-year stint as assistant director and instructor in Hawai'i's new Outward Bound School, which, in turn, included my first real exposure and training in conflict resolution. It was taught by certain Native Hawaiian elders in a small town called Miloli'i on the south Kona coast where we kept outrigger canoes for the ocean segments of our 24-day wilderness expeditions. We incorporated their teachings into the courses we were leading through potentially risky rainforest, ocean, and mountain environments.

Ho'oponopono, this traditional indigenous method for resolving disputes in extended families, means "to make things right." It is millennia old and found in various forms throughout Polynesia and Micronesia. Like so many older cultures, many of which are disappearing, Hawai'i had its own way of managing conflicts, one developed over centuries of feudal and internecine fighting. This was how Hawai'i resolved disagreements while people were reloading for their next fights.

Ho'oponopono fascinated me. The idea of people sitting together under the guidance and choreography of an elder peeling back the substantive and emotional layers of a problem and seeking to restore harmony in families and communities struck me as sensible and highly productive.

Organizing and leading 24-day wilderness learning expeditions led me to "conflict management" and "ADR." I applied for and won a job as executive director of one of the first Department of Justice-funded community mediation centers.

The newly created Neighborhood Justice Center of Honolulu (NJCH), established in large part by US Attorney General Griffin Bell in the wake of the 1976 Pound Conference, was advertising for an executive director. It didn't pay much and didn't have a real caseload or secure financial future, but it did have a small coterie of freshly trained mediators who were as enthused about mediation as I was about *Ho'oponopono.*

I considered myself lucky, maybe even serendipitously blessed. I went to mediation trainings and took to it fast. It seemed to combine the two worlds of ideas and actions perfectly. I learned quickly because I was intensely interested.

I also got fine advice from more mentors and business *consiglieres* and became reasonably proficient in navigating the braking and acceleration required in my new leadership role: caseload development; fundraising; managing a small professional staff and a coterie of volunteers; and marketing, not just for the NJCH but for the whole idea of mediation as a valuable addition to American law and society.

This then led to an offer and an appointment by the chief justice of the Hawai'i Supreme Court to help develop and direct a newly established Center for ADR. Our local courts knew they wanted this but didn't really have a way to push it. My job was to be a mediation catalytic converter.

Over the next decade, my organizational and mediation interests expanded and would eventually lead to a stint as president and CEO of the Keystone Center, which focused on consensus-building strategies for technically and legally complex energy, environment, and public-health controversies. I had started out thinking I would go into aquatic biology, diverted into the social sciences, and now came back to those origins with new strategies and tools.

Over the years I have been especially intrigued by applying whatever mediation skills and experiences I have accumulated to public-policy matters and one particular strand of conflicts I'll call "SIPSIDs" which is code for "Science-Intensive Politically Snarky Disputes." Many of these involve major collisions over plans, regulations, and laws that seem to bring outraged advocacy groups, defensive government agencies, bunkered business leaders, and scientific and technical experts into sharp-elbowed fights.

I liked working on these kinds of conflicts and helping lawyers and experts deal with their inevitable conflicts, confronting the limits of their authorities, beliefs, and certainties and still looking for ways to avoid the risks and uncertainties of adverse political or legal decisions. It carried forward the basic notion of disputants trying to create mutual value and becoming the architects of their own solutions.

Most of these disputes are intensely political and imbued with actual or impending litigation. I have learned that careful processes, patience, better communication, and improved relationships are essential but insufficient to deal with many of these skirmishes. Coming to grips with the veracity of competing claims and defenses is often necessary, and finding a way to get a plausible set of facts on the table in the midst of highly charged debates is one starting point.

I have no delusions about any of this and don't believe scientific facts are the center of the universe. Matt Cartmill, a professor of biological anthropology at Boston University, put it well: "As an adolescent I aspired to lasting fame, I craved factual certainty, and I thirsted for a meaningful vision of human life—so I became a scientist. This is like becoming an archbishop so you can meet girls."

Still, confronting factual disagreements that are part of the conflict narratives people tell us is one door into the emotional and political center of many arguments about freshwater security, GMOs, agricultural practices, ozone depletion, hazardous geothermal energy emissions, and even helping disputatious native Hawaiians develop a vision of their future and a proposed new constitution for some future sovereignty arrangement.

Daniel Patrick Moynihan, a US senator, ambassador, and sociologist, famously said everyone is entitled to their own opinion, but not to their own facts. Moynihan was wrong. In the now-instantaneous world of tweets, posts, blogs, memes, and accusations of fake news, everyone asserts that his or her own facts are the ultimate truth. When they learn their truth may not be fully triumphant or immutable, or may not win the day, small *rompecabezas* go off. Cracks appear, shifts occur, and opportunities become apparent.

Some disputes feel like tin cans or tightly capped bottles with highly pressurized contents. Sometimes, my job is to just be a good can opener, release the pressure slowly, and prevent unnecessary spillage. Or maybe even to use the contents to make a flavorful or at least nutritious meal. But I also have no illusions. Some of it is political sausage-making, stuff that is better not put on full public display.

In certain cases, I feel like I am working somewhere between extortion and bribery. One side wants something. The other side wants to offer something. It's an awkward dance. I help them with that as gracefully as possible.

To exert a positive force, I have endeavored to further evolve my craft, not just with a focus on facts but a certain style of communication and diplomacy. I want people to tell their stories. If they are in a rage, I let them do that and listen carefully until it's time to pivot. The pivot point comes when people are repeating themselves, when they have actually not just "listened" but absorbed what their counterparts are saying, or when they are frustrated or exhausted.

I have learned to avoid embarrassing anyone in front of others. I ask hard questions in private. And living and working in a largely Asian and Oceanic culture, I am particularly sensitive to saving, managing, and assuring "face." And though timing is important, I have learned to bring outside metaphors, analogies, and occasional humor to the table when they may have relevance to the problems at hand. I try to do this with subtlety and without detracting from the stories others are unfolding or substituting my own for theirs.

I also use silence. I have learned at long last to ask questions—and then shut up and listen. In traditional *ho'oponopono*, the mediator is called a *haku*, which is the braided lei many Hawaiian people wear on their heads for important occasions. *Ho'oponopono* has time outs, periods of intentional quiet, and moments when everyone must confront whatever responsibility they carry for the issue at hand. The *haku*, or mediator, must try to be the "braider" of their stories into possible solutions.

Like all my colleagues in this volume, I keep as one of my main goals helping people move beyond their immediate hurts, the self-righteousness of starting positions, and their overt or *sotto voce* hungers for revenge. And like others, I have learned to be a chameleon. Each situation is unique. In the words of Frank Sander (another mentor to many of us), "let the forum fit the fuss."

That means having a few different mediation and facilitation choreographies at the ready for different fusses. It involves directing discussions as necessary and with carefully chosen trajectories and usually with a "less is more" attitude.

If I am working in the four corners of courts and litigation, I often lean toward more evaluative and muscular approaches to resolution. In business boardrooms, I change the vocabulary and talk the way many business professionals prefer when they have a dispute. Business people don't seem to care for the words "conflict" or "mediation" until they are in court. Until then, I will encourage "strategy development," "internal alignment," "project planning," or "analytic forecasting." In other settings, I may be purely facilitative in style.

The challenge is always to start with "huh," evoke stories, be patient, ask questions, keep both unwarranted optimism and unchecked pessimism at bay, and stay especially alert for places where pragmatic outcomes can be discussed. To be clear, there is inevitably a moment in all matters when people have talked enough and are dithering. This moment comes through from spoken words, facial expressions, body language, or direct comments. Sometimes, it's just my own gut instinct. If that instinct is wrong, the parties will tell me.

Then it's time for me to call the question and start the solution-braid. Built on what is coming through the noise surrounding a central conflict, that decision and its ideal moment in any choreography is often intuitive, simply a piece in the opaque, sodium-colored gray zone.

All these tendencies are now as much a part of my personal as well as professional life. I think it is what the Japanese mean by the realm they call *wabi-sabi*, an outlook built on "not knowing" but recognizing and taking comfort from the obscurities, asymmetries, and irregularities life presents. In Japan, *wabi* connotes a quality of solitude. *Sabi* is the acceptance of transience and imperfection. It is a far stretch from the dualities and "binary-isms" of my youth.

At heart, I am a dilemma manager, though I do other things as well. When I succeed at helping people tame a snarky problem, resolve a dispute, align into a new strategy, heal old wounds, or simply get on with their lives, I feel like a blessing has happened to them and me. Admittedly, plunging into other people's confusions is a peculiar, maybe aberrant way to make a living. Nonetheless, it is what I do, and by some fluke, I like doing it.

My satisfactions come in many ways. I like seeing people gain higher clarity on the problems they are experiencing. I like it when they move from judgments to "huh?" I feel truly useful when they get "unstuck" and move on with other parts of their lives. I like it even more when, in the right circumstances, old hurts are healed, vexed disputants create robust plans for the future, and people come away feeling that they accomplished something important.

Once, after helping a group of regulators, business professionals, and community leaders sort out a very complicated water problem, the group gave me a little plaque that said, "Blessed are the peacemakers, for they shall never be unemployed." There is a small truth to that, especially now that so many ex-judges and retiring senior lawyers have hung out shingles as mediators and arbitrators.

But in the end, it isn't about the money. Money calms the nerves but never brings happiness. I have come to relish working in the gray zone of human affairs, the wabi-sabi place that is neither precisely good nor bad nor right or wrong but always a mix of entanglements in which people struggle with human dramas and behave at their very best and worst.

In this yin and yang world, binaries still exist but have acquired enough plasticity that we can handcraft new third stories, which optimistically we believe can hold for a time. One of my colleagues once told me to never underestimate the power of a new and better-expressed ambiguity to resolve old ambiguities that have grown tired or conflictual. That turns out to be sound advice.

While I sometimes secretly yearn for a life that might have more direct and tidy lines between causes and effects and life's good and bad days, I have become more porous and comfortable in a world of unknown-unknowns. I don't dream of a better place beyond this one. There is no Valhalla, no Elysian Field, and no shining city on a hill. Nor do I believe in eternal damnation, perdition, or rebirth. We are what we have done and now do.

In the face of adversity and uncertainty, my father-in-law used to repeat a Japanese proverb: *Shikata ga nai.* "It cannot be helped." I have no delusions that what gets done in the moments I am proudest of will be remembered. Still, it feels like honorable work that cannot be helped.

3

How I Found My Groove

By Howard Bellman

◆

My mother was gifted. Insightful. Within moments of meeting someone, she was capable of giving the compliment they desired or deflating them with surgical precision. If she knew a bit of your history, she could sum you up in a few words and pretty much characterize you for life. On top of that, she had a famous sense of humor. She could make you laugh from the soles of your feet on up and enjoyed a good belly laugh herself, which meant that whether she was skewering you or making your day, the presentation had a diplomatic quality. She just seemed to see and hear more acutely than most, and have a capacity to get to the core quickly. I like to think that those were two of her gifts to me.

Until I started high school in 1951, we lived in the working-class neighborhoods of Toledo, Ohio. In those days, I was not formidable in appearance and was the only Jewish

---

Howard Bellman has mediated in nearly every category of disputes, with concentrations on labor, the environment, and public policy. His practice has been nationwide and international. He has held leadership positions in professional organizations, taught courses and lectured at universities around the world, and published in scholarly and professional journals. He served as secretary of the Wisconsin Department of Industry, Labor and Human Relations and commissioner of the Wisconsin Employment Relations Commission. He received a law degree from the University of Cincinnati and an LLM in labor law from New York University.

kid within bullying distance. There was a lot of verbal crap flung in my direction, not to mention a lot of punching and wrestling on the way to school and back. Otherwise, from the first through the eighth grade I kept my distance, and the others did the same. When I came home with my wire-rimmed spectacles all bent out of shape, my mother counseled that the other kids were jealous. My father explained how he punished his assailants.

My father worked very hard and constantly, and by my high school years had taken us out of those neighborhoods and into a lovely home of our own in a neighborhood with plenty of Jewish families. The Jewish kids there had generally grown up together, however, and my place in the society of my peers was possibly even more tormented and undesirable than it had been before. However, toward the end of high school, for reasons I do not recall, I learned to play the drums and even led a dance band that performed at the YMCA and a few high school events. (It was OK to be playing at the dances in the gym. I wasn't compromising any dating opportunities.)

Everything changed in college. I was in Cincinnati, without a reputation and a would-be musician. In short order I met two extremely sophisticated sophomores who encouraged me, and within weeks, I was playing, mainly the jazz of that era, all around the city. My Toledo persona was history. I continued to play the drums a lot throughout my undergraduate years, and despite my less than admirable academic performance, I grew an ego.

Eventually, I was able to assess my musical career potential and enrolled in law school for another round of academic mediocrity on my part. In law school, I weaned myself off the drums, self-assessed once again, and headed for the labor law program at another law school. (The weaning included some coffeehouse folk music performances featuring the political songs of Pete Seeger and the like. Union organizing and the plight of workers were at the leading edge of liberal politics at the time.) Labor law was an easy segue and, thank heaven, where I landed. I found what I cared about *and* what I might be good at. Unprecedented.

After graduation, I moved to Detroit as a bottom-rung attorney at the regional office of the National Labor Relations Board, as content as a "pig in shit." It was the era of Jimmy Hoffa and Walter Reuther and the Big Three automakers all at their most powerful, and I was reinforced by an office replete with supportive managers and colleagues who were glad to see me realize my potential. (It was a sort of encouragement I had not received, or earned, in college or law school.) I moved quickly up the ladder and found that I was not inclined to become a litigator (the indicator of success in that office) or a member of a law firm (the other success indicator). While I was very glad to remain immersed in labor relations, I was not disposed to sign on with a union or a management law firm. As I saw it, there were too many villains on both sides. I like to think I was inclined to a definition of "success" that emphasized personal integrity over wealth and power, that being a "hired gun" for unions or management was contrary to my nature, and that I was a "natural" neutral. But maybe I was attracted to acceptance by a broad range of individuals and segments of society, and where is broad acceptability more a component of success than among mediators and arbitrators?

I took a position at the bottom at the Wisconsin Employment Relations Commission (WERC). That job included work as an administrative law judge, an arbitrator, and a mediator. I would be neutral as can be, in a very small agency in a state in the midst of leading the nation into what I saw as enlightened labor policy for public employees. There I learned to mediate from very skilled senior colleagues and received enormous support from the three commissioners who were appointed to lead the agency. (Still a well-placed pig.) After nine years of that, in late 1974, I was appointed by the governor to the commission that heads the WERC and served in that capacity for two more years.

The WERC is my alma mater. It is where I acquired my skills and values. To this day, as I work in a multitude of other settings and sectors, what I absorbed there grounds my practices. We were mediating between unions and employers, assisting them as needed to achieve collective bargaining agreements governing future wages, hours, and working conditions. The process was transactional and allowed the parties to maintain their fundamental, albeit conflicted, belief systems. It relied heavily on the knowledge and interests of the two parties, and it was legitimized by statutes and venerable American public policies. Our objective was "labor peace," not optimal public or private enterprises, workplace democracy, or fair compensation. It was closure—strike avoidance. We worked day and night, near and far, in whatever weather miseries Wisconsin provided. We were proud of our service but asked for no recognition.

We understood that ideally the parties negotiated successfully without our help, and that the less we were needed the better, both in general and during the course of a particular mediation. It would be perverse to insinuate any dependence on mediation into the parties' practices. The grief and the glory were theirs. Ownership of the dispute and its settlement terms belonged to the parties, but we were there when they called. We found conflicts within the caucuses, breakdowns in communication, problematic assessments of alternatives to settlement, limited repertoires of possible settlement terms, the need for a referee, and a myriad of other barriers to agreement that mediators are well positioned to address.

We also practiced in a broad variety of settings. Even though I was limited to labor-management negotiations for collective bargaining agreements to determine wages, hours, and working conditions, I worked with symphonies and ballet companies, foundries and factories, teachers and firefighters, university faculties and grave diggers. The construction industry and the printing industry were communities with cultures of their own. Despite the obvious superficial commonalities, the enterprises and the workforces required adaptations. In hindsight, it was a preliminary for adaptations to come.

There was no obvious intellectual activity at the WERC. There were no books to read, no academics to examine or explain us. We understood that, according to the traditions of our work, if we were ethical, we would do well. If we were truly and slavishly "neutral," we would enjoy an excellent reputation and continued success, as we defined it. As I did that work, especially in state and local government labor negotiations and as an appointed agency head, I think some sensibilities about governing and real politics seeped into my worldview and laid some groundwork for my later work in public-policy mediation.

When I resigned from the WERC to help found the Wisconsin Center for Public Policy (WCPP), a private nonprofit research institute, I saw an opportunity to initiate a practice as a labor-relations neutral and to advocate for some experimentation and innovation in labor relations conflict management. WCPP, which was generously supported by Herb Kohl, a businessman who would later serve in the US Senate, was billed as a think tank. Some of us did some respectable research, but it was also something of a staging area for Democrats waiting to run for office. Election campaigning and related operations were the coin of the realm.

The research at WCPP moved me toward a more intellectual approach to my work, and I began teaching labor law at the University of Wisconsin in 1978. (In later years I taught dispute resolution courses there. In 1995 I began teaching dispute resolution theory at Marquette University in Milwaukee at its Center for Dispute Resolution Education and its law school.)

Around this time, friends who were still leading state agencies asked if I might mediate disputes in the caseloads of the Department of Natural Resources (DNR) and the Public Service Commission. Tony Earl, the DNR secretary, had observed my mediation of a collective bargaining agreement with a union of state employees while he was heading another department. He wanted a consensus-based resolution of a very complicated waste-load allocation dispute. No such thought had ever crossed my mind. I had no idea what the term "waste-load allocation" meant. (It turns out that in this context, "waste-load allocation" means the load of pollutants each discharger of waste agrees to release into a particular waterway.)

This was the late 1970s, and the field, later described as alternative dispute resolution, was in its earliest stages. Neighborhood justice centers were opening. (I served on the board of one.) Frank Sander, the Harvard Law professor known as one of the founders of ADR, visited me. He was considering mediation as an adjunct of the courts. Family counseling and divorce professionals were seeing mediation as superior to litigation. (I am embarrassed to recall that in 1981 I spoke at a conference of the Association of Family and Conciliation Courts and said of their concept and use of the term mediation, "You can't paint it green and call it grass." Clearly, I was a naïve purist and did not anticipate the expansive connotation of "mediation.")

Probably because I had accumulated a caseload of environmental disputes due to my friends in government, the Ford Foundation provided generous support for that work and invited me to gatherings of others in that emerging practice area. I don't know which was the greater gift, and to this day I treasure the friendships and professional support of the colleagues I met then.

My new colleagues generally were not former labor mediators, and some were not lawyers. Some were planners, and some came from other disciplines. Worse yet, they were comfortable with non-agreement-seeking public engagement processes. They did not share my assumptions, and their ideas of best practices seemed heterodox and dubious. While I believed that disputes were best resolved by stakeholders, these practitioners seemed to be working on behalf of authorities who would ultimately determine outcomes. Moreover, they displayed a facility with butcher paper, masking tape, and colored markers that felt gimmicky to me, much less serious than the risky and demanding business of agreement-seeking "real" mediation. Their work seemed passive and too easy. Perhaps I was evolving, still naively protective of the doctrines of my earliest training.

I needed reassurance of my professionalism, of my grasp of when, how, and why mediation works. My entry into new conflict realms and teaching at the university level required diligence in that regard, and those new colleagues and their writings were there for me. Not competitive, despite the very limited demand for the work that we all wanted, we argued earnestly and elevated one another and revealed, among so many things, that being grounded differently, being mainly academics or mainly practitioners, was our advantage.

I learned a lot from adapting to work in non-labor mediation and from the others on that frontier. Jerry Cormick, Gail Bingham, Susan Carpenter, Peter Adler, and Lawrence Susskind come to mind. I met Linda Singer, Michael Lewis, and Margaret Shaw. I discovered journal articles that I reread to this day. Lon Fuller, Frank Sander, Stephen Goldberg, Lawrence Susskind, Joseph Stulberg, and Leonard Riskin provided me with explanations and values and eventually personal counsel.

Fuller, who was grounded in collective bargaining, explained in scholarly terms what I had experienced. I recall that I found his article to be a wonderful gift, implying that there was serious intellectual thinking to be done about the work in which I was engaged. It elevated my work. He argued that mediation is more apt when determining norms (transactions) than in norm enforcement (settling disputes arising out of asserted legal and contractual rights). I agree with that, despite the fact that mediation's great growth strongly suggests otherwise. Fuller emphasized the role of the parties' enlightened self-interest and the importance of working well with the agents of the stakeholders. Those points, and others, were confirming of my labor mediation experience.

Sander and Goldberg amplified and reinforced the labor mediators' belief that mediation is only one element of a repertoire of strategies to be applied where they are apt, not an end in itself. Riskin gave us a nomenclature with which we could communicate more effectively and explained that even within mediation there is an array of strategies to be mastered. He asserted wisely that the notion of "real" mediation is of no more value than an official definition of pizza. Stulberg and Susskind examined the elusive concept of neutrality and the challenges to true professionalism that lie in how we define success.

It seems in retrospect that a fundamental result for me was an acquired comfort with unresolved doctrinal ambiguity. My grounding has not changed. My labor mediator roots are deep and reassuring. But, decades later, I have come around some, and I think I've gained flexibility, which supports versatility.

To be effective in environmental disputes. I not only needed to shift from the two-party model to a multi-party process. I had to operate within the very complicated and profound consequences of not achieving closure. The laws and regulatory regimes had to be recognized, as did the societal, ecological, and political impacts. I found that the "environmental" rubric covered a very broad and undefined variety of conflicts, many of which were caught in a seamless web of political and social issues that were critical to their settlement, e.g. not-in-my-backyard siting conflicts.

The environmental work also took me into a variety of conflicts based on contentions by American Indian tribes regarding their sovereignty and treaty rights. There were plenty of cross-cultural interactions in my labor cases, but none that were so explicit. Opportunities to work in Canada, England, Bulgaria, Czechoslovakia, Poland, South Africa, Japan, and some of the nations that were reborn following the collapse of the Soviet Union, were also invaluable sources of insight as I attempted to explain and apply my American perspective. Twice a year for many years, students from six African countries came to the Marquette Center for Dispute Resolution Education, where I continued teaching, and they kept me humble and curious about my work here in the United States.

When I drafted rules and regulations for a national labor mediation agency in Bulgaria, I had been the head of such an agency in Wisconsin. As the work went on, I became increasingly aware of how our policies and practices were rooted in our laws, economic system, and mores regarding labor-management relations. In my recent work at the University of Amsterdam helping establish a public mediation program, I have experienced how a culture seemingly similar to our own can view conflict profoundly differently and yet suffer the same undesirable consequences of impasse—and benefit, as we do, from mediation.

Eventually, arrogance suggested that if I could have success as I defined it (i.e., voluntary agreements on a broad spectrum of environmental conflicts), I could probably transplant my doctrine and skills, with my ability to flex and accommodate a little, to pretty much any sort of dispute. I decided that I would not involve myself in the divorces of others, but otherwise I was ready to wade into any subject matter, and I did. (It was my presumption that family conflicts were not only beyond the scope of my training but exceeded my capacity to deal with overt emotions. Much later, this presumption was tested when I provided mediation in a number of clergy sex abuse matters. I believe that I can claim some success in those cases, but I also experienced a sense of burnout that was new to me.) My thought was that mediation, like writing, was a cross-cutting process and skill and that there was nothing particularly environmental or labor-related about it.

I returned to state government in 1983 when Tony Earl, my friend at Wisconsin's Department of Natural Resources, became governor and appointed me secretary of Industry, Labor and Human Relations. It was a department that included a broad variety of programs, including safety codes, equal rights, workers' compensation, unemployment insurance, workforce training, and a great deal more. Our new administration inherited a scandalous deficit in the unemployment insurance fund that could be overcome only by raising taxes in a very selective manner. The governor believed that should be done on the basis of an agreement among both political parties and both chambers of the legislature. He saw it as a mediation, and he knew me as a mediator. I met publicly and privately with the legislative leaders, and we got it done. My belief in the potential of the process was reinforced. I spent the remainder of the governor's four-year term learning a lot about managing in government and regulating. I also attempted to manage a state office of dispute resolution from my position as a cabinet secretary.

When we failed to gain reelection, I returned to my eclectic practice, hoping that my time as a Democratic public official hadn't compromised my acceptability as a neutral, and was invited by Gail Bingham, who was at the time leading an environmental conflict resolution program in the Washington, DC-based Conservation Foundation, to affiliate with her program. It was my great good fortune to join the small number of individuals acting as convenors and facilitators in negotiated rulemaking processes being initiated mainly by the Environmental Protection Agency (EPA). I began with work on regulations developing at the Nuclear Regulatory Commission and over the years worked with the EPA, the Department of the Interior, the Department of Agriculture, the Department of Energy, the Federal Trade Commission, and the Department of Education as well as their counterparts in a number of states throughout the country. (I was also very fortunate to become the favorite mediator of Tommy Thompson, the Republican governor who put me out of my position with the state and whom I had worked with successfully in the unemployment compensation negotiations while he was the minority leader in the State Assembly.)

Regulatory negotiations were mainly the brainchild of Philip Harter, a conflict resolution colleague and administrative law expert who recognized and wrote about the potential for substantially reducing delay and elevating the quality of, and compliance with, administrative rules by inviting stakeholders to participate with the regulatory agency in the drafting of those rules. The process of determining whether such negotiations were apt (convening) and the actual management of the processes that went forward (facilitating) were more than intriguing to me. They seemed to be familiar components of mediation that might be informed by political savvy.

Obviously, the convening process in which the conflict at hand is assessed for mediation feasibility is in many ways an enlarged and explicitly identified version of the assessment most mediators make at the threshold of their engagement. What seems peculiar to these large-scale, multiparty, policy-making negotiations is that the assessment includes the extremely critical determination of what parties should participate as negotiators if a proper settlement is to be obtained. It's not a matter of plaintiffs and defendants, unions and employers, or spouses. Rather there is the need to identify and bring to the negotiations both obvious and less well-known entities that are critical to the efficacy of the negotiations. I believe that having worked among political actors, activists, and affected communities has given me an advantage.

Indeed, negotiated rulemaking exposed how the more established mediation processes worked, as if by examining an elephant one came to understand the components of a mouse. As the anatomy of the process was expanded to include more players, it became both necessary and easier to see that anatomy. It established that the same anatomy occurred in small group mediations, but without explicit reference.

Moreover, negotiated rulemaking reinforced my view of mediation as a cross-cutting process. Its application to environmental rulemaking was soon recognized as appropriate to regulating an array of administrative responsibilities. The process put a premium on the importance of grasping political realities, a skill that I felt I had acquired as a government official. And most importantly, by its participative nature, negotiated rulemaking seemed to promise to enhance liberal democracy, vindicating the preference that I shared with Lon Fuller for the mediation of transactions rather than settling rights-based disputes. Last, negotiated rulemaking required mediation that Riskin describes as facilitative/broad, which also comported with the labor mediation doctrine that I had absorbed years before.

Negotiated rulemaking also resonated with the political traditions of Wisconsin. Beginning in the early twentieth century, Wisconsin was a political laboratory mainly influenced by the economist John R. Commons, who led us to believe, among many other things, that government policies informed by stakeholders of all perspectives were most likely to serve us well. (Sadly, we seem to have left all that behind recently.) The department that I led was the inheritor and implementor of that wisdom, and I was a true believer.

An affiliation with the National Policy Consensus Center at Portland State University allowed me to work in Oregon, where progressive politics were supporting such approaches to public policy making on the state level. It provided an opportunity for me to think more systematically about what I had done and what I had learned.

Actually, mediation has always provided an abundance of time for self-assessment. Sitting in airports and airplanes, driving my car, and standing by in the halls of public buildings have provided a lot of opportunities to wonder about what happened to me. Why do I seem to be pretty good at this? Am I talented? Why am I able to work well with individuals and organizations I disapprove of and, at times, even admire them for their skills? Why am I uncomfortable co-mediating, except with Susan Podziba? How does this process work? Why do I like it so much? Is there a personal factor that argues against formulaic theories? Does it coincide with my growing up as a marginalized observer of ordinary people? Does it coincide with my politics?

What about the pure enjoyment—the psychic payoff? What else has done that for me? I'd say playing jazz in college. There seems to be a real analogy there. Or a metaphor. Or an explanation.

On the surface, neither jazz nor mediation is subject to a consensus definition; but both are mainly ensemble performances, and, in my experience, they are both essentially improvised performances. A jazz musician draws in the moment from what bandmates are playing and a repertoire acquired from years of performing and listening to the performances of others. To that is added the musician's skills with an instrument, mood, and taste. A mediator also has a repertoire of responses learned from training and experience that is called upon in the moment without much cerebration. (The rests are as important as the notes.)

In mediation, perhaps "taste" is better referred to as "judgment," and like taste, it is augmented by perceptive powers, mainly listening. I think talented jazz musicians and mediators have an "ear" that takes them beyond what may be gained from training, study, and practice. I think that gift has its origins in their early environment and even genetics. Perhaps it should be referred to as intuition. How many superb musicians come from unmusical homes and neighborhoods? They may sit down and play without a lesson or the ability to read musical notation. (As I mentioned at the start, I think my mom had a fine "ear," and maybe that was one of her gifts to me.)

I think training comes from all of one's experience, not only so-called formal training and mentoring. Among jazz musicians and mediators there are those who are "natural," those who are "technical," and those who enjoy the excellence that comes of both talent and training. There is valuable work to be done by all of these mediators, and I hope they are deployed optimally. I worry, though, that some mediators, talented and otherwise, have become "overtrained"—that their intuitions have been smothered by lessons, doctrine, "recipes," and the fear of "errors." Some jazz listeners have observed that contemporary musicians, who are far more likely to be conservatory-trained than their predecessors, never drop a beat or miss a note. And thus they lose the feature that is at the heart of the idiom, the essential quality that brought jazz to the attention of conservatories in the first place.

Both jazz and mediation are creative processes producing unanticipated new outcomes, even for familiar undertakings. The tune has been played a thousand times, but never quite like that. It's just the latest collective bargaining agreement, but it responds very well to the present environment.

The success of the ensemble performance, in both cases, depends on a shared understanding of underlying structure (chord progression, negotiation principles). That explains why we must smuggle training into our discussions with some parties, and why working repeatedly with some is such a pleasure. We anticipate them, and that augments our capacity to respond artfully. (I understand that some great jazz musicians, known for their rapport while performing, have had no use for each other off the bandstand.) At their best, both performances capture the ironic potential of orthodoxy and discipline combined with freedom. They are artistic, creative, informed by study and practice, and elevated by talent. My belief that my work has features that exist in art elates me.

Extending the jazz analogy, negotiated rulemaking seems like an opportunity to move from playing in a quartet to leading a big band. No longer a few others to make music with, but many more. Leading is a different responsibility, more than collaborating and contributing. But the core improvisational, creative process is there, even though there is a score-like agenda, and agreement remains the preferred outcome. There are more players to cope with and therefore a more explicit structure to create and follow (negotiated ground rules), but the relationship between agreed-upon underlying structure and creativity, realized by presentations and listening, is still key. And the potential for cacophony is truly present.

Many factors contributed to my capacities as a practitioner. There was my mom's influence, however it was transmitted, combined with my early years on the periphery. Then there was the excellent mentoring and doctrine that I received from the mediators I worked with early on and the lessons that I receive to this day from generous colleagues. Finally, there is my teaching and the writing of the field's great scholars. It seems to me that these factors, combined with my time in responsible positions in government as well as my inclination toward expanded democracy (as in industrial democracy), give me a particular advantage in regulatory negotiations as well as other matters of public importance. (My cases included school district desegregation, the restoration of rivers, statewide school funding disputes, intergovernmental conflicts of many kinds, etc.). Maybe being a Midwestern American male of a certain age and era is relevant. Perhaps those factors combined to place me in a niche, like a piano player who, despite the prevailing fashions, prefers to play in a certain style.

That's all speculative and intellectual. It's an analogy that can be strained and extended even farther to prove its aptness, but none of that explains the sizzle. The thrill of it isn't only in its outcomes, but in the performance itself. Justice and good policies are great when they result, but "life is on the wire," and when you go to a mediation not knowing what to expect or to a gig wondering how your bandmates will perform and something beautiful happens, the payoff is visceral. It's rooted, I believe, in the essential element of improvisation, the riskiness of it, the sense of yourself after you stepped onto the wire, pretending perhaps to be confident, and find your way safely across the chasm. Vince Lombardi, the ultimate font of wisdom in Wisconsin, told his players that celebrating in the end zone is unbecoming and that they should act as if they'd been there before. I get that, although I will admit to the impulse. (It wouldn't be cool.)

For me, another important source of enrichment is the support, provocation, inspiration, and camaraderie of colleagues. In 1987 and again in 1996, Frank Sander invited a group of mediation practitioners and scholars to informal two-day conferences in Maine that left us wanting more. We were peers, eager to learn from each other, and the format exceeded our expectations. In 1998, under the auspices of the Western Justice Center, led by our colleague Bill Drake and located in Pasadena, California, a near replication of that group reconvened and initiated a series of annual meetings, mainly in the Boston area, that continues to this day. Individuals have come and gone from our ranks—too often, sadly—but because we are diverse in our practices and career paths, we continue to elevate each other in remarkable ways. Just as my early exposure to Fuller elevated my sense of my work, the opportunity to interact with these successful, busy, thoughtful colleagues also contributes to what the work means to me.

Finally, mediation, like jazz, is undefined, so to forecast its future requires confidence as to what "it" is, and such confidence seems naive. I believe that the wonderful potential of the mediation I have practiced is transactional and holds promise for enhancing democracy and public policy, although I suspect that this is only one of the niches that mediation will occupy. I have never been one to describe mediation as a "cause" or a path to social justice. That has always seemed dreamy to me. Nonetheless, for my mentors and peers—and for me—mediation has been a central and meaningful element of our lives. In contrast, for many recent entrants to the field, it is work that promises a good lifestyle to entrepreneurs and the semi-retired. Jazz lovers have referred to certain performances, and certain musicians, as "commercial," and never with admiration. The implication is that careers designed mainly to gain popularity and financial return do not deserve the respect due to those who would advance something more, something of worth.

I fear, though, that in the wake of the coronavirus pandemic, mediation's commercial potential will be what comes to the fore. The Great Depression of the 1930s and World War II contributed enormously to my worldview and that of my mediation peers. The coronavirus pandemic is likely to do the same for those now entering the dispute resolution field. Our current interest in videoconferencing and all things online that allow us to work, albeit remotely, seems of particular currency and promise. In recent years, probably due to necessity and the patient and tactful treatment I have received from Colin Rule, I have become less resistant to some online dispute resolution processes. But my belief that face-to face interactions are the heart and soul of mediation persists. I worry about the convergence of decreased face-to-face mediation and the commercialism to which I have just referred.

We have always asserted that mediation is a time-and cost-saver. Now we can reinforce that claim by offering remote service and exploit the seductiveness of leading-edge technology as well. Will the primers and webinars on videoconferencing technology that promise, at least implicitly, to "grow your practice" prescribe best practices and eclipse our interests in democracy and public policy? Will we reassess the proper mixture of the technical and the intuitive or "natural?" Or will the mediators of the future be the masters of their instruments *and* the providers of the greatest value that is the potential of their work? I cannot say, but to those new to mediation and the field in general, I wish all that I have enjoyed: the joy of shared performance, inspiring and supportive colleagues, endless exploration and learning, and the occasional thrill of a challenging undertaking ending in success for all concerned.

4

Mediation and My Life: Moments and Movements

By Lela Porter Love

◆

Backstories

Long before I had ever thought about mediation—much less considered it as a career path—I had several memorable experiences, ones that I now understand influenced

---

Lela Porter Love is a professor of law and director of the Kukin Program for Conflict Resolution at Benjamin N. Cardozo School of Law in New York City, where her program has been ranked by *US News and World Report* among the top 10 law school programs in the United States in dispute resolution since 2000. In 1985, she founded Cardozo's Mediation Clinic, one of the first clinical programs to train law students to serve as mediators. She serves as mediator, arbitrator, and dispute resolution consultant in community, employment, family, human rights, school-based and commercial cases. An active educator and participant in dispute resolution activities, she regularly conducts mediation training programs and courses both domestically and internationally. During her year as chair of the American Bar Association's Section of Dispute Resolution, she initiated the first International Mediation Leadership Summit in the Hague. She has written widely on the topic of dispute resolution, including co-authoring three law school textbooks. Among her books are *The Middle Voice: Mediating Conflict Successfully*, co-authored with Joseph Stulberg, and two collections of stories about mediations: *Stories Mediators Tell and Stories Mediators Tell—World Edition*. The International Academy of Mediators gave her a Lifetime Achievement Award in 2012. The American College of Civil Trial Mediators gave her a Lifetime Achievement Award in 2010, and in 2009 she received the "Front Line Champion" Award at the Association of the Bar of NYC on Mediation Settlement Day.

my later choices. They became stories I told about justice and dispute resolution processes.

At Palm Beach Private School and Home, 1959: Injustice

I was in fourth grade and just beginning to be sensitive to peers—and relationships with boys. I was sweet on one boy but wore the bracelet of another, which signified a connection. One day, one of the boys in the class held out my chair as I approached my desk. I was pleased by this seeming courtesy. But when I went to sit down, the chair was swiftly removed and I was suddenly on the floor, shocked. Classmates found this funny and laughed, and then I did, too. I was impressed by the joke, even though I was the butt of it.

Later that same day I was home for dinner with my parents and siblings. Wanting some fun and wanting to share the joke played on me, I went to my father's chair and held it for him. He looked very pleased at my good manners. When he went to sit down, I whisked the chair away, and he fell to the floor. No one spoke or laughed. There was an awful silence. I was taken upstairs and spanked—even though that was unheard of in my family. I got no dinner. I thought I was very unjustly treated, and I never forgot how that felt. Much later I learned that at the time, my Dad (who seemed very athletic, playing tennis every day at 64) had had back and heart issues, and the fall I caused was scary for my parents. I never had the chance to tell my story, nor did I have the full picture at the time. The disinterest in my "side" of this incident—and my not being informed about the details of my Dad's health—are what made this stand out as a never-to-be-forgotten injustice.

On the Road in Tanzania, 1970: a Justice Event

The scene remains vivid in my mind. I had recently arrived in Tanzania to work for a development project sponsored by Harvard University and the Max Planck Society. My work was to be starting a jam-making project, as Tanzania imported jam but enjoyed an abundance of sugar and fruit. Before my work began, I was riding in a Land Rover down a rural road. Sitting in the front seat next to the driver, I was the sole White female, the only person who was not a local Tanzanian, and the only one in the car who did not speak Swahili beyond "Jambo" ("Hello").

Suddenly what seemed to be rocks were thrown at the windshield. The driver slammed on the brakes, and all the men jumped out of the Land Rover to chase the children who had thrown the rocks (though it turned out that the rocks were actually dried cow dung). I was left alone by our vehicle on a dirt road in Africa.

A little time went by. I started to wander up the road in the direction the men had gone, and then a crowd of people with raised machetes came running toward our car. That was pretty scary. Before they got to me, though, village elders—each of whom had an umbrella to mark his station—came toward the car along with the men I was with and a group of three boys, who seemed to be the ones who had thrown the cow dung.

Everyone—men, women, and children—converged on a flat open area near the car, and the villagers, their machetes down, made a circle with the elders, the boys, and the men from our car in the middle of the circle. I was off to the side but a part of the circle around the men, boys, and elders.

The elders asked the men what had happened, and the drivers recounted: the cow dung was thrown at the car; it could have killed everyone by shattering the windshield and causing a crash; this was especially bad with a visitor (me).

The elders asked the boys what had happened.

The boys said that they were just playing—no harm was meant, and the men chasing them acted like they were going to kill them. (All this was translated for me by someone from our car.)

Next the elders said to the boys, "What should be done?"

The boys said they should receive a certain number of blows each from a stick. I forget the number of blows—it was more than three, and they were real blows. The boys took their hits right in the middle of the circle. Then everybody shook hands with everybody—including the boys. This took a long time; *everybody* shook hands with everyone. The atmosphere was positive. The tension was gone.

I had never witnessed such a satisfactory justice event. Everyone told their story and retained their dignity, the community seemed healed—and I never forgot it. Knowing what is possible in heated conflict with proper interventions sets the bar high in terms of goals. This event primed me to want to get similar healing results.

At George Washington University, 1980: Teaching Philosophy of Law and a Clinic

I was employed by George Washington University and its National Law Center in 1980, and part of my job was teaching an undergraduate course on the philosophy of law. In preparing for the course, I remember being struck by a description of the adversarial system as one in which two sides fight as relentlessly as possible on opposing sides, each saying the worst about the other and the best about themselves, so that a neutral person in the middle, judge or jury, could best decide the truth. This description was in keeping with some of my trial practice training at

Georgetown Law School. While my law school education had neglected philosophy, I had been well taught to use theatrics that could sway decision-makers. For example, it was important to consult and touch my client as often as possible to indicate I liked and trusted them and valued their input (regardless of whether I felt that way). Using such techniques, whatever trust and credibility I, as a lawyer, might have would be shared by my client. Such tricks, however, struck me as the opposite of seeking, much less finding, truth or justice. Recalling the injustice I felt when I was punished for the joke I played on my father, I was leaning toward an approach where disputants educated each other about their perspective and agreed on a just outcome, as had happened in Tanzania.

This perspective was enhanced by further exposure to literature about alternatives to litigation in preparation for teaching the philosophy of law course. New ideas from the 1976 Pound Conference, particularly Frank Sander's multi-door courthouse, which featured, among other processes, mediation, were influential. In 1980 I had no firsthand experience in mediation or formal consensual dispute resolution procedures. What I did learn firsthand that year was how to establish a successful law school clinic by starting a small business clinic where law students at the National Law Center represented businesses. This became a springboard for developing a very early mediation clinic in 1985.

At a Community Dispute Resolution Center in Brooklyn, 1983: Taking Mediation Training

In 1983 I moved to New York with the plan to get part-time work as a lawyer and explore mediation and arbitration—the two key alternatives to litigation that I was inspired about following my George Washington philosophy of law course. For mediation, I signed up for the basic training at the Brooklyn Mediation Center, a training delivered by Josh Stulberg and Margaret Shaw, two masters of their trade. I was mesmerized learning how a philosophy or vision of conflict resolution could be put into nuts-and-bolts practice. Whether it was a neighbor dispute, a landlord-tenant matter, or a family fight, I liked "putting the rubber to the road" to give disputants an exciting path to transform their often-dangerous conflict into an opportunity to create a better future. In a 24-hour training I learned how to conduct a mediation: how to begin, how to listen, how to develop an agenda, how to generate movement, how to caucus, and how to bring closure. It was these very elements I would spend decades exploring once I had begun a Mediation Clinic and had (in 1986) joined with Josh Stulberg as a trainer. But what works as an elegant and simple theory in a classroom doesn't always work in practice. Still ahead was the trial by fire.

Cases and Turning Points—Seeing How Theory Plays in Practice

Arbitration in New York Civil and Small Claims Court

In 1983, at the same time I was pursuing mediation, I signed up as an arbitrator for New York Civil and Small Claims Court Programs, wanting to explore and compare various roles of neutral interveners. Civil court paid a small per-case stipend to arbitrators, and small claims arbitration was volunteer work. I recall that the only memorable feature of a very short training for arbitrators in Small Claims Court was that I should never tell parties my award because the court, in such a case, "did not have the resources to protect the arbitrator." (The court mailed out notices of the arbitration award a few weeks after the hearing.) The few times I broke this rule, I was very sorry I did. Once a party knew your opinion or award, all they wanted to do was change your mind and change the outcome, which could get uncomfortable, if not dangerous.

I found arbitration difficult. The two sides always told very different stories, and I had to find the "facts" very quickly. I often worried that I was wrong in terms of understanding the truth of the situation, though I took some satisfaction in providing the best procedural due process I could devise. That meant I was careful to explain the process in an opening statement; gave each side uninterrupted time to explain their case and present their evidence; welcomed questions about what had been said and asked my own; and mainly tried to be respectful of each party. In the civil court program, six arbitrations were scheduled in one morning or afternoon window, and the result was that most cases settled either before or at the scheduled arbitration time. The attorneys were there with their files and were prepared to present a case, and consequently the settlements flowed easily, though, as an arbitrator, I did not participate in the negotiations. These early settlements made the program seem like a success, though they did not, *per se,* enamor me of the arbitration process. In small claims court, a rapid fire of cases resulted in the need to make fast decisions, as the court clerks were eager to process paperwork so they could leave on time. The speed that was needed to keep the court functioning contributed to my feeling that arbitration was "arbitrary," but even putting that feature aside, I was haunted by thinking that if I knew everything about a case, I might have made a different decision.

Leaving the courts after arbitrations, and particularly after dark, I worried about being followed or accosted by disputants in a way I would never worry if the service I provided had been mediation. Nothing of that sort ever happened, though I did usually take the precaution of traveling home with another arbitrator. In my teaching career,

I spent a fair amount of time comparing and contrasting arbitration and mediation (my husband joked that my gravestone would say "she knew the difference between arbitration and mediation"), and, in addition to more usual markers of difference, I never forgot the feeling of being an arbiter who probably made at least one side angry or unhappy and who might have made the wrong decision because the "facts" I found were only my best guesses of what had transpired. Mediation, in contrast, offered the possibility of achieving a "win" for all parties.

Mediation at the Brooklyn Mediation Center—Community Cases—and the Mediation Clinic at Cardozo Law School

My first mediation cases, immediately following the training program in 1983, were community cases at the Brooklyn and later Manhattan Mediation Centers, community dispute resolution centers under the umbrella of the New York Peace Institute. The cases involved everything from neighbors disturbed by noise or cooking odors to family members with issues about children or unpaid debts or housing, or fights between parents about kids, disputes between landlords and tenants, and even "love" triangles. These were labeled "minor" disputes by the legal system, but they definitely were not minor to the disputants.

I recall one tenant coming in and placing a mouse on the mediation table and former friends violently shouting at each other or throwing their drinks or pens at each other or (often) breaking down in tears. Once, when a funding cutback for the courts resulted in a plan to cut the armed court officers at the Brooklyn Mediation Center, a mediator strike was organized. In other words, the cases were not easy because disputants were passionate and often angry, and that made a community center a wonderful place to learn the art and science of mediation. If you could do it there, you could do it anywhere.

What was most exciting was that the theory of mediation I had so loved when taught by Josh Stulberg and Margaret Shaw worked in practice. Time and again, after telling their stories, parties would come to some accommodation. For me, it was like an addiction—to take something difficult and bad and help change it into something workable, good, and promising.

By 1985 I had proposed to Cardozo Law School the creation of a Mediation Clinic. Cardozo's dean, Monroe Price, embraced new ideas and quickly agreed to establishing one. The most difficult hurdle for the clinic was convincing Mark Smith, the then-director of the Brooklyn Mediation Center, to allow a law school program in his center. Mark thought that law students might import an "attitude" of arrogance and adversarialness that would be disrespectful to his staff and counter to the philosophy of the center. Because our agreement was that Mark retained the power to exclude any law student who didn't behave, he gave it a try. That first year we had one arrogant law student who was disrespectful toward the center staff, but armed with the threat of expulsion, Mark and I were able to teach the student some manners.

In a school with many popular clinics, the Mediation Clinic became the most sought-after clinical program in the school, thanks to the remarkable opportunities it offered students. I had the privilege of seeing cases from the vantage point of being a mediator myself as well as that of introducing law students to the practice and watching them apply the theory in the service of disputants. Result: the practice of mediation was even more exciting than my dives into theory had been.

Trust and Estate, Commercial, Family, and Other Cases

When I was a student at Georgetown Law School, one of my achievements had been to receive recognition for the highest grade in Trusts and Estates—due, I think, to the fact that my mother, my only surviving parent, died during the course of the semester, and I was acutely attuned to the various issues raised. So whenever I had the chance, I would mediate cases involving family disputes over wills and trusts. In family cases there was always the legal issue (e.g., did the testator, the maker of the will, have testamentary capacity? Was the testator unduly influenced?), but then there was a plethora of non-legal issues (the conduct of holiday events, the distribution of photographs or other items of non-monetary value, sleeping arrangements for children with aunts and uncles, how various children addressed the elders). Nearly always, principles collided, and the need for equality—equal shares from parents—had to be balanced against the principle of need—shares should be adjusted according to need (e.g., where descendants needed money for education). A stand-out moment for me was addressing the Committee on Trusts and Estates of the Association of the Bar of the City of New York and seeing the surprise on attorneys' faces that helping clients address non-legal issues in mediations, in my judgment, was critical to making acceptable deals that settled cases and sometimes allowed family members to reconnect with each other. By the time I was addressing bar committees, it seemed obvious to me that attorneys should uncover and help clients deal with all the issues that were blocking resolution—not just the legal causes of action—so the surprise of committee members was a surprise for me.

I served on the panel of the US District Court of the Eastern District of New York and in that capacity, as well as getting random referrals, would mediate commercial cases. Were such cases "all about money" or were they, like the trust and estates cases, frequently about relationships and non-legal matters that, if resolved, would provide momentum for the resolution of money issues? I usually found that concerns about respect, a need for recognition and sometimes apology, or some symbolic adjustment that showed care, could spark momentum toward a monetary agreement.

The Long Island Cases—It Works in Smaller Cases, but Does It Work in "Big" Ones?

"Have you read Owen Fiss?" That question was asked as I shook the hand of the Salvadorans' civil rights attorney on the morning of the first day of mediation about a situation between the Town of Glen Cove and Salvadoran day laborers there. The question was particularly apt given the constitutional questions raised by the case. Yale Law Professor Owen Fiss was "Against Settlement"—the title of his brilliant article (Fiss, 1984)—so it was either a harsh or a funny way for an advocate to start a mediation. I replied, "I believe you will be pleasantly surprised." And after the mediation he was.

The Owen Fiss moment came in 1992, after tensions between immigrant day workers and the town had brewed in Glen Cove, Long Island, for four years. A large group of workers gathered daily to meet up with contractors and agree on a day wage on a busy street in Glen Cove early in the morning, and the city responded by passing an ordinance that prohibited pedestrians from soliciting employment from someone in a motor vehicle and also prohibited motorists from hiring workers from their vehicles. A class-action lawsuit followed alleging the ordinance violated constitutional rights of freedom of speech and of equal protection. Write-ups about the situation in major media, as well as the cost and delays of litigation, heightened tensions. An Immigration and Naturalization Service raid on the gathering place for workers and employers (the "shaping point") exacerbated the situation.

As memorable as the Owen Fiss comment was the way the two Salvadoran day laborers started the mediation: "It is such an honor to have such very important people come to listen to our problems." The warmth and appreciation of the two class members created a glow that infected the rest of the day and created a positive trajectory for the dispute. By day two (one week later), options were created to resolve the litigation: a collaboration to craft a new ordinance that would further the town interest in early-morning traffic safety on a busy thoroughfare and insure the constitutional rights of the plaintiffs; a plan for translating public notices into Spanish and ensuring that the city soccer field would be available for all; a commitment that the police would have diversity training, some Spanish language ability, and a protocol for dealing with non-English speakers in crisis situations; the provision of a platform for the police to address community interests at Salvadoran meetings; and ideas for a new shaping point.

The same principles guided the conduct of this case and the conduct of other types of cases: involving the real parties (the Salvadoran plaintiffs—despite their lawyers not wanting to do that initially) and giving them a platform to speak, setting up the room (we had a round table in the public library), and arranging comfort coffee and food to maximize chances of success (we began each day with coffee and breakfast snacks, partially to ease what might be different arrival times of the different cultural groups), addressing all issues (not just the legal causes of action), being mindful of the agenda structure (we started with the "easy"—or easier—issue of the use of the city soccer field by the Salvadorans who couldn't read the English postings about playing and signing up), and so on. These formulas for practice worked across the board: in mediating class-action litigations, community cases, trust and estate matters, workers comp, EEOC, and commercial cases.

In 2009, I mediated another class-action suit involving another Long Island town and its Section 8 Housing program. A class of minority plaintiffs challenged the administration of the town's program because it resulted in discriminating against Black and Hispanic applicants by favoring applicants who lived within the town. Again, the mediation began (after an opening statement by the mediator) with an actual plaintiff recounting to the town's Section 8 program administrator what it had been like to apply for the program. The plaintiff's sad and moving story brought the administrator to her side—an administrator shocked to be sued after all her efforts. Later the same day, the administrator opened her files to the plaintiffs' attorneys, shortcutting a long discovery process and thereby building trust. Balancing inconveniences, one session was held out on Long Island, and the second was held in the fancy law offices of plaintiffs' *pro bono* attorneys in Manhattan. The Long Island session allowed for the town to share its files with the plaintiffs' attorneys. The Manhattan session was a distributive, positional bargaining session about the remaining—and big—issue of the amount of money to be paid to the plaintiffs. The sides traded offers and counteroffers of monetary amounts that didn't appear likely to converge. When town officials realized that the plaintiffs wanted a seven-figure settlement, they announced that such a settlement would be the end of the town's participation in the housing program because it exceeded the six-figure cap on the town's insurance. "If the settlement of this case is more than the town's liability limits, then we will be forced to shut down the Section 8 housing program." What a bad result that would be for the *pro bono* counsel! As the mediator, bringing the parties back to their interests—a housing program that best served poor constituents and was "doable" to run—was sufficient to resolve the issue, even though a seven-figure settlement would have enhanced the litigation track record of the *pro bono* counsel. The case settled for an amount of money just south of the town's policy limits thanks to uncovering the BATNA of the town's exiting from the Section 8 program altogether. Asking the *pro bono* counsel the simple question of whether they wanted to be responsible for shutting down a housing program for persons in need worked magic. They did not.

These Long Island cases strengthened my belief in ensuring that the parties are given a platform to speak so that their issues (not just legal causes of action) are addressed and their voices can inform the process, in providing a neutral and comfortable setting with arrangements for food and adequate breakout space, a thoughtful speaking order, an invitation to discuss all issues of concern, respectful listening, time for reflection and creative problem-solving in uncovering and highlighting the underlying interests, in trying to build an adequate information base before jumping to option creation. These were the lessons I had learned from community cases, and they still applied in large multi-party, multi-issue cases. Learning about George Mitchell's mediation in Northern Ireland, where he used similar standard practices, reinforced those lessons.

Louisiana Workers' Compensation Cases and EEOC Cases

In 1992 and 1993, Josh Stulberg and I were asked to provide a skill-building workshop and a training manual for mediators in the state of Louisiana's Workers' Compensation Program. Prior to the training or writing, we asked to observe cases and had the exciting opportunity to travel around Louisiana and participate in a variety of cases.

Going into this assignment, I worried that the training and practice I was used to might not serve well in worker's comp cases, which were dominated by attorneys and insurance adjusters, often together with the one lone worker seeking compensation sitting by a lawyer who didn't want the client to speak. I was used to an emphasis on parties, rather than professionals, and didn't know how sessions overbalanced with professional representatives would play. But what we found was that the same principles applied. Let the parties speak! We were given the chance to observe and participate in cases while we were in Louisiana, and we wove our case experiences into the training program.

In one case, for example, a worker seeking considerable compensation was given the floor. "You don't think I have a serious back injury?" she asked. "Let me describe my evenings. I have to lie on the floor of *my* kitchen while my daughter-in-law, whom I hate, cooks dinner in *my* kitchen. Everything is *wrong* for me—the smells, her using my pots and pans, the food she cooks, but I am immobilized and helpless in my own kitchen due to my back." It was not the stack of papers that convinced the insurance adjuster about the severity of her injury but the worker's passion in telling her story and the details that just could not be fabricated.

Consequently, we emphasized in the training allowing parties to speak, setting up the space with everyone on the same level around a conference table (instead of using the traditional hearing room, where the neutral sat elevated and apart), and using familiar techniques to generate movement (reality-testing, thoughtful agenda-setting, exploration of the BATNA, and the like). I came away impressed that what worked in "small" cases and worked in "big" cases (e.g., the Long Island cases) also worked in cases dominated by (sometimes jaded) professionals.

Articles, Textbooks, and Stories Mediators Tell—Inspiration and Impact

"The Risks of Riskin's Grid" with Kimberlee Kovach

There was a time in my career when I wasn't that interested in dispute resolution-related writing. What I wanted to say was already being well said by others—by Frank Sander, Josh Stulberg, Baruch Bush, Lon Fuller, Carrie Menkel-Meadow, Roger Fisher, and other of my hero pundits. But when I was sitting on a panel at an Association of American Law Schools meeting sometime after 1994 (when Len Riskin had first published his grid of mediator orientations) and I saw Len Riskin draw and describe his grid, I realized that the narrow evaluative mediator he described was not a mediator as I knew it at all but was more related to an arbitrator.

That moment propelled me into writing, in 1998, with Kimberlee Kovach, "The Risks of Riskin's Grid" (Kovach and Love, 1998). Kim and I thought that if mediators took on a decisional or evaluative role, this would undermine parties communicating with each other because they would be trying to convince the mediator and also undermine the creation of self-determined outcomes. I thought criticizing the "evaluative" mediator would be an unpopular stance, but, given my love for mediation as I understood it, I felt it was a worthy "hill to die on." From that point on, I was led into academic arguments and debates. After that article, I wrote many more, plus book chapters, commentaries, tributes, magazine columns, training and teaching manuals, and letters to editors. What stand out as a few major endeavors follow.

The Middle Voice *with Josh Stulberg*

I conducted mediation trainings from 1986 to the present, using the framework and content from Josh Stulberg's book, *Taking Charge/Managing Conflict* (Stulberg, 1987). What a pleasure it was for me to be invited to work on a new book with Josh based on *Taking Charge* but modified by our long experience in training mediators. In 2009, *The Middle Voice: Mediating Conflict Successfully* (Stulberg and Love, 2009) was published.

Dispute Resolution: Beyond the Adversarial Model *with Carrie Menkel-Meadow, Andrea Schneider, and Jean Sternlight*

Starting in 2005, writing a series of textbooks with a wonderful team of co-authors (the "chick book" until Michael Moffitt joined the team in 2018), provided a unique learning opportunity—both in negotiating with co-authors and in broadening my own horizons and perspectives on the ADR world.

Stories Mediators Tell *with Eric Galton and* Stories Mediators Tell: World Edition *with Glen Parker*

I love stories, and I love mediation, and I long wanted to marry the two to share these passions. I believe my best project to date is the publication of two books of stories told by mediators (Galton and Love, 2012, and Love and Parker, 2018). Not only were the books well received, but since their publication I have enjoyed many story-telling events around the world with mediators sharing their adventures. So many remarkable breakthroughs happened in private mediation rooms—never publicized. Understandings grew, long-standing hatreds abated, and deals were born. Telling the stories seemed like a magical gift to the world. I felt the stories opened a window to the private mediation rooms, allowing an adversarial world to take a deep breath and appreciate another, better way to address conflict.

Other Moments in My Career

Giving Cardozo's International Advocate for Peace Award to Archbishop Desmond Tutu of South Africa; former President Jimmy Carter; former senator and Northern Ireland peace negotiator George Mitchell; Peter, Paul and Mary; and Paul McCartney (to name a very few of our luminaries) were "highs" in my career. Bringing these people visibly into the camp of Cardozo's "advocates for peace" enhanced a sense that we had a real movement toward human collaboration.

A course on mediation at Central European University in Budapest every summer since 2000 has created an international community of scholars and mediators and friends. Serving as host for the International Mediation Leadership Summit in the Hague in my 2009 chair year of the Section of Dispute Resolution of the ABA felt like the crest of a powerful wave that gathered mediators worldwide before sending them to their many shores. Since that event, many events and publications have brought the international mediation community closer together. I remember pausing at the Peace Palace during the event and thinking, "I can stop here. This is the peak." Or, in St. Petersburg, at the International Legal Forum in 2018, placed between the minister of justice from Serbia and the assistant minister of justice from Russia in a plenary session on "The Future of the Legal Profession," I thought that if Russia and Serbia are moving toward mediation, this field has come far. And I have been very lucky to be along for the ride.

A Full Circle "Peace Train"

One night I was driving with a close friend who said, "I'm going to play something for you," and he cued up "Peace Train" by Cat Stevens. I had never heard it, and I hit repeat over and over. Both the spirit and the words captured something about what I was striving for, what made me happy. Moving in some Darwinian or Teilhard de Chardin progression toward relations between people that embody understanding, collaboration, and the possibility of unity, I smiled as Cat Stevens sang:

Oh, I've been smiling lately,
Dreaming about the world as one...
Oh, Peace Train take this country...
Something good has begun.

References

Fiss, O. M. 1984. "Against Settlement." *Yale Law Journal* 93(6): 1073-1090.

Galton, E. and L. P. Love, eds. 2012. *Stories Mediators Tell*. Chicago: American Bar Association.

Kovach, K. K. and L. P. Love. 1998. "Mapping Mediation: The Risks of Riskin's Grid." *Harvard Negotiation Law Review* 3: 71-110

Love, L. P. and G. Parker, eds. 2018. *Stories Mediators Tell: World Edition*. Chicago: American Bar Association.

Stulberg, J. P. 1987. *Taking Charge/Managing Conflict*. Lanham, MD: Lexington Books.

Stulberg, J. P. and L. P. Love. 2009. *The Middle Voice: Mediating Conflict Successfully*. Durham, NC: Carolina Academic Press

5

What Am I Doing Here? Field Notes on Finding My Way to Mediation

By Ian Macduff

─────◆─────

I.

"It is quite true what philosophy says, that life must be understood backwards. But then one forgets the other principle, that it must be lived forward."
—*Søren Kierkegaard*, The Diary of Søren Kierkegaard

Ian Macduff is director of the New Zealand Centre for ICT Law at Auckland Law School. He taught at Victoria University of Wellington for a number of years and until June 2016 was associate professor of law and director of the Dispute Resolution Initiative at Singapore Management University. He worked for the World Health Organization in Sri Lanka on their "Health as a Bridge to Peace" program between 1999 and 2006 and has been a practicing mediator for more than 30 years, working in commercial, environmental, policy, intercultural, family, online mediation, and other fields. He is a member of the Independent Standards Commission of the International Mediation Institute and a member of the IMI's Task Force on Intercultural Mediation accreditation, a member of the Global Organizing Committee of the Global Pound Conference series, and a fellow of the National Center for Technology and Dispute Resolution. He is also editor of *Essays on Mediation: Dealing with Disputes in the 21st Century* (2016), co-editor of *Ethnic Conflict and Secessionism in South and South East Asia* (2003); and contributing author of *Dispute Resolution in New Zealand* (1999), *Guidelines for Family Mediation* (1995), and *An Asian Perspective on Mediation* (2009).

The inherent risk in a project such as this collection of chapters, is that we, as narrators and constructors of the diverse stories of our becoming involved in dispute resolution, find more coherence to the narrative than might in fact be true. This, however, did not necessarily trouble Bruce Chatwin, from whom I borrow the title of his last book, published posthumously: *What Am I Doing Here?*

Even in the opening essays of that book, written while Chatwin was in hospital, terminally ill (though he may not have conceded that), he sought an exotic explanation for his illness in a "very rare Chinese fungus of the bone-marrow." And through many of his other books and essays—in particular perhaps his most famous, *The Songlines*, written in 1987—the narrative served a larger purpose, which was to underpin his thesis about the fundamentally nomadic nature of the human species . . . in turn, an explanation to himself and long-suffering friends and family, as to why he was constantly on the move, when he wasn't imposing himself on someone's hospitality.

Only some 10 years after Chatwin's death were a number of his previously unpublished essays and papers collected by Jan Borm and Matthew Graves under the title *Anatomy of Restlessness*, highlighting both his nomadic quests and his hypothesis about the human imperative of constant mobility. It's a collection, however, that seamlessly mixes the fictional, the autobiographical, and astute social commentary.

In the following paragraphs, I will endeavor to trace some of the leads I found myself following, ending up in mediation though not initially knowing that's where I was headed—if only because mediation was something that belonged, at the time, either in the arcane world of labor relations or in the remote worlds of non-Western societies. There will be—as in Chatwin's writing and that of another favorite author, Patrick Leigh Fermor—a great deal of shameless name-dropping, though in this case my aim is not to establish academic credentials but rather to make one core point about my own version of this pathway: it was the people I met along the way who *were* the path.

> He aha te mea nui o te ao
> *(What is the most important thing in the world?)*
> He tangata, he tangata, he tangata
> *(It is the people, it is the people, it is the people)*
> —*Maori proverb*

II.

I blame my sister's undergraduate anthropology texts from the year she spent at Auckland University in the mid-1960s. On the bookshelves at our parents' home in New Zealand an alluring array of texts appeared, and the one that stays with me is Raymond Firth's 1936 classic *We, the Tikopia*, a sociological study of kinship in Polynesia. My imagination about the lives of others had already been captured by *National Geographic*, to which my family had a subscription. In the anthropology texts, the formalizing of the *National Geographic*'s relatively brief (and now dated) excursions in the form of a discipline of study seemed infinitely more interesting than what was on offer in the final year of my high school.

Once I started at that same university myself in 1966, the texts remained on the shelves but were displaced in my attention, if not in my interest, by the imperatives of a double-degree program in law and history and German. This was, however, the mid-'60s, and even in far-off New Zealand there were signs of ferment in academe. While hair grew longer and jeans displaced the "smart casual" norms, the occasional new academic appointment from the United States and United Kingdom brought news of a loosening of the stranglehold of intellectual and social convention. For whatever reason, anthropology—the discipline and the university department—held a perceived promise of critical and personal exploration of what we'd now probably refer to as "the other," though I doubt that the term was used then. At that time—around 1968—the university established a department of Sociology and made its first professorial appointment—not without dissent, I recall, within the more established disciplines of anthropology, history, and political science, where people must have imagined that they had the territory of social sciences already covered.

My own program of study didn't involve formally taking up anthropology, but in (I think) my second year in the law school, the faculty appointed someone who had spent time in Singapore, Malaysia, and Papua New Guinea and introduced to some of us wide-eyed wanderers the subject of the anthropology of law. This, I suspect, is where the fever took hold, one that led, in due course, to works that are now very familiar to those who have been around mediation for long enough: Laura Nader's *The Ethnography of Law* (1965) and *Law in Culture and Society* (1969), Simon Roberts's *Order and Dispute: An Introduction to Legal Anthropology*, Cathie J. Witty's *Mediation and Society: Conflict Management in Lebanon*, and others.

Fortuitously, the then-mandatory subject jurisprudence was seen by instructors as sufficiently flexible in its agenda that some of those studies in legal anthropology could be brought in—to the horror, it must be said, of the more conventional and positivist of other professors, for whom sociology and anthropology could only be contaminants of the analytical purity of "real" jurisprudence. Nevertheless, here we came across Karl Nickerson Llewellyn and Edward Adamson Hoebel on *The Cheyenne Way*, P.H.

Gulliver on *Disputes and Negotiations: Social Control in an African Society*, Leopold Pospisil on *The Anthropology of Law* (and, more broadly, on legal pluralism). While not expressly on legal anthropology, Bronislaw Malinowski's 1922 study of the patterns of trade in his *Argonauts of the Western Pacific* was seen rightly as the work that established ethnographic methodology even if we would now see many of his attitudes toward his subjects as, at best, paternalistic and, at worst, plain racist.

Sometime during that period I bought my first text on anthropology (while still pursuing the conventional pathways of law and history)—John Beattie's *Other Cultures of 1964*. This remains on my shelves as a study (perhaps dated, though I see it is still in print) of the "big" questions anthropologists ask, as well as, in the second part, specific studies of social ordering, kinship, law and political organization, and economics. History and biography are risky territory when read backwards in the search for explanations or excuses, but what stands out in reviewing that earlier reading is the continuity between the anthropologies of law and social ordering and the earliest influences in the development of modern mediation and "alternative" dispute resolution. The possibility of dispute resolution without the formal intervention of law or through the intervention of non-judicial third parties at least provided a procedural alternative to litigation—even if, as we have seen over four decades of development, modern mediation has developed its own kinds of formalism.

It will also come as no surprise to many that, despite law being essentially about interpersonal, social, and political ordering and the management of disputes and conflict, precious little attention was ever given to those issues. I think it was an American jurist named Holland who said something to the effect that, "if you can think about something that is related to something else, without thinking of the thing to which it's related, then you have a legal mind." And here's the prime example: at least in that era, the study of law was effectively devoid of any attention to the reasons for law. The doctrinal jurists had set the agenda for the study of law; and now others—the anthropologists and sociologists—were presuming to have something to say about law and conflict. The stage was set for the appearance, through the 1970s, of the twin threads of critical legal studies and studies in dispute resolution and—crucially for the development of "alternative" dispute resolution—a critical concern with access to justice.

III.

A parallel branch of my reading habits which continues to this day is travel literature (anthropology without the footnotes, if you will). This of course is a wildly eclectic field and marked by significant variations in quality so, at the risk of sounding elitist, I underscore the "literature" part of that description: there is, in the best of the writers, a quality of writing that matches the depth of observation and humanity of engagement with the lives of others. Think here of Mark Twain, Johann Wolfgang von Goethe (on his travels in Italy), Wilfred Thesiger, George Orwell (down and out in Paris and London), Norman Douglas, Freya Stark, Colin Thubron (in Damascus, Tibet, Russia, central Asia, and elsewhere, an outstanding writer as well as traveler), Patrick Leigh Fermor, Laurie Lee, William Least Heat-Moon (see his wonderful *Blue Highways*), Alexander Frater (chasing monsoons), Paul Theroux (in his less grumpy modes), Jonathan Raban, Bruce Chatwin (though, as I've mentioned, the boundaries between fiction and fact are, at times, as blurred in his observations about travels as they are in his autobiographical moments), William Dalrymple, and Pico Iyer. I'm less inclined to include in such a list those whose style is redolent of the "I'm here and you are not" smugness—especially if "here" is some envy-inducing location in Tuscany or the south of France or central Vietnam. But the best of travel literature can, I think, rank alongside the more formal cousins in anthropology in providing humanistic, empathetic, and thoughtful insights into the diversity of our shared condition.

IV.

There's a third strand to this story, expanding on one word in that previous sentence, and that is the development through the 1970s and into the 1980s of "humanistic legal education." By this time, I was teaching at law school in New Zealand, treading the line between the persistence of doctrinal law and legal education and the potentially destructive power of critical legal education that was threatening to undo a number of American law schools. Shaping this, too, were the disruptive (before Silicon Valley co-opted the word as its catchphrase) influences of feminist and minority and/or indigenous legal theory.

Three features of the time were, I think, outstanding influences: one is the engaging power of critical ideas that allowed, or even demanded, that law and other institutions be constantly re-examined; the second was the appearance in scholarly journals of a more reflective and engaged scholarship; and the third was the networks of colleagues who, even before the connecting power of the Internet and email, began to find each other. In the field of humanistic legal education, which today is perhaps less important as those ideas have become more mainstream, academics such as James Elkins, Jack Himmelstein, and Elizabeth Dvorkin began to write about thinking about law and legal education "from the bottom up," as it were. Much of this work sought to bridge the familiar gap in legal education between the practical and the theoretical—or, as William

Twining called it, the tension between "Pericles and the Plumber" (Twining, 1967).

As James Elkins noted in his law review article "A Humanistic Perspective in Legal Education":

> The teacher with a humanistic perspective recognizes what the traditional teacher ignores. The humanistic teacher takes the effort to discover who the student is and what unique gifts she has that will help her pursue the life of a lawyer. By taking the effort to know her students, the humanistic teacher concentrates less on the curriculum, the skills, and the body of knowledge transmitted in legal education than does the traditional teacher. Instead, more time is spent teaching and learning the process of participation in an individual, personal, and subjective world of law and legal practice. In other words, the emphasis shifts from merely teaching the skills of a lawyer to teaching the law student to be a whole person. (Elkins, 1983:494-495)

If one feature can be extracted, even in retrospect, from the changes in legal scholarship in the 1970s, it was a change in the cast of characters who were now part of the story of law and disputing: law and disputing became far richer than simply the domain of legal doctrine and those who managed that narrative and now was peopled by those whose lives were intimately—and not always constructively—affected by it. If anything, it was that kind of shift that helped make mediation possible in that the notions of agency in the worlds of disputes and resolution permitted—even required—the active presence of those whose disputes they were. While I might not have seen it at the time, the shift that was taking place, at least enough to permit the parallel development of mediation, was from the earliest ruler-centered dispute resolution (the divine right of kings) to rule-centered processes (the rule of law and of centralized justice) to disputant-centered processes in which disputants acquired agency in their own conflicts.

One example of this came from the world of criminology rather than law, in a seminal article by Norwegian criminologist Nils Christie writing about "Conflicts as Property" (Christie, 1977). The argument of that article became one of the core foundations of restorative justice and community empowerment movements, at the heart of which of course are actors other than just the familiar agents of state authority. There's a combined critique in this and related work: a critique of the presumed unique expertise of conventional authority, and an institutional critique that makes possible the imagination of alternatives to usual structures of power. Those familiar with the emerging literature on mediation will recognize a kinship in Carrie Menkel-Meadow's title, "Whose Dispute Is It Anyway? A Philosophical and Democratic Defense of Settlement (In Some Cases)" (Menkel-Meadow, 1995).

V.

". . . I'm glad you stood in my way."
—*Leonard Cohen,"Famous Blue Raincoat"*

The preceding four sections of this chapter have set out some elements of the intellectual and bookish parts of my indirect route to mediation. If I extract the key elements of this exploration, they would have to be, first, the discovery through anthropology and travel literature of ways of doing things (governing, social order, dispute resolution, economic life, art, and so on) radically different from, but as effective in their context as, those that formed the core of "conventional wisdom;" second, and related, the first glimmerings of pluralism, cosmopolitanism, and diversity and—though not then named as such—multiculturalism as shaping forces for the emerging "alternatives" to legal formalism and litigation; and third, the underpinning critical stance toward one's own ways of life or law.

Beyond those more intellectual elements, however, the enduring value came in the form of a network of authors, colleagues, and friends, a kind of parallel universe to life in the law school. I still recall, with some poignancy, seeing a student in the early 1980s at the University of California at Davis wearing a lapel badge with the words "Is there life after law school?" This parallel network indicated that there was almost certainly life alongside law school . . . and one poised to invade, in due course, as the marginal became mainstream and the "alternative" was dropped from descriptions of dispute resolution.

In the course of a sabbatical leave in the United States in 1980, I was in effect passed from one colleague to another, initially with Jack Himmelstein in the humanistic legal education universe at the City University of New York (later at Columbia Law School). The overlap between critical legal education and the emerging world of mediation led to an introduction through Jack to Gary Friedman in California—another lawyer who had moved from conventional legal practice to pioneering work in mediation. Oddly, in both cases, there was another introduction but from outside the worlds of both law and mediation: by pure coincidence I had been introduced to Edith Stauffer (1909-2004), a practitioner and trainer in Jungian psychosynthesis and forgiveness who was based in Pasadena but visiting Wellington. On hearing of my nascent mediation interests and plans to go to the United States, she said, "Well, you must meet Jack and Gary." Gary also insisted that I should meet a friend and colleague, Harry Sloan, who had quit dentistry to lead workshops at the Esalen Institute at Big Sur—and it just happened that I'd already booked into one of his workshops on "Choosing to Change." If one were to believe in synchronicity, this might be it.

While in California I arranged to meet Carrie Menkel-Meadow, who was based at that time in San Diego. The initial contact was—perhaps oddly—through feminist legal theory, which I was teaching as part of a jurisprudence course, though with some apprehension about presuming to represent that critical voice in legal theory. Carrie, as will be well known to readers, has become one of the significant practitioners and authors in the field of dispute resolution and, on occasion, a colleague in Singapore.

There were, I think, two outstanding aspects of this period: one was the emergence of a network of colleagues, both in universities and mediation practice, who sought to combine a commitment to the emerging values of mediation and dispute resolution with a critical evaluation of the field, and the other was the opening up of academic publishing—whether in existing journals or new ones—to the study of non-doctrinal legal practice.

On my return from sabbatical to Wellington and Victoria University, I met Ted Becker, who was himself on leave from the political science department at the University of Hawai'i. Ted had been teaching a course in dispute resolution at UH and, over the course of several conversations, the plan emerged for me to go to Hawai'i during a university vacation to meet yet another in this network, Peter Adler. Peter, a fellow author in this volume, was at the time the director of the Neighborhood Justice Center of Honolulu. He might have been a little surprised (but nevertheless was welcoming) when I turned up on the doorstep to announce that I planned to apprentice myself to the mediators in the center for the next few weeks, which I did. Recall that this was 1981 or 1982, before there were established training programs and standards in mediation. Over the course of about a month, I shifted—thanks to the welcome offered by the center's mediators—from being a mere observer to taking on a co-mediation role, across an array of domestic, neighborhood, consumer, and commercial disputes.

Through Ted and Peter I met John Barkai, a professor in the School of Law at the University of Hawai'i and another pioneer in developing courses in dispute resolution and negotiation—and in forging links between domestic and international conflict resolution.

As I write these paragraphs, I also recall the many occasions on which students in my courses in mediation and dispute resolution have asked about the career path to get into this kind of work, especially as my own path led to teaching in Italy, training for the World Health Organization in Sri Lanka, a mediation conference in Buenos Aires, workshops for the World Health Organization in Geneva, and annual workshops in Cologne, all of which must have seemed impossibly exotic. Writing this now allows me to realize that, apart from the acquisition of a solid foundation in mediation training, the essential component is the network of colleagues and mentors—which makes the work of the Young Mediators' Initiative (and the app-based mentoring scheme set up at the International Chamber of Commerce's annual mediation competition) in 2019 so vital.

Professor John Paul Lederach, who was initially at the Eastern Mennonite University and subsequently at the Kroc Institute for International Peace Studies at Notre Dame University, a prolific author and widely experienced practitioner in conflict resolution, has used the image and metaphor of "nets" to think about the "entanglement" in and resolution of conflict in Central America (Lederach, 1991: 165-186). There are three points I take from this: the first, as Lederach intended, is the reliance on the "folk" language of actors in disputing, rather than on formal models of analysis, to understand and explain the processes observed; second is the important shift in thinking from conflict or dispute "management" to thinking of the dynamic of entangled and convoluted relationships; and third is the importance of nets and networks in supporting the work and growth of those of us who have taken this path.

For those reasons, too, this section of my chapter needs to be a kind of sustained appreciation for those with whom I crossed paths, several of whom are fellow authors in this volume.

VI.

At the heart of his 1979 wonderful collection of essays, *Mind and Nature: A Necessary Unity*, Gregory Bateson ponders "What is the pattern that connects the crab to the lobster and the primrose to the orchid, and all of them to me, and me to you?" Central to this question for Bateson is conversation—and not only what we might normally take to be a shared reflection on a topic or question but also a conversation about conversation itself, which Bateson called "metalogue," a process in which participants not only address the shared question but think about the structure of how they go about that engagement. Such metalogues are central to his 1972 collection of essays, *Steps to an Ecology of Mind*, in which he engages with the reader on a dizzying array of questions—as well as on the process of thinking itself.

The point of this reference and concluding section is twofold: first, to extend the metaphors from both Lederach and Bateson into the theme that, for me, exemplifies mediation practice; and second, to point to the direction that much of this work is now taking, in the virtual networks of the Internet and online dispute resolution. I will be brief on both.

First, as Bateson also asks when thinking about the "pattern which connects," we can (and should) ask what connects the natural to the cultural, the other to me, the familiar to the strange. And as Lord Bhikhu Parekh has observed, "We approach [others] on the assumption that they are similar enough to be intelligible and make a dialogue possible, and different enough to be puzzling and make a dialogue necessary" (Parekh, 2006: 124).

If I think about the intellectual and literary influences I referred to at the outset, they largely turn on finding the familiar in what is different, the normal in what might seem alien, and even the comfort in what might seem dangerous. Equally, the value of the network of colleagues and friends is that it served to support what was, at least at the outset, seen to be a delinquent form of professional activity. Does it stretch the analogies and metaphors too much to say, with Lederach and others that, unlike law's rendering of what is normal and normative, mediation becomes an exercise in constructing a Batesonian "pattern which connects?" Watch an experienced mediator at work, if you can, and observe the pattern of questions and interventions that disentangles the messed-up version of the net, and—ideally—mends the rips and tears in that net, which may then restore or reconstruct a pattern of connection between the parties, even if only sufficient to arrive at a working and workable outcome.

One of the enduring features and challenges of mediation is that it has fostered—through private dispute resolution—a kind of "distributed" decision-making. While this has, on the one hand, served the ends of freeing parties to be authors of their own outcomes, it has also freed them from the normative anchor of legal and constitutional motherships. That relationship and tension between center and periphery, public and private, formal and informal, substance and process is unlikely to go away any time soon. Indeed, it becomes an even greater issue in the world of information technology-based, at times algorithm-driven, online dispute resolution which is the field that—at the time of writing—largely preoccupies me. One of the leading authors on the contours of contemporary networked society, Professor Luciano Floridi, goes so far as to refer to a "distributed morality" as a feature of the changing patterns of moral agency—to which both private settlement and arm's-length dispute resolution contribute, the latter rendered increasingly necessary with the spread of online, cross-border commerce, and austerity-driven economies in the institutions of justice, as well as wider commitments to the use of digital technologies to enhance access to justice for hitherto remote and disadvantaged communities (Floridi, 2013: 727-743). The question arises then as to whether, and if so how, to create a degree of normative coherence to the processes of social ordering that emerge in this online context. It's a long way from dispute resolution and social ordering in pre-industrial societies, which provided some of the inspiration and moral courage to those laying the foundations for modern mediation, to an online world in which "social" ordering and governance are moot points (even if, at its most optimistic, it is called "social media").

Picking up on an earlier thread in this chapter, on the central role of networks of colleagues in creating pathways and connections, I can add that my own participation in the development of online dispute resolution over the last two decades has involved a strongly connected and widely distributed collection of ODR "pioneers." The significant difference between this online network and the one that fostered my original adventures in mediation is that I met most of these colleagues only "in real time" when I attended the annual ODR Forum in Paris in 2017. Many of them, of course, knew each other well, both in virtual and physical spaces, as it's largely a northern hemisphere group at this stage; but the ease and immediacy of online communication meant that the social bonds were already established, professional and personal reputations known, and trust reinforced by the network of mutual connections.

Having begun with a borrowed question—"what am I doing here?"—I find that we are now in the practical and metaphorical position that "here" can be "here, there, and everywhere." "Here" is the world of familiar, everyday, face-to-face interactions, in which we seek to turn a "blooming, buzzing confusion" of disputes into orderly and agreed results. "There" is the more complicated world, across borders, outside the familiar, in someone else's physical, national, and cultural space, in which our pursuit of agreement and understanding is likely to be mediated or muddied by differences in perception, language, and priorities. "Everywhere" is the non-physical space of the Internet, not yet three decades old and both unfamiliar because of the rapidity of changes wrought and yet entirely familiar as it's the world many of us occupy for much of our time, through email, web searches, social media, and, mobile communication. The single—and simple—point is that context matters. Context shapes relations, perceptions, and communication preferences. And context matters when we shift from the reasonably familiar world of our own comfort zones into someone else's territory and then into the contemporary world of virtual negotiation and interaction.

When we think and talk about mediation, whether as mediators, trainers, or commentators, we probably end up with two kinds of questions. The social, legal, and political question centers on the contributions that mediation can make to access to justice, social peace, efficiency and economies in justice systems, disputant autonomy and responsibility, and so on. The second question is the more personal one—why do *we* mediate, why do *we* prefer to work this way? If I draw together some of the threads of the preceding paragraphs and experience in mediation, my own responses turn on the challenges of working in culturally diverse settings (which are the ones that have taught me the most, especially about naïve and culturally limited assumptions I might have relied on); working out ways to foster essential conversations; and—at a more existential level perhaps—eliciting mutual recognition, even if only enough to arrive at a workable outcome.

One example may illustrate this. A couple of decades ago my wife and I were asked to run a workshop on conflict resolution at the University in Pisa, where I was visiting professor at the time. The participants—whose identities must remain confidential—were all men, all military, all recently involved in violent and bloody conflict with the other groups represented in the room. We had one instruction from the workshop organizer: don't talk about the war. After most of a day spent exploring conflict and resolution in generalized terms, and with little engagement around the room, one participant stood up—perhaps at some risk to himself—and said, in effect, "We have spent the day not talking about what it is we need to address. Please help us find a way to talk to each other." This was the moment at which we realized that the preceding process of dialogue on conflict and resolution had made it possible for one person to take that kind of risk; and those are the breakthrough moments that explain mediation's appeal.

The traditional, conventional, cultural, and now online versions of mediation capture, for me, some sense of what it means to be connected to others. In the emerging world of online democracy, Jay G. Blumler and Stephen Coleman suggest that two versions of democracy or participation are captured (Blumler and Coleman, 2001). One is the "inert and sulky" version of minimal (and complaining) engagement. The second conception, they write, "envisages the active citizen, enabled by effective, accessible technologies as well as effective, accessible representative institutions, to feel democratically empowered."

The latter, I hope, is what we're doing here.

References

Blumler, J. G. and S. Coleman. 2001. *Realising Democracy Online: A Civic Commons in Cyberspace.* IPPR/Citizens Online. March 1, 2001. https://www.ippr.org/publications/realising-democracy-online-a-civic-commons-in-cyberspace.

Elkins, J. 1983. "A Humanistic Perspective in Legal Education." *Nebraska Law Review* 62(3): 494-525.

Floridi, L. 2013. "Distributed Morality in an Information Society." *Science and Engineering Ethics* 19(3): 727-743.

Lederach, J. P. 1991. *Of Nets, Nails, and Problems: The Folk Language of Conflict Resolution in a Central American Setting. Conflict Resolution: Cross-Cultural Perspectives.* Edited by K. Avruch, P. W. Black and J. A. Scimecca. New York, Westport, CT, London: Greenwood Press.

Menkel-Meadow, C. 1995. "Whose Dispute Is It Anyway? A Philosophical and Democratic Defense of Settlement (In Some Cases)." *Georgetown Law Journal.* 83(1995): 2663-2696.

The National Center for Technology & Dispute Resolution. "Fellows." Accessed September 17, 2020. http://odr.info/fellows/.

Nils, C. 1977. "Conflicts as Property." *The British Journal of Criminology* 17(1): 1-15.

Parekh, L. B. 2006. *Rethinking Multiculturalism: Cultural Diversity and Political Theory.* 2nd ed. New York, NY: Palgrave Macmillan.

Twining, W. 1967. "Pericles and the Plumber." A lecture delivered at Queen's University of Belfast. Published in shortened form in *Law Quarterly Review* 83(3): 396.

6

Born to Mediate

By Lucy Moore

◆

As an only child of warring parents, I began mediating at a very early age, probably before I can remember. Early on I was aware of being in the middle, where listening seemed to be my main job. Later, as I began to see and empathize with both my parents, I tried interpreting one to the other as best I could. I was beginning to appreciate the many shades of gray that I would later learn to love.

Lucy Moore has been a mediator, facilitator, consultant, and trainer since the late 1980s. Formerly a partner at the nonprofit Western Network, she is now the principal of Lucy Moore Associates, often working with multiple parties and multiple issues. Her focus has been natural resources and public-policy disputes, and her clients have included federal, state, and local agencies, tribal governments and communities, public-interest organizations, and industry. The subjects of the disputes have been wide-ranging, from water rights and air quality to mine reclamation and endangered species protection. With her strong background in Indian country, many of Moore's cases involve tribal interests and parties. Moore has mediated high-level federal disputes, facilitated large public meetings, trained EPA staff in "Dealing with Difficult People," and offered cross-cultural alliance building workshops with Hispanic and Native colleagues. In 2015, she received the Sharon Pickett Award from the Association for Conflict Resolution, granted to honor advancement of the cause of environmental protection through writing and the effective use of alternative dispute resolution. Moore's memoir, *Into the Canyon: Seven Years in Navajo Country* (2004), won Best Memoir from Women Writing the West. She is also the author of *Common Ground on Hostile Turf: Stories from an Environmental Mediator* (2013), in which she tells the stories of 10 of her most challenging cases.

As I aged and gained some verbal skills, I could offer sympathetic responses, and by 12, I was refining skills, sometimes using shuttle diplomacy. Did I like my mandatory career? No. I resented both parents for using me in this way. On the other hand, I did not protest, refuse, or resign. It was probably a survival mechanism, a way to find approval and love from both parents. In high school and college, my skills were honed so that friends unloaded their problems on me. I was the one who seemed to be able to explain or at least surmise why someone said that, felt that, acted like that. I could often suggest a way of wording a difficult message, dealing with a troubled relationship, or identifying the sticking point between two people. I never thought of this as mediation. It was just what I did, what I had always done.

I graduated from college in 1966, a time of turmoil, with more turmoil to come. I had no career plan, but I was drawn to the big issues that needed attention—poverty, civil rights, the Vietnam War. Our generation was ready to spring into action, via the Peace Corps, VISTA, War on Poverty, and Legal Services programs. As newlyweds, my husband and I headed for the Navajo Reservation, where he had an important role to play as the first attorney in one of the reservation towns, Chinle, Arizona. I, with my degree in modern English and French history and literature, had a less clear path.

It did not take long to realize that this corner of the country was tragically behind mainstream America in health, education, economic opportunity, and participation in the basics of democracy. Most painful of all was the systematic assimilation of Navajos into the White culture. Children as young as 6 were removed from their homes and put in government boarding schools, where they were forbidden to speak Navajo and lost all contact with the stories, traditions, and practices of their culture. Class pictures from those days show very somber Indian children, with mainstream haircuts and clothes, staring out into this foreign world with sadness and confusion.

I approached this world full of idealism, energy, and compassion, ready to save everyone I encountered. I quickly learned, however, that no one needed to be saved, and certainly not by me. I responded with patience, watching and listening for opportunities to be useful. I was a Head Start teacher's aide and a school bus driver. I sold vehicle insurance to Navajos who were victimized by off-reservation dealers who charged triple the going rate. I helped start a daycare center, and finally I ran for justice of the peace and was elected to two terms. With jurisdiction over non-Navajos on the reservation, I handled traffic tickets, served as coroner, tried misdemeanor cases, and held preliminary hearings for felonies, all without a law degree. I also had jurisdiction over Navajos as well as non-Navajos for the purpose of registering voters, which I did by the hundreds, and marrying people, which I often did in my backyard, with dogs yowling and small children running around.

Being a justice of the peace as a 24-year-old was not something I planned, but it seemed oddly relevant given my early years as a mediator. And yet, fun as it was to bang my gavel on the hollow-core door that served as my desk, declare a scofflaw guilty, and collect $100 on behalf of Apache County, I was uncomfortable coming down on one side or the other. There were too many sides, too many ways to look at the problem.

Those seven years were life-changing for me. I learned how to survive and then thrive in a foreign culture. I learned to be comfortable in my own (White) skin. I learned how to be helpful on their terms, not mine. Without protest, I sewed Joseph and Mary costumes for the Head Start Christmas pageant, I helped 5-year-olds make paper Pilgrim hats and Indian headdresses to celebrate Thanksgiving, and I organized an Easter egg hunt on a freezing, windswept mesa top, where the grandmas shoved the kids aside to fill their flour sacks with needed supplies for the family. Where I could, I advocated for the inclusion and honoring of Navajo culture, and I formed relationships that have lasted more than 50 years. Chinle laid a foundation for my future work as a mediator and consultant in cross-cultural alliance-building.

In 1975, now a family of four, we left Navajoland and moved to Santa Fe, New Mexico. I was deeply, achingly homesick for the reservation. Although Santa Fe is a multicultural place with Hispanics, Native Americans, and Anglos, I missed Navajos, mutton stew, and fry bread, the endless horizon, the huge bowl of a sky, even the world-class mud in the winter and the unspeakable dust storms in the spring.

I told myself I would eventually melt back into the Anglo scene from which I had come, that this strange White world would soon not look so strange anymore. I knew this was true, and it made me sad. I was a different person, more aware of the world around me, and more willing to not have all the answers. I wanted to be sure I did not lose that part of myself that was forged in Chinle, that part that had learned how to survive and thrive in another culture.

I Become a Mediator, Officially

Wanting to stay connected to Indian country, I joined a nonprofit dedicated to empowering Indian communities legally and economically. Like me, John Folk-Williams, coincidentally a college classmate, had recently arrived in Santa Fe. We solicited proposals, evaluated projects, and advised foundations on what kinds of project would have the most impact. Eventually we formed our own nonprofit,

Western Network, and began researching water conflicts in the West, often involving tribes that were seeking ways to defend fast-disappearing water rights. I was on the phone all day, talking to people entangled in nasty, often years-long conflicts over water rights, management, and use. Of particular interest for me was Tucson, then embroiled in a huge battle for groundwater. As a rapidly growing city in the desert, it had no choice but to stick a straw into the aquifer and start sucking. The impact on neighbors was significant as the water level began to drop. The Papago Tribe (now Tohono O'odham Nation) was seriously affected and filed suit to defend their aboriginal water rights. Nearby pecan growers and mining operations joined the fray, and soon it was a multi-lawsuit, mudslinging mess.

As I talked to people over a period of months, I began to hear a hint of optimism. There was someone who stood in the middle, taking no side, listening to everyone and brokering agreements. Congressman Morris Udall was mediating the conflict in his district. I had a revelation. I wanted to be Morris Udall when I grew up. All those years of being in the middle—as an only child, as a friend, as a justice of the peace—finally made sense. I was a mediator.

By the early 1980s, visions of Morris Udall still dancing in my head, I had helped Western Network transition into a foundation-funded environmental conflict resolution firm. We saw the need for forums where parties in conflict over natural resources—tribes, Hispanic communities, federal, state, and local agencies, and others—could come together in a safe, facilitated setting. Here they could engage in dialogue, get to know each other, develop a bit of trust, and hopefully explore paths forward that focused on their common ground and shared needs, rather than on their painful history and the debilitating fears that drove them apart.

In an early effort to educate a state agency about the value of mediation, we offered our heavily subsidized services to the New Mexico Environment Department to conduct a regulatory negotiation. Weary of the usual way of developing regulations—promulgation followed by lawsuits—the agency was happy to have us pilot this new process that brought together all the parties likely to sue and anointed them as regulation drafters. This was how I came to be known, for a short time, as the Queen of Lust (Leaking Underground Storage Tanks, the subject of the mediated regulations). The agency was delighted, and we were elated, with the success of the process: regulations acceptable to all and not a single lawsuit.

Experience was our main teacher, and we learned critical lessons from each case. John and I had minimal training but were able to apprentice to some outstanding practitioners, including Ben Moya and Howard Bellman, who also served on our board. We benefitted enormously from other board members who brought a wealth of ideas, inspiration, and connections. Many thanks to Gail Bingham, Dick Trudell, Luis Torres, Craig Barnes, Chris Carlson, Lee Kapalowski, Fred Anderson, Roberto Chené, Oscar Rodriguez, and so many more.

Slowly we began to gain credibility as facilitation and mediation professionals in the Southwest, but we could not ignore growing criticism of our role from the very people we were trying to help. We may have seen ourselves as saviors, bringing our talent and our funding to help disempowered, struggling communities have a voice and take their place at the negotiating table where decisions impacting their lives were made. But through painful discussions with local land-based people, we began to understand the region's complexities and our lack of accountability to those we were serving. Like so many outsider do-gooders, we had waltzed into a new landscape, steeped in history and conflict and laced with intricate relationships, with little knowledge of where we were. We raised substantial outside funding to pay ourselves to help local communities, whose members were themselves experts—about the natural resources, about their challenges and their needs—and had the capacity to deal with complex situations themselves. If we had taken the time to listen, learn, and build relationships, a valuable partnership might have ensued. As it was, we looked like one more carpetbagger.

We were *entremetidos*, those who get in between, who butt in where they are not wanted, they said. Why didn't we take our bags of money and go back where we came from? How dare we raise money "off the backs" of poor northern New Mexico communities? We used our Ivy League credibility with the Ford Foundation. It was easy for us to go "knock on that door." "Do you think that door would ever open for us?" they asked. If we at Western Network wanted to be useful, we would help them gain access to the big money, let them determine how best to spend it, and support them in their efforts however we could. We were defensive in the beginning, but these passionate voices were compelling, and we began to understand the truth in what they were saying. We were acting disrespectfully at least, and perhaps unethically at worst.

We learned to listen to that client community and become their allies, partnering with them on their priorities, and sharing leadership in project planning and implementation. We used our influence to bring major foundations to Santa Fe for a meeting with community leaders to air these grievances and help foundations understand the darker side of philanthropy in poor communities. The result was a multi-million dollar grant from several foundations to the New Mexico Community Foundation for grassroots projects. These lessons, painful as they were, were critical as my career developed. Listening to those on the ground, those whose lives are impacted, and empowering them to take a role with other parties in the design of a process, for me became fundamental principles.

I also saw during this period examples of local leaders who brought people together and helped them find their own resolution to conflict. Happy as I was to call myself a mediator, I understood that there were certain situations where I needed to step aside. Since then, I have watched with admiration as those local leaders—sometimes secular, sometimes religious—work, often quietly behind the scenes, to make peace and heal old wounds. These are "cases" better handled by those intimate with the issues and known by the parties. Sometimes I have been asked to support local leaders by providing neutral facilitation of a difficult meeting, or by making a connection with a stakeholder or decision-maker, or by simply coaching. Playing this role is precious to me, and I know that it is based on my understanding of the landscape—geographical, political, cultural, economic, etc.—and the resulting trusting relationships.

By the 1990s, Western Network had weaned itself from foundation funding and shifted to a for-profit firm. Foundation funding was seductive, but those years had hurt our credibility with those we were trying to serve. We decided that if we indeed had something to offer those in conflict, they should be willing to pay for it and we should be able to make a living at it. Fee for services was a cleaner way to do business. We continued our work, but with a new commitment to accountability not only to clients but within our own organization as well. We took a critical look at our internal structure, and made a commitment to include as staff local New Mexicans who aspired to be part of the conflict resolution field. We mentored our talented secretary Rosemary Romero to become a mediator, replaced her with a young Navajo, and hired two other Native New

Mexicans, Aron Rael and Richard Pacheco, as interns. Our work life, internal and external, was enriched immensely by opening our doors to those representing the communities and cultures around us.

In 1999, unable to support our expanded staff, Western Network dissolved, each of us principals moving to private practice. I am still a solo practitioner, focusing on natural resources and public policy disputes. My mediation cases are usually multiparty, multi-issue, and include tribal or other traditional land-based interests. I also design and facilitate public processes of all kinds, including scoping processes for environmental impact statements, forest plan revisions, endangered species designations, and more.

A particularly satisfying part of my current practice is being part of a multicultural training team. With Hispanic and Native American colleagues, we respond to requests from agencies, nonprofits, and communities that are struggling to develop meaningful alliances with partners across a cultural divide. An environmental organization may find itself at odds with a traditional community that they see as a natural ally to combat development. A nonprofit board may have trouble soliciting board members or staff of color, although their mission relates directly to those communities. Given my years with the Navajo and my experience working with land-based communities, I am drawn to these cases, where I am part of a team that can bring the full landscape of multicultural dynamics to life. For me, those conflicts that are rooted in our identity, our shared history, our shared pain and responsibility are profound. If we can work through the trauma and see each other as humans engaged in struggle, we can develop a relationship, share fears and dreams, and perhaps find that elusive common ground. Although they are more dramatic in cross-cultural situations, these truths apply to every case for me.

My Brand of Mediation

Each of us is different. We come to conflict resolution for different reasons, on different paths, at different times. Unlike many colleagues, and most young practitioners entering the field, I did not go to graduate school. I learned from mentors, from life experiences, and from struggling in the trenches of conflict, developing a set of beliefs and practices that are mine.

My idea of the mediator role shifted radically during a long-weekend workshop with Gary Friedman, a lawyer and mediator from Mill Valley, California. Gary taught us to trust our instincts at the mediation table. He believed that contrary to much training of the day, the mediator is an active player in the room, not a neutral robot whose inner life has no place in the process. I learned from him to take my own temperature during the mediation. If I felt uneasy, anxious, distracted, bored, or a host of other emotions that I might scold my professional self for indulging in, I should see it as a barometer for what is happening in the room. Depending on the situation, I have learned to honor my emotions and even bring them into the conversation. If my mind is wandering or I am inexplicably anxious, I might say, "Let me interrupt for just a moment. I have to confess that I am not able to focus on this conversation. Maybe it's just me, but I want to ask if anyone else is having the same trouble. Is there something that's not being said here? Is something missing?" Almost always someone will echo my feeling and suggest that we need to shift gears and consider another angle, or back up and get back on track, or name the elephant in the room.

Gary also suggested that as mediators we enter a room with the hope that everyone, including ourselves, will be the "best version of themselves." Just holding that image, he said, could nudge participants into a place where agreement was more possible. At first, this seemed wacky, smacking of New Age thinking that had invaded Santa Fe. But I gave it a try, and although I can't say definitively that it works, it does put me in a good frame of mind for handling the group. With my newly opened mind, I even went so far as to adopt a method from Cesar Milan, the dog whisperer whose TV show focused on clients with naughty dogs. Cesar teaches the owners to take an attitude that is "calm and assertive." Yes, I have learned that entering a room of unruly humans with that commitment to be "calm and assertive" works wonders. For the most part, they settle down, alert, ready to work. . .waiting for a treat, I suppose.

I am grateful that my life experience has given me a credibility with Native Americans and other communities for whom land, water, and cultural rights are so crucial. I am eager to take a case involving these interests—often in conflict with agencies, industry, environmentalists, and more—and feel that this is where my talents are best used. I am proud of being able to manage a fair process, but I also am very aware of my deep affection for Indian country. Once, I was accused of being "pro-Indian" by non-Indian participants in a difficult case involving Bureau of Indian Affairs school operations. I realized that I had not extended my sensitivity to the non-Indians and that they had suffered deep pain and guilt as they listened to the trauma of their Indian counterparts. It was an important reminder to give everyone at the table attention, care, and sensitivity—regardless of race, ethnicity, age, or any of the other identifiers. Trauma is difficult for everyone.

There are certain cases where the parties may be traditionally on opposite sides but have the desire to work together and are willing to be vulnerable, even when in some shark-infested waters. They understand instinctively that the relationship is primary if the substantive work is to succeed. These cases are a dream for me. The head of the

New Mexico Office of the State Engineer, responsible for water rights in the state, came to me in the 1990s needing help in negotiating a water rights settlement with the Navajo Nation. "I think I need a wedding planner," he began as I looked around nervously. "We are going to need to 'get married' in order to come to a good resolution, but I don't know how to take the first step, how to approach my future in-laws." With some trepidation, the bride's and groom's representatives came together to begin discussions. Four years later, a $900 million settlement gave security to irrigators in the basin while providing badly needed water to underserved portions of the reservation. The vows were said, the cake was served, and smiles were seen all around.

And I am lucky to have another (unlikely) dream case. This one involves contamination of natural and cultural resources surrounding the Los Alamos National Laboratories (LANL) in northern New Mexico. Beginning in the 1940s and lasting decades, LANL developed, tested, and disposed of extremely toxic, hazardous, and radioactive materials, with serious impacts to soil, water, and sacred sites belonging to four Native American pueblos. Part of the Superfund Act calls for making the public or a tribe whole in cases through restoration, replacement, or, as a last resort, compensation for the damage. The process is painful for the pueblos, reducing their cultural resources and sacred sites to commodities, to be valued only monetarily. This conversation lies ahead in this multiyear process, but we are laying the groundwork with data-gathering and analysis and by nurturing trusting relationships among the parties.

Why do I look forward to these monthly meetings on this painful subject? Because those at our negotiating table have developed a level of trust and appreciation that is remarkable. Natural enemies—Department of Energy, LANL, four damaged pueblos, the US Forest Service, and the state of New Mexico—work through difficult technical material and a host of challenging decisions: how much data is adequate for settlement talks? How will pueblo cultural data be gathered and kept confidential, safe from the grasp of the Freedom of Information Act? What projects will make up a settlement package, and how will the four pueblos share the benefits of those projects?

I marveled at a recent going-away party for the DOE representative at the table who was being transferred. He had been part of the group for many years and was well liked. As we broke up, a pueblo representative went over and gave him a big bear hug. "I'm going to miss you, bro," he said, and they exchanged good-luck wishes. This group understands that they are all working for the same goal—a fair resolution that will bring some wholeness to the damaged pueblos. They know they are not personally responsible for the situation they are in, and they are grateful to share the negotiation table with committed, caring fellow human beings.

If this kind of case seems tailor-made for me, there are those with challenges that seem designed to drive me crazy. I have had a handful of cases where a righteous zealot blocked consensus, clearly participating in bad faith, never intending to give even an inch. Often arrogant and uninterested in the human beings they share the table with, they cannot tolerate even the smallest concession. I hate to admit it, but under these conditions, my all-encompassing, welcoming heart slams shut. I have pled with their higher-ups to replace these people, citing concern with bad faith, usually to no avail.

Challenging cases for me often involve a preponderance of data and reliance on science, to the point where there is no room for relationship-building, exploration of history, sharing of values and world views. These cases feel heartless to me, and my efforts to inject the nontechnical aspects are often met with skepticism and seen as a waste of precious time. I have learned to bring in that softer, human focus at the beginning, with a day or two of relationship-building before the participants leap into the technical morass. I am careful not to frustrate them with too much "Santa Fe woo-woo" (as I was accused of at one EPA training in Dallas) but ask them to spend some time learning about each other. Once they begin exchanging stories, they understand the value of this foundation, and the skepticism ends.

I have had a few cases that are just plain sad, so sad that I cry in the car on the way home, and when I get there, I make myself a stiff martini. Mt. Taylor, an elegant, gently sloping conical peak in central New Mexico, is a sacred mountain for six local tribes. But the Mining Act of 1872 gives anyone the right to explore and develop mineral resources, no matter the ownership or designation of the surface lands. After years of struggle, tribes won the Traditional Cultural Property designation for Mt. Taylor from the federal agency that protects important cultural sites and properties in the United States. The Mining Act, however, made the designation moot, and uranium companies applied for permits to drill on Forest Service lands on Mt. Taylor.

Section 106 of The Historic Preservation Act requires any federal agency to consult with tribes or others who may be impacted by a development proposal. But in this case, neither the tribes nor the agency had the power to deny the mining permit. They could negotiate only trivia, cajole, plead, pray for some considerations—avoid this spot where artifacts are found, drill farther away from this stream, move your access road a few yards to the south—but the company held all the cards. These sessions were painful for the tribes, who made it clear that by participating they were not condoning the mining but simply trying to make the impact on them and their culture a little less severe. My belief in the power of relationships is tested in cases like this. The painful history of exploitation and the prospect of further degradation of what is sacred made it difficult for tribes to share a table with the mining company. At each meeting, I allowed them to speak of the seriousness of the loss and plead for consideration, and difficult as it was for the company representatives to listen, I saw them take it in and be moved. Friendships were unlikely to emerge, but respectful, meaningful exchanges happened, and company representatives made concessions to the tribes that they might not have made otherwise.

Exploring Principles

A case like the one above makes me face the difficult question: can or should a mediator be an agent for social change? Personally, I am an advocate for social change, but professionally, my responsibility is to create and maintain a fair process. I trust that with the right parties at the table, that fair process will produce an equitable outcome. But I am left with a tension between a yearning for a more just society and a commitment to mediator ethics that forbids any bias. My answer is to add a bit to the definition of "fair process."

For me, to treat parties *equally* is often not enough. Some at the table may not have the capacity to participate effectively because of language or cultural barriers, inadequate financial resources, or lack of technical understanding of the issues. To treat them equally with corporate lawyers, environmental activists, and agency experts feels to me like abuse. We owe it to all our parties to be sure they have what they need to be fully engaged with a strong, clear voice. I see nothing biased in figuring out how to provide gas and daycare money, finding an interpreter, tutoring between meetings, or offering other assistance to enable a participant to fully represent his or her interest. It may also mean holding meetings in locations and facilities that are culturally comfortable and taking field trips to see the impacted resources and better understand the community's situation. We may make adjustments to the agenda, spending extra time on introductions to focus on the importance of relationship and even beginning the meeting with a traditional prayer in a Native language. Interestingly, after dozens and dozens of meetings like this, never has a participant of a different faith complained and asked for equal time. There seems to be an understanding and even appreciation of this cultural practice as something offered on behalf of the group as a whole. Taking extra time for introductions can bring some objection, but usually all agree it is worth it in the long run. I see all these proactive steps as a way to make the dialogue more inclusive by empowering those voices inherently disadvantaged at a mainstream negotiating table. Those participants who are comfortable in the mainstream culture are not diminished in their power; they simply have more capable negotiators on the other side.

A footnote: The tables can be turned. I heard a tale of woe from a utility company executive. His mainstream, be-suited attorneys were completely thrown off their game when visiting a traditional Navajo community to negotiate a transmission line right-of-way. They arrived with a PowerPoint presentation to find the community had no electricity. The interpretation of their serious technical presentation into Navajo took forever and included moments of hilarious laughter. And, the kicker: they of course could not refuse the community's invitation to stay for lunch, which turned out to be a great (and slimy) delicacy: sheep intestine stew. The local community came out ahead on that negotiation.

Speaking of "tweaking" the core principles of mediation, I have a couple of suggestions. I would like to see a tenet that speaks to honoring and respecting the humanity in each other. One could argue that this is understood to be part of procedural fairness, but for me it deserves to stand alone. Procedural fairness speaks to a process that treats parties equally, with ground rules that seek order, civility, confidentiality, and good faith. I am left with a rather mechanical set of rules that ignores our vulnerability, our need for trusting relationships, our need to be connected, human to human, our capacity to take courageous steps toward resolving conflicts. I am not sure how to articulate this in a set of principles. Perhaps it could be an understanding or an assumption underlying our processes.

I would also like to see a core tenet relating to sustainability. Too often, we mediators put all the energy up front, and have nothing to offer in the way of implementation, sustainability, monitoring, follow-through, enforcement, and revisiting the mediated agreement. We are focused on the resolution of the conflict, and too often, once those signatures are on the dotted line, we breathe a sigh of relief, shake hands all around, wish the parties luck, and ride off into the sunset. The water rights settlement between the state of New Mexico and the Navajo Nation was ratified by necessary parties and funds were allocated by Congress, but persistent objections from non-Indians in the basin are working their way through lower courts. Ground has been broken on the major water project that was the key to the agreement, so practically the "wet" water will flow. The "paper" water rights are still being contested. I would have liked to continue my role with a mediation effort with the basin residents, who had not, by the way, been part of the state-tribal negotiated settlement. But there was no vehicle for this to happen.

Finally, what about the sustainability of our beloved profession? I would like to see in print a commitment to grow our field by recruiting and supporting those who share our passion for resolving conflict. Not every practitioner can or wants to add this to their job description, but to elevate the need in importance would help. I have always loved to mentor those who aspire to do this kind of work, especially those with limited access and connections. As the end of my career looms, and as my experience grows behind me, I am more committed to mentoring than ever. I find enormous enjoyment in connecting with those who are young, energetic, and passionate about the work. Mentees come to me in a variety of ways. They may have read my book and been intrigued by the stories I tell. We may meet at a conference, or through one of many webinars I give to graduate classes around the country. I engage the students, answering questions, learning about their passions, giving career advice, and telling particularly provocative stories from my career. It is so satisfying to spend time with their enthusiasm and curiosity, and they help clarify for me why I am a mediator.

To be in the middle is an honor for me. I always feel grateful that this diverse bunch of disputants has allowed me to stand there, trusting that I will manage the difficulties that lie ahead fairly and with sensitivity. I love the moments when I can defuse a dangerous moment, identify a roadblock, bring warring voices together, offer lightness or insight when needed most. I could not be happier with this career—the one I was born into, the one that Morris Udall showed me, the one that has given me so much to think about these past 35 years.

7

My Passage to ADR

By Geetha Ravindra

◆

Childhood

My involvement in mediation and dispute resolution is closely connected to my family background and culture.

I was born in India and moved to the United States at the age of 2. My father, the eldest of nine children, comes from a small village in the state of Karnataka, in the southwestern region of India. His parents were farmers, and while they were not educated, they appreciated the importance of a good education and strongly encouraged my

---

Geetha Ravindra, who is currently director of workplace relations for the Fourth Circuit Court of Appeals, is an attorney, mediator, and trainer with more than 25 years' experience in dispute resolution. Before joining the Fourth Circuit, she worked with the Federal Emergency Management Agency's ADR division providing mediation, training, large-group facilitation, and other organizational development services. She served as the first mediator for the International Monetary Fund from 2012 to 2018, as director of the Department of Dispute Resolution Services at the Supreme Court of Virginia from 1996 to 2007, and managed the Dalkon Shield Arbitration Program at the Private Adjudication Center from 1992 to 1996. She has taught mediation at the University of Richmond School of Law and the College of William and Mary Law School, mediated family cases for the Richmond City Juvenile and Domestic Relations District Court, and served as a mediator and trainer for the World Bank and other federal and state agencies. A past chair of the American Bar Association Section of Dispute Resolution and past president of the Virginia Mediation Network, she is a certified Supreme Court of Virginia mediator and a certified organizational ombudsman practitioner.

father to go to college and pursue a career in engineering. My mother, one of six siblings, was raised in a very conservative family. Although she was not given an opportunity to complete her college education for fear this would make it harder to find a suitable groom for her, she embodies characteristics that cannot be taught, such as kindness, grace, and compassion.

Leaving India for the United States, with very little money and no job or relatives to support them in their new country, took great courage. Like many immigrants, my parents were motivated by their desire to give their children a good education, a job and home earned honestly, without resorting to bribery, as well as the opportunity to succeed based on merit, not connections. Coming to America shaped the course of my life.

Growing up as a first-generation American of Indian origin, I straddled two continents, mediating between the Eastern and Western cultures. We celebrated Hindu festivals, attended services at our temple, and studied our religious texts. Service to others, humility, devotion, gratitude, respect, honesty, and hard work are among the key principles I was taught at a young age. I was supported in my academic pursuits, such as the debate team and Model UN, but because my parents could not understand and did not condone many aspects of American culture, I was precluded from enjoying many social activities. My interactions with boys were always restricted; I often had to explain to my American friends why I could not date or go to a school dance or sports event. Getting teased for being different, feeling isolated from peers, and compromising what I wanted became my normal state of being. I struggled to balance peer pressure and respect for my parents' wishes, lashing out at times but ultimately conceding. In the Indian culture, respecting your elders is your duty, and being mindful of what society, especially the Indian community, thinks about you and your family is very important.

Two primary tenets of Hinduism, karma and dharma, have also informed my life and my work as a neutral. Karma is the concept that every action has a reaction: good deeds beget positive consequences. Dharma is the principle of responsibility. We all must fulfill our respective duty, which includes roles as a parent, spouse, student, and member of society. The notion of what is "right" has generally been determined collectively in my life, not individually, as I am always conscious of the impact of my actions on others. I continue to weigh the appropriateness of my behavior and actions in terms of their alignment with Hindu values, and I am always mindful of my responsibilities in whatever role I hold—mother, wife, daughter, mediator, teacher, or administrator.

My fear of disappointing my parents far outweighed my personal interest in fitting in, but my childhood experiences also stimulated an interest in family dynamics and motivated me to be more open-minded with my two children as they were growing up. It has also made me an empathetic sounding board for a number of Indian youth who have been unable to talk to their own parents and has helped me in my work as a mediator in international organizations with people who have experienced challenges related to assimilation and cultural stereotypes.

The tension between my traditional upbringing (and my parents' expectations) and my own self-determination came to a head when I was considering colleges and a career path. Because I skipped second grade, I was only 16 when I finished high school, and I was not permitted to leave home for college. My parents insisted that it would not be appropriate for a girl to be autonomous at such a young age, so I attended the University of North Carolina at Charlotte while living at home. I was very upset about being unable to pursue my dreams of attending a more reputable college and negotiated a promise from my parents that I could leave home for graduate school. Eager to gain my independence, I completed my undergraduate degree in three years.

Most Indians are drawn to the fields of science, technology, engineering, and mathematics (STEM), as we are taught from a young age that this will lead to jobs that provide a secure and prosperous life. I, however, was never interested in math and science. I loved English and history, actively competing in debate and original oratory throughout high school and college. I served as the chair of the Student Government Legislature in college and often dreamed of becoming prime minister of India.

After several visits to India during my teenage years, I became convinced that my purpose in life was to bring about social change. The first time that I felt I truly belonged somewhere was when I visited India at age 9 and was overjoyed that everyone looked just like me. During each visit to India, my heart would swell with sadness at the sight of the rampant poverty and anger at the politicians who took bribes and precious funds from projects that were supposed to build schools, roads, and hospitals. My sense of purpose to right all of India's wrongs grew stronger as I matured. I read the autobiography of the father of India, Mahatma Gandhi, and was struck by his commitment to *ahimsa*, respect for all living things and avoidance of violence, and peaceful conflict resolution. Gandhi inspired me to strive to become a lawyer and an agent of change.

Law School

Toward the end of my final year of college, my parents were surprised and disappointed to learn that I wanted to become a lawyer instead of going into medicine, engineering, or computer science, but they eventually supported my decision. Challenging my parents was not easy, but I was older and felt that I needed to have voice in the decision that would affect the rest of my future, even if it made them unhappy. I enrolled in UNC-Chapel Hill Law School.

As the first person in my family to enter the legal profession, I had no mentor or role model. Not wanting to appear ignorant next to my classmates, many of whose parents or family members practiced law, I had no idea where to turn for advice. I was also young, 19, and felt tremendous anxiety as I adjusted to living away from home for the first time while competing with students who appeared far more confident and had far more life experience.

I felt this lack of guidance most strongly when I started my job search for a summer internship. Like most of my classmates, I had envisioned getting an offer from a law firm, but despite my good grades and best efforts during interviews, I was never offered a position. I began to second-guess my decision to pursue a legal career and, as the only Indian woman in my law school, worried whether my ethnicity played a role in my marketability. Eventually, I decided to broaden my options and applied for and received an IOLTA (Interest on Lawyer Trust Accounts) scholarship that provided a small stipend to work with a nonprofit organization.

Among the options I explored was the Private Adjudication Center (PAC), a nonprofit dispute resolution organization affiliated with Duke University's School of Law. I had never heard of what was then known as alternative dispute resolution, or ADR, but it sounded interesting. Rene Ellis, the PAC director, selected me as the center's summer intern. I attribute my good fortune of entering the field of dispute resolution to this first job and will be forever grateful to Rene and the PAC for opening this door.

Career Path

The PAC custom-designed dispute resolution services for clients. It was a small organization, but it was doing groundbreaking work. As a summer intern, I worked on cases related to the Toyota Reversal Arbitration Board, which was designed to give dealers a user-friendly process to address sales credit disputes.

I was also introduced to the Dalkon Shield Arbitration program, which the PAC hired me to help manage upon my graduation, an innovative and highly effective application of ADR in resolving a mass tort. More than 300,000 claims were filed against A.H. Robins Company for injuries related to the Dalkon Shield intrauterine device. The manufacturer was bankrupted, and a trust fund was established. I noted the privacy, efficiency, and voice that the women in these less formal Dalkon Shield arbitration hearings received. I had discovered my calling. ADR gave me the opportunity to listen and understand the objectives of clients, custom-design fair and informal processes that offered procedural justice, and partner with parties in reaching solutions that met their needs and interests. I also had the pleasure of meeting colleagues in my work with the PAC who continue to be lifelong friends, including David Hoffman, Daniel Bowling, Edith Primm, and Bobbi McAdoo.

After working with the PAC for three years, I moved to Richmond, Virginia, with my husband so he could begin his internal medicine residency at the Medical College of Virginia. The PAC permitted me to work remotely because the Dalkon Shield Trust was also in Richmond. With the luxury of working from home, I decided to start my family. I took the Virginia Bar exam as well as mediation training to become a Virginia court-certified mediator.

In 1996, when I was 27, Rob Baldwin hired me to serve as director of the Department of Dispute Resolution Services at the Supreme Court of Virginia. The trust and confidence Rob had in me as an entrepreneur seeking to expand mediation and other ADR services in the state allowed me to blossom and grow as a professional. While I was very aware that I was an anomaly in the dispute resolution community—being an Asian American—I felt empowered to innovate and expand the ADR programs and services we offered litigants in the court system.

Early in my time at the Supreme Court of Virginia, an unauthorized practice of law (UPL) complaint was filed against a family mediator. This raised a great deal of fear, concern, and outrage in the mediation community. Mediation had begun in the community centers in Virginia, and most mediators who had received their training in the facilitative model of mediation strongly resisted the suggestion that mediation could be deemed the practice of law. However, with increasing numbers of attorneys and retired judges serving as mediators, as well as the demand for more evaluative mediation services, the pressure for all mediators, regardless of background and training, to provide legal analysis in mediation grew. Working with a committee of judges, lawyers, mediators, and the Virginia state bar's ethics counsel, I developed "Guidelines on Mediation and the Unauthorized Practice of Law" to assist mediators in distinguishing between providing information and providing legal advice.

The guidelines, intended to support ethical mediation practice, were the most comprehensive effort to clarify these issues and provide direction where none existed before, but they were not popular in Virginia and around the country. Attorney mediators, in essence, were concerned that the guidelines were too restrictive and would impede commercial and private mediation practice, while mediators who were not attorneys feared that the distinctions between what attorney and non-attorney mediators could do would give attorneys an advantage in the marketplace.

Despite the challenges of drafting the guidelines, I appreciated the opportunity to address this sticky issue with transparency and in collaboration with the Virginia state bar. The ABA Dispute Resolution Section later passed a resolution declaring that mediation is not the practice of law, and the Society of Professionals in Dispute Resolution (SPIDR, which later merged with other organizations to become the Association for Conflict Resolution), created a committee to study the issue. No further UPL complaints were filed against certified mediators in Virginia during my tenure as director of the Department of Dispute Resolution Services.

I left the Supreme Court of Virginia in late 2007 because of a change in leadership and reduced support and funding for ADR. The Department of Dispute Resolution Services, which I had headed for 11 years, was downgraded from an independent, highly visible department and subsumed under another larger department. The decision to leave was difficult, as I loved my job and knew that it offered the unique ability to be an instrument for ADR policy and program development.

In leaving a secure position to start a private mediation practice in 2008, I knew I was taking a big risk. Most of my career up to that point had been as an administrator, and I had to build my mediation practice from scratch, relying on my mediator certification, hundreds of hours of training, and the professional networks and excellent working relationships I had developed over the years. As one of the few Asian American neutrals in Virginia, I recognized that my ethnicity, combined with my lack of traditional legal experience, affected my marketability. I provided mediation and training services for several state and federal agencies, including the US Navy and NASA, as well as the

Richmond Juvenile and Domestic Relations District Court. I also taught mediation and advocacy in mediation as an adjunct professor at the University of Richmond's School of Law and the College of William and Mary School of Law.

In 2010, I joined the World Bank Group's roster of mediators and became enamored with the internal justice system of this international organization. I provided mediation, large-group facilitation, and conflict resolution training and supported organizational development initiatives around the world. In 2012, I was selected as the International Monetary Fund's first mediator and was given the opportunity to build the Mediation Office there as part of an internal justice system to informally address employment disputes.

The staff of the IMF are international civil servants who do not have access to the US court system. As a result, their only recourse for work-related concerns is provided by the IMF's internal rules and dispute resolution systems, which include mediation as an alternative to a more formal grievance process. As the head of the IMF's Mediation Office, I integrated my administrative and mediation expertise and greatly appreciated the autonomy, resources, and opportunities I had to innovate.

Working at the IMF, which includes 3,000 staff members from more than 150 countries, was the first time in my career that I truly felt I fit in. I never had to be self-conscious about my Indian background, as I had been in my other jobs; my "differences" actually gave me credibility with colleagues from around the globe. People saw me as culturally competent and familiar with the dynamics of the Western work environment. I was mediating between cultures, languages, values, and expectations in the context of employment disputes. The hierarchical nature of international organizations, the high education level of staff members, the conflict-avoidant culture, and the vulnerability of staff because of visa status were just a few of the issues I encountered.

As part of the network of mediators and ombudsmen of the United Nations and related international organizations (UNARIO), I attended annual meetings with dispute resolution colleagues from other UN organizations where we shared common challenges and ideas. These exchanges were enormously helpful. Only a small number of individuals have the privilege of serving as a neutral in the internal justice system of an international organization. Many are working in a country other than their country of origin, and most are multilingual. This cadre of neutrals is highly sophisticated in their understanding of dispute resolution, multi-cultural issues, and workplace challenges for managers and staff in international organizations, and I learned a great deal from my colleagues in UNARIO. For example, drawing from a similar program at the World Bank, I developed a unique program for the IMF called Peers for a Respectful Workplace.

The most challenging aspect of my work at the IMF was being an effective "inside–outsider." As a mediator, I knew that remaining neutral and impartial in all my interactions with staff and managers was critical, but because I often had to engage with key decision-makers in the legal and human resource departments, I had to be careful that these working relationships did not create any perceptions about an alignment with management. As had been the case in my childhood, my IMF responsibilities placed limits on my social life: to avoid any possible misunderstanding of my loyalties, I never had lunch with staff members or managers and went out of my way not to develop any personal relationships with them. I had wonderful staff in my office whom I worked with closely, and I regularly met people during mediations, trainings, and meetings, so I never felt alone. I walked this fine line throughout the almost six years that I served as mediator at the IMF, and I believe it helped me be more effective.

Another challenge at the IMF was that although I always emphasized the confidentiality of mediation communications in describing the benefits of the mediation process, I quickly realized that I could not honestly assure parties complete confidentiality. Confidentiality was outlined in the "Agreement to Mediate" and in the IMF's "Mediation Rules", but there was no real way to enforce it. Staff talked to staff about their experience in mediation, whether they could trust the mediator, and the nature of settlements they reached in mediation. Managers talked to managers about the effectiveness and utility of the process and whether they had used it successfully in certain employment matters. Confidentiality could also be waived on a "business need to know" basis, such as when several people had to be informed of mediation agreements to allow implementation. This reality made ensuring that the mediation process was fair and constructive even more critical, since even just one negative experience could have damaged both the program and my own reputation. Whether or not others honored the confidentiality of mediation discussions, I always did. I hope and believe that my strong advocacy for the fundamental principles of the mediation process, particularly confidentiality, helped maintain the integrity of the program.

I loved working at the IMF, but the position of mediator there has a limited term and is nonrenewable, and I moved on to the ADR division at the Federal Emergency Management Agency (FEMA), where I worked in organizational development and conflict management. Under the leadership of Cindy Mazur, FEMA's ADR division has grown and helped the agency fulfill its mission to assist survivors of disaster. More recently, I joined the Fourth Circuit Court of Appeals, serving as its director of workplace relations.

The Development of ADR in India

Over the past 15 years, I have been involved in the development of dispute resolution in India, training lawyers and retired judges in mediation and educating members of the bench and bar about the benefits of mediation. I have been thrilled to be able to able to take my knowledge and skills to my motherland—and to feel my professional and personal worlds converging.

Visiting the first court-annexed mediation program in Chennai (also known as Madras, the capital of the state of Tamil Nadu off the Bay of Bengal), after a cadre of mediators had been trained there was incredibly rewarding. High court judges overwhelmed by their dockets described the volume of cases as akin to the weight of a large elephant, and their strong appreciation for the relief mediation offered made me think of the ADR revolution in the United States after the Pound Conference of 1976.

In introducing the Western model of mediation in India, which has a rich history of informal processes analogous to mediation, I had to be careful to adapt certain aspects of the training to Indian legal culture. Insisting on the neutrality of mediators in India, for example, would not have lent credibility to the program: Indian litigants feel comfortable working with professionals that they know and trust and whose subject matter knowledge and expertise, as well as reputation, are well respected. In addition, while self-determination is appreciated, the parties in India generally expect the mediator to provide some direction and evaluation. Indians are often distrustful of private proceedings and insecure in making decisions for themselves. Often decisions cannot be made in one mediation session, as parties might have to consult with their extended family. In small jurisdictions that have only one judge, requiring that the judge who handles the mediation cannot later hear the matter if a resolution is not reached is simply not feasible. Mediator ethics training in India, where bribes have been part of the culture for centuries, had to emphasize the inappropriateness of accepting money or tips and the need to avoid conflicts of interest, topics we would not cover in the same way in the United States.

Over the past decade, the number of court-annexed mediation programs around India has grown extensively. The dispute resolution community there is grappling with a variety of issues such as quality-assurance, enforceability of mediation agreements, program evaluation, credentialing, and continuing-education requirements for mediators. Having played a small part in the evolution of ADR in India brings me great fulfillment, and I maintain contact with several colleagues in India and discuss barriers to the expansion of mediation in private matters as well as other programmatic issues.

Reflections on My Mediation Practice

Over the past 25 years I have mediated general civil, domestic relations, truancy, child dependency, and employment disputes. Of these, I most enjoy working on cases that involve family and employment matters. While seemingly different, family and employment cases both involve relationships that have enormous repercussions for the lives and well-being of the parties and their extended families.

Children are resilient, but if parents don't develop and practice good communication and collaborative problem-solving skills, their children's physical and emotional health can suffer. These key skills can be modeled and explicitly discussed in mediation. As a mediator who is also a wife and mother, I try to stand in the shoes of the parties and understand the frustrations and concerns expressed. My primary goal is to model good communication, support collaborative problem-solving, and help people manage feelings of anger, betrayal, loss, and fear.

The challenging family dynamics in my own childhood make working on family cases especially interesting for me, and I know my experience has helped me help others. My parents wouldn't let me date in high school, as I mentioned, but not just because they didn't approve of Western teenage ways: they wanted me to marry a man from our caste and region of India. I understood how important it was for them that I marry someone who shared our language and customs and was from a good family with similar values. My father pre-screened several young men who met certain criteria, and I had a chance to meet with a few of them. My husband and I spoke only a few minutes before we were betrothed a few weeks later, and I'm happy to report that we have been married for 30 years. I am fortunate to have a good marriage, but over the years, many Indian couples struggling with challenges in their marriage have turned to me for help.

In the Indian culture, divorce has a strong stigma. Even if a couple is incredibly unhappy and argues all the time and even if there is physical and psychological abuse, they must remain married to avoid losing face in the community. Reflecting on the religious and cultural reasons that keep Indians in unhealthy marriages, the typical sources of discord such as meddling in-laws, dowry and financial troubles, the imposition of inequitable patriarchal expectations, and poor communication, I wrote a book, *Shaadi Remix: Transforming the Traditional Indian Marriage.* My goal is to provide some insight into how Hindu marriage traditions can be adapted for the younger generation. I also share questions that can help couples assess compatibility and outline dispute resolution options such as mediation. While my work now is primarily focused on employment matters, I still get calls from people needing assistance in family matters.

Employment cases are close to my heart because I know firsthand what a positive—and not-so-positive—work environment is. In employment matters, workers often feel a sense of identity that makes conflict quite emotional. Most of us spend more time at work than we do at home, and the relationships, reputation, experiences, and expertise we build at work are valuable to us. We have a strong need to feel recognized for our efforts and to know that the work we do is meaningful. When our job security or ability to succeed at work is threatened, we invariably react very strongly. In both family and employment matters, communication, trust, respect, financial security, roles, and responsibilities all come into play. My personal journey enables me to meet people where they are in employment and family matters and help them find solutions that are right for them.

Reflections on My Programmatic Work

In addition to the great satisfaction I get from the actual work of mediation, I enjoy program administration and leadership. I thrive on the adrenaline of responsibility and multi-tasking and enjoy coordinating and networking with a wide variety of people. I also enjoy creating new initiatives that will support efficiency and promote awareness and effective use of conflict resolution processes.

In 2015 I had the privilege of serving as chair of the American Bar Association's Dispute Resolution Section, an honor I never imagined. I have been active in the section since the early 1990s, and it has been an excellent source of information, friendship, and networking. While there were many important projects I led during my year as chair, the most exciting for me was coordinating the Asia Pacific International Mediation Summit.

The Dispute Resolution Section had coordinated an International Mediation Summit at The Hague in 2008. As the first chair of Indian origin, I was eager to expand knowledge-sharing between dispute resolution leaders in the United States and Asia. The Asia Pacific Summit required 18 months of planning and collaboration with dispute resolution colleagues in several countries, and more than 200 dispute resolution professionals from 18 countries participated. Justices from the Supreme Court of India, the chief justice of Singapore, and leadership from Hong Kong, the United Nations Commission on International Trade Law (UNCITRAL), and the American Bar Association were also in attendance. The Asian participants enjoyed engaging in discussions with ABA members who shared their insights, experiences, and program models that have been successful in the United States, and many US participants said they gained a greater understanding and appreciation of mediation program development in Asia. I have great hope that the section will be able to continue to promote this kind of cross-cultural exchange.

Reflections on Mediation Tenets

The basic tenets of mediation such as neutrality, self-determination, procedural fairness, and confidentiality generally hold true for me even after 25 years of practice, but I have also come to appreciate the art of mediation.

Like most mediators, I was taught to leave my opinions and beliefs at the door when I start a mediation. Having served as a mediator for more than two decades, though, I know that I can never be completely neutral and unbiased. I feel the greatest tension between my values and my role as a mediator when I observe what I can only describe as injustice, a tension I've experienced in cases where one party appears to take advantage of another or the agreement seems inequitable. When I feel this tension, I remind myself that it is not my conflict and that I shouldn't judge whether a resolution is fair. As long as the parties are competent, have access to counsel, are exercising self-determination, and are making an informed decision, I cannot allow myself to be drawn into questioning the appropriateness of an agreement.

One of the greatest weaknesses I have as a mediator is that I carry my cases and clients home with me in my thoughts. I have difficulty disconnecting and worry about the impact of the conflict on the well-being of my clients and, if the case is an employment one, on the organization. I revisit the mediation discussions in my mind and examine my approach, considering whether different questions or strategies might have led to a better outcome. I describe myself as not impartial, but multi-partial, caring for a fair process and positive outcome for all.

I have learned to honor my intuition as a mediator and try to mediate from my heart. Often when I demonstrate vulnerability in mediation—at times by sharing my personal challenges—my clients begin to feel comfortable with uncertainty and risk-taking. Training in conflict coaching has taught me to replace fear of the unknown with curiosity. I have learned to be more self-aware, try to lean into discomfort with silence to allow for reflection, actively consider the parties' feelings, and observe what is influencing them. I question why I am using a particular approach and understand that I must be genuine to be effective. Through deep listening and removing mental distractions of other matters, I ask myself what is really happening in the conflict. I listen to the text with my rational mind and listen to the subtext with my heart. I listen for unspoken assumptions and dilemmas and try to be authentic in naming what is going on. I worry less about looking and speaking like an expert mediator and focus more on being in the moment with the parties.

My conflict coaching training and ombuds training have complemented my mediation skills training to make me a more holistic mediator. I treat every case as a new challenge and opportunity, even when the issues and the subject matter are similar to those in previous cases. If my energy level and care for the clients ever decline, I know that it will be time for me to stop mediating.

Conclusion

I became a lawyer because I wanted to make a difference in people's lives, and I love the human connection that dispute resolution provides. I can have my finger on the pulse of the parties' emotions and on the negotiation process, and I often can sense how close to (or far from) resolution we are. The personal satisfaction that I achieve every day through this work comes from knowing that I have helped reduce clients' stress and anxieties by addressing their concerns in a constructive manner, and my reward is seeing clients happier and more hopeful about the future. When people who began the dispute resolution process feeling angry, scared, frustrated, or distrustful walk away from the mediation table talking, laughing, and feeling more positive, my heart sings.

My favorite observations include the shift in parties' body language—from turning away to facing each other directly, from speaking only to me to speaking directly to each other. The lightbulb moments that mediation often stimulates, as well as the genuine apologies that are shared, are priceless. Through my mediation and facilitation work, I have seen individuals and teams transformed. This is important to me because I am at heart a peacemaker. I want people to be happy at work or in their marriage and to thrive.

As I reflect on my professional journey, I recognize that while nothing I did was exactly planned, everything I did has been connected to my goal of serving others. I feel truly fortunate to have held key positions in amazing organizations, and each role has built on the others. I have experienced dispute resolution from almost all angles—as an administrator, a mediator, a professor, a consultant, an ombudsperson, a coach, an internal provider, and an external provider, at the state, federal, and international level. They say if you love what you do, you will never work a day in your life, and this is certainly true for me. Every morning I'm eager to see what challenges and opportunities the day will bring, and I look forward continuing to learn, grow, and contribute in the years to come.

8

Crosscurrents

By Nancy A. Welsh

◆

I have always felt caught in crosscurrents of identity, never entirely settled in one place or the other. I suppose that the resulting discomfort has motivated me to try to understand the different currents tugging at me. Yearning to understand—and yet also wanting to find my own voice, to be heard and respected—these are my internal drivers. They match some of what I see as key aspirations of our

---

Nancy A. Welsh is professor of law and director of the Dispute Resolution Program of Texas A&M University School of Law. She was previously the William Trickett Faculty Scholar and professor of law at Penn State University, Dickinson School of Law. A leading scholar and teacher of dispute resolution and procedural law, she examines negotiation, mediation, arbitration, judicial settlement, and dispute resolution in the United States and international contexts, focusing on self-determination, procedural justice, due process, and institutionalization dynamics. Welsh presents nationally and internationally and has written more than 60 articles and chapters that have appeared in law reviews, professional publications, and books. Welsh is also co-author of the fourth, fifth, and sixth editions of *Dispute Resolution and Lawyers* (2009, 2014, and 2019). She succeeded Harvard Law Professor Frank Sander as co-chair of the Editorial Board of the *Dispute Resolution Magazine*, conducted research as a Fulbright Scholar in the Netherlands, and served as chair of both the ABA Section of Dispute Resolution and the AALS Alternative Dispute Resolution Section. Before joining the legal academy, she was the executive director of Mediation Center in Minnesota and practiced law with Leonard, Street and Deinard. She earned her BA *magna cum laude* from Allegheny College and her JD from Harvard Law School.

field—providing people in conflict with a forum in which *they* can hear each other, be heard, and find their own way.

I have working-class roots. My maternal grandfather emigrated from Italy when he was a teenager and became a coal miner in West Virginia. My maternal grandmother was only 5 when she arrived in this country from Italy and was only 15 when she married my 27-year-old grandfather. She bore nine children. Warm and loving, my grandmother never learned to read or write. When she visited us, she taught me simple crochet stitches. I taught her to read simple words. I never remembered those stitches; she never remembered the words.

My mother, the second-youngest in her large family, slept with her sisters four to a bed in their company-owned house. My grandmother had to take in a drunken boarder to make ends meet, and my grandfather had to stop work after he was injured in the mine. That sounds pretty grim, but my mother also told us stories of learning to play the piano and violin, being popular and doing well in school, and laughing and dancing with her siblings.

After high school, my mother moved in search of a better life. Erie, Pennsylvania, had substantial populations of Germans, Poles, and Italians who were relatively recent immigrants, but these snooty "city people" made my mother feel like a hillbilly, a hick. My father, who has lived his entire life in Erie except for a few years of military service in Okinawa, was smitten with the raven-haired, laughing young woman he met at a gathering spot for Catholic singles and soon asked my mother's father for permission to marry her. My mother, to this day, believes that my father's German and Polish family was unhappy that he married an Italian.

By the time she met my father, my mother had a good job as the secretary for the chief engineer at the telephone company. Because of her fast fingers and excellent writing skills, she had risen out of the typing pool quickly. I think she enjoyed her job. But remembering how difficult it had been for her when all the potential jobs were occupied by "women flashing their diamond rings," she quit as soon as she was married. It was time to be a wife and mother.

Born about a year later, I grew up in Erie, an industrial city in what is now known as the "Rust Belt," with its best days long past. We knew it as "dreary Erie, the mistake on the lake." From my mother—and from Erie—I inherited an identity as a have-not, likely to be discounted, someone who would have to work for everything she got.

And yet I also went to Harvard Law School—a very different identity. But I'm getting ahead of myself.

For a very long time, my identity also was tied to my religion. Catholicism permeated nearly every aspect of my life. My parents were and are devout Catholics, and I attended 12 years of Catholic school, with uniforms, nuns, crosses on the walls, and religion class every day. I was mesmerized by the Catholic saints, especially the martyrs, finding great romanticism and mystery in their lives.

Even as I write these words, I think to myself how much they evoke both a 1950s ethos and the draw of mystical medieval traditions.

But I am also female, with a decently logical brain (probably due to my data processing father), and I have the eldest child's tendency to want to lead—a set of identities that did not fit well with Catholicism or Erie. I had lots of questions about the rules I was supposed to follow and the dogma I was supposed to believe. I preferred books and the company of wise and cosmopolitan authors as they explored new worlds and (at a safe distance) the complexities of the human condition. I liked thinking, trying to understand why things worked as they did. I wanted to make a difference, to be important somehow, not just exist or survive—and there was no place, in Erie or Catholicism, for a girl with those sorts of preferences and ambitions.

I suppose you can see from what I've written thus far that the crosscurrents I felt had a lot to do with being female. Indeed, when I was born, my parents expected a boy. They had chosen only one name: Michael. (My father still cannot explain why he suggested the name Nancy.) My brother arrived just 18 months later. (My sister, who is nearly seven years younger than I am, took a little longer.) As the oldest daughter, I certainly played the "little mommy" role. I mediated between my younger siblings. Sometimes I mediated between my parents—and sometimes I still do. More often, however, I mediated among these different sources of identity that defined me.

As I grew up, the larger world intruded on my insular, tradition-bound cocoon. On the television and in the pages of *Life* magazine, I saw and read about what was going on—in the rain forests of Vietnam, as Walter Cronkite announced every night the number of American soldiers killed that day; in the South, as African Americans marched; on college campuses, as young people amassed and shouted and surged against school officials and armed police. There was conflict—exciting, important conflict—out there. People were fighting, martyring themselves, even, for democracy, for equal rights, for the right to be heard and counted. This conflict was different and attractive—direct, aggressive, demanding change. It was not the solitary, weakening conflict that an individual feels as she remains largely unseen and struggles to fit in.

Then in 1973 and 1974, Watergate struck. I was in an all-girls Catholic high school, but with a different breed of nuns. They were inspired by Vatican II, ready to cast off many of the traditions of the Church and become more relevant in the world. They invited debate, introduced us to other religious traditions, and even created an independent study for a girl who hungered to read the great books. With these women and the rest of the nation, I watched the Senate and House Judiciary Committees' hearings and deliberations. Representatives William Cohen and Barbara Jordan, Senators Howard Baker and Sam Ervin, Republicans and Democrats, all asked hard questions and sought the truth. The US Supreme Court forced Nixon to turn over his tapes. As in 1968, our democracy seemed at risk. It was a time of unsettling sound and fury.

But it was also an inspiring time. Smart and brave leaders, many of them lawyers, were helping us face tough issues and find our way through. In a June 1973 hearing, Senator Baker said, "The central question at this point is simply put: what did the president know, and when did he know it?" That was exactly right, and I realized I wanted to be able to think as clearly and cleanly as that, to cut through the sound and fury. That is when I decided I wanted to be a lawyer. Lawyers were leaders, questioners, advocates—and they had played a big role in making changes I thought were important, like establishing students' First Amendment rights. When I learned that a mere 2 percent of the lawyers in the country were female, the deal was sealed.

You may notice that to this point, I have not referenced any particular desire to be a peacemaker or mediator. Yes, I mediated at home sometimes, and I sort of mediated between my different identities. I asked questions. I tried to understand. But I was drawn to the people advocating for change, finding the truth, moving us forward through crisis. I wanted to be one of *them*.

So in high school and college, I became involved in politics on a small scale. At others' urging, I ran for president of Allegheny College's student government. I wanted students' voices to be heard. After knocking on every student door on campus, I won and became the first woman to lead the organization. I met with college administrators and advocated for students, but this was 1976 and 1977 at a small college in a small town in northwestern Pennsylvania. I was disappointed to learn that most students cared more about the cost of using the school's washing machines than the bigger issues facing their college. The few students motivated to use student government to achieve larger goals were the Young Republicans. They were my nemesis, but I have to admit a certain grudging admiration for them. Besides being ambitious, they were disciplined and patient. My supporters and I made a few reforms—and put on some great concerts—but then I moved from student government to the college radio station and professional radio and even considered broadcast journalism as a career.

But I still wanted to work for change, to be the one making a difference, not just reporting it. I had done very well in college and had impressed the faculty with my service as a student leader, my double major in English and political science, and my senior thesis. I also did well on the LSAT. (I "prepared" for the test, by the way, by going to the movie *Animal House* the night before. That would never work today.) I ended up at Harvard Law School, which was quite the feat for a nerdy, working-class girl from Erie, Pennsylvania, a coal miner's granddaughter whose parents had not attended college. My parents were proud and happy for me.

Harvard, though, was a culture shock. The students were nothing like my college classmates or my family or the people I knew in Erie. Harvard Law's students had lived; they knew the world, sometimes because this was their second career or because they came from a much more worldly social class. They read and cared about the news, they were ready to compete, they knew they mattered, they intended to be noticed and, if necessary, would force change. The faculty also were nothing like my previous teachers, many of whom had been grateful to have a student who was motivated to engage and learn. These professors had active lives outside the classroom, with research, consulting work, and television appearances. They did not identify primarily as teachers and mentors, preparing us to perform as lawyers. They were confident that we were smart and would find our way. Indeed, our job was to live up to *their* institution, "the" Law School.

And what about that demanding mistress, the Law? Like most law students, I found learning to read judicial opinions much more difficult than reading and analyzing novels or textbooks. In addition, the exciting concepts involved in Constitutional Law represented just one minuscule part of the legal curriculum. Most of the common law's foundational principles involved private property-related rights and obligations, contracts, or determining liability after accidents. Changing the world was not its primary focus. Rather, we learned the elements of legal causes of action and defenses, identified key facts that could affect application, and ultimately prepared to help clients achieve their self-interested goals. Sometimes, legal analysis and argument felt like dancing on the head of a pin to determine who would win or lose an ultimately inconsequential battle. Even working with Harvard's Prison Legal Assistance Project to help prisoners in parole revocation hearings or monitoring and researching potential legislation for the Washington, DC office of the American Civil Liberties Union ultimately did not seem to provide for meaningful forward movement. In the case of the prisoners, we were placing bandages on much bigger problems—and at the ACLU, we were caught in Washington DC's large web of big egos and self-interest.

But it was at Harvard Law School that I was first introduced to mediation. All 1Ls had been required to read Charles Dickens's *Bleak House*—an interesting way to introduce future lawyers to the effect of law and legal institutions. (Clearly, some people at Harvard had their doubts about our current legal structures.) I participated in a mediation training that took place on the weekends and mediated disputes in small claims court. I also took an elective course taught by Professor Frank Sander titled "Interdisciplinary Approaches to Dispute Settlement." I did not know that Frank was a central figure in dispute resolution. I knew only that I enjoyed his class and, very uncharacteristically, enjoyed taking the final examination because it required us to identify the disputing parties' interests and goals and figure out how to help them resolve their dispute. *This* felt creative and meaningful, although I had no idea what career path would allow me to use the concepts and skills that Frank taught.

Upon graduation in 1982, I joined the Minneapolis law firm of Leonard, Street and Deinard to practice civil litigation. I was drawn to Minnesota's progressive history and Minneapolis' Midwestern pace and personality. Leonard, Street was a medium-sized firm, with accomplished partners and a social justice history that remained an important part of the firm's culture. Three very talented Jewish lawyers had founded the firm after they had been rejected by the city's white-shoe law firms, and the firm was very involved in the labor movement, the creation of the Minnesota Civil Liberties Association, and protection of northern Minnesota's environment. Leonard, Street also had made a woman one of their partners well before any other firm in town. I liked the tradition of this firm.

By the time I arrived, though, medium-sized law firms faced a dilemma. They had to become smaller, boutique firms or grow substantially to become more corporate, full-service firms. Leonard, Street chose the latter course. I had wonderful mentors, made good friends, learned the craft of lawyering, and settled all my cases. I never used mediation, but in one case in which I represented a third-party defendant with minimal exposure, I played the role of quasi-mediator because it was in my client's interests for the case to settle—and sooner rather than later.

A large federal securities class action, a case that was in discovery and motion practice for five years, also played an outsize role in my life as a junior lawyer. I was part of a team of lawyers and legal assistants who spent countless hours combing through documents, preparing clients for depositions, and researching and writing motion papers. Finally, we went to Philadelphia for the trial, empaneled a jury, made opening statements, and began putting evidence into the record. The judge, known for settling cases, required the lawyers and clients to meet with him—repeatedly. After four days, the case settled. Despite my belief in settlement, I was crushed. I *wanted* that case to go to trial. That is what we had prepared for, and I could not believe how much time, energy and creativity we had wasted. There had to be a better way. I knew what it was.

In 1986, I left the firm to join Mediation Center, a non-profit organization founded by the Hennepin County Bar Association, that provided mediation and other dispute resolution services, conducted negotiation and mediation training, and probably most important, served as a resource and catalyst for the development of dispute resolution in Minnesota. Bobbi McAdoo was executive director. I was director of mediation services, responsible for overseeing our roster of mediators, marketing our services, consulting with private and public entities, conducting trainings, and mediating my own cases.

This was an exciting time. I received additional mediation training from CDR Associates, with masterful demonstrations of how people's interests could open a productive path to solving their problems. With mentoring and encouragement from Bobbi, I mediated cases large and small—contract, employment, environmental issues, public policy. It was exhilarating to give people the opportunity to explain what troubled them, show that I was listening and really understood what they cared about, and then help them identify and use their underlying interests, tempered with realism, to arrive at a workable solution.

We also were involved in systemic change. Mediation Center played a key role in persuading Minnesota's legislators to allow Hennepin County's courts to pilot the use of mediation for civil cases, provided the services for the pilot, and worked closely with the state to design an evaluation. Although we believed in our process, we did not know what the results would be. They turned out to be good. The parties rated mediation as fairer, more efficient, and more satisfactory than traditional adjudication (Kobbervig, 1991).

This evaluation led to statutes and rules requiring lawyers and clients to consider dispute resolution and authorizing Minnesota judges to order the use of mediation. Mediation Center then began conducting training and continuing education programs, for judges assessing cases for their mediation potential, lawyers representing clients in mediation, and the many lawyers, mediators and others who wanted to serve as court-connected mediators.

It was a heady time. Even those who decided after the training that they were not cut out to be mediators told us they appreciated learning a new way to interact with their clients and opposing counsel. I also was tapped to advise the Minnesota Supreme Court regarding mediator ethics requirements and procedures. The state of Minnesota had institutionalized dispute resolution in its courts and had developed innovative rules and procedures. We were leaders.

During this time, in 1989, I became the executive director of Mediation Center. I recall three particular moments of reveling in the center's—and my—leadership role. The first occurred on a quiet day in the office as the snow sparkled outside. I leaned back in my chair and reflected that after a lot of work, we had reached and were riding the crest of a wave. It was exciting and wonderful. The second moment occurred at one of the annual spring conferences held by the ABA Section of Dispute Resolution. As I sat with Bobbi in the audience for one of the workshops, I realized that she and I could and should be in the front of the room and people would be interested in what we had to say. They could even learn from us. The last moment occurred when I met with Bobbi, Jim Coben, and some of Mediation Center's trainers, debating whether we had something we could write about. Would anyone want to know the story of mediation's institutionalization in Minnesota? Jim was doubtful, but I was sure we had something worth sharing. My writing began.

With Bobbi, I wrote about Minnesota's experience. We wrote for lawyers, for judges, for academics. We wrote about the steps we had undertaken. We wrote about the results of empirical research that Bobbi had conducted to learn how Minnesota lawyers perceived the courts' mediation process. But as we reviewed those results, I began to fear that the wave I'd reveled in earlier, that wonderful wave, was crashing. Increasingly, especially in the personal injury mediations that then dominated the courts' civil dockets, defendants were not showing up. Lawyers—not their clients—were doing most of the talking. Lawyers were choosing litigators with substantive expertise as their mediators and expected reality-testing, not facilitation of the parties' dialogue. Increasingly, mediation was being conducted in caucus rather than joint session.

Wait. The mediation that I had helped institutionalize, the process that fit with what I cared about, involved enabling people to talk productively, getting at their underlying interests, and helping them figure out whether they could reach a solution based on those interests. Of course, discussions in a court-connected mediation should inevitably include the law, but the process was supposed to offer more than that, something that served the people involved by incorporating their voices and enhancing their self-determination.

Again, I felt conflicting currents. I was a mediation advocate, but this was not what I had advocated for. I decided that I needed to research, to write, to try to understand what was happening, to determine whether I *deserved* to be upset as the mediation process adapted to fit the culture of the courthouse. I also wanted to be sure that lawyers understood mediation's potential.

I had been teaching as an adjunct law professor at Hamline University School of Law and had recently experienced exhilarating intellectual discussions at the Salzburg Seminar in American Studies, an invitation-only global conference held in Salzburg, Austria. I had enjoyed leading Mediation Center for nearly a decade, but it was time to throw my hat into the ring to try something new—the legal academy—to affect policy regarding mediation and help law students understand the process. Frank Sander and Len Riskin agreed to serve as references, as did Bobbi and federal judge Ann Montgomery.

Penn State University's Dickinson School of Law offered me a tenure-track position as assistant professor of law. Dickinson had a long and storied history as a private and independent law school and had produced many of Pennsylvania's best lawyers. In 1997, Dickinson had become part of public Penn State University. The law school had a vibe that was both warm and ambitious, committed to teaching while being part of a major research university.

It was difficult to leave Minnesota. I had come to love the state, the Twin Cities, cross-country skiing, and camping on the North Shore. I had made many wonderful friends, some of whom had introduced me to my husband,

Eric. Our two sons had been born in Minnesota. But in 1998, I headed with my family back to Pennsylvania.

In my first few years at Penn State Dickinson, I focused on researching and writing articles that would help me—and, I hoped, others—figure out whether mediation was being misused in the courts. First up: the principle of self-determination. What did it mean, exactly? How were ethics codes in Florida, Minnesota, and Virginia dealing with the effect of mediator evaluation on the parties' self-determination? How likely were the courts to understand and seek to protect self-determination? I concluded that courts were very unlikely to care about protecting parties' self-determination or even understand the concept and that the courts' interest in docket reduction would translate into a strong presumption favoring the enforcement of mediated settlement agreements, no matter what approach the mediator used. At most, the courts might rescind mediated settlement agreements that were clearly coerced by a mediator's behavior, but how likely was a court to find that a mediator, with no power to impose solutions, had coerced a party's agreement by conducting reality-testing, even strong reality-testing? To protect self-determination, I proposed that every mediated settlement agreement should be subject to a three-day cooling-off period. Even my friends were troubled by my proposal, because it could encourage people to back out of agreements. But I thought self-determination ought to trump finality.

Because I had concluded that courts would not care about self-determination, I decided to focus in the second and third articles on something that courts should care about: justice, particularly procedural justice. Somewhat to my surprise, I concluded that mediators' evaluative interventions could be entirely consistent with procedural justice, depending upon when such evaluation occurred and how it was delivered. I also concluded that lawyers' domination of mediation sessions, speaking on their clients' behalf, also could be entirely consistent with procedural justice, as long as clients could observe that they were being given voice and their lawyers sufficiently understood what was important to them. And finally, I concluded that the use of caucuses would not necessarily undermine perceptions of procedural justice as long as enough was done in joint session to permit the parties to make a judgment about the even-handedness of the mediator. In my final article in this trilogy, I reported the results of a relatively small qualitative empirical research project involving interviews with parents and school officials involved in special-education mediation sessions. The results suggested that both parents and school officials cared most about the procedural justice offered by the process and making meaningful progress toward resolution. Also, they appreciated *both* facilitative and evaluative interventions, as long as such interventions provided for procedural justice and productively moved discussion toward resolution. Events occurring during caucus turned out to play a very significant role in the parents' and school officials' perceptions.

Every academic hopes their scholarship will have some effect. The first article of this trilogy ("Thinning Vision") influenced state ethics codes and the Uniform Mediation Act, and it was recognized as the third most-cited article in the *Harvard Negotiation Law Review*'s first 10 years of publication. The second and third articles ("Making Deals" and "Stepping Back Through the Looking Glass") brought procedural fairness to the fore in discussions of mediation.

By the end of this exploration, I felt that I had a much more realistic picture of how court-connected mediation could encourage dialogue and surface parties' interests while also permitting lawyers' likely dominance and mediators' use of both caucus and evaluative interventions. I also had come to realize that many people in disputes, at least those in civil litigation, did not necessarily expect the same expansive sort of voice and self-determination that I did.

I was promoted to professor of law with tenure in 2004. A few years later, I was named the William Trickett Faculty Scholar. Over the years, I have continued to return to court-connected mediation—writing about potential misuse of the mediation privilege, whether and how the process addresses prejudice, and even how mediation could be integrated into the treaty-based arbitration process used to resolve disputes between host states and foreign investors.

In 2006, I had the good fortune to be granted a sabbatical and named a Fulbright scholar to explore the Netherlands' institutionalization of court-connected mediation. Even more fortunately, my husband and sons were able to share the experience of living in The Hague. The Dutch institutionalization of court-connected mediation was inspired by the US experience but instructively different. For one thing, their model of mediation tended to be more facilitative and interest-based. Judges stood ready to decide cases if the parties' "self-test" revealed that their dispute would be resolved with the answer to a legal question. More generally, the Dutch conflict resolution culture provided people with access to many more "paths to justice" than in the United States. In court, Dutch trials were more like periodic conversations with a judge. And the Dutch Ministry of Justice had tapped a single well-respected judge to lead the institutionalization of court-connected mediation, in contrast to the decentralized experience of the United States.

Following my sabbatical, Len Riskin and I wrote an article proposing that someone, courts or lawyers or mediators, should be required to ask the parties what model of mediation they wanted and what issues they hoped to address. On the other hand, Bobbi McAdoo and I wrote an article suggesting that court-connected mediation had to serve courts' goals, not vice versa. Looking back, it's clear that I was still searching for how mediation fit in civil litigation and whom it should serve. More crosscurrents.

Meanwhile, I was growing tired of the crosscurrents I felt inside, as a proponent of mediation who constantly critiqued it. My next steps might have been different if I had been able to experiment with different approaches to institutionalizing the process in the courts, but Pennsylvania was not particularly fertile soil for this. Pennsylvania's state courts had not embraced mediation, except for certain types of divorce and child custody matters, and even in that substantive area, Pennsylvania already had court adjuncts called "divorce masters" who behaved very much like mediators. My most direct engagement with mediation in Pennsylvania—e.g., mediating cases and conducting training outside the law school—was with the US District Court of the Middle District of Pennsylvania and with the Pennsylvania General Counsel's Office.

My law school also was embroiled in conflict that seriously affected my life as a scholar, teacher, colleague, mother, wife, and human being. More crosscurrents. Around the time that I had been awarded tenure, Penn State's president tried to move the law school from its historic home, one that had been guaranteed by contract to continue "in perpetuity," to State College, where Penn State's flagship campus is located. All hell broke loose, with enraged law school alumni, battles in the press, law students being asked difficult questions by potential employers, a lawsuit, and a debilitating sense of uncertainty. The warring parties finally agreed on one law school but with two locations, one in Carlisle and the other in State College.

I was told that I had to move to State College. I did not want to move—I had a husband and young sons who were happy in their work, schools, and friends—and ultimately I didn't. But there were many more disruptions: moving to a temporary building next to the Pennsylvania Turnpike, teaching by videoconference with some students in the room with me and others in the "remote" classroom two hours away, traveling between Carlisle and State College to develop relationships with students and colleagues, and then going through another upheaval when Penn State decided to have two entirely separate law schools. Adding to the turmoil were the horrible revelations about football coach Jerry Sandusky's abuse of young boys and the potential cover-up by top Penn State officials.

These events certainly were distracting. But they also were instructive, as I experienced the challenges of dispute resolution. I was in the midst of a major conflict, but without meaningful voice. I was one of the faculty's most productive and cited researchers, but because I had chosen to remain in Carlisle, I was stereotyped as insufficiently focused on achieving a world-class profile for the law school. Ironically, for a time, I lost my own self-determination. At various points during those years, I proposed that Penn State bring in outside neutrals—mediators, facilitators, whatever—to help us work through our issues. That never happened, which was also instructive.

In retrospect, I see that much of the turmoil was probably the inevitable result of merging two organizations with different cultures and different hierarchies. Just as a human being has to go through the awkward stage of puberty, Penn State Dickinson had to go through a painful period of adaptation. It was made worse, though, by Penn State's decision to create two locations, one in the favored spot on Penn State's flagship campus aiming for global impact, the other located on a satellite campus presumed to be focused primarily on teaching local students. The structure and stress almost inevitably resulted in competition and even warfare.

At about this same time, I had also become distressed over the direction that the dispute resolution field was taking, especially in terms of arbitration, as that process became more of a business and less of a calling. Increasingly, dispute resolution organizations were working with companies to insert mandatory pre-dispute arbitration clauses into take-it-or-leave-it contracts and thus force consumers and employees to waive their right to go to court or join a class action. The Supreme Court was encouraging this abandonment of the courts through a series of cases declaring a federal policy supporting arbitration.

Like mediation, arbitration originally was created as an act of party self-determination. Disputing merchants preferred to have their contract disputes decided by one of their own, rather than a judge. But an arbitration clause in a contract negotiated at arms-length between two sophisticated businesspeople is quite different from an arbitration clause hidden in a form contract between a company and one of its consumers or employees. I began researching and writing on this topic, with a focus on procedural due process, structural bias, and dispute system design.

I was also elected to the council of the ABA Section of Dispute Resolution and in 2010, began working with several colleagues, including Lisa Amsler, Homer La Rue, Larry Mills, and Tom Stipanowich, to organize a series of roundtables on consumer and employment arbitration that would involve all the different stakeholder groups. We hoped that developing relationships, sharing information, and identifying issues would create some opportunities to "move the ball forward." Indeed, our consumer arbitration roundtable informed some of the research later conducted by the Consumer Financial Protection Bureau (CFPB) as it decided whether to bar mandatory pre-dispute arbitration clauses in consumer contracts for financial goods and services.

Once again, I was playing the role of dispute resolution advocate while also critiquing a process. I became chair of the section in 2016 and very much wanted this leading dispute resolution organization to play a catalytic role, to protect the integrity of arbitration by limiting the use of mandatory pre-dispute consumer and employment arbitration. Many within the section supported such a position. But many others felt that arbitration was being unfairly maligned, and some urged that they did more as arbitrators in debt-collection matters to ensure fairness to debtors than courts would have. Ultimately, the section supported ABA policies critical of mandatory pre-dispute arbitration in certain—but not all—sectors. The section also gained permission from the ABA to submit comments strongly supporting the rule proposed by the CFPB to require reporting and transparency regarding the use and results of mandatory pre-dispute arbitration.

Before this, I had not thought a lot about the need for more transparency regarding institutionalized dispute resolution. But it makes sense. The outcomes of private arbitration receive expedited judicial enforcement—thus borrowing the coercive power of the state. There should be transparency regarding the numbers of cases going to arbitration, the parties involved, the neutrals serving as arbitrators, the parties' perceptions of the fairness of the process, and the outcomes. The same is true for mediation, especially when it is imposed by the courts. Transparency—regarding both arbitration and mediation—has become my most recent focus in terms of scholarship, and it dovetails with those urging greater attention to access to justice, particularly as more people come to court without lawyers or find themselves diverted to private dispute resolution processes.

In 2017, I also made another major transition. I retired from Penn State Dickinson and joined the faculty of Texas A&M University School of Law as professor of law and director of the "Aggie" Dispute Resolution Program. It's been exciting to experience the rough-and-tumble, the diversity, and the sense of possibility that exists in the very large, very proud, and very "can do" state of Texas. I am lucky to have a wonderful group of colleagues in the Dispute Resolution Program, each with one foot in dispute resolution and the other in a substantive area of law or practice; lucky to be at a law school that requires all its students to take a course in dispute resolution and regularly integrates negotiation, mediation, arbitration, and dispute resolution skills into substantive courses; lucky to be in a state that has fully endorsed court-connected mediation and is now experimenting with online dispute resolution. And I am most lucky to have a supportive husband and family collaborating with me in this latest adventure.

And what about those crosscurrents? I don't think they will ever be fully reconciled within me. I am one of those people drawn to promising concepts: the mysticism of Catholicism, the clarity of law, the possibilities in mediation if you listen for people's underlying interests. But I am sufficiently logical and realistic to acknowledge that these promising concepts also need to fit within larger structures. Sometimes there will not be a fit. My hope is to help with the times when a fit *is* possible, but only if we care enough to work for a balance that will keep the promise sufficiently alive.

References

Kobbervig, W. 1991. *Mediation of Civil Cases in Hennepin County: An Evaluation.* St. Paul, MN: Minnesota Judicial Center.

9

Three to Tango: Reflections of a Mediator

By Johnston Barkat

♦

When India was partitioned in 1947, my mother was living with her brother in Agra, India, and my father was living in Sialkot, in the Punjab region, in an area that had become Pakistan during one of history's greatest mass migrations, involving displacement of 15 million people and mutual genocide costing the lives of more than one million people. The effects are still felt in the region, with continuing clashes over the disputed territory of Kashmir and lack of

---

Johnston Barkat is an internationally recognized expert in the field of mediation and preventive diplomacy who also advises companies on corporate social responsibility. He serves as the mediator for the International Monetary Fund and previously served as assistant secretary-general heading the United Nations Ombudsman and Mediation Service. At the United Nations, he served as a moderator and negotiator to help achieve international consensus to reduce hydrofluorocarbons, which was agreed upon in October 2016 in Kigali, Rwanda. He also chaired the interagency effort to develop a systemwide Mental Health Strategy and continues to serve on the UN steering committee that developed a global action plan to reduce violence caused by religious extremism. Barkat has taught negotiation and mediation at Columbia University and has had leadership roles in the Association for Conflict Resolution and the International Ombudsman Association. He is a fellow of the American Bar Foundation and also received the Front Line Champion Award, presented to those who have made a significant impact on the field of mediation and have helped others through their commitment to the effective practice of mediation. He received his PhD from Columbia University, an MPA from Pace University, and a BA from The King's College.

clear progress toward peace. In August 2018, Pakistan's foreign minister expressed that he was hoping for eventual progress and resumption of peace talks with India, but that "it takes two to tango."

It was amid the post-partition aftershocks that my parents married in 1955. Seeking a place to pursue education and start their life together, my father ended up coming to the United States in 1958 to study at Tennessee Temple University. My mother, a nurse, sold her gold wedding jewelry—a big sacrifice from an Indian perspective—so that my father could travel ahead to continue his studies and establish himself in the United States. Eventually, when I was 2, my parents moved to affluent Westchester County, New York, where my father began teaching psychology at a nondenominational religious college. This was where I eventually received my undergraduate degree.

Life and history did not place me in a clear identity group. I cannot remember many other people of color attending my largely homogenous school, and our town did not have a significant Indian or Pakistani community. While one might assume that this made me feel like an outsider, I felt at home and at ease. After all, it was essentially all I knew. In hindsight, the fact that my school had no significant minority representation probably facilitated my acceptance by others, who felt no real threat. As a result, I felt as accepted, or not, as any other child would be in that community and that school—on issues other than my heritage or skin color.

Our family was Christian, and as a result I attended a rather conservative college with separate male and female dorms and prohibitions against smoking, drinking, and even dancing. However, it was only about 40 minutes from New York City, which clearly had more progressive and liberal views of the world. Also, I was raised in a house that was the home base for many guests and visitors from around the world, which helped introduce me to other religions and ways of life. An interest in different countries and cultures was also sparked by travel with my family during summers and my father's sabbaticals. So even my conservative religious upbringing—where litmus-test behaviors such as drinking and smoking were frowned upon—was continually challenged. Most importantly, making regular trips to—and then living and working in—New York City exposed me to a mosaic of people from all backgrounds and reinforced my belief that no matter how different, people can find ways to live as neighbors or even friends.

I think my ability to take pleasure in finding connection and commonality with people who differed along religious and racial lines might have been an important factor in sowing the seeds that eventually drew me to mediation. While pursuing a master's degree, I met a classmate who was preparing to become a mediator. I was re-evaluating my career path at the time, and the idea of being someone who bridged divides matched my abilities and resonated deeply with my values.

My first mediation training consisted of a two-weekend course designed to prepare participants to serve as community and court mediators. Like most basic mediation courses, it laid out a series of moves to guide aspiring peacemakers, like steps to a basic box-step dance, in the framework of a two-party mediation in which both sides politely follow those steps. Then, after a period of co-mediation, mediators were launched into the courts and community to help provide a forum for the fair resolution of disputes. Community and court mediation was like going to boot camp. Cases involving all imaginable issues, people, and temperaments were presented to a mediator who had been shown the basic steps to a dance he hadn't mastered.

I remember one of my first cases. The year was 1995. It was late in the day, and I had been mediating for nearly two hours. The parties were a woman of color and a White man, neighbors in a high-density apartment building in Yonkers, New York. I envisioned a linear process: each side would tell his or her story, and I would reframe the issues, leading to a transformative problem-solving discussion. But the case had taken an unusual turn since our last session. The woman had found chicken bones and feathers at her front door, and she was petrified. Trembling with fear, she accused her neighbor in no uncertain terms of placing a hex on her. The man unleashed his views about her "Third World culture," how she was "uneducated and stupid" and a "hysterical woman." She responded in turn. Things quickly spiraled out of control.

While I did my best to hold the parties to the ground rules and ask open-ended questions, I was not prepared to handle the degree of offense and animosity between them or their rapidly escalating emotions. There I was, a relatively new mediator, trying to contain screaming parties and dealing with issues of race, social status, power, culture, religion, cultural beliefs, and sexism. The basic introductory steps I had been taught to conduct a mediation seemed woefully inadequate for dealing with real life heightened by conflict.

The situation reminds me of when I first tried dancing salsa socially after only six months of lessons. As I watched the couples moving smoothly on the floor, I realized that the classes allowed me to replicate steps I had learned but did not equip me to incorporate any artistry, style, or improvisation into my movement. I was essentially robotic in a situation requiring intuitive creativity. Mediators, likewise, have to respond quickly and creatively to unpredictable situations.

Having experienced the potential of mediation and my own limitations, I realized that I wanted to learn more than a few prescribed steps to the basic dance. I reflected that if

I wanted to be a more effective mediator, I needed to learn why people fight, what their defense mechanisms are, what makes people intractable, how their biases form, and what draws them into destructive conflict cycles. Knowing that, I reasoned, would enable me to find more creative ways to extricate people from their conflicts and help them plot new, more productive paths.

I ended up pursuing my doctorate in the social-organizational psychology department at Columbia University and studying with Morton Deutsch. Deutsch, often credited as the father of conflict resolution theory, was the director of the International Center for Cooperation and Conflict Resolution at Teachers College. Mort was a skilled mentor, and he treated students and colleagues alike with respect and kindness.

My doctorate was structured in such a way that I also had to qualify in a second academic area, so I studied in the international transcultural department under my other mentor, Gita Steiner-Khamsi. Through Gita's strong international experience, I deepened my understanding of the transference of learning across cultures.

Guided by such mentors and a combination of both areas of study, I became immersed in historical international case studies and experimental psychological research that helped me deepen my understanding of why people get into conflict, what barriers inhibit resolution, and what role culture plays in the equation. For the first time, I began to feel as if I could move beyond the basic steps of the mediation dance to a more advanced level where I could draw on deeper knowledge, improvise more, and handle a broader range of more complex and unpredictable cases.

At the time, I was working as an ombudsman at Pace University, helping resolve conflicts involving students, faculty, and staff. Apart from the usual academic and interpersonal conflicts, a university is fertile ground for almost any conflict—not only internal ones, but political ones originating from as far as the Middle East.

In 2002, controversies erupted about the construction of a wall between Israel and Palestine, and throughout the world groups polarized in support of, or opposition to, the wall. I was asked to moderate a community town hall meeting on the issue. Knowing how such meetings can sometimes devolve into incendiary political statements and verbal assaults with people demonizing those who take other views, I struggled to come up with an approach to allow voices to be heard, prevent escalation and violence, and create conditions in which the sides might be able to hear and perhaps learn from each other. I adopted a model from Laura Chasin at the Public Conversation Project (now called Essential Partners), who had long experience bringing women together from opposing sides of the pro-life/pro-choice debate in Boston. Laura and I had frequently discussed her work, and I was intrigued by how we might use elements of her model in such a potentially volatile situation (Chasin, Herzig, Roth, Chasin, Becker, and Stains, 1996).

On the day of the event, in addition to local participants, protesters representing both the Israeli and Palestinian perspectives, all of whom felt passionate about the situation, were bused in. Once inside, participants self-segregated, sittings on opposite sides of an aisle, much like the relatives of the bride and groom at a wedding, to hear a panel present different views of the conflict. An open town-hall-style time for questions followed the presentations. I asked the participants to avoid making political statements, frame their contributions in the form of a question, ask what they were genuinely curious to learn from the other side's perspective, and be mindful of time to allow as many people as possible to participate. When introducing the method, I explained that the idea was not to quash the passion of viewpoints but to channel it toward productive communication so people could not only express their own concerns but could genuinely hear those of the other side. As participants approached the microphones with their index cards, staff from my office helped them frame their questions, and then each participant had a moment at the microphone. Throughout the event, I tried to keep the group focused on the core issue from the questioner by reframing the essence of their concern.

I don't claim the process worked perfectly—it was a tense meeting. The discussions were sometimes heated, and the arguments were strong, but we got through the event with no violence, minimal grandstanding, and perhaps even a little learning. Later, we were asked to repeat the event, which gave us an opportunity to try to refine the approach.

Regardless of what method we use to mediate or moderate conflict, understanding more than the basic steps of mediation is critical. We need to understand at a deeper level what dynamics and processes create conflict or inhibit their resolution so that we can choose the right tools and process for each conflict. A process that helps participants frame their questions on index cards may work in a public dialogue hosted by a US university but may not be the right strategy with two neighbors from a high-density housing project in Yonkers who are screaming at each other. With experience and a deeper study of conflict and its resolution, mediation improvisation and artistry became easier to incorporate in meaningful and effective ways, providing me with the agility to respond both substantively and creatively but with consistent results.

As I continued to hone my craft, I found myself increasingly mediating at the intersection of culture and religion. Life also brought these lessons home in very real ways during that same time. The period after the attack on the World Trade Center on September 11, 2001, was a tense time for the world. It also became a time I first felt a sense of dread about the violence that can erupt in the aftermath of such events. People were expressing their outrage to anyone who looked remotely "Middle Eastern," and the verbal and personal attacks were escalating. My fear was not for myself. I was keenly aware that my young daughters, despite the Germanic features of their mother, also inherited South Asian coloring and the features of my side of the family. With every incident I read about, I became more and more concerned and aware how vulnerable they were to the potentially displaced anger from all of those who felt violated by the attacks. Walking down the street with them became an anxious experience for me internally, while I struggled to maintain a lighthearted facade for my daughters. This experience sometimes resurfaces when I am involved in mediating conflicts involving directed anger and hatred toward cultural, ethnic, or religious groups. It gives me a very personal touchstone to empathize with such situations, which can often start with small incidents and escalate quickly.

Years later, having accrued experience with hundreds of cases as an ombudsman as well as a court and community mediator, I ended up working for international organizations such as the United Nations and the International Monetary Fund and mediating for related agencies, economic commissions, peacekeeping missions and programs such as the UN Environment Program and the UN Office on Drugs and Crime. Accordingly, mediation practice regularly involved people in different countries and often from different religious groups or ethnicities.

The role of religious and cultural identity was strikingly clear in a challenging mediation I conducted in South Central Asia. In the spring of 2013, I was approached about a longstanding, seemingly intractable conflict among about 70 people in a politically sensitive and volatile region of the world. The nationals of the country were at odds with the local leaders of an international organization who were trying to implement changes that were perceived to infringe on rights long enjoyed by the locals.

It was an intriguing proposition. The case had festered for months, gradually worsening over time, with other resolution attempts proving futile. Anticipating that I might spend some time in that region, I decided not to shave in order to appear more familiar. Soon I had a salt-and-pepper beard that would make any Brooklyn hipster envious. Eventually, arrangements were finalized for me to mediate. After traveling halfway around the world by plane, Learjet, helicopter, and finally, armored vehicle, I found myself in one of the most dangerous places in the world with a seemingly impossible task. Due to the volatility of the situation, I was assigned a protective detail.

Fortunately, I had included one of my most senior staff members on the trip, which cut the interview time with the group in half. While the issues predictably involved people feeling disrespected because they felt that their input and views were not adequately considered, we soon found an additional dimension. While most of the group were from the same religion (Islam), they were divided along sectarian, denominational, and nationality lines. What looked from the outside like a homogeneous group with a common religion from the same region could be viewed through another lens as diverse, fractious, and potentially explosive.

After interviewing each individual, we gathered about 25 representatives in a small conference room. The group was tense, and several forcefully articulated their grievances. At one point one of the men banged the table, his body shaking, and yelled out that the object of his anger "was acting against the prophet and against Islam." The disputants were angry, and their rhetoric was escalating and tugging on religious trigger-terms. This was not two neighbors arguing over noise and chicken bones. Out of the corner of my eye I saw the hand of my protective guard move toward his firearm. As the tension in the room quickly escalated, my protector leaned toward me and whispered in my ear, "Sir, it may be a good idea to leave the room. They are getting too agitated."

From his perspective he was right. I considered this for a moment, though, and whispered back, "Not yet."

Fortunately, I had more experience to draw on than in my fledgling days and was able to engage in a constant back-and-forth, ensuring that the representatives knew I heard and understood them, validating their emotions, and reframing their language and accusations in ways that felt true to them but changed the tenor and focus of the exchange. I knew better how to leverage the power of the mediator and better understood how to distinguish those moments that required a strong intervention from ones that benefited from letting the parties vent. When their anger needed to be aired, I was able to recognize that this was a necessary stage to express their frustration before more constructive stages could begin. And I also recognized that there was an element at play where those designated as the negotiators needed to show their constituents that they were committed to taking the opposition to task. This was also done in a very specific cultural context with its own norms. In that context, righteous anger and the drama of the debate were a part of the negotiation dance. Slowly the tension in the room began to diminish. In the end, we were able to get the parties to redirect their focus from the people across the table to the issues they were frustrated by.

The sessions continued for several more days and ended with all parties signing a mediation agreement. I asked them how they would seal an agreement in their culture. They said first they would mark and seal the agreement with a religious prayer and then they would sacrifice a goat and prepare a feast to share together. I paused, struggling to suppress images of a goat being slaughtered, and agreed to their proposal. Fortunately, our helicopter had to leave too soon for them to arrange the sacrifice, and the goat lived to see at least another day. But we did mark the agreement with a ceremonial prayer. That symbolic prayer became an important part of the agreement, for in that moment the conflicting parties who began with so much anger came together united around their area of commonality.

Part of me is tempted to let the story end here, leading a reader to believe that my mediation skills were exceptional. But mediation is also a great profession in which to learn humility. I'll never forget the conversation with a team of three representatives who approached me the night before we reached that agreement.

"Sir," they said, "We have watched you carefully and thank you for bringing us this far in our negotiations. We have agreed to resolve this issue if you think it is best." And before I could let any of this go to my head, they added, "Because you have a white beard, in our culture this means you are wise. Everyone has agreed to accept the agreement if you think it is fair." Nothing brings you down to earth more quickly than being told that a mediation was successful, in part, because your beard game was strong.

In this case, as often in my practice, I struggled to adapt my Western mediation training to a culture that understood mediation differently. As much as I tried to minimize my role and have the parties negotiate their interests, it became evident to me that they saw the mediator as similar to a village elder. In such situations, the elder might try to ensure that interests are expressed and met, but ultimately the parties want the elder to approve their agreement. In essence, this gives them permission to forgive, to save face, and let go of the conflict. So finally, when the parties had crafted an agreement that met all their interests, they came to me and said it was acceptable—provided I agreed it was a good solution. After much internal struggle, I told them what I felt it addressed and what I felt might still need to be worked on, and then I indicated it was a good resolution. It was all they needed to hear, and they happily embraced their agreement. There are times, such as in this instance, that people need permission to move from fighting to détente. For the mediator, knowing when and how to differentiate the moments when the parties decide from those when the mediator directs or gives permission can be critical. In this case I was looking for an approach that addressed their interests while also finding a way for them to move on from the conflict and save face.

In every case I mediate—whether successful or not—I learn much about people who are in conflict, how to improve my practice, and even a lot about myself. The focus on myself as a mediator is not a self-indulgent exercise. The process of self-reflection is a tool to sharpen my skills and become a more effective mediator. When I co-mediate, I always take time to debrief and seek feedback from my co-mediator on what I could have done better. And when I mediate alone, as is most often the case, I also frequently survey participants and ask for feedback on what worked and what could be improved in the process. Questions I ask include whether the parties believed I was impartial and whether they felt heard and respected. I seek to know what helped move them toward learning about themselves or the other party and what moved them toward resolution—or what created obstacles or impasse. And I often reflect on what I was feeling during the session, what buttons of mine were pushed, where I felt I was effective or, more frequently, where I felt I could have done better.

One of the most important elements that helps me be more confident in strategy development is grounding my practice in theory and research about psychological dynamics and group processes. From this body of knowledge we know a lot about what keeps people from accepting what would satisfy their needs; we understand the dynamics of distrust and how individuals and groups repair and rebuild breaches. Theory and research have been especially helpful in situations where a counterintuitive approach might be called for. When, for example, is it better to refocus a party on himself instead of the other side? What to say in caucus, and what to say (or have them say) in front of the other side? My approach is increasingly guided by a better mix of instinct and learning-based strategies.

In almost every case I find myself incorporating social psychology into my practice. Awareness of my presence in a conflict draws me to research on social facilitation and mere presence, which suggests that people's performance may be affected simply by the presence of others, and a phenomenon like the Hawthorne effect, suggesting that groups' performances are enhanced when being observed but may revert later.[1] These studies prompt me to use my listening and acknowledgment of parties, my "presence," to better manage the mediation process. And when I sense there may be deference to the mediator's view, such as in the complex case where the parties sought my view, I test even more carefully to ensure that offers are genuine and potential agreements are durable. Furthermore, knowing that objective self-awareness research has found that people are more aware of how their behavior aligns with internal values when seeing themselves in a mirror or hearing their own voice guides me to use mirroring questions, reframing, and paraphrasing more intentionally.

Likewise, reactive devaluation research shows the power of the messenger over the message. This has guided me at times to use shuttle mediation to allow proposals to be better received than if delivered first by the other party. Attribution error studies, which highlight how people attribute their own behavior to external or environmental forces but attribute the behavior of others to character, personality, or internal traits, has also been a useful tool to help disputants reflect on judgments they may be making about others and help them better reflect on their own actions. And research on apologies and forgiveness helps craft genuine statements of remorse that authentically repair some of the perceived harm experienced by a grievant. This kind of grounding in theory has provided solid steps that allow me to more substantively and creatively find ways to enhance my mediation.

If a new mediator is like someone learning steps to a dance, the accomplished mediator is more like an Argentinian tango dancer. Argentine tango came to me later in life, after salsa and swing dance. Other than its obvious sensuality, it did not initially appeal to me. It seemed slow and a far cry from the overt energy and excitement of salsa or swing. But in 2015, I was finally persuaded by instructors and friends to give it a try and began to see another side of it.

It is the most intellectual dance I have discovered. In tango, you don't just walk up to someone and invite them to the floor, as you might in other social dances. Rather, you start with a *mirada,* a scan of potential partners from across the room. If your gazes meet and are held for a moment, then the invitation, or *cabeceo,* the slightest nod of the head, is initiated and responded to in kind. The leader then walks around the dance floor and approaches the partner, who does not stand until she is sure no signals have gotten crossed and the invitation was indeed intended for her. The dancers are expected to dance three short songs with the same partner, a *tanda*, after which, during a short interlude, the leader returns the follower to her seat and the ritual begins again. If between any of the three songs in the *tanda* the leader or partner does not want to continue, he or she simply says, "thank you." This can be a way to express that the dance is not working for one partner. These rituals involve subtlety and face-saving for both partners and can be easily missed by a casual observer.

During the dance itself, a leader in tango—like other social-partner dances—must navigate the floor to ensure their partner and others are not injured and must be a choreographer to initiate the partner's moves. However, in tango, the leader must always be aware of what foot the partner's weight is on relative to one's own. You are leading the movement of four feet.

This can work beautifully when both partners are skilled and in synch with each other. However, there have been times when I was paired with a partner who was at a different level, or unable to maintain her own balance, or was an excellent dancer who just didn't connect well with me. I recall one moment on a dance floor when my overly ambitious partner made a slight misstep that brought us crashing to the floor. I could have blamed her, but as the leader, I was responsible for navigating the floor, regardless of her skill level or how she responded to my lead.

The mediator is like that leader in Argentine tango. Essentially this means being fully and intuitively aware of what is going on with each of the other parties—down to the slightest, almost imperceptible, shift of weight. Mediation, as in tango, requires that deep sense of mastery of subject, artistry, and improvisation. It requires that degree of intuitiveness. A mediator must sense the situation, but, more important, must know how to seamlessly respond when the weight shifts occur, to guide the next steps toward something that advances progress. It can be hard to perceive movement toward resolution from the outside, but these elements of mediation have served me well. However, unlike in tango, the mediator has the added complexity of being the leader of at least two partners—the disputants—at the same time. You are essentially balancing the weight and trying to coordinate the dance of six feet. In mediation, it seems, it takes three to tango.

Not long ago I mediated a conflict at an international school that involved parents on one side and school administration on the other. It was as intractable as any international political conflict I have mediated. After weeks of meetings with lots of anger and frustration, I brought representatives together for a joint session. With only 45 minutes left before the session began, I struggled as I reflected on what might nudge these disputants toward resolution when traditional attempts seemed to be failing. The attribution errors were plentiful on both sides, and I sensed that there was incongruity between their actions and their shared values. These two theories, minimally, were at play, and I needed to find a way to tap into their commonalities to thaw the ice and find a way to have them humanize the other side and hold a mirror to themselves so that they could ultimately communicate better. Then in a flash of inspiration, I realized it was Valentine's Day. I ran across the street, got some heart-shaped chocolates from a drugstore, and then laid out red construction paper, scissors, markers, and chocolates at the spots of each representative. When they arrived, the sides did not make eye contact with each other, and the mood was tense. After they were seated, I told them that because it was Valentine's Day, I would like them to cut out hearts from the red paper. Then I gave them questions I asked them to respond to on the hearts. The questions included why they worked at the jobs they did, what hopes they had for the children, what environment they ultimately wanted in the school, and what ideal interaction they envisioned to work together. As each one shared, many were moved to tears, and they began to bond over their shared concern for the children and the school. School officials heard how much the parents had sacrificed for their children and how they cared to help make the school successful, and parents heard how the officials entered their profession because of their deep love of children and commitment to dedicate their life to improving education. It was a stretch to use this approach, but I felt confident of my underlying strategy (my reflective questions) and in using the creative approach (having them make hearts and articulate answers to the questions). It is also a technique that probably would not have worked well in many of the international cases I have been involved in. But it was the perfect improvisational catalyst for these disputants.

It bothers me that many mediators are not well prepared for complex mediations. Unfortunately, there is no advanced education required of mediators to ensure their continued and deeper learning or education in conflict resolution to sharpen and strengthen their practice. Most additional learning is self-selected, and many mediators simply assume that their previous roles—as judges, lawyers, or other professionals—will provide the necessary skills. While skills from prior jobs might sometimes be useful, many times mediators are caught off-guard by situations in which their professional training does not help them develop a deep understanding of the causes or provide clear guidance toward a particular strategy to fit a specific case.

I also believe that the best mediators learn the subjects of the cases they handle, even if that requires a deep-dive crash course in preparation. I recall cases where I had to immerse myself in new subjects in science, employment law, intellectual property, or trademark patents.

One of the most memorable cases involved facilitating a global environmental agreement at a time when countries were at an impasse on how to phase out hydrofluorocarbons (HFCs). When first approached, around 2014, I recall feeling completely out of my element because I knew none of the technical details of this complex issue. HFCs are what make our air conditioners cold, but they also have some unfortunate environmental side effects that have prompted a global call to find alternatives. This dispute had many elements, from concerns about fairness and cost to developing countries that would be required to change their technology to the effectiveness of replacements, since the existing HFCs worked well in countries with high ambient temperatures. Between sessions I would try to immerse myself in information about the relevant science, technology, and a host of related issues. It was a dizzying experience during which I learned more than I ever wanted to about refrigeration and the environmental impact of how we cool our homes and workplaces. In 2016, after two years of work, while still swimming a bit out of my scientific depth, I was able to sit with environmental ministers from participating countries and probe with somewhat reasonably intelligent questions that reflected a basic understanding of their complex, and often technical, concerns. The ability to immerse myself deeply in new spheres of learning is one of mediation's great charms.

Mediation can sometimes appear deceptively simple to those who do not do this work. However, in my experience, the ability to find the thread that leads to resolution from a tangled web of conflict is not easy. When it works well, it can transform. And when it doesn't, it reminds me that I still have much to learn.

Nevertheless, my practice continues to mature, and from each case I reflect on, I develop more options for the next. My early cases found me in reactive mode, driven by the parties and responding frantically to each change of direction. Over time, with the acquisition of experience and intentional study of the field, I was able to better ground my practice in research and theories. As my grounding deepened, I was able to see the possible spaces for more flexible approaches that provided the creativity to pivot and improvise in the most complex cases. I no longer focus on the basic steps to the dance. They are certainly still there and foundational. But now I can take joy in the artistry, improvisation, and creativity that I can incorporate into challenging mediations.

These days some of my greatest joy also comes in paying forward the example of my own mentors who guided me both professionally and academically. Their openness to seeing and nurturing talent in their students or employees is a lesson I have not forgotten. I have tried to continue that legacy with students, interns, and staff who have worked with me over the years. Their successes, and there are many, are ones I celebrate and take pride in. They inspire me to continue to take on interesting and challenging work—and to partner with them as I do so.

Beyond the challenge, I also find the work to be deeply satisfying and meaningful. It is work that at its best guides disputants to resolve conflict, rebuild relationships, learn new skills, and reflect on themselves. And it is work that has allowed me to step into breaches and brawls and help restore a measure of mindfulness and peace to moments of chaos. I have learned much about people but, more important, as I have reflected on my own role as a mediator, I have learned more about myself. If you ask those who know me best, you would probably hear that I am a bit more patient, a better listener, less judgmental, and more forgiving than

I was earlier in life. The professional lessons of my craft have influenced who I am and how I move in the world. And it is through this work that some of my deepest and most meaningful moments of personal growth continue.

So the profession I ended up choosing because it embodied my values has not only found some small ways to make the world a little better for my children but has made me a bit better for the world. I often tell my daughters that any path they choose in life is fine with me, as long as they try to remember three things: do something you love, treat others with respect and dignity, and leave the world a little better than you found it. In mediation, I have been blessed to have found such a calling.

Notes

[1] The phrase "Hawthorne effect" has its origin in studies conducted in the 1920s and 1930s at the Hawthorne Works, a Western Electric factory outside Chicago. The Hawthorne Works had commissioned a study to see whether workers would be more productive in higher or lower levels of light. The workers' productivity seemed to improve when changes were made but slumped when the study was over. Subsequent analysis by Henry A. Landsberger suggested that the productivity increase happened as a result of the motivational effect on the workers due to the interest being shown in them by the presence of the researchers.

References

Chasin R., M. Herzig, S. Roth, L. Chasin, C. Becker, and R. Stains, Jr. 1996. "From Diatribe to Dialogue on Divisive Public Issues: Approaches Drawn from Family Therapy." *Mediation Quarterly* 13(4): 323-344.

10

A Sort of Career

By Chris Honeyman

◆

A book about careers in mediation inherently invites some introspection from a contributor. And the concept of a career rattling around in the minds of most readers may be one that is relatively logical. In this conception, one starts a professional career as a result of detailed postgraduate study of relevant material, with successful passage through some kind of relevant academic institution culminating in a suitable degree (in our field, typically a

---

Chris Honeyman, who is managing partner of Convenor Conflict Management, has served as a mediator and arbitrator and in other neutral capacities in more than 2,000 disputes since the 1970s as well as being a consultant to numerous academic and practical conflict resolution programs in the United States and abroad. Since 2003 he has been co-director of the Canon of Negotiation Initiative, an effort to find the essential sources of understanding of negotiation among more than 30 fields and make them coherent to people with other specialties. From 2007 to 2013, he served as co-director of Rethinking Negotiation Teaching, a major project to revamp the content and methods of negotiation teaching worldwide. From 2004 to 2009, he was the lead external consultant to ADR Center (Rome), the largest dispute resolution firm in continental Europe, with a particular focus on design of the center's multinational projects in Europe, the Middle East, Africa, and the Caribbean. From 2004 to 2008 he served as an evaluator to a team of six US and European law schools, aiming to design better methods of aligning American and European teaching of negotiation and other forms of conflict resolution, and from 1990 to 2006 he was director of an extensive succession of Hewlett Foundation-funded research and development programs. Honeyman is co-editor of *The Negotiator's Desk Reference*, the *Rethinking Negotiation Teaching* series, *Negotiation Essentials for Lawyers* and *The Negotiator's Fieldbook*.

law degree or a PhD in a social science, with some rather alarming people having achieved both). The career itself is then a canny progression through some kind of ladder of promotion, with just enough lateral or other unexpected jumps to keep things interesting. I regret to say I have none of these elements.

I've long had a vague conception that I have had two quite different careers as a mediator. Writing for this book has pushed me to make that more explicit, to myself as well as to a reader. In these terms, the "first career" consisted primarily of lots and lots of real live cases. About half of these were not nominally "mediation" cases at all, but since I always tried to settle arbitration or administrative law cases and was fairly often successful at that, I have never made a sharp mental distinction as to what the real work was based just on what the file number said.[1] The vast majority of my "straight" mediation cases, meanwhile, have been fairly typical labor-management disputes, predominantly in the public sector. From the parties' point of view I was essentially interchangeable with peers who were also mediating every week in similar cases. Later, my more practical work shifted toward consulting, but that element ramped up only after I had already been a full-time practitioner for 25 years.

My attitude to this work, however, was definitely not interchangeable with my peers': my real interest was elsewhere, not centered in the cases at all. I was basically doing the cases because (a) for reasons below, they were my entree into trying to understand a bunch of societal forces that seemed to me worth an effort, and (b) I had to make a living.

A Practical Life

My attitude toward a career may be peculiar, but at least I came by it honestly. In my family, going back at least a couple of generations, I can find hardly anybody who has *had* a career according to the standards above, though they have often had interesting work lives. Nothing in my family history programmed me for programmatic success, in any field. So it's entirely appropriate that I encountered mediation while avoiding two other careers.

One was as a lawyer. There was family pressure on this, starting in London, where I grew up and where it took the form of encouragement to become a barrister (rather than a solicitor). The pressure centered on taking up an occupation that promised some degree of predictability and a decent living. I was unmoved, for reasons that may be entertaining but will not fit the space constraints here. The other was as a scholar. I was an undergraduate at the University of Chicago, then as now a sort of production facility for new academics. The concept that someone might theoretically want some other kind of career barely entered those cloistered precincts. I assumed upon graduation that I was doomed to become a political scientist.

I had enough respect for the brilliant members of that discipline I had already encountered to doubt whether I was their future peer. Yet none of them seemed to have a persuasive explanation for the central questions then on the undergraduate mind, which revolved around why we had to have Richard Nixon as president and why we had to be in Vietnam at all. And I was uncomfortably aware of the trenchant comment in David Halberstam's book *The Best and the Brightest*, looking around a roomful of Kennedy's advisors, that nobody in the room had ever run for sheriff (Halberstam, 1972). I thought at least I could avoid that kind of error. I resolved to try to get myself some sort of job at the sharp end and try at whatever junior level to actually govern somebody for a few years before training "properly" in political science. To me, this meant applying to join the federal civil service.

Luck enters here. When I graduated, I pursued my then-girlfriend (and now wife) from Chicago to Milwaukee, where she at least had a job and I was no more unemployed than I would be anywhere else. I took the federal entrance exam, did OK, and checked out the local offices of various federal agencies. There were not many, because there were huge regional offices of everything in Chicago, only 90 miles away. But the National Labor Relations Board had a full-scale regional office in Milwaukee, to cover Wisconsin as well as the Upper Peninsula of Michigan, because otherwise the Chicago and Detroit offices would have been unmanageably large. I interviewed there. The person interviewing me was one of the few Black professionals I had seen in the federal offices I had visited (this was Milwaukee in 1972, remember), and he had been promoted to a position of some consequence, as the compliance officer—i.e., the hard-nose who goes after repeat violators of the law. So I thought it was interesting when he appeared for the interview with an Afro out to here and a zoot suit.

This was promising: it suggested that the NLRB was not a typical federal agency. The interviewer also laid emphasis on the fact that the NLRB's field professionals, even at the most junior levels, had labor-law alleged-violation cases of their own to investigate, and in union representation matters, ran their own hearings as well as on-site elections. This, moreover, involved an array of every kind of industry that was "in commerce" (the standard for which was low enough that it could be met by a large gas station). This, too, was promising: it suggested that I would be working with (and studying) a pretty diverse cross-section of the society and the economy.

I concentrated my efforts thereafter on the NLRB. I offered to work in any of its 30-plus regional offices, with very few exceptions, one of which was Detroit. They offered me a job, in Detroit. I took it. In one of many career ironies,

I thus learned to practice law without a license; or at least, to apply labor law as a neutral, including conducting my first federal hearing at the age of 24.

I would have conducted that first hearing at 23 if I had not discovered I was reasonably good at mediating cases so they did not have to go to hearing. At this remove, I hesitate to speculate on why I developed quite early on a good record at settling cases. Perhaps it had something to do with conspicuous interest in hearing what everyone had to say—for which I deserve no credit, since it fit my underlying (and undisclosed) reason for being there. I deserve no credit for the second quality—conspicuous neutrality—either, since my neutrality could reasonably be seen as the product mostly of indifference to labor-management relations. Indeed I was probably the rare NLRB hire who had not only not majored in any related subject but had never bothered to take a single course in it. The self-confidence (or at least the ability to fake it) gained from having been born in one capital city and having grown up in another, with sophisticated rhetorical combat the default mode at family dinner parties, also helped. In Detroit, I felt up to the challenge of dealing verbally with just about anybody.

So I learned the law by learning the law, following the famous formula; and though I never found the law to be something I particularly wanted to pursue, legal work pursued me, for more than two decades in all. (Without a whole lot of enthusiasm, during about one-third of my work time in a later job I served as an administrative law judge. For 19 years.)

But to be out and about with the parties, investigating cases, hearing the stories that the parties and their witnesses told me—many of them true!—and then trying to settle each case rather than have it go to a formal disposition: this was entertaining, and much of the work was mediation, no matter what the agency called it. The mediation aspect was especially fun because it allowed for applying some creativity and responsiveness to the parties' peculiar (sometimes *very* peculiar) circumstances, which the legal solutions definitely did not. The work also usefully involved learning something about the world beyond the federal government. The life and times of the people who managed, worked in, and fought each other in meat-packing plants, retail stores, hospitals, trucking fleets, and lots of other places—even all the department chairs of a liberal arts college, once—leavened the central element of heavy industry. For an education in the basics of conflict and how it's handled, I could have done worse.

Yet the point of this analysis is, virtually no analysis was involved: I was not organized enough to actually have a plan, or a theory, much less a career in mind. I was just putting one foot in front of the other. But in the way of first jobs everywhere, I tired of this after a few years, and began seeking alternatives.

The chief federal mediator in Detroit at that time was David Tanzman. He was good enough to talk to me and tell me how his profession worked, though he plainly thought a fellow who came from the rule-oriented NLRB was unlikely to make a good federal *mediator*. But his key phrase, if it was intended to dissuade me, had the opposite effect: "Mediation is the only profession that has no tools, and no rules." I was the child of a photographer and a writer; grandchild of an actress; nephew of a Mississippi towboat captain; and so on. An occupation that combined a regular paycheck and health insurance (both of which I had come to appreciate) with opportunities for creativity seemed more promising than most.

I went off to pursue a job as a mediator elsewhere. I found one, with the state of Wisconsin. And the next time I saw David Tanzman he proceeded to prove his point. Back in Detroit a year or two later for a conference, I ran into

Mr. Tanzman in the hotel corridor even though I had just seen his name all over the papers as mediating the city-wide teachers' strike, which had been going on for days. This case was a big deal, because thousands of people staying home with their children disrupted production across the whole auto industry. The union had offered to go back to work if the employer agreed to refer all unresolved contract items to binding arbitration. But the publicly elected school board was damned if it was going to turn over its authority to some unelected arbitrator.

I approached Mr. Tanzman with all the deference customarily given in labor relations to persons of authority and seniority: "What the hell are you doing here? You're supposed to be *working*." He was good-humored: "Oh, we're done for now. They're going back to work tomorrow. It'll be in the papers tonight."

Based on the last public positions of the parties, I expressed surprise. Mr. Tanzman beamed: "They've agreed to *binding* mediation." Now the arbitrator in me was more than surprised: "That's a contradiction in terms. It can't exist!" His reply was "It does now!" (Anecdotally, I'm informed that some people today treat that as a term of art, describing a particular kind of practice. But that was the first I, and to judge by Mr. Tanzman's evident pleasure at his ingenuity, anyone else, had heard of it.)

No tools, no rules indeed. That moment has come back to me many times since, when I've been confronted with parties who *could not* be persuaded to do anything that had the remotest connection with logic. On those occasions I've tried to honor his wisdom.

I arrived at the Wisconsin Employment Relations Commission in its heyday. The year 1978 represented a sea change in the agency's domain: new legislation had suddenly given rural public-sector unions real power; the legislature knew this was coming and actually funded the agency to double its staff. All the new hires were designated mediators by job title, but it's far from irrelevant to my "mediation career" that the job was never more than roughly half mediation, and that's if you count mediating cases that started out with quite a different kind of docket number. The administrative-law work represented a promotion compared to the role I had held at the NLRB but was conceptually related. The arbitration work was more fun because it allowed for more variation in style to accommodate the parties' realities, and it was surprisingly autonomous by comparison with the legal role. It was also entertaining that, then as now, there were very few 29-year-old labor arbitrators around. (A good 15 years later I complained once to one of the best-known arbitrators in the United States that most of his peers still regarded me as a young pup. He replied that they still regarded *him* as a young pup. He would then have been a bit over 60.)

But the mediation work was the most creative part of all, and the part I enjoyed most. Along with my equally junior colleagues, I was out six or seven nights a month, generally to hamlets on back roads and generally till way after midnight, mediating between extremely liberal teachers' unions (or rural county-employee unions) and extremely conservative school boards (or rural county governments). The new legal structure banned strikes but allowed either party to force the other into package-final-offer arbitration. A burst of game-playing and strategic creativity on both sides promptly ensued. Our elders and betters had learned mediation when final-offer arbitration was available only to big "bargaining units" such as the Milwaukee police, and told us the great thing about it was that the parties hated it because of the loss of autonomy involved—so the threat of final-offer arbitration worked like a charm for getting them to be realistic enough to settle.

We new mediators had a different experience: we found ourselves in tiny places where there were no rewards on the public-employer boards for saying yes to the unions. Militancy on the union side meanwhile reflected years of hearing "Our position is no to everything" (the verbatim response of at least one employer I remember from that era). In our junior but, we thought, more situation-specific view, the parties *loved* the opportunity to grandstand, almost as much as they loved the opportunity to blame the result on an unelected arbitrator. So getting them to actually agree on a contract involved a lot more creativity than we had been led to expect. This learning helped develop skepticism toward the received wisdom of our field, which in turn paid off not only in my approach to subsequent writing about principles of mediation ethics and qualifications and so on, but even before that—especially the first time I had to decide a case that challenged all the accumulated "knowledge" of my field. More on that shortly.

Within a few years, however, I had learned the job. My mediation track record was considered at least adequate, my contested-case decisions ditto; and in contrast to some of my peers, my decisions were almost always on time. In short, the job was no longer a huge challenge and I was getting a little bored.

A novelty offered itself: a tiny Wisconsin state environmental agency had recently been set up to handle the increasingly difficult problem of starting new landfills without triggering years of NIMBY disputes. Borrowing concepts from Wisconsin labor law, the enabling statute required negotiations between the landfill operator and a committee of affected local governments, with final-offer arbitration at the behest of either party if the other proved unreasonable—but also with a legal process available, one that could result in obliterating one party completely if they did *not* negotiate. When the agency got its first case of the legal-challenge type, it had no staff member who could conduct the hearing and issue a proposed decision. They asked if they could borrow one of ours, *ad hoc*. The commission offered the case to the staff, with the *proviso* that the person taking the case would not be paid extra—and there would be no corresponding reduction in regular caseload. No one else on the staff was bored enough to take that deal, but I was. The case became my introduction to "context matters."

It took me many more days than my usual to write that decision.[2] Not just in the state but nationally, this was a "case of first impression," as far as I was ever able to find out—and my attempts to apply the superficially analogous reasoning and precedents in labor law failed a basic concept of workability under these new circumstances. I wrote, after all, as a by-now experienced mediator who had often had to navigate the real world of bargaining. So I found myself laboriously writing my way around the labor law "precedents," meticulously parsing the history back to 1935, and articulating why I felt the apparent precedents did not apply. I issued the (proposed, but public) decision with some trepidation and awaited the inevitable appeal from the losing party and the probably scathing disposition of the Waste Facility Siting Board (an august body whose members were appointed directly by the state's governor).

And it sailed through. "*Of course* that's how it has to work" said the board's sole professional staffer, when I was later free to talk with her about the case. I went on hearing and proto-deciding the occasional case for the Waste Facility Siting Board for several more years. But it was this first case that forced me not just to grumble (as in our early mediation experience) but to articulate in writing that what my peers and I had been told by our superiors was eternal verity was so until just one or two of the parameters of circumstance changed.

The discovery that I could write in this vein and survive led quite directly to my first academic writing. And though almost all of my subsequent writing has been on mediation or negotiation rather than law or arbitration, it was the fact that I had a job that mixed all these functions in any given workweek that made writing seem a natural extension of my mediation role. In turn, many years' rapid switching between neutral roles has made each type of work inform the others, so I am more likely to this day to perceive commonalities and overlaps than hard distinctions between these forms of work.

A Practitioner Starts to Theorize

About the same time as the case just mentioned (i.e., 1984), the then-Society of Professionals in Dispute Resolution (SPIDR) attempted a code of ethics for mediators across our increasingly sprawling field. The code, as initially drafted, was influenced by the perceptions of some leading family and environmental mediators, and set terms for what a mediator should do that included notions such as a mediator's responsibility to balance power between the parties where it was drastically unequal and a mediator's duty to go find parties of interest who did not seem to be represented. Power-balancing and hauling in unrepresented parties were things my labor mediator colleagues found *un*ethical. In our world, one operative phrase was "the lion's share goes to the lion." And to us, employees who did not think the union represented their interests had the right to try to organize a new union or to vote the union out, or alternatively, to get political within the existing union and try to replace its leadership—but no right to intervene at the bargaining table otherwise. A schism was threatened in a profession that had barely formed *as* a profession.

Emboldened by my practical case decision on "context matters," I wrote a couple of papers about biases and other ethical issues in mediation, arguing in part that in so diverse a field, a principle of disclosure (rather than more specific ethical commands) would be the only workable basis for such a code. I was slightly surprised to find the papers accepted for publication.[3] The SPIDR ethics code, when completed shortly after these articles were published, also shifted in the direction of disclosure as the core ethical principle—though it contained no cites, so I cannot claim to have been influential in the matter. However, the combination of circumstances encouraged me to tackle a new problem.

Back at the shop, trouble had been brewing for a while. As noted already, and uniquely among our peer agencies around the country, every staff member was expected to serve as an arbitrator and an administrative law judge in addition to mediating. This meant the agency had to have people who could not only keep a roomful of factions working together but write intelligible decisions when mediation was not going to work. The agency paid badly, and the night-after-night mediation work, with limited promotion opportunity and no compensation for overtime, took a toll. Almost all my contemporaries were lawyers who were readily employable by management- or union-side law firms. There developed a high level of turnover. But not all their replacements were of equal talent at our specialized work, despite good records in law school and in their prior employment. The agency discovered the hard way that it had hired a clutch of mediator-arbitrators, some of whom did OK with the parties but seemed unable to get a coherent decision together, let alone get it out the door on time, and some of whom could write OK but could also meet extensively and earnestly and kindly with parties in mediation without anything much happening.

By that time, I had been appointed to a semi-supervisory role with an urgent current assignment to try to retrain several of our newer hires. I proposed to the agency chieftains that I actually *study* mediation and try to figure out what we were doing wrong in training. They agreed, though of course with no reduction in my caseload.

I started by scheduling myself to take two weeks of experienced-practitioner summer crash courses at Harvard Law School, largely because I had heard of the Program on Negotiation's use of role-plays in training and wanted to learn how to design them. I took the opportunity to go and talk to two of the most famous scholars our field had produced, then or now—Roger Fisher and Frank Sander. I explained my agency's practical problem and asked them how one might go about responsibly studying how mediation actually worked. They considered the problem—and said they had no idea.

I found this oddly encouraging: if *they* had no idea, this meant (to me) there was no set methodology, which meant (to me) I could invent my own and not be clearly wrong from the outset. No tools, no rules, why not? Of course, it did not occur to me to ask any of the esteemed senior scholars in the Program on Negotiation who came from disciplines *other* than law. Perhaps an economist or a psychologist might have given me a different answer.

I did talk to an organizational studies scholar: Sander said I might profit by talking to a younger woman who had recently gotten her PhD at MIT by studying mediators at work—Deborah Kolb. I followed his advice. I have asked Debbie's advice many times since and have profited from it greatly. But Debbie did not tell me how to conduct the study.

The study I actually concocted led to a lot of writing elsewhere, and the details are not necessary here.[4] What *is* necessary to note is that the publication of the first resulting article in the house journal of the Program on Negotiation at Harvard became pivotal to my career, in two contradictory ways. I was a midlevel staffer at an agency that had a definite pecking order. This had been tacitly acknowledged to depend primarily on (a) one's personal reputation with repeat-player parties and (b) one's professional adroitness in managing political self-promotion in state government while appearing devoutly nonpolitical. Publication in a "prestige" venue was not within this scheme of things. Plainly, it gave me a new source of some sort of influence, but one that was hard for my superiors to gauge, let alone re-establish their superiority over. Not all of them reacted well. Perhaps this reflected the fact that unlike my three earlier published articles that had passed without local alarm, this one actually talked about our agency. Who was I to dare to describe our agency's functioning—even in terms more flattering than otherwise?

Retribution followed promptly, though it proved more comic than serious: I was informed that my use of the office secretaries for typing these academic works was improper and was henceforth disallowed. (This particular gambit died of absurdity within a year.) But the palpable envy of some (not all) of the people I had to report to, when this paper was published in the *Negotiation Journal*, did not go away. It became the first stone in a wall that eventually separated me from them professionally to the point where I had to leave. At the same time, that article became a turning point in a gradual process of developing credibility and contacts among scholars, and eventually I gained enough of these that I was able to construct a whole new career-within-a-career.

There is a step-by-step quality to this which, if someone were to study it in retrospect, might look as if it were planned. Thus, for example, talking with Debbie Kolb about her first book and about my observations over the time I was preparing a publishable version of my own study led her to suggest that I join the Law and Society

Association. I did, and after sitting in the back at two of their conferences, decided it was time to introduce myself properly. I thought a bit of research *on researchers*, done "live" at their next conference, might be different enough to interest them. A colleague from Wisconsin, Dan Nielsen, was willing to play opposite me in a role play we concocted together; a federal mediator who was more research-friendly than most, Christina Sickles Merchant, was willing to mediate the case "cold" in front of an audience. Now we needed researchers who were willing to put their own perceptions of what was happening to the test, again "cold" and in public. I was able to persuade four of the leading mediation researchers of the day to join in this effort only because one of them—Debbie Kolb!—agreed first. The others trusted her (they certainly had no reason to trust me, at the time). The resulting sessions were, I think I can honestly say, original, and they were videotaped. The Program on Negotiation decided to sell copies of those tapes and kept them in their catalog for 20 years.

I have met academics who became lifelong colleagues after they bought those tapes to use in their own teaching. Of the four scholars who had participated, I later worked with three multiple times over many years (I would have loved to work with the fourth, too, but she shifted her research interests away from mediation). And some of the people who formed the audience became colleagues later, too. But I cannot credit myself with any foreknowledge or even strategy here. One foot in front of the other . . .

At roughly the same time, however, the quality control work that I had just published started to take off—first, in the Commission on Qualifications that SPIDR had set up to follow its Commission on Ethics, then, in a very practical effort in the Boston courts. By the time the Boston effort had succeeded, it became possible to mount a national project, with me as laboring oar and general dogsbody and three nationally renowned public-policy mediators on the initially small steering committee.[5] Frank Sander served as steering committee chair.

We had no idea then that what became known as the mediation Test Design Project would run for five years or grow to a cross-disciplinary and practically diverse steering committee of more than two dozen. In the event, the project produced multiple publications including a full special issue of *Negotiation Journal* (Vol. 9/4, October 1993), and had the side effect of introducing me not only to an array of scholars in different disciplines concerned in one way or another with mediation but to the entity that was then the central funder of innovation in the field. I will not belabor the point that after a few years of very tentative and economical funding of the Test Design Project, the Hewlett Foundation very kindly proceeded to fund me for a substantial, and increasingly well-resourced series of other projects. These varied in topic, but all depended on the ability to draw quite diverse kinds of professionals into working together, and on mediating the inevitable disagreements.

This kind of work became the center of my self-definition as a mediator, and so it has remained, long after the foundation declared victory for its conflict resolution program and went home. But that project, together with Hewlett's insistence that it was working to build institutions that could survive, not to fund individuals, also taught me to build teams and work with ongoing institutions. This counterbalanced my "cowboy" tendencies.

Technically, this "second" mediation career has mostly been as a mediator of transactions rather than disputes. Its overall objective is to help build up systems and structures of conflict handling rather than to dispose of open conflicts as such. In other words, I have been trying to get people to work together, and sometimes build enduring relationships, who ordinarily would never have met each other, let alone entered into multiyear projects together. I stayed engaged in my original variety of mediation work for quite a while; there were 20-plus years, all told, in which case-handling remained my central focus. But as of this writing, I have been in the field for 47 years. So, again in retrospect, my self-image as primarily a case-handler accounts for less than half of my time in this field. Another way of saying this is that as "mediation career #2" gradually emerged, the traditional cases began to fade in personal importance to how I saw myself as a professional.

Mediating "Intellectual Transactions"

By the late 1990s, I had gone into private practice and gotten out of all my quasi-legal and most of my mediation casework (and, in at least the first part, without regrets). I went on arbitrating (at a lower cases-per-year rate) for another 15 years or more and mediated those cases whenever the parties would let me, and enjoyed that. But over time, that work, too, gradually faded in personal importance. Six years ago at this writing, I took my name off the last panel I was on.

I might have remained in that whole line of practical work as long as I did partly because something in helping actual parties with concrete problems still resonated, but certainly the fact that it was a part of my economic existence was a strong factor. In the several years since "the numbers" showed that I really did not need that source of income any more, I have not felt my sense of self to be suffering any. (Full retirement could turn out differently, but that's a bridge I have not yet had to cross.) Meantime the work I might characterize as "intellectual transactions" or "systems and structures" continues to fascinate me.

The *Theory to Practice* project,[6] with its many subprojects over five years, crystallized my approach to working with mixed groups of scholars and practitioners to produce something new. Two subsequent long-term projects, each of which took on a single huge topic, have become central to this effort. Both have had a quality of intellectual investigation about them, as well as systems/structure building, perhaps because you can take the kid out of the University of Chicago but you cannot take the U of C out of the kid. Both have also had long-term individual and institutional partners—Andrea K. Schneider and Marquette University for one project, James Coben (along with Sharon Press and a rotating cast of others) and the Dispute Resolution Institute at Mitchell Hamline School of Law.

The first, the *Canon of Negotiation* initiative,[7] has been the result of a whole lot of mostly academic colleagues agreeing that we had yet to really try to integrate the wisdom of all of the many disciplines and practice specialties that make up negotiation, and therefore mediation. A first phase, 16 years ago and starting with 20 younger, "second-generation" scholars and practitioners, found two dozen subjects that were not being taught outside their domain of origin—law, international relations, business schools, or planning, or whatever—but should be. The second round netted 80 such topics, from almost 30 disciplines and subject fields. By 2017 that 800-page text in turn had been replaced—with two volumes, and 1,500 pages (Honeyman and Schneider, 2017).

The other large-group project was *Rethinking Negotiation Teaching.*[8] This set out partly to address the overrepresentation of American ideals in the field and the consequent failure in application of many of our teachings when they became exposed to very different societies. So the team structured that project around three meetings, deliberately moving farther and farther from US culture; thus Rome, then Istanbul, finally Beijing. In not much more than five years this resulted in four books, several special issues of journals, and a whole lot of experimentation in teaching in multiple countries.

What's next? Well, I have some ideas, and even plans, but since this book is about the contributors' personal motivations and experiences, those are for another day and a different venue. Here I will simply say that my personal enthusiasm for mediation has been centered in using its skills to do something new. I honor those mediators, no doubt the vast majority, for whom it's all about the people, whether defined as the immediate parties or in grander societal or "bringing peace" terms. But I should acknowledge that my own motivation is different, tied to the opportunity to work on something in which intellectual output may have some useful practical consequences. If I had arrived at my professionally formative early 20s at a different time, my attention might have been drawn by some other line of work entirely.[9]

Thus it was a matter of luck, not talent, that I happened on mediation just as it was breaking out of its twin straitjackets of labor relations and traditional diplomacy and becoming applied more generally. It was luck that the first mediator I met had so engaging a way of describing his work, and luck that the agency that then hired me combined sophistication and dysfunction in ways that encouraged new thinking. And if the field, like so many, had then hbecome thoroughly developed and "routinized,"[10] I might not have had enough fun with it to keep at it.

Or perhaps my personal motivation is not quite as distinctive as I may think. I can remember exactly when I first articulated a theory of how a mediator actually worked. It was a summer night in 1985, three o'clock in the morning, at an all-night coffee shop on the outskirts of Stevens Point, Wisconsin. I had been observing one of my colleagues mediating a labor dispute that night, the same Dan Nielsen mentioned above. He was one of five mediators—all of whom, I thought, were better labor mediators than I was—who were part of the study I had concocted. He asked whether I had any conclusions yet. I did. I laid them out—or at least the first, tentative, incorrect-in-many-ways oral draft. He considered this, and responded, "If you're right about this, you're going to take all the fun out of this profession."

His answer suggests something about mediators other than me. My belated riposte is, "Oh, no, I'm not." And on behalf of all the creative colleagues I've worked with since then to try to improve our understanding of mediation, *we're* not going to take all the fun out of this, either. There's still far too much doubt about what the right thing to do is in any given circumstance; far too much room for creativity; and plenty of room, too, for personality and just plain weirdness. With any luck at all, mediation as a field will learn to do still better work for the parties and the public than it already has, and with any luck at all, for the mediators ourselves, it will go on being, well, fun.

Notes

[1] In that, I was typical of my working milieu, so there was nothing distinctive about my approach thus far. I have written elsewhere about the reasons behind my then-agency's peculiar habit of allowing or even encouraging a case to mutate from an arbitration or legal case into a mediation; see Honeyman 2006.

[2] See Troy Area Landfill v. East Troy, "Selected (Public) Decisions," Convenor, accessed April 5, 2020, https://www.convenor.com/selected-public-decisions.html.

[3] Along with subsequent papers on the same theme, they are reproduced at https://www.convenor.com/mediation-ethics.html, accessed April 5, 2020.

[4] See "Key Publications," Convenor, accessed April 5, 2020, http://www.convenor.com/assessing-mediators.html; see also "Assessing Mediators: A Bibliography," International Mediation Institute, accessed April 5, 2020, https://www.imimediation.org/practitioners/feedback-guidelines-reviewers/.

[5] Two of them, Linda Singer and Michael Lewis, were respectively also the chair and a member of the SPIDR commission. The third, Howard Bellman, is one of the contributors to this book.

[6] See "Theory to Practice," Convenor, accessed April 1, 2020, https://www.convenor.com/theory-and-practice.html.

[7] See "Canon of Negotiation," Convenor, accessed April 1, 2020, https://www.convenor.com/canon-of-negotiation.html.

[8] See "Rethinking Negotiation Teaching," Convenor, accessed April 1, 2020, https://www.convenor.com/rethinking-negotiation-teaching.html.

[9] And in fact, in the months before fatefully taking the federal service entrance exam, I had toyed with becoming a city planner, to the point of writing up a theory of a new urban transportation system based on widespread distribution of city-owned bicycles. (This went nowhere, of course. I thought I had a solution for the inevitable theft problem, predicated on fleet orders big enough to justify manufacture of a model on which no part would fit any other type of bike. But a solution to the cost problem was decades away, and as history has shown, depended on Internet billing; meanwhile the vandalism problem self-evidently has yet to be solved.) I quit the urban planning field before even starting in it, though: a few days at the field's main national conference persuaded me this was not going to be fun.

[10] Routinization threatens, but has not yet taken over, perhaps partly because of efforts to alert our colleagues to the threat. See "Penn State Law Review Special Issue, Vol. 108, No. 1," Convenor, accessed April 5, 2020, https://www.convenor.com/penn-state-law-review-special-issue.html.

References

Halberstam, D. 1972. *The Best and the Brightest*. New York: Random House.

Honeyman, C. 2006. "Worlds in a Small Room." *Journal of Dispute Resolution, Vanishing Trial Symposium Issue* 2006 (1): 107-118.

Honeyman, C. and A. K. Schneider, eds. 2017. *The Negotiator's Desk Reference*. St. Paul, MN: DRI Press.

11

We Can Work It Out

By Colin Rule

◆

"...there is no such thing as a conflict that can't be ended. Conflicts are created, conducted, and sustained by human beings. They can be ended by human beings."
—*Former senator and Northern Ireland peace negotiator George Mitchell*

When I was growing up, I remember encountering *The Morton Downey Jr. Show* for the first time. The syndicated television program centered around Downey, an irate, chain-smoking host in a cheap-looking television studio

---

Colin Rule is CEO of Mediate.com. In 2011, he co-founded Modria.com, an Online Dispute Resolution (ODR) provider based in Silicon Valley that was acquired by Tyler Technologies in 2017. From 2017 to 2020 he served as vice president of ODR at Tyler and from 2003 to 2011 was director of ODR for eBay and PayPal. He is the author of *Online Dispute Resolution for Business* (2002) and co-author of *The New Handshake: ODR and the Future of Consumer Protection* (2017). He serves on the boards of the Consensus Building Institute and the PeaceTech Lab at the United States Institute of Peace and is currently co-chair of the Advisory Board of the National Center for Technology and Dispute Resolution at UMass-Amherst and a fellow at the Gould Center for Conflict Resolution at Stanford Law School. He co-founded Online Resolution, one of the first online dispute resolution (ODR) providers, in 1999 and served as its CEO and president and worked for several years with the National Institute for Dispute Resolution in Washington, DC, and the Consensus Building Institute in Cambridge, MA

screaming at his audience and guests, generally working himself into a frenzy of anger about whatever outrage or hypocrisy was the chosen topic of the day. Downey would stalk the stage, tapping his ashes into a large silver ashtray, occasionally blowing smoke into the face of one of his guests in order to rile them up. He'd accuse anyone who made the slightest progressive argument of being a "pablum-puking liberal" and would frequently interrupt others mid-sentence by shouting "ZIP IT!" into their faces from inches away. Often he'd urge his guests to fight with each other on stage, even goading them on several occasions to come to blows.

But the aspect of the show that really made an impression on me was the audience. His diehard fans referred to themselves as "Loudmouths." They loved everything about Downey's act. They'd bring homemade signs to his shows with slogans urging Downey on, trying to draw Downey's ire so he could deliver them a personal dressing-down. When Downey would go on a rant, they'd stand up and cheer—almost like spectators at a professional wrestling match. The camera would pan the faces of the smiling and elated audience members (many of them young white men) as Downey's rants escalated and the veins popped out of his forehead. They knew it was all staged (they must have known), but they clearly loved it. In interviews, they'd explain that they loved "The Mouth" because "he's not afraid to open his mouth ... he's not afraid of anybody."

For some reason, Downey's popularity profoundly disturbed me. I couldn't take more than 10 or 15 minutes of the show before I was extremely disquieted. What did it say about human nature that this man had such an audience? What was it about his absurd ranting that commanded such attention? But because it fascinated and horrified me in equal measure, I would flip over to it on occasion.

To me, Downey's ranting seemed like playing with fire. I was raised as a Unitarian Universalist and from my earliest days was surrounded by the community at First Unitarian Church in Dallas. I looked up to many of the adults in that church and saw a future for myself in their lives. Although Unitarianism is free from any prescribed belief system, the principles undergirding the religion—such as the inherent worth and dignity of every person; justice, equity, and compassion in human relations; acceptance of one another; understanding that everyone is on their own search for truth and meaning; and the shared goal of a world community with peace, liberty, and justice for all—made an early and indelible impression on me. Downey seemed to be entirely devoted to the opposite.

Unitarianism asks its members to figure out their own faith. In response, as I crafted my personal theology, I had little confidence that humans were anything other than the smartest monkeys around. We're all riding this little blue rock out in space for a fairly short period of time, trying to make sense of our existence and bring some meaning to our lives. We like to think of ourselves as reflections of the divine—enlightened and rational—but any cursory observation of current events provided me plenty of evidence of the limits of human enlightenment. People seemed to me easily confused, manipulated, and set against each other. My studies in school documented how hate and fear could easily metastasize into nationalism, jingoism, and racism. History offered a long parade of leaders who had appealed to the devils of human nature to achieve their (often selfish) ends. But there were others who spoke to the angels of our nature: the ones who led from love, which seemed to me to be the one thing that made our lives have meaning. I came to believe that there was no higher calling than working to promote understanding, tolerance, empathy, and peace. We're all stuck on this rock together and none of us can leave, so we had better learn how to get along.

When I was in eighth grade I wrestled with depression, and at one point it got bad enough that I dropped out of school for a few months. In retrospect, I think I was uncomfortable in my own skin, and it was making me feel lonely and ostracized. But during this period I discovered a new community on a local bulletin board system (BBS) called "Eclectic." This was long before the Internet, so to access this community you had to dial up via a modem, and there were no pictures—only text. I spent many hours each day talking with my new friends on Eclectic about politics, books, philosophy—really anything that captured our attention. Eventually I asked my Mom if I could host a party for my online friends at our house and she said yes, not knowing anything about them but knowing I needed some social interaction.

When the day of the party finally arrived, I was nervous and excited. The first person who showed up was a 50-year-old Vietnam vet named Ed who arrived on his Harley dressed all in leather. The second person who showed up was a local nurse in her mid-30s named Cynthia. The third person was an engineer from Texas Instruments named Don. Thirteen-year-old me was (understandably) terrified, so after saying a quick hello I ran back to my room and hid while my mother served iced tea to them in our backyard. Eventually someone showed up who was sort of close to my age (probably 15), and we hung out together until the party ended and everyone went home. Then we all logged onto Eclectic and everyone raved about what a great time it had been. Remember, this was long before the Internet was associated with cyberbullying, or child exploitation, or racial intolerance. This community welcomed me at a time when I didn't feel as if I belonged anywhere. To a kid painfully aware of his awkward appearance, the connections on

Eclectic, which were intellect-to-intellect, felt almost more genuine and more authentic than in-person connections, inevitably influenced by first impressions around attractiveness and age.

By high school I had become a competitive debater. I uncovered my skill in public speaking as my shyness receded and my Eclectic friendships faded away, so by my junior year I was traveling around the country to dozens of debate tournaments, steeped in a community with its own elaborate terminology and ruthlessly competitive mindset. In a way, the debate community was similar to Eclectic, because debate is all about your mind; it doesn't matter what you look like, as long as your brain is sharp enough to make the winning argument. All the elite teams on the national circuit spent their summers at various institutes reading books, "cutting cards" (e.g., gathering evidence), and educating themselves about every nuance of the selected topic for the year, and I was no different. I gave myself to it fully.

In debate you never know what side of the argument you're going to be on. When you walk into the room, you know the general topic (maybe improving water quality, or improving agricultural yields, or improving retirement security), but you might be put into the position of arguing for ("political stability is good") or against ("political stability is bad") a proposition. The competition isn't about the truth, *per se*, it's about who is the better debater. We called debate "mental football." The goal was to win, to be more agile in your arguments, and to get the better of the other side. The truth was beside the point.

I remember one debate round in New York City where my opponents, an inexperienced team from Alaska, proposed an expansion of funding for the Peace Corps. In the first cross-examination I got them to admit that their proposal would increase economic growth, so I spent the rest of the round speed-reading the various apocalyptic scenarios that would trigger, scenarios they did not have the evidence to rebut. We won the round handily, but I as I was packing up my boxes of evidence, I had a queasy feeling: I had always wanted to be a Peace Corps volunteer. I believed the Peace Corps was a good thing for the world. But I had just spent two hours using my talents to convince the judge otherwise.

Debate teaches very useful skills. There are many lives to be lived where you argue as your profession, and most of my fellow debaters assumed that future awaited them. Whether in the law, or politics, or even business, competition ("winning at all costs, truth be damned") is at the heart of the job. I was recruited to some of the top programs in the country to continue my debate career, with the assurance that my continued success would open doors in these professional pathways. But I also had a sense that being a professional arguer wasn't a career that would a) make me happy and well-adjusted, or b) make the world a better place. So I applied early to Haverford College, a small school that had no debate program. Acceptance by Haverford marked the end of my career as professional arguer (although my wife might say I have retained my amateur status).

I fully embraced Haverford from my first day on campus. I felt a resonance between my Unitarian values and the values of Haverford's intentional community, which was influenced by its long association with the Quakers. Haverford's honor code, all-campus plenary meetings, and decision-making by consensus felt like hard, noble, worthwhile work. I found that the public speaking skills I'd gotten from debate were useful for things other than just winning arguments. I was the kind of kid who loved staying up until the wee hours talking about the state of the world, exploring how we could promote more understanding, empathy, and respect. I even ran a weekly campus speaker series called Collection, in which I brought in a spectrum of speakers to explore those themes further. I focused my academic studies on becoming a peacemaker, even though at the time I was more than a little unclear about exactly what that meant.

I majored in political science (with a peace studies concentration), aiming to look at politics through the lenses of sociology, anthropology, and social psychology. During my sophomore year, I was lucky enough to gain a seat at a mediation training conducted on campus by the Friends Suburban Project, and I was immediately entranced; to me, mediation seemed like practical peacemaking, much more useful than the political science books I had been poring through in my intro poli-sci classes. After the training I went on to co-lead the campus mediation program (called Communication Outreach), which focused on disputes between students, faculty, and staff, and eventually I got elected president of the Student Council, where I got deeply involved with the big identity-based conflicts on campus. I took every class on dispute resolution I could in the course catalog, devouring any ADR-related book I could get my hands on. I wrote my thesis on student-run collegiate mediation programs, all the while sending out query letters to dozens of dispute resolution organizations, introducing myself and asking for information about their activities. (Note to the younger generation: this was what we did back before the Internet.)

One of the organizations I came across in my research was the National Institute for Dispute Resolution (NIDR) in Washington, DC. Since my fiancée was already in DC, during my senior year I had plenty of excuses to visit NIDR and do research in their (somewhat unorganized) library. After graduation I talked my way into an unpaid internship at NIDR, and a few months later a position opened up, so they hired me as an Information Services Specialist (I guess so I could help organize the library). At NIDR I had a chance to work on many diverse projects that advanced ADR, including the "Building the Collaborative Community" and "Statewide Offices of Mediation" initiatives, two efforts aimed at expanding the use of dispute resolution in state and local government. I also handled all the external information requests, usually connecting unhappy lawyers with local mediation trainings. I attended my first ADR conferences during this period—the Society of Professionals in Dispute Resolution (SPIDR), the National Conference on Peacemaking and Conflict Resolution (NCPCR), the National Association for Mediation in Education (NAME), and the American Bar Association's Dispute Resolution Section—and felt a real kinship with the community of mediators. I felt: these are my people. They are appealing to the angels of human nature. They are trying to get people to understand each other and trying to promote peace and empathy. I decided then that I wanted to spend my career working with and becoming one of them.

After NIDR my wife, Cheryl, and I signed on with the Peace Corps to be English teachers in Eritrea for two years. I joined the Peace Corps thinking I'd be a peacemaker but quickly realized once I arrived in the rural Horn of Africa that many more fundamental challenges, such as water, food, and education, demanded our attention before I'd be getting around to any hands-on peacemaking. I went to Eritrea expecting to teach and take care of people but really I spent all my time learning and being taken care of. Seeing my culture (and my privilege) from a distance fundamentally changed my view of the world. Even though my service was many years ago, I still feel a deep connection to Eritrea and Eritreans, and serving in the Peace Corps is one of the best things I've done with my life.

After we returned to the United States I signed on to get a master's from Harvard's Kennedy School of Government (in conflict resolution and technology, because I am a nerd) while also studying for an ADR certificate at night from the University of Massachusetts-Boston, where I did my first small claims mediations. The Kennedy School was light on conflict resolution courses, so I cross-registered at Tufts University's Fletcher School, Harvard's law school, and its business school to round out my dance card. I was an insufferable broken record with my fellow students, going on and on about the wonders of mediation and facilitation. In retrospect, I can see that I was chomping at the bit to get started as a full-time dispute resolver.

During my studies in Massachusetts I took a position at Larry Susskind's Consensus Building Institute (CBI), where I served as business manager for the newspaper *Consensus*. I thought that with a degree in public policy, multiparty dispute resolution and facilitation might be where I'd start to hone my skills. The work CBI did was very interesting and inspiring, but it was clear I'd have a hard time breaking in. Most of the facilitators at CBI (and other multiparty firms) already had doctorates or extensive scientific/technical backgrounds. I found myself handling administrative tasks (e.g., taking notes, managing mailing lists) instead of working with disputants.

One thing that had remained a constant since my Eclectic days was my love of technology. I never thought of technology as my profession, as it was more of a hobby. But here is the thing: every organization I worked with eventually started to give me more technical responsibilities because I enjoyed them, I was good at them, and I added value. One of the friends I had made at NIDR was John Helie, who started the online discussion forum Conflict-Net. Based on my Eclectic experience, I took to Conflict-Net right away. By the time I graduated from the Kennedy

School six years later, the Internet was in full bloom, and John had evolved ConflictNet into Mediate.com, which was the largest online resource for mediators. John and his co-founder Jim Melamed invited me to join Mediate.com as general manager, so I resigned from CBI and moved my career full-time onto the web.

Mediate.com gave me an excuse to keep attending all the ADR conferences as an exhibitor, but it also introduced me to many skilled practitioners, because I was building and maintaining their websites. Over the next few years I had a growing number of discussions around how one would go about resolving disputes over the Internet. eCommerce was expanding rapidly, which meant more disputes between people who had never met and would never meet in person. Just up the road at UMass-Amherst, Ethan Katsh had started a pilot program resolving disputes on eBay, and he had launched the Center for Information Technology and Dispute Resolution (CITDR). Because I was both a dispute resolution acolyte and a technology-loving nerd, this was right up my alley, so I got as involved as I could get. I started writing about ODR (articles on Mediate.com and on my new blog, ODRNews) and developing ODR software, and eventually I convinced the Mediate.com founders to let me spin off a new company focused on ODR, OnlineResolution.com. Online Resolution was one of the first ODR providers, and I hired a small team to figure out how to make the company work. I raised money from friends and family and got to work learning how to run a startup, mostly by trial and error.

Michael Lang, a giant in ADR, was working with me at Online Resolution designing our ODR training for mediators. At one point, I remember, he said he needed more resources to build out the curriculum he had designed. I looked up to Michael because of his ADR experience, but I was the CEO, so I had to draw the line. We didn't have more resources we could devote to the effort, and I told him so.

After a lengthy negotiation over the telephone in which I didn't budge, Michael started chuckling. When I asked him what was so funny, he said (in an amiable tone), "Colin, I have shoes older than you."

"That may be, Michael," I said, "but you're still not getting any more money for training."

Michael got a contract with Jossey-Bass to write a book on ODR, and we all volunteered to help him. He gave us chapter assignments and told us to have drafts by the first of the year. Come the first of the year, none of us had written a word. As a result, Michael decided to cancel the contract. But I called him and asked if I could take over the project, and he graciously agreed to introduce me to his editor. That was how I got the chance to write my first book, *Online Dispute Resolution for Business* (Rule, 2002).

I did some work on multiparty disputes during these years, helping resolve complex environmental and energy-related disputes (such as the Cape Wind development in Nantucket Sound). I even brought ODR into the picture by co-creating the "Online Public Disputes Project," which applied ODR tools to multiparty, complex disputes. But I couldn't get any sustained traction in the multiparty space—it was too hard to break in. I also started to get calls from schools that were interested in having me teach: Ethan Katsh asked me to teach a course at UMass-Amherst, and I taught a full 40-hour course on ODR at Southern Methodist University.

In 2003, out of the blue, I got a phone call from a senior vice president at eBay. He had found my book on Google, and he wanted to talk to me about coming to Silicon Valley. After two trips out as a consultant, eBay hired me as its first director of online dispute resolution.

Joining a huge Internet company moving at full speed was quite an education. Over the next few years I led the creation of eBay's ODR platform, the eBay Resolution Center, and then moved to PayPal (which was owned by eBay) in 2005 to build out the PayPal Resolution Center. Eventually the eBay and PayPal resolution centers grew to resolve more than 60 million disputes per year around the world in more than 16 languages.

I continued to write and teach on ODR during my time at eBay, serving as a fellow at both the Center for Internet and Society and the Gould Center for Conflict Resolution at Stanford Law School, which was just up the road. eBay and PayPal gave me a huge platform to experiment and learn about ODR and to travel the world to learn how ODR could be adapted to different cultures. Eight years later, I was able to secure a license to some of the ODR technology I had helped to design at eBay and PayPal, and with my colleague Chittu Nagarajan, I co-founded a company called Modria.com to apply those technologies in new areas. Over the next six years, from 2011 to 2017, Modria grew to become the premiere ODR platform in the world, resolving millions of cases in Asia, Europe, and North and South America. Modria's technology managed (and manages) the largest caseload for the American Arbitration Association (the New York No Fault caseload) and handles online property tax appeals in the state of Ohio and cities such as Nashville, New Orleans, Atlanta, Durham, and Gainesville. During this period I co-authored my second book with my friend Amy Schmitz, entitled *The New Handshake: Online Dispute Resolution and the Future of Consumer Protection* (Schmitz and Rule, 2017).

Throughout, I continued to write, speak, and teach about ODR, offering full-credit courses at schools such as Pepperdine University, Santa Clara University, and Stanford University and guest lecturing at schools such as Harvard, Yale, New York University, Cornell, the University of Southern California, Northwestern, and many others. I kept blogging and writing book chapters, articles for law reviews, ADR journals, and publications such as *Dispute Resolution Magazine* and *ACResolution*. Along with Ethan Katsh, who is generally acknowledged as the father of ODR, I became something of a spokesman for the emerging field. In cooperation with my colleagues and fellow fellows at the National Center for Technology and Dispute Resolution,[1] we held annual ODR conferences all around the world and expanded ODR into new areas and applications.

From its inception, ODR was global because eCommerce crossed boundaries and cultures so fluidly. This fit with my values: perhaps influenced by my Peace Corps experience, I wanted to do work that built global connections and spread empathy across borders and boundaries. I thought ODR was an important evolution of ADR practice, in some respects the future of ADR, and that I was the "ADR nerd" who could help the field through this period of evolution. This work also felt very much in line with my Unitarian-instilled values around equity, justice, and compassion.

In 2017 Modria was acquired by Tyler Technologies, a multi-billion-dollar public company that develops software for local government. Tyler is the leading provider of court case management and e-filing software in the United States, and it positioned Modria as an integrated court ODR system to promote early resolution in family, small claims, and minor criminal caseloads. The Tyler-Modria Court ODR system is now deployed across the United States in states such as Nevada, Texas, California, Ohio, New Mexico, and Georgia. The ODR field is expanding more rapidly than ever, which is very gratifying. The COVID-19 pandemic has raised ODR's profile even further, as all mediators are being forced to become online mediators.

A friend of mine jokes that dispute resolution is like the dentist's office: no one walks around daydreaming about visiting the dentist, but if someone has a toothache, all they can think about is getting to the dentist. He says it must be depressing dealing with angry disputants all the time, but I explain that I enjoy it because I can help them resolve their problem and end the aggravation and annoyance. At base I don't like conflict—it makes me feel anxious and unhappy—and I like being able to help other people resolve their conflicts so that they won't have to feel that way. And I get great satisfaction from being part of the dispute resolution field and carrying the torch forward.

I also have loved working to build a new field from scratch. To be present at the naming of a new discipline, to start one of the first providers, to write one of the first books, and then to see it evolve into a global movement, one that has the potential to significantly expand access to justice for people all around the world, is enormously satisfying. For some time, I suspected I might be the person who knew the most about ODR in the world, which felt like a real gift. And even now, as ODR grows beyond me in directions I could never have imagined, I'm honored to have played the role I did.

I do have political opinions, and opinions about how people should treat each other, and I do sometimes have to work to keep those opinions from interfering with my role as a dispute resolver (and as a trainer). Even though Morton Downey Jr. is long gone, his intellectual heirs have definitely kept that angry and confrontational message (and methodology) alive, and I sometimes find it a challenge to empathize with its adherents. But much of my work these days is at the systems-design level, and I rarely serve as a neutral in conflicts between individual parties. As a result, I don't have to struggle with maintaining impartiality.

I know that our recent political palpitations, especially the conflict-exacerbating actions of the Trump administration, have shaken some of my colleagues' and mentors' confidence in conflict resolution practice and methods. This period has unquestionably been jarring, but I don't share that concern. I believe there's a time and a place for everything, and one can resist now while acknowledging there will be a time soon for reconciliation. At some point, when the pendulum swings back from fear and division and the country again hungers for healing and understanding, I am confident our work will be more important than ever.

Technology is changing the way we interact with each other. So it makes sense that it will also have a massive impact on how we fight and how we resolve our fights. We can't keep resolving disputes the way we've been resolving them and expect that to work in a world that is changing so radically. We must take all the lessons we've learned over the past six decades of dispute resolution practice and integrate them into a vision for the future. People are just as complicated when they communicate over technology as they are when they communicate face-to-face.

We also can't think that the challenges of the future are so new that we can't learn from the past. We have to learn to leverage the growing power of technology to make peace and build understanding, instead of letting it drive misinformation and conflict, and we need to take our wisdom and experience and play a formative role in building these systems for dispute resolution. We need to embrace the power of the tools that technology is offering us and learn to leverage their benefits and mitigate their challenges. We can't just sit on the sidelines saying "Call us if you have a conflict."

The pandemic is moving us toward a world where we reserve face-to-face interaction only for our most intimate friends and family members, and it's clear that the bulk of our professional and public lives will take place online. Before long, I believe, the idea of driving to the doctor's office or to the courthouse will seem as antiquated as getting your water from a well. Along with electricity and water, access to the Internet will be a new utility—a new human right, even. Our identities will be seamlessly online and offline, and navigating from one to the other will be entirely normal. I can even envision a world where technology is designed in a way that builds human empathy and understanding. Algorithms will monitor enormous amounts of data from the Internet and social media in real time to identify escalating conflict early, so we can intervene effectively and prevent the outbreak of violence. Global networks (maybe delivered to every corner of the planet by low-orbit satellites) will provide access to opportunity and education for more than a billion people who have previously been disenfranchised solely as a result of their geographic location.

We will physically live in communities we choose, surrounded by the people we love, but technology will enable us to interact instantly with all other people around the planet. This frontier is where online dispute resolution starts to blend with the field of peace tech, which I've observed through my work with the Peace Tech Lab at the United States Institute of Peace. We're still in the Wild West phase of the Internet, with technology unleashing profound and destabilizing change, but eventually we will civilize cyberspace, and I am confident we will harness its power to open a new era of greater peace, justice, and happiness for everyone.

I see my work as moving the practice of dispute resolution and peacemaking into the future. I have always believed that you shouldn't work to impress your peers— you should do work that would make your heroes proud. My heroes are the people who built the field of dispute resolution. Their work inspired—and inspires—me and cleared the way for my professional path, so my objective is to advance their values and aspirations for what conflict resolution can achieve in the world. I believe I have a window of opportunity to continue their work, so I will do the best I can during my time at the tiller. And then I'll hand it over to the next generation.

Notes

[1] The National Center for Technology and Dispute Resolution, odr.info, supports and sustains the development of information technology applications, institutional resources, and theoretical and applied knowledge for better understanding and managing conflict.

References

Rule, C. 2002. *Online Dispute Resolution for Business: B2B, ECommerce, Consumer, Employment, Insurance, and Other Commercial Conflicts.* San Francisco: Jossey-Bass.

Schmitz, A. J. and C. Rule. 2017. *The New Handshake: Online Dispute Resolution and the Future of Consumer Protection.* Washington, DC: American Bar Association.

12

Bashert: How I Found Dispute Resolution and It Found Me

By Andrea Kupfer Schneider

◆

My story of how I got involved in negotiation and dispute resolution began in my first year of law school with a class in negotiation. I don't recall why I chose this elective in the first-year curriculum. Perhaps I thought it fit with my interest in international law. Perhaps it seemed close to a business school course, which interested me because I was still contemplating trying to get a joint degree (an idea I

Andrea Kupfer Schneider is a professor of law, the inaugural director of the Institute for Women's Leadership at Marquette University, and director of the Dispute Resolution Program at Marquette University Law School. Her most recent books include *Negotiating Crime: Plea Bargaining, Problem Solving and Dispute Resolution in the Criminal Context* (2019, co-authored with Cynthia Alkon), *Negotiation Essentials for Lawyers* (2019) and *The Negotiator's Desk Reference* (2017, both books co-edited with Chris Honeyman), and *Smart & Savvy: Negotiation Strategies in Academia* (2017, co-authored with David Kupfer). Her textbooks include *Dispute Resolution: Examples and Explanations* (2008, with Michael Moffitt) and *Negotiation: Processes for Problem-Solving* (2014), *Mediation: Practice, Policy & Ethics* (2013), and *Dispute Resolution: Beyond the Adversarial Model* (2005) with Carrie Menkel-Meadow, Lela Love, and Michael Moffitt. She is a co-author of two books with Roger Fisher, *Beyond Machiavelli: Tools for Coping with Conflict* (1994) and *Coping with International Conflict* (1997). She has published numerous articles on negotiation, ethics, pedagogy, gender and international conflict, is a founding editor of *Indisputably*, the blog for ADR law faculty, and started the Dispute Resolution Works-in-Progress Annual Conference in 2007. In 2017, the ABA Section of Dispute Resolution gave her its award for Outstanding Scholarly Work.

later dropped). Perhaps I signed up for the course because I subconsciously thought it fit my personality or family background. Perhaps, as in so many choices students make, first impression and convenience played a part: the course sounded interesting and fit perfectly in my schedule. Whatever the reason, I am confident that at the time I had no idea it would change the trajectory of my career. In retrospect, I think it might have been *bashert*, which is Yiddish for "destiny." Something I was meant to find.

Getting to Dispute Resolution
Harvard Negotiation Project

Roger Fisher, who usually taught the negotiation course, was on sabbatical that year, so Bruce Patton was the professor, and he was a terrific teacher. I enjoyed the class immensely and realized that I wanted to do much more work in this area. To figure out how to accomplish that, I met with Elizabeth Kopelman (later Borgwardt), a 3L who was Roger Fisher's research assistant. Liz, who wound up hiring me to replace her, later became a mentor and coauthor. I was very excited to step into her shoes.

I met Roger Fisher for the first time in the fall of 1990. He was almost a foot taller than I am, and that day he looked both daunting and friendly. He peered down at me. "I understand that you are to be my research assistant," he announced. And that was that—it was meant to be.

Working for Roger for the next two years was a whirlwind of everything from class preparation to research on current events to preparation for his Senate testimony and his other high-end commitments. Because of Roger's focus on international events, those two years confirmed for me my interest in conflict resolution and how international law was only one piece of the puzzle of how countries should relate to one another.

For example, in December 1990, after Iraq invaded Kuwait, the United States was still debating whether to send troops. I worked on Roger's Senate testimony, and he allowed me to co-author an op-ed piece with him and Doug Stone, who was then an associate at the Harvard Negotiation Project. The op-ed in the *Boston Globe* pointed out that Saddam Hussein was not crazy—and that "crazy" was too glib a label to give to other leaders when we disagreed with them. Hussein, I learned, did not just show up in Kuwait and claim the oil but set forth his claim in elaborate and law-based arguments: 1) that Kuwait was really a 19th province of Iraq, as the Western powers that had drawn the maps after World War I had gotten it wrong (which was not a crazy point at all) and 2) that Kuwait had been tunneling under Iraq to steal its oil. If even supposedly "crazy" Saddam Hussein was claiming that he was permitted to act under international law, having a legal standard from which to negotiate must be vital. This also made me realize that one key challenge in negotiation is to listen and try to understand the other side—even when you think they are absolutely wrong.

I also appreciated that Roger's perspective on the Middle East was quite different from mine. I had visited Israel and back in 1990, I pretty much viewed Israel as the hero in any narrative (a view that has become far more nuanced in the last 30 years). Roger didn't necessarily disagree, but he had much more appreciation for the views of the Arab countries, which helped fill in my narrative.

By the time I became a teaching assistant for the Negotiation Workshop in January of 1991, I was hooked. Bruce Patton again took the lead—this time in teaching all the teaching assistants how to teach. And even though the workshop was harder and more time-consuming than anything I had ever done, I loved it and decided that this was my future career. I've always felt blessed to have figured out this part of my destiny by the second year of law school because with that clear direction, I could map out my next steps more thoughtfully.

Looking back, I'm amazed that I realized so early on my desire to build a career in negotiation and be a law professor. I had come to law school thinking that I would like to be in-house counsel for IBM, which at the time was the largest company in the world, and travel around the globe. Of course, in retrospect, my choice seems entirely logical. My mom, dad, and stepmom are all professors, and their knowledge and experience in their respective fields have served me extremely well over my career. I've co-authored a book with my dad about negotiation in academia, focusing on faculty in medicine and science. And I was pleased to be able to guest lecture about the Nuremberg trials in my mom's class on the Holocaust, after she came down with the flu while I happened to be home. When I later got the opportunity to see her teach, I realized how similar we were in running a classroom. This would not be surprising to anyone outside the family, but I still remember being shocked to understand that I had really grown up to be her.

In my third year of law school, I was the head teaching assistant in Roger's undergraduate class "Coping with International Conflict." In addition to learning the course materials, I learned how to hire other students and manage a team. I also got to see the thoughtful analyses that we had presented to diplomats and the Senate the previous year be used by undergraduate students with the same understanding and effectiveness—a great lesson in how good theory and clear concepts can be applied in many different contexts. As Roger used to say, the students would be able to learn about South Africa or India and Pakistan, but perhaps more important, they would also realize that they could negotiate more effectively with their roommates and their families.

This lesson has really stuck with me. Settings and applications will change, but good frameworks and theories can be applied across the board and provide insight and support, even for someone who is not an expert in that context. In some ways, this is what a mediator does—providing process expertise regardless of substantive knowledge. This recognition has given me the confidence to expand my "context" past where I have direct experience. Working on the materials for this class also led to my first two publications in the field, both with Roger and other colleagues: the popular book *Beyond Machiavelli: Tools for Coping with Conflict* and the textbook *Coping with International Conflict: A Systematic Approach to Influence in International Negotiation*.

Stanford and Interdisciplinary Learning

I had marvelous good luck when Robert Mnookin, who was then a professor at Stanford Law School, visited Harvard in my second year. After I took a family law class and worked with him in the January workshop, he, too, became a mentor who helped shape my career. Bob was very clear and direct about what it would take to become a law professor, and I went about "checking those boxes" for the remaining time at Harvard. I worked on the *Harvard International Law Review*, kept striving for better grades, published two student notes, and secured a coveted clerkship with Judge Irving Kaufman of the Second Circuit. When Judge Kaufman died late in my third year of law school, shortly before I was to start my clerkship, it was Bob who fortunately provided my soft landing and offered me a teaching position at Stanford for the fall of 1992, turning adversity into an opportunity.

The semester at Stanford was eye-opening for all sorts of reasons—from learning about how different faculties operate and get along (Stanford was quite different from

Harvard) to the amazing interdisciplinary focus of the Stanford Center on Conflict and Negotiation (SCCN) in the 1990s. I also was exposed to yet another take on the world of negotiation. Each of these lessons informed my future work. In particular, SCCN was renowned for working with leading lights in the emerging field of behavioral economics and psychology, including Lee Ross, Amos Tversky, and Daniel Kahneman. Although my undergraduate work had been interdisciplinary, law school perhaps inevitably focused on cases, case studies, and law reviews about and from lawyers. This was true even in the negotiation class. Being at Stanford was a key reminder that interdisciplinary work was crucial to creating negotiation theories that were robust and applicable.

The semester at Stanford also gave me a distinct comparison between the kind of writing and theory and practice that Roger was producing and what was happening at Stanford, with its high-end empirical work. Harvard was best known (in negotiation) for Roger's famous book *Getting to Yes*, which is easy to read, with no citations, and is still assigned in classes around the world, having sold millions of copies. On the other hand, the wonderfully rich and empirically based *Barriers to Conflict Resolution* produced by Stanford was not being assigned in any law school classes, let alone being read by practicing lawyers (Mnookin et al., 1995). It would take years before this material would be "translated" for law school use and then popularized by Kahneman's own later writing. For me, this was a realization that there was a whole world of research that *could* inform best practices in negotiation but would not unless and until people were actually reading it. This was a lesson I put into action years later with Chris Honeyman, creating and editing *The Negotiator's Fieldbook*, followed by *The Negotiator's Desk Reference and Negotiation Essentials for Lawyers*, translating theory into practice (and in my dispute resolution textbook, co-authors, Carrie Menkel-Meadow, Lela Love, Jean Sternlight, and Michael Moffitt, I found partners who were equally committed to interdisciplinary readings and approaches).

Visiting in DC

Fast forward: I returned to the East Coast from Stanford, worked in Washington, DC, for two years at a law firm where I continued to conduct trainings in negotiation (my law firm, first skeptical about an associate who wanted to teach, later hired me to do that), and then landed a position visiting for one year at George Washington University's Elliott School of International Affairs. Roger had connected me with a group of international negotiation scholars based in political science and involved with the School of Advanced International Studies at Johns Hopkins (SAIS), George Mason, and other intellectual centers addressing issues of international relations from their own disciplinary perspective. This group's monthly lunch meetings provided me another opportunity to get different perspectives on topics I enjoyed so much. I was honored to join professors Bill Zartman, Saadia Touval, and others who added to my reading list of "things I should know." Saadia was instrumental in connecting me with the Elliott School when people there were scrambling to fill a last-minute opening in their international law offerings. (I remember feeling that this connection I had built, too, was *bashert* because I had already decided to quit my law firm within a few months. I was clear with the lunch group about my goal to teach, and Saadia remembered that when this job opened up.)

And so I ended up teaching international law and international conflict resolution to undergraduate and graduate students in political science. The classes were terrific, but in some ways, the conversations each day with my new colleagues in the political science department were even more instructive in how different disciplines do research and approach the world (for example, the empirical research on the Supreme Court done by political scientists was fascinating to me, as they often focused on overall voting patterns while in law school we had primarily focused on legal reasoning).

Landing at Marquette

The visiting position lasted only a year, so in 1995, I went on the teaching market for a full-time faculty position. I landed a job at Marquette, where I have been since the fall of 1996. I've taught dispute resolution and negotiation almost every year since then and have also moved through a series of additional classes that have continued to inform my thinking about dispute resolution. When I arrived at Marquette, I focused on international law (and international conflict, based on the undergraduate course at Harvard). Over time, I have also taught human rights, European Union law, and art law but slowly settled into dispute resolution, negotiation, international law, and a seminar of rotating topics—all topics that I have chosen, written about, and loved. Against my will (but a switch I am now totally delighted with), I shifted out of international law more than a decade ago into teaching ethics. Other classes now include Restorative Justice and Alternative Criminal Processes.

On reflection, this seems like a pretty straightforward path into academia and a steady career of writing, teaching, and training in the field. Yet many of us have noted family influences on our choice of field. Did they perhaps also play a role?

Family Matters

My parents divorced and remarried when I was relatively young, bringing our combined families on each side to six kids (my children have more than 20 first cousins!). I was the eldest of my parents' "core four," so there was no question about my being in charge or acting like the mom as we navigated the divorce and realignment of our family. (I am sure that each of my siblings has stories of me bossing them around, and I am also sure that I still do that now at times.) And, as the eldest, I was usually the one to manage communications between parents who did not necessarily want to communicate with each other. My guess is that this responsibility trained me as a mediator, developing my ability to hear a point of view even when I did not agree with it. Arguments among the kids (and sometimes with the adults) were loud, vocal, heated, and probably quite healthy in getting everything out. Although I still don't think I went into dispute resolution because of all of this, I do think that this early experience gave me a better understanding of how different people, including myself, manage—or do not manage—anger.

In my first-year negotiation class at Harvard, managing anger was the personal skill that I worked on. A bit of background: each year, the negotiation class professors called on psychologists to work with the class for a few sessions so that each student could identify one interpersonal skill the student wanted to improve and work on it with a psychologist. Students created a scenario that required this skill and then were videotaped showing different responses, exercises designed to help us be more in control and effective. I knew that I could express anger in family relationships, particularly with my youngest sister, since she and I were quite good at pushing each other's buttons until we were both in tears. And I'd seen anger between divorced parents who were still parenting four children. So

I was good on that. What I knew I needed was the ability to express anger professionally. How do you tell someone, such as a boss or a colleague, that what they did was out of line?

This was the skill that Bruce Patton worked on with me, work so impactful that I can still recall it clearly. It was okay to be angry, and it was okay to share that fact—it just needed to be deliberate and purposeful. I loved watching the videotape of me reacting to Bruce (who had learned how to push my buttons) with cold, calm disappointment rather than out-of-control rage. This was another moment when I realized how, in teaching negotiation, you can push people to be a better version of themselves. And it inspired (and still inspires) me to encourage personality stretching. It also reminds me that we are not "set" at age 25, an idea that is very useful both in teaching negotiation and in teaching ethics.

Academic Concentrations

My ongoing work as an academic has focused on three main areas. Both their origin and their possible futures, I think, are worth exploring.

International Law and Conflict

In high school I competed in debate and speech and after my freshman year discovered that I loved extemporaneous speaking. Extemporaneous speaking, as an event, was a competition in which each participant was given a question, 30 minutes to prepare a speech, and seven minutes to deliver it. The questions could cover any domestic or foreign current event, so performing well required a lot of advance work. For background, I regularly read the *New York Times*, the *Economist*, the *Christian Science Monitor* (which in that day was known for its foreign policy coverage), the *Wall Street Journal*, and *The Financial Times*, among other publications. My teammates and I cut out relevant articles and created huge files about each country/leader/crisis and toted those around to different competitions. In retrospect, I realize that pre-Internet, we created our own portable Wikipedia that we could dive into at a moment's notice. My best friend and I, who traveled to state and national championships together, were both quite talented. I doubt that anyone who knows me today would be surprised to learn that I won trophies for talking, but I didn't recognize then that this exercise—researching and delivering a very short speech in a very short time—would serve me better than almost anything else I've ever done.

It also gave me a terrific grounding in international affairs, which led me to apply to the Princeton School of Public and International Affairs for my major in college. And, although I hadn't been out of the country until my junior year in high school, traveling abroad became a pursuit in and of itself. The summer after my sophomore year at Princeton, I went to Paris to work in the regional government, at the Préfecture de la Région Ile de France, and was captivated by the debate over allowing EuroDisney into the outskirts of Paris and the fear that it would ruin French culture. This, perhaps for the first time, showed me how different people view the world differently depending on their own experiences and perspectives (what I now understand to be partisan perceptions).

In my junior year, and as part of a "task force" class titled "US Policy toward Greece & Turkey," we took a trip to Greece and Turkey over spring break. Again, speaking first with one group of politicians and then another (who opposed most of the policy initiatives of the first group) was eye-opening.

In my senior year, realizing the value of in-person visits as well as wanting more travel, I set about (successfully) persuading Professor Frank von Hippel that the "task force" for which I was the senior teaching assistant should go to Europe. The class was called the "Conventional Defense of Europe," and for our trip, we visited not only the headquarters of NATO and SHAPE (the Supreme Headquarters of the Allied Powers in Europe) in Belgium, but also US troops stationed at the Fulda Gap, the geographic trip wire for an East German invasion of West Germany; NATO and Warsaw Pact officials in East and West Berlin; and Warsaw Pact and Polish officers in Warsaw. This was invaluable, firsthand learning: I met all the individuals involved in executing military and political strategies, people whom I had only read about, and learned directly from them about their challenges, concerns, and thoughts.

I realized that when we visit other countries and other cultures we learn much more than book learning (and that even book learning sticks better when we have people, places, and experiences we can attach to it), so in my teaching today, I create the same opportunity for my students. I started in 2008 with a trip to Europe to study international courts and for the last 10 years have taken students to Israel to study the Israeli-Palestinian conflict up close. My students and I also went to Cuba when it opened in January 2016 and, most recently, to Northern Ireland in early March 2020.

Even though I know that most of my law students will not go into foreign relations, I think learning about international conflict helps with lawyering in general. Realizing that things are not black and white, that headlines are only part of the story, and that there are multiple interpretations of any event allows students to reflect on conflicts and problems that are not their own and to apply the tools that we teach. This is true of issues with clients, problems in society, politics, and other big matters. Hoping to show how conflicts taught in the classroom can be used in real life, I usually end my Dispute Resolution class by giving students a dispute system design challenge such as advising the police department about designing a civilian complaint system (an exercise that seems especially relevant and important in today's troubled world).

One last note on the international focus of my career. For my senior thesis at Princeton, I wrote about the Musée d'Orsay. I wanted a thesis topic that would get me back to Paris and combine policy with art history, which was my quasi-minor, and my French professor suggested writing about the new museum—again, *bashert*. Looking back now, I realize that my research focused on decision points and conflicts in the creation of the museum. I loved writing the thesis, and the book that grew out of it, and I still love visiting the museum. The topics most interesting to me at the time were the debates (and therefore negotiations) about the starting and ending dates of the collection, the interior architecture of the museum, and the role of outreach and history in the museum. My research allowed me to interview the major players involved in these decisions, and—once again—reinforced my recognition that everyone has their own view of what happened and why.

I learned two important things about negotiation in working on that thesis. To conduct the research, I had to cobble together funding for a trip to France from four or five different university departments, related organizations, and alumni groups, which meant I had to create a negotiation plan and ask for what I needed to make the trip happen. I also had to learn how to get interviews with all the important players. Once I landed one "side," landing the other was easier. (I managed to get an interview with a journalist from *Le Figaro* through connections with my French professor, for example, and then told the journalist from *Le Monde* that it would be a travesty if I talked only to the more conservative paper.) Only later was I able to name the negotiation concepts that helped me persuade everyone to talk to me in the short three weeks I was in Paris.

Women and Negotiation

I was relatively oblivious to gender differences in negotiation until I took the law school negotiation course. On the one day devoted to differences, I remember watching a video from the 1980s that provided advice on how women could negotiate more effectively. I don't actually recall what it said, I just recall feeling appalled and surprised. Who were these women who needed advice on being assertive? As I have often said in my presentations on gender, no male member of my family—no husband, brother, father, or son—has ever worried that the females in his life were not being sufficiently assertive. And while this is mostly a joke, I realize that I was raised with stories about strong women in my family succeeding at negotiation and bending rules that were seen as sexist.

I used to call my grandmother, Mama, an anti-feminist feminist. On the one hand, it was important to her that I could cook, had kids, and wore heels. On the other hand, she herself was a math teacher who then was my grandfather's accountant—and fully supported my career from the start. She would tell me stories about her aunt, my Great-aunt Rayah, who was a doctor for the White Army in the Russian revolution and later emigrated to the United States. Great-aunt Rayah delivered both my mom and uncle and then helped my grandmother bend the rules to keep her job. Back in the day, female teachers were supposed to quit the moment that they got pregnant—but then return to work immediately if they wanted to keep their job. This rule did not work for my grandmother, or her aunt. Mama, apparently twice, did not quit her job until she was showing and couldn't hide her pregnancy—she needed the money—and great-aunt Rayah then duly explained the "premature" births to the school system. Of course, since the babies were "fragile" each time, my grandmother had a doctor's note saying she could not return to work for several weeks after the birth. These women created their own maternity leave policy.

My grandmother also told me stories about her mother, Anna (my namesake), who had come to America on a boat from Russia by herself at age 15 and then worked to bring the rest of her family over. My favorite story of my great-grandmother's successful negotiations was when she went to a store (after it went bankrupt during the Depression) and literally sat on the furniture she had purchased to ensure its delivery. (And as a child I was told that I was a great negotiator myself when I convinced my younger brother to clean my room each week for 10 cents, pocketing the remaining 15 cents that my parents paid me to do it.)

Other gender stereotypes also did not seem to fit me. For example, I loved building things in the workshop at my dad's lab and constructed and wired a dollhouse for my sisters rather than playing with the dolls myself. (In eighth grade, when I asked my mom for a doll, since I didn't yet have one, she explained that I had broken them all when I was younger.) And I loved math and science all the way through high school. I switched to social science only after taking—and not understanding—a linear algebra class at Carnegie Mellon as a high school student. (In retrospect, I wonder whether in another era or with another professor I would have had more encouragement and mentorship to stick with it, but that's just speculation.)

In short, it had never occurred to me that I would negotiate differently because of my gender. My first research project about women and negotiation was to rerun Gerry Williams's 1976 study on negotiation styles, in which he found that legal negotiators behaved primarily either in a cooperative or a competitive manner, with 65 percent of lawyers falling into the cooperative style (Williams, 1983). His original study had not even had enough women in the sample pool to pull out any negotiation differences, so I wanted to run a new study to see if there were. By 1999, I had completed what I thought would be enough law review articles for tenure and turned to working on the longer project of running this study. In 2001, I had the results and could demonstrate that lawyers assessing the behaviors of other lawyers barely found any gender differences at all. So I moved away from the topic of gender, convinced that there were negligible gender differences, if any.

Yet a few years later, when the book *Women Don't Ask* came out, I was troubled by the results (Babcock & Laschever, 2007). It indicated that younger women at the start of their careers were not negotiating the terms of their employment. This caused some reflection on my part and prompted me to do additional research. I realized that I, too, had not negotiated my first salary offer. I don't think that was related to the fact that I was a woman, but rather that no one had told me that I should negotiate. (Perhaps that itself was gendered?) I also wanted to think about the broader lessons: When should we negotiate? How should we be trained? How do we even create the expectation that you should negotiate? My next research project examined whether my own law students were negotiating upon graduation. I discovered to my delight that the women were negotiating at the same rate that the men were and were getting just as much or more money.

This helped me realize that blanket guidelines about how all women negotiate are far too broad. I also noted that most research focused on assertiveness, rather than additional negotiation skills. My research since that time has tried to home in on the contexts in which we see stereotypes at play as well as the far more common situations when gender is just one more difference negotiators have that may—or may not—affect how we negotiate. It's also made me realize that negotiation skills cannot remedy everything. Early articles would blame pay inequity on women for not negotiating harder, for example, but we know that such structural inequities cannot be fixed by negotiation alone.

Ethics

More than a decade ago, I was asked to take on teaching ethics to allow a junior colleague to be able to teach international law. At first I pushed back—I was not interested in ethics. But now I love this class—perhaps this was *bashert* again—destiny found me, and I was willing to grab it. I was ready for a new challenge and enjoy being exposed to a larger percentage of the student body since this is a required class. I've used the problem method, talking about what actual lawyers would do in a challenging ethical situation, a teaching methodology that ends up being close to how I have taught dispute resolution classes.

Dispute resolution focuses on more effective ways to resolve conflicts—how we want our students and future lawyers to communicate with each other and with their clients to be able to "get" more, protect their reputation, and behave in ways that allow them be good people. Similarly, international law focuses on how countries should behave toward their own citizens and toward other countries (with the emphasis on "should"). Thus, the focus on legal ethics fits quite well as I can talk about the world we want and how thoughtful (ethical) decision-making promotes that vision. It's not that we can eliminate conflict between countries or lawyers or clients—it's that we can handle it better.

Some commentators have suggested that ethics professors should not do more than teach the rules of professional responsibility, that they should make sure that students know the rules and that's all. Because students need to pass the Multistate Professional Responsibility Examination (MPRE) to pass the bar, this is an understandable priority. There is also a natural hesitation on the part of teachers who don't want to be accused of trying to challenge family or personal religious values.

We could assume that law students are sufficiently moral by the time we get them or that it's already too late—their morals are already set—but I think this is a dodge for several reasons. First, the more we know about brain science, the more we know that brains and moral decision-making are still evolving when people are in their 20s. Second, there are plenty of "legal" situations in which morals come into play, such as the tension between loyalty to a client and a risk to public safety. And then there are circumstances, such as conflicts of interest, where morals are not the key but rather, understanding what the ethical rules are and what client obligations we have are crucial. In short, I think we have the opportunity in these classes to talk about what type of person each student wants to be and discuss the challenges to that goal that might arise in terms of financial pressure, family strife, career concerns, and stress—all of which can lead to poor decision-making.

Criminal Context

In some ways, this leads directly into my most recent foray into a new subject area—criminal law and alternative criminal processes. I started learning about restorative justice from my colleague Janine Geske, who started the restorative justice initiative at Marquette, when I sat in on her classes and visited a prison with her and our students. When Janine retired, I co-taught this class for several years until we found a talented alumna to take over. And, after colleague Cynthia Alkon approached me about writing together, we published the first textbook on alternative criminal processes for use in law school called *Negotiating*

Crime: Plea Bargaining, Problem Solving and Dispute Resolution in the Criminal Context (2019). I am not the only person to believe that our current criminal justice system is broken, with far too many mistakes, injustices, and racial divides. And I hope that applying a dispute resolution lens to that problem might be a slightly new way to help move sorely needed reform in the right direction.

Conclusion

Looking back on my career, I see a few themes. From my lawyer grandfather, I was taught early on that curiosity and humility will lead to taking pleasure in a life of learning. If we assume there is more out there, we must continue to push ourselves out of our comfort zone, out of our discipline and push ourselves even out of the country. I have regularly sought out perspectives and experiences that are different from my own. My best friends from college and I did not share religion, region of the country, or political views when we all showed up freshman year, and that, to me, defined a good college experience.

I still try to purposely engage with different people. On our student trip to Cuba, for example, I strongly disagreed with a law professor who spoke to my students about international relations, but I was intrigued by her perspective. That empathy, maybe even humility, continues to stretch me, and I try to convey to my students the importance of challenging themselves. This is not to say that I'm not opinionated. I know I am. And I know I'll be more persuasive if I'm genuinely inquisitive and understand the other side.

The study of dispute resolution has given me a home for my interest in other people and places. It gave me frameworks and theories to structure my curiosity and understand why and how these concepts could be useful. I probably would not have been so compelled to work, teach, and write in this field unless something in it resonated with me in some innate, profound way. And the colleagues in the field—my mentors, co-authors, co-bloggers, and friends—are like the soulmates that *bashert* implies.

I have had many opportunities that seem like luck, and I have also been prepared to embrace them to create my own destiny. I have found mentors all along the way; through my choices, tried to open doors rather than close them; and have been willing to take risks or try new routes. Sometimes, I've responded yes to an invitation that pushed me in a new direction. Other times, as in creating the *Indisputably* blog or the dispute resolution works-in-progress conference, I've created the community I desired. I've tried to practice what I preach to my students—to listen, be open, be curious, and assume there is more to learn—while also being prepared to persuade and assert myself to move forward and take advantage of opportunities. I feel blessed to have found my *bashert* in dispute resolution.

References

Arrow, K., R. Mnookin, L. Ross, A. Tversky and R. Wilson, eds. 1995. *Barriers to Conflict Resolution*. New York: W. W. Norton.

Babcock, L. and S. Laschever. 2007. *Women Don't Ask: The High Cost of Avoiding Negotiation—and Positive Strategies for Change*. New York: Bantam.

Williams, G. 1983. *Legal Negotiation and Settlement*. Minneapolis: West Publishing.

13

Synchronicity, Paradox, and Personal Evolution

By Thomas J. Stipanowich

◆

Dispute resolution has been the overriding preoccupation, passion, and shaping influence in my adult life and career, and I am very grateful for the privilege of being a part of this field. My career coincided with four decades of the Quiet Revolution in dispute resolution, since I started law practice in 1980 and within a year was engaged in multiple major arbitrations and one of the first mediations of a complex construction dispute. Since the mid-1980s I've been a dedicated educator and scholar with a "circle of activity" that regularly included experiences as an arbitra-

---

Thomas J. Stipanowich is William H. Webster Chair in Dispute Resolution and professor of law at Pepperdine University as well as associate dean of the Straus Institute for Dispute Resolution, where he teaches courses in negotiation theory and practice, mediation, arbitration practice and advocacy, international commercial arbitration, and international dispute resolution. He has also taught contracts, commercial law, remedies, Anglo-American legal history, and property. A leading scholar, speaker, and trainer on conflict resolution topics as well as an experienced arbitrator and mediator, he is on the executive committee of the International Task Force on Mixed Mode Dispute Resolution Processes co-sponsored by the International Mediation Institute, the College of Commercial Arbitrators, and the Straus Institute and was an advisor on the ALI Restatement of US Law on International Arbitration. He has also served on the Advisory Board of the New York International Arbitration Center and the Academic Council of the Institute for Transnational Arbitration.

tor, mediator, or facilitator. The latter half of my career has been associated with two important institutions with educational missions—the International Institute for Conflict Prevention & Resolution (CPR) and the Straus Institute for Dispute Resolution at Pepperdine School of Law. My unique journey has involved a series of meaningful coincidences that Carl Jung might have claimed as examples of "synchronicity." I've also become aware of some of the paradoxes that regularly confront and challenge actors in the fields of conflict resolution: the need for self-understanding and self-management as a critical component of constructive human interaction and the importance of personal commitment and positive action in a fraught and riven world.

◆

I was raised in a household of teachers. Education was not only highly valued; it was—and is—our mutual calling and a way of making the most of our lives by enriching the lives of others. My first year of life was spent in a Quonset hut in the "vet village" at Northwestern University, where my father was working on his doctoral degree, but my earliest memories are of Macomb, Illinois, a college town situated midway between Samuel Clemens' boyhood home of Hannibal, Missouri, and the region around Springfield, Illinois, where Lincoln practiced politics and rode the circuit. Family life centered around Western Illinois University (WIU), a regional center of learning in the heart of an ocean of corn and soybeans, as well as the wider community from which my parents sprang.

My parents came to WIU as the first in their families to attend college. My mother's family funded her education as a top priority, but because my father's family was always on the edge of poverty—a situation exacerbated by a costly court battle over family assets—he self-funded college, in part by renting and running a gas station for a year after high school. Dad's ambition produced three degrees and eventually led to a professorship in the mathematics department at WIU; Mom was an instructor in home economics. Despite their academic calling, both my parents remained active in the wider community, in their church, service clubs, and local organizations.

From the ages of 3 to 17, I attended classes on the Western campus—first at the Home Management House as a guinea pig for young women practicing parenting on preschoolers, and later in the university's Laboratory School. The Lab School was a place where future teachers could hone their skills or observe children in the educational environment; over the years I was followed around by teams of observers at least half a dozen times and was interviewed and given tests on camera. The Lab School also gave me the opportunity to take college courses and engage in a wide variety of activities including vocal and instrumental music, art, theater, creative writing, and journalism.

Evenings at home tended to follow a pattern. Dinner table conversation would hinge on the events of the day—an anecdote about a student or faculty member, a joke, song, or teaching tool my father had used that day, the challenges surrounding the latest recipe in my mother's home economics class, or my own stories from school. After supper, my father would invariably retire to the sofa with student math papers spread about him. My mother would, like as not, work on a lesson plan in the dining room. I spent many evenings drawing or doing homework at an antique classroom desk, complete with inkwell holder. As young children, we had bedtime fare that was heavy on biography; my father, when not sharing recollections of growing up in the "movie town" of Culver City, California, during the golden age of Hollywood, would regale us with episodes from the lives of Euclid, Archimedes, Newton, Gauss, Napier, and others—a juvenile version of his History of Mathematics class.

As I grew older, however, the joy that my father had expressed about teaching was overshadowed by the weight of obligation he took on as chair of his department. For almost a decade our nightly routine was regularly marred by the pain my father shared at our evening meal about the difficult issues, personalities, and office politics he had to deal with. More than 50 years on, my brother and I still recall our own shared agony as we listened to his recapitulation of the day's challenges, battles, and betrayals. My father always had a mercurial temper, and the constant stress of his situation led to migraine headaches and outbursts that affected us all. Even my mother, who habitually sought to pour oil on troubled waters, could do nothing to remedy the situation.

Looking back, I have the benefit of a better understanding of the role of emotional intelligence in our lives and relationships. At the time, however, I was led to feel two things: a visceral desire to avoid or ameliorate conflict, and, given the gut-wrenching reverberations of my father's experiences with departmental trench warfare, a strong inclination to pursue a career outside higher education. But my parents also instilled in me a commitment to making the most of myself and an obligation to make the world a better place—as my father put it, to "pay my way." Eventually, this commitment led to my calling as an educator.

———◆———

The first momentous independent decision of my life was to leave my hometown and enter the program in architecture at the University of Illinois, from which I would eventually obtain bachelor's and master's degrees. The choice reflected my desire to find a vocation that allowed me to make use of my diverse interests and skills, including my love of drawing and design, my fascination with history, and my strength in math and science. The rigorous and highly varied architecture curriculum was a kind of academic decathlon, and I explored several areas of concentration including architectural design, architectural engineering, city planning, and architecture history (along with design, my favorite subject, and the focus of my graduate teaching assistantship). My apprenticeships with architecture firms, however, were disappointing; I came to realize that the tedious process of design production and drafting was much less joyful than other creative endeavors. (One summer, for example, I spent my days at a drafting board in an architecture firm and nights and weekends playing featured roles in musicals with a repertory company; as I explained to an interviewer from a local newspaper, I lived entirely for the latter.) Still unsettled on a specific career path, I used the opportunity provided by a postgraduate European traveling fellowship to study planning and preservation of the urban landscape at the Institute of Advanced Architectural Studies at the University of York. There, a lecture on city planning by a noted attorney reinforced my instinct that a law degree would greatly expand my "tool box" and afford me a wider range of career choices. (Not incidentally, I had recently read and been personally moved and inspired by Carl Sandburg's *Abraham Lincoln: The Prairie Years*, detailing that remarkable Illinoisan's evolution as a trial lawyer and politician.) When I told the professor heading the institute that I intended to return to the United States and become a "creative lawyer," he guffawed, "Don't you know that's an oxymoron!"

But while architecture school was for me a virtual smorgasbord, law school initially seemed to present me with a single cold dish, served repeatedly. The classes felt like a throwback to those overpopulated foundational courses for college freshman, affording little personal interaction with professors. I had no creative outlets as respite from the relative drudgery of reading, class preparation, and formal writing; focused on success in law school, I had given up my outside work as an illustrator/graphic designer and my participation in vocal groups and dramatics. In desperation, I flew to Denver late in the spring of my 1L year to explore opportunities with architecture firms. Unexpectedly, my visit persuaded me that while the prospects for young architects were very poor, combining backgrounds in law and architecture was much more promising. Moreover, multiple leads directed me to an Atlanta-based boutique firm with a highly regarded national practice specializing in engineering and construction law. Thereafter, my law school experience was wholly reframed as preparation for that practice, which would eventually bring me to the cutting edge of change in the resolution of conflict. I also benefitted immensely from the mentorship of a favorite teacher, Professor Thomas Morgan, whom I assisted with research for a new edition of his widely used text on professional responsibility.

———◆———

Like many aspects of life, my experience in law practice entailed a great paradox. On the one hand, I was immensely troubled by many aspects of my experience as a "litigator," which for me consisted of long periods of mind-numbing boredom punctuated by moments of sheer terror. (Did I miss that filing deadline? Will opposing counsel blindside us at the hearing?) All too often, my assigned role ended up being that of a mercenary in a battle of attrition rather than a constructive problem-solver; the costs and delays associated with legal process sometimes exceeded the real benefits my clients sought or obtained. For example, one of my cases involved a dispute that had been tied up in litigation for almost a decade, and I was the third lawyer who had been assigned to the case. (As my counterpart at the client's company suggested, only half-jokingly: "Perhaps this time around, you should pay me!") By the time I was able to take depositions, one key witness had passed away and others' memories had faded. Although my client, who had been pressing a claim, "won" the bench trial and at last received compensatory damages, I was appalled by the many years of delay in obtaining justice. Representing another client, we spent almost five difficult years in adjudication to resolve a host of disputes surrounding the renovation and expansion of a hospital. Despite receiving what in the legal system would be termed a "home run" (full compensatory damages, attorney's fees, and punitive damages), the president of our client company wrote to say that although he appreciated that we had obtained for his business all that the law would allow, he was disappointed. He explained that the cost, both in human terms and in lost business, had been staggering. Surely, he concluded, there had to be better ways of resolving disputes for people and businesses.

Paradoxically, these experiences were the beginning of my own wisdom regarding the limitations and pitfalls of the legal system. My client's implied admonition to seek more suitable and effective strategies for resolving conflict became the lodestar of my career. As fortune would have it, construction practice was becoming a proving ground for out-of-court dispute resolution processes, and I made the most of the opportunity to garner considerable experience as an advocate in binding arbitration and other choice-based processes. (Among other things, I observed that while arbitration offered parties opportunities to construct effective alternatives to litigation, sometimes arbitration ended up being just as expensive and time-consuming as going to court.) In 1981, my first year of practice,

I had the good fortune to participate as an attorney in what may have been the first mediation of a major construction dispute. It was a new experience for all the participating lawyers, although our client had engaged in mediation on the labor front. Given the complete absence at the time of trained mediators, the parties chose a senior partner from a noted Chicago architecture firm to facilitate negotiations. Although the mediation failed to settle the case, I understood the potential of the process for promoting more effective and appropriate ways of resolving conflict, especially in ongoing relationships. These experiences provided a critical foundation for my later work as a scholar and teacher with a foot in dispute resolution practice.

———◆———

Several senior lawyers in my law firm taught courses at Emory Law School and Georgia Tech. In truth, despite my earlier resolve to avoid becoming embroiled in the kind of destructive faculty politics that my father experienced, I realized that being a classroom teacher was something that appealed and came naturally to me; the opportunity to someday teach as an adjunct was one of the things that had attracted me to the firm. Those opportunities, however, seemed a far-off dream for a young lawyer embroiled in multiple major cases around the country. So when Tom Morgan, my former law school professor and mentor who was then serving as dean of Emory Law School, inquired whether I had any desire to teach, I demurred on the basis that I was, regrettably, too busy to teach a law school class. "Tom, I am not talking about being an adjunct," he responded, "but about becoming a full-time professor of law." In a moment, my life changed. Nothing ever felt so right. My disillusion with trial practice was now coupled with the belief that I was called in a direction more in keeping with my personal values and my desire to make the world a better place. From then on, I was seized with the idea of becoming a teacher/scholar, and with the help of Dean Morgan and others I bent my efforts energetically toward that goal.

A year and a half later I joined the law faculty at the University of Kentucky in Lexington. From the very start, I never doubted that my decision to become a teacher was the right one—indeed, that I was an educator "in my bones." I loved being part of an academic community and eventually developed a repertoire of courses including contracts, commercial law, mediation, dispute resolution, construction law, and legal history (a parallel to my father's course on the history of mathematics). I relished the chance to create a classroom environment that was challenging but pleasurable rather than intimidating and to encourage students to reflect carefully upon the human costs and consequences of legal advice. I felt privileged to play the role of mentor and advisor to students, and I was enthusiastic about developing a respected and coherent body of scholarship on alternatives to litigation. Finally, I found that the role of teacher/scholar provided diverse opportunities to give play to my wide-ranging interests and energies and still gave me time for my family. My life became a continuous cycle of teaching, researching, writing, consulting and policymaking on a national stage, arbitrating, and, eventually, mediating (with emphasis on construction and commercial cases).

Early on, I had no concept of what lay ahead, or how fortunate I was to be riding the wave of major movements in the landscape of conflict resolution—but my intuition was that I was onto something important. The 1976 Pound Conference and Frank Sander's evocation of the "multi-door courthouse" were still recent events, and only a handful of scholars and teachers were beginning to focus on dispute resolution topics. My own experience in practice equipped me with a long list of potential writing topics; whatever other challenges I might have had as a young scholar, I never lacked for challenging subjects that were receiving growing attention among practitioners. Most of these concerned hot topics in commercial arbitration that drew directly on my own practical experience, including arbitral awards of punitive damages and the handling of multiparty disputes in arbitration. I also took steps to overcome the dearth of information on perceptions and practices regarding arbitration by garnering and analyzing data from hundreds of experienced lawyers. My work caught the attention of two eminent scholars at Northwestern University, Ian Macneil and Richard Speidel, who invited me to join them in writing what eventually became an authoritative five-volume treatise on US arbitration law and practice entitled *Federal Arbitration Law: Agreements, Awards and Remedies under the Federal Arbitration Act*. My own contributions to this massive project focused on many aspects of arbitration process and procedure and were mightily influenced by my own experience with arbitration. When the treatise was published in 1995, I noted with irony that my only encounter with arbitration in law school had been a single paragraph on the final page of the textbook used in civil procedure class, which described arbitration as a simpler, more efficient adjudication process that permitted parties to avoid crowded court dockets and other incidents of litigation in the courts. As our book evidenced, its expanding use as a private alternative to litigation was also changing the very character of arbitration. In another paradox, this evolution tended to move arbitration processes closer and closer to a litigation model.

As noted above, actual experience in the field always provided a critical foundation for my understanding of the dynamics of dispute resolution procedures. Although my clear and abiding priority was my educational role, I could not imagine writing about or teaching arbitration topics without having personal experiences in practice. My own views on the importance of experience may, however, be something of a rarity among law professors. One evening at dinner with a prolific arbitration scholar, he asked, "You actually do this stuff, don't you? I mean, arbitrate?" Only after I responded did it occur to me that my questioner had little or no firsthand practical experience.

By the mid-1990s I was convinced I knew pretty much all I needed to know about arbitration and was thus primed for a rude awakening. I was appointed as one of several "public members" (representing the interests of public investors) on the Securities Industry Conference on Arbitration (SICA), a policy-making body that debated and proposed reforms in the rules governing investor-broker arbitration regulated by the US Securities and Exchange Commission. I quickly came to realize that the experiences and expectations I brought from the arena of commercial arbitration—that is, of arbitration as a choice-based process—were often of little or no value in an arbitration system in which individuals found themselves battling with major companies in a forum that they had no choice but to accept. My involvement in SICA served as a crucial counterpoint to my commercial experience and forced me to wholly readjust my image of the dispute resolution landscape to acknowledge the fundamental dichotomy presented by negotiated commercial dispute contracts and contracts of adhesion. My fully awakened concerns about fairness issues in consumer and employment arbitration systems—systems made possible by a series of Supreme Court decisions stretching federal arbitration law beyond its original intended scope—prompted me to accept the role of academic reporter and chief drafter of the Consumer Due Process Protocol developed by a diverse group brought together by the American Arbitration Association. The protocol was intended to be developed as a set of guidelines governing any arbitration administered by the American Arbitration Association (AAA) under the terms of contracts for consumer goods or services. I jumped at the chance to play a central role in the protocol's development because I believed that for cases in the AAA system, the protocol could serve as a bulwark against overwhelming corporate leverage in the contracting process. I also envisioned the protocol as a establishing a basic "floor" of procedural fairness—a kind of community standard—that could influence the development of other rules and standards, and perhaps even encourage judicial decisions interpreting and enforcing arbitration agreements. I am convinced the protocol had an important impact on consumer arbitration, including some aspects of the Revised Uniform Arbitration Act, for which I served as an academic advisor. But although the protocol was a force for the good of the general public, we drafters sadly failed to anticipate the development of class-action waivers in connection with arbitration under standardized consumer and employment contracts.

———◆———

Having been impressed by the potential of mediation upon my first experience back in 1981, I watched with great interest as mediation came to the fore as a strategy for resolving cases in litigation and was captivated by the concept of neighborhood justice centers and other community mediation programs. These, I believed, embodied the spirit of the Pound Conference and our Quiet Revolution by opening up the justice system and engaging not only disputants but the entire community. Toward the end of 1990, I concluded a speech by suggesting that our region, the bluegrass region of Kentucky, would benefit by having a community mediation center. With the backing of lawyer and non-lawyer volunteers and the Kentucky Supreme Court, I took the lead in establishing a 501(c)(3) nonprofit entity called the Mediation Center of Kentucky, created a board, began visiting court-connected mediation programs in Atlanta and other cities, sought out expert guidance on procedures and protocols, and brought in leading trainers to prepare the first cadre of mediators. Once the center was up and running, I stepped back from a leadership role but continued to mediate cases. Almost three decades later, the center is still in operation under the auspices of the administrative office of the courts; my only personal regret is that, like many court-connected programs, the "gravitational pull" of the legal profession has severely limited opportunities for non-lawyers as mediators.

My own mediation practice developed around my expertise in resolving engineering and construction disputes and expanded into the larger commercial realm. I loved the flexibility of mediation and the room for creativity in helping parties devise solutions, including tailored process options such as final-offer arbitration. What I most enjoyed, however, was facilitating parties' efforts to restore or improve personal and working relationships—something that was not always uppermost in parties' minds by the time they had "lawyered up" and positions had hardened. Focused on the special opportunities of early, "real-time" mediation in the context of long-term relationships, I took on work as a "standing neutral" during the course of construction projects and facilitated resolution of jobsite issues before they spiraled into legal disputes. My "upstream" focus eventually extended to facilitating project partnering by bringing together key members of the design and construction team to share organizational and individual priorities and specific concerns, laying the groundwork for early resolution of issues during the progress of the project. At the time, my own experience and broad-based surveys of lawyers, architects, engineers and other construction professionals and construction gave me reason to believe that real-time approaches like these would be the future of construction conflict management and the ultimate evocation of the Quiet Revolution.

By the late 1990s, I strongly felt the need for a new challenge. Through the Mediation Center and other initiatives I'd hoped to construct an institutional framework in which law students could develop skills and insights for conflict resolution, and eventually to establish a multi-faceted academic program. It became clear, however, that my very hidebound law school was unlikely to support such a venture—at that place, I would remain a "one-man band." I concluded, moreover, that for all of the effort I had spent trying to make a difference in the culture of dispute resolution practice, I felt I was reaching only a relatively small and self-selected audience. It was time for a big change.

The Center for Public Resources was a Manhattan-based nonprofit organization founded by a group of Fortune 1000 corporate counsel in 1979. Its amorphous title reflected the fact that the founders envisioned several discrete missions for CPR, but it was not long before the organization's focus was on promoting alternatives to the high cost and perceived risks of litigation. As the CPR Institute for Dispute Resolution, the organization engaged and received financial support from more than 400 of the world's leading corporations and law firms. It convened leading lawyers, academics, and thinkers in topical working groups; developed books, guidelines, and procedures for the resolution of business-related conflict; hosted national and international conferences; sponsored panels of distinguished neutrals; gave awards for outstanding initiatives and writings in the field of dispute resolution; and published a magazine,

Alternatives. This unique organization first came to my attention when a young in-house lawyer loaned me copious materials from a CPR-sponsored workshop on minitrial, which I promptly photocopied; I was astounded at the quality and breadth of information on private dispute resolution processes, and I resolved to become involved with CPR. My opportunity came in 1987, when one of my early writings received the prize for best professional article at CPR's annual meeting at the University Club in Manhattan (a truly heady experience for a young scholar), and I was invited to be an affiliated scholar of the organization. My engagement with CPR eventually resulted in my designation in 1998 as academic director of a Hewlett Foundation-funded commission of more than 50 leading arbitration experts that produced the book *Commercial Arbitration at Its Best: Successful Strategies for Business Users*, co-published by CPR and the ABA Sections of Dispute Resolution and Business Law.

In 2000, I was recruited to replace Jim Henry at the helm of CPR, and at the beginning of 2001 I left my chaired professorship to become the second president and CEO of the organization. It was a dramatic leap, requiring me to give up tenure, but I was confident that CPR would provide an unparalleled platform for promotion of creative conflict management in law and business practice at a high level. My romanticized image of the position had emphasized its scholarly, creative, and educational aspects, but very quickly I found myself immersed in other things: leadership, management, and administration, fundraising, and maintaining relationships with a wide range of people. The organization I inherited needed new momentum, new sources of revenue, improved staff morale, more effective teamwork, and a revamped board of directors. To effectively address these needs I had to work and act differently. Learning to manage myself was the first and greatest challenge, especially in the months following the September 11 attacks, when everyone in New York City seemed to exist under a cloud of despondency. Although the first two years at CPR were among the most difficult and challenging of my life, working alongside colleagues old and new (including my friend and mentor Peter Kaskell and my remarkable right hand, Peter Phillips), and with the immeasurable support of my wife, Sky, I was able gradually to promote critical changes and move CPR forward. The board of directors was transformed by bringing on an outstanding and fully engaged group of general counsel, and we were able to launch a number of new initiatives, including an International Business Mediation Congress in The Hague aimed at promoting greater use of mediation in the European Union. We also sought to build partnerships in other parts of the world and responded to the request of the China Council for Promotion of International Trade to cooperate in the creation of a new US-China Business Mediation Center. To recognize the role of corporate counsel whose companies were using effective conflict management practices as well as to address serious revenue concerns, we created an annual Corporate Leadership Award; Ernst & Young's Kathryn Oberly and General Electric's Brackett Denniston were among the first awardees. CPR's financial picture improved dramatically, and when our Madison Avenue lease was up we were able to move to new and larger offices elsewhere in midtown.

In the course of five years at CPR I changed markedly and developed new capabilities as a leader. The reality, however, was that despite being at the head of an international dispute resolution "think tank," I felt I was losing touch with developments on the ground: I profoundly missed the opportunity to teach, write about, and practice dispute resolution. As president of CPR I made many dozens of speeches and conducted workshops for leading companies and law firms, participated in national and international initiatives, and even co-authored a new dispute resolution text for law schools. Deep down, however, I realized that my true calling was as a full-fledged, dedicated teacher and scholar; I still longed for the experience of leading a major academic program uniting dispute resolution theory and practice.

———◆———

In the spring of 2005 I met with the leadership of the Straus Institute for Dispute Resolution at Pepperdine School of Law for the purpose of exploring a joint training venture. Not long after we initiated discussions, Straus Director Professor Randy Lowry announced his resignation to assume a university presidency, and the talks about institutional cooperation gradually evolved into a personal discussion with his associate director, Professor Peter Robinson, who raised the possibility of my joining the Pepperdine faculty and working together at Straus. Peter's openness and willingness to explore a collaborative role impressed me greatly. When approached by Pepperdine regarding the faculty position some time later, I felt encouraged to propose that Peter and I jointly engage in a rather unconventional "co-directorship" of the institute; this arrangement would enable me to leave day-to-day administration to an able and trusted partner while concentrating on my own teaching, scholarship, and projects. In mid-2006 that vision became a reality, and Sky and I moved from the East Coast to the Pepperdine campus on a mountainside in Malibu, California.

My years as a chaired professor of law at Pepperdine and academic director of the Straus Institute have been among the happiest and most fulfilling of my adult life, thanks in large part to the wonderful community of which I've been a part. My renewed participation as a teacher and scholar was a privilege and blessing; I had the opportunity to reflect regularly on approaches to teaching dispute resolution skills and to encourage constructive and reflective approaches to problem-solving by tomorrow's lawyers and make fuller use of my creative energies. I also experienced greater satisfaction with my impact on our field and its future.

At Pepperdine, my scholarly work focused heavily on trends in the evolution of arbitration and mediation practice in the United States and internationally, with special emphasis on the unintended consequences of procedural developments as well as the impact of globalization, the revolution in information technology, and current research on human cognition. In my renewed practice as an arbitrator, for example, I observed that arbitration procedures were "drifting" increasingly toward a litigation model. My 2007 keynote speech on that subject set the stage for an important national initiative that eventually led to the *College of Commercial Arbitrators Protocols for Expeditious, Cost-Effective Commercial Arbitration*. The protocols were distributed by DuPont general counsel Tom Sager to all the top lawyers at Fortune 1000 companies and played an influential role in US arbitration practice. This "modern" work is juxtaposed against several historical research projects regarding conflict and its resolution. These included a study on relational conflicts between Warner Brothers Studios and each of three famous actors (James Cagney, Bette Davis, and Olivia de Havilland) during the golden age of Hollywood—a project that benefitted greatly from Olivia de Havilland's sharing of personal recollections. Most personally satisfying, however, is my research on Abraham Lincoln as a problem-solver and manager of conflict during his life and career, a project inspired by his admonition to fellow trial lawyers to "discourage litigation" in favor of efforts toward informal problem-solving and negotiated resolution.

These scholarly efforts are just one aspect of my engagement as co-leader of the Straus Institute, a unique center comprising a broad academic curriculum and vaunted professional skills training. The Straus Institute's academic curriculum consists of more than 40 courses on conflict management and dispute resolution, none of which were regularly taught when I was in law school. I could comfortably teach no more than a handful of courses—negotiation, arbitration practice, international commercial arbitration, courses immersing students in international dispute resolution practice in Europe and in China, and, most recently, a capstone course on ethical and practical challenges in dispute resolution. As a teacher, my greatest joy is engaging with and preparing young graduate students from all over the world to be responsible and reflective lawyers, dispute resolution professionals and problem solvers. At recent proceedings celebrating the signing by nation states of the Singapore Convention, I was pleased to see that I was in a room with no less than six of my former students who are practicing or teaching in places such as Ecuador, Korea, Hong Kong, Serbia, Singapore, and Qatar. I have also taken the lead in organizing and hosting conferences and symposia on diverse topics: women negotiating their way in the entertainment industry, efforts at forgiveness and reconciliation in South Africa, innovative conflict management approaches in business, and teaching dispute resolution. In addition, I conducted a series of filmed interviews with Archbishop Desmond Tutu, special master Kenneth Feinberg, and others. These projects and others benefitted from the involvement of more than 50 individuals who make up the Straus Institute's Council of Distinguished Advisors, a group of lawyers, dispute resolution professionals, corporate general counsel, and leaders of dispute resolution organizations from all over the United States and abroad that I brought together in my first months at the Institute to help credential, enhance, and offer valuable advice for our program. It was also during this time that I began drawing and painting again in the service of the institute, producing posters of Lincoln, Gandhi, and others with quotations that I am told have inspired mediators and problem-solvers around the world.

After a highly productive and satisfying decade at Pepperdine, new challenges emerged. In 2016, acknowledgment of the Institute's reputation and continued success prompted university directives to significantly increase the number of students in our graduate programs and collaborate in the establishment of three new online master's degree programs, two of which were solely focused on dispute resolution. In addition, the relatively streamlined and autonomous decision-making processes to which we were long accustomed were replaced with new layers of administration and stricter regulation; having for so long piloted a highly maneuverable frigate, it sometimes felt as though we were submerged in the command chain of a lumbering aircraft carrier. Meanwhile, a valued colleague began stepping back from his role as day-to-day manager of the institute after many years of service, necessitating the development of a new leadership team to meet new challenges. During the current period of transition and change, I've again focused on reflective self-management as a critical part of my efforts to employ the same skills in interpersonal communication, problem-solving, and conflict resolution that we teach in the classroom. In these efforts as in the classroom, my ongoing studies of the life and career of Abraham Lincoln as an exemplary lawyer and leader are an invaluable source of insight and inspiration.

Four decades into the Quiet Revolution in dispute resolution, it is natural for those of us who have shared the experience to examine and reflect upon our era and our personal and institutional legacies. For me, the greatest joy has come from engaging with many outstanding individuals in efforts aimed at improving human interaction, moderating or ending conflict, and restoring or enhancing relationships. Our greatest accomplishments as a field include the development of mediation, which is sometimes employed as a highly flexible and valuable method of dispute resolution and relational transformation, and the establishment of academic and professional training programs that promote reflective and effective practices in negotiation, mediation, arbitration, and other approaches.

Yet despite unprecedented study and experience with the promotion of peacemaking and problem-solving, our successes are limited. Although we have devoted substantial attention to the employment of mediation and arbitration, lawyers have too often severely limited the flexibility and utility of these processes by imposing a "litigation mentality," and in-house counsel too often abdicate their choice-making role. In addition, the challenges we face are seemingly more daunting than at any time in recent memory. For the typical US citizen, the ability to obtain "justice" may be as elusive as ever, both in the public and private realm (although recent experimentation with online platforms suggests new ways of overcoming the barriers of time, distance, and cost). Moreover, even those who have devoted considerable time and effort to the resolution of conflict seem unable to narrow the vast divisions—economic, political, social, cultural, religious—in our society and in the world at large. Current national and global trends are alarmingly evocative of historical periods of mounting hostility leading to armed conflict, such as the years preceding our own Civil War or the two World Wars.

Although I am often tempted to throw up my hands in the face of current events, I tell myself that it is precisely now that I must take heart and act. I have been given skills and insights to influence and constructively channel human interaction and must press forward even if I sometimes feel that my impact is limited to individuals or small groups. I think of my teacher parents, especially my father, and I am grateful for their example. As an educator and facilitator of conflict, I have the opportunity to influence (directly or indirectly) other practitioners and teachers around the world, to focus attention on outstanding exemplars of ethical living and leadership (such as Abraham Lincoln), and to model the behaviors this field seeks to inculcate. In these efforts, self-awareness and self-management are central. Who I am and who I intend to be—my essential makeup, my core beliefs, and the themes that animate my life—are more important than ever.

14

The View from the Helicopter

By Lisa Blomgren Amsler

◆

Experiencing life as an "other" brought me to this field—not as much an "other" as is experienced by people of color, LGBTQ individuals, immigrants, or those other-abled, but enough to make me want to understand how our systems contribute to human conflict and shape how we handle it.

Family

My parents met when they were flying for Northwest Airlines (now Delta); Dad was a pilot, and Mom a stew-

---

Lisa Blomgren Amsler (formerly Lisa Blomgren Bingham) is distinguished professor and Keller-Runden Professor of Public Service at the Paul H. O'Neill School of Public and Environmental Affairs at Indiana University, where she has served on the faculty since 1992. Amsler is also the Saltman Senior Scholar at the William S. Boyd School of Law at the University of Nevada, Las Vegas. She received the Abner Award from the Association for Conflict Resolution for excellence in research on labor and employment relations in the public sector (2002), and the Rubin Theory-to-Practice Award from the International Association for Conflict Management for research that affected practice (2006). The American Bar Association honored Amsler for Outstanding Scholarship foundational to the field of dispute resolution (2014). She is a fellow of the National Academy of Public Administration Labor and Employment Relations Association. In 2019, she received the Dwight Waldo Award from the American Society for Public Administration "for distinguished contributions to the professional literature of public administration and recognition of a distinguished career as author, educator, and public administrator." Her research addresses dispute resolution, mediation, arbitration, dispute system design, collaborative governance, and public engagement, with more than 130 published works.

ardess. Dad was Swedish-German from Boise, Idaho. His father had abandoned him when he was 10, and at 16 Dad lied about his age to get into World War II. After the war ended, he stayed in the Pacific for five years, playing jazz sax in Manila bars and trying to start businesses with surplus military planes before coming back to the United States to attend college on the GI Bill. Mom was a Sicilian and Romanian Jew from a turbulent family who grew up in Queens, New York; like others before her in her family, she did not go to college. When they married, Northwest Airlines fired Mom because this was the 1950s, before the Civil Rights Act of 1964. Dad had low seniority, so he suffered repeated layoffs.

I was the firstborn in Michigan in 1955. Laid off and responsible for a wife and baby, Dad gave up on the airlines and took a corporate pilot job, a move that Mom complained all her life was a big mistake. My parents loved each other, and they also fought. They were both youngest children and had trouble managing money. My sister (3 years younger), brother (7 years younger), and I grew up moving from place to place like Army brats.

From the Deep South to Long Island: Culture Shock

The first home I remember is Mobile, Alabama—and the first place I felt like an "other." Mom hid the fact she was part-Jewish, and Dad hid his serious leftie leanings. On November 22, 1963, I was in third grade when the principal announced that President John F. Kennedy had been assassinated. All my classmates clapped. I cried, because I knew my parents loved the Kennedys. Disapprovingly, my teacher said, "Go to the ladies room and compose yourself." I did not understand—why was I crying and everyone else clapping? While I did not realize what it meant, I was in an all-White segregated elementary school in the Deep South.

Less than a year later, Dad was transferred to New York's LaGuardia Airport. We moved to an Oyster Bay rental house, and I entered an integrated fourth-grade classroom with my Southern accent and manners (stand up when the teacher calls on you, say, "Yes Ma'am" and "No Ma'am"). After school, I would face south in the back yard and cry, missing home where I could wander alone in the swamp, catch lizards, tadpoles, and crayfish, climb mimosa trees in full bloom, and eat pine nuts out of pine cones with the neighbor kids.

By spring, though, I had a new friend, Grace, who was Black and had a heart condition and an identical twin who was fine. She invited me to spend the night but despite my protests, Mom said no. Why not?

That fall, I moved away from Grace to a nearby suburb, Syosset, where I again felt "other." I remember being embarrassed in fifth grade—I tried to defend the Deep South when we talked about the Civil War. I prided myself on being a good student, but I was wrong *in school*. It was traumatic. I did not want to mediate between North and South. I just wanted to understand.

In moving to Long Island, we suddenly had close contact with all Mom's extended family, including Grandpa Bennie Bonacio, a musician and composer who played in Paul Whiteman's big band and Broadway shows. We also discovered new cultural traditions like traditional Sunday Italian family dinners, at which I heard complaints about the musician's union. Meanwhile, like Grandma's family, Mom's sister and her husband were practicing Jews active in their temple. We all celebrated Passover at their house. At our home, Easter was about the "God of Chocolate."

I loved meeting my first cousins, but we became separated after our family boycotted my cousin's bar mitzvah in a dispute Mom never explained. There was something called the "Mandel Madness," in which people would "ghost" each other, as it is now called. Things also became challenging at home. Dad, working as a pilot, was away a lot for days at a time. Alone with us, Mom was physically and verbally abusive. I later learned that Grandpa Bonacio had hit her a lot. In an "accident" before age 2, I had ended up in the hospital with a fractured skull and broken collarbone. I think my sister bore the brunt of it because unlike me, she had no medical record of previous injury. I have survivor's guilt for not protecting her. I did not try to mediate—I was afraid of Mom.

In contrast, my sister and I spent several largely peaceful summer vacations, without our parents or brother, with my Dad's family in Idaho. His Aunt Lou had a cabin by a lake in the Rockies—it was bliss. Grandma Carrie, who was of German ancestry, did not like Mom because she was a Jew (although Mom, like her children, had never practiced any religion). The summer that I was 12, Grandma Carrie and Aunt Lou had my sister and me baptized in a Boise Episcopal church. This irritated Dad because he was an atheist. The family conflicts over culture, religion, and ethnicity made me want to understand why people cared about all this stuff. Why was there so much drama?

I was lucky—we lived in Syosset until I graduated from high school. While I was in college, my siblings lived in two more states and three more houses between middle school and high school.

Escape

I babysat and saved money to escape back to Idaho the summer after ninth grade, this time alone. Aunt Lou was a tremendous influence. She gave me the gift of freedom and introduced me to Emerson, Krishnamurti, and the Theosophical Society. I discovered Buddhism. I began to have a frame for thinking about conflict, tolerance, and peace. She took me to the Grand Tetons. She let me use her lakeside cabin in the mountains for three weeks, driving up on weekends to make sure I was alive and did not starve. I was 15; it was the summer of 1970. I read about the long conflict between England and Scotland, the Berrigan brothers, the Kennedys. I meditated by the lake.

When I returned home to Syosset, it was back to conflict in the house, but by high school I had new friends, which made a huge difference. They introduced me to social justice, picketing for the grape workers, political protests, strikes at our school. Many in this social circle had a passion for writing and language. I also had wonderful courses—Greek tragedy, the Bible as literature, Shakespeare. My philosophy teacher, William Cawley, was a Jesuit-trained conservative with a crewcut. His capacity for logical argument gave him power over conflict, and watching him debate teenage long-haired radicals about Plato or St. Thomas Aquinas made me want the perfect 19th-century gentleman's education. After I decided to graduate a year early, a librarian at Syosset High steered me toward her alma mater, Smith College, a women's school. Smith accepted me early decision when I was 16.

College

Smith had no distribution requirements. I double-majored in ancient Greek and philosophy. It was all about conflict—the *Oresteia* and the *Iliad*, Plato's *Symposium*, the battle of ideas between Platonic forms and Aristotelian empiricism, and the New Testament in Koine Greek on Christianity and Rome. A religion course on Hegel was transformative. His dialectic gave me a language to think about conflict: thesis, antithesis, and synthesis. This was not simply logic. Synthesis meant it was possible to resolve a conflict between ideas, to take them together to a new level. The dialectic was a language for how systems evolve. I did my honors thesis translating the fragments of Heraclitus—he who said you can never step in the same river twice, and everything is change. As have Eastern scholars, I argued that he was a mystic like Lao Tzu. Smith College was empowering. Now, in conflict I could both reason and synthesize. And my wonderful housemates became my lifelong friends.

All was not peace in college, though. In the fall of my sophomore year, Dad lost his temper at work when skipped over for a long-promised promotion and he left his job of 17 years, so there was chaos at home. In January, my roommate's brother was shot to death at work. A week after that, Grandpa Bonacio died from a heart attack a few months after becoming a conductor for a small orchestra—he had no retirement pension and needed to keep working. Three generations of men struggling to earn a living, support families, or be able to retire in peace. I questioned whether the system provided workers with job security, safety, and justice.

Becoming a Lawyer and Dispute Resolver

My Smith professors in the philosophy and classics departments advised against going to graduate school. Hegel and Heraclitus were not in vogue, and I probably would not be able to find an academic job teaching ancient Greek. Realizing I did not want to spend my life talking about dactylic hexameter, I defaulted to law school, something I had first discussed with my father when I skipped a year in high school. I was engaged to my first husband, who had a year left in college in Connecticut. I got a day job as a legal secretary and attended the University of Connecticut School of Law at night, transferring to the day division after a year.

I discovered dispute resolution in law school through civil procedure, contracts, and labor law. Cornelius Scanlon, an accomplished labor mediator, taught contracts.

Peter Adomeit, a member of the National Academy of Arbitrators, taught civil procedure and labor law and became my mentor. At Smith, I had discovered Hegel; in labor law I encountered a system for workplace democracy that presented in reality the dialectic process between labor and management. I loved it.

I became a systems thinker in labor law. Later in life, after I became an academic, one of my former law partners said that listening to a talk I gave at Yale Law School was like watching someone in a traffic helicopter. I appreciated his metaphor, because in retrospect I was searching for the big picture, trying to understand the system that was producing conflict—in employment, in my family, in the North and South, nationally in the late 1960s and early 1970s—like hovering high enough to see crashes and resulting jams in the flow of traffic.

In 1978 during my second year of law school, Professor Adomeit introduced me to the Connecticut Education Association (CEA). There I worked for in-house counsel on cases of first impression argued before the Connecticut State Board of Labor Relations. Remembering my grandpa and both parents encountering work challenges related to both labor and management, I decided to become a labor lawyer. Workers' rights are political rights. A functioning labor law system can provide workplace justice. That experience brought me to mediation, arbitration, and dispute resolution.

After law school graduation in 1979, I joined a "silk stocking" general practice law firm's labor law department as an associate. Now the largest in Connecticut, it represented primarily public-sector management (school boards, municipalities, later the state). Both my mentor Peter Adomeit and CEA colleagues reassured me it was a firm of high integrity and well regarded by unions: I would not be viewed as a union-buster. For the next 10 years, I served as chief spokesperson and advocate in countless hours of negotiation and mediation, and in numerous grievance arbitration, fact-finding, and binding interest arbitration hearings. I argued three cases before the Connecticut Supreme Court, winning two. On two occasions, I represented employees instead of management, one in an age discrimination complaint and another in a Social Security disability case, settling one and winning the other. It was deeply satisfying to help people in individual cases—yet not enough. Individual cases rarely make for system change.

By 1983, I was getting close to the partnership decision, and my husband wanted to do his dissertation research in Sweden. We applied for Fulbright fellowships. When I approached the firm for unpaid leave to accept a six-month Fulbright, it voted to dock me a full year's credit toward partnership. Knowing that the previous year the firm had granted a two-year unpaid leave with full credit toward partnership to a male litigator to serve as a public defender, I objected. My mentor advocated for me in the partnership, which then reduced the time docked to six months. After I returned to the firm, I was made partner in 1986.

In July 1986, I also gave birth to our first son. I was the first woman partner to have a baby and return to practice. Trying to juggle motherhood, 70-hour work weeks, and a post-doc spouse commuting between Hartford and New Haven was a challenge. The turning point for me came during the annual "pie-cutting" in 1987, a full partnership meeting at which the firm set prospective percentages each partner would receive of the profits in the coming year. At that time, the firm cut the pie democratically. Each partner read aloud the percentage they set for every one of the partners. The firm then averaged all partners' votes to determine each partner's share of profits. My 1986 stats were in the top quarter of the partnership for billable hours and cash receipts, despite my having had a baby by C-section and taking five weeks of maternity leave.

The firm voted me a compensation in the bottom quarter of the partnership. If the basis had been seniority, that would have seemed fair, but it was not. One partner voted the same compensation for all three women partners, regardless of individual productivity statistics or seniority. A litigation partner later told me that junior male partners "had a family to support." I had a new baby and a husband on a post-doc; I, too, had a family to support. A third partner told me in the hallway, "Lisa, you can be a good mother or a good lawyer—you can't be both." Title VII did not apply because I was an equity partner, not an employee. In 1986, being the first woman partner in a big firm to have a baby and return to full-time law practice was no fun. I told my husband I would leave for whatever academic job he chose. In 1989, he was hired by Indiana University (IU). I had no regrets about leaving law practice.

When we arrived in Bloomington, I planned to stay home with my son, have another baby, and recuperate from law practice while my husband worked toward tenure. However, Peggy Intons-Peterson, the first female chair of the IU psychology department, was concerned about my career as a "trailing spouse" and set up networking meetings for me. Terry Bethel, a labor law professor at the IU School of Law and a National Academy arbitrator, told me it was unwise to take a complete hiatus from my professional identity. I became a lecturer in legal writing and research. IU opened a door to a new career direction: teaching, with dispute resolution practice.

I mediated or arbitrated dozens of labor cases. Most challenging was an expedited *pro bono* Olympic sports arbitration over an elite athlete's allegedly positive drug test. If I ordered that the athlete be permitted to compete, the International Olympic Committee (IOC) had the authority to reject my decision and could even disqualify the entire track and field team. I had never before encountered an arbitration system that lacked finality *and* allowed my award to harm innocent third parties. I published my first article as an academic about this system.

Becoming a Scholar

In 1992, I was invited to apply for a tenure-track position across campus at Indiana University's O'Neill School of Public and Environmental Affairs. By then, in addition to my position at the law school, I had two sons (a 5-year-old and an 8-month-old) and a practice on the side as a negotiation trainer, facilitator, mediator, and arbitrator. The deans of both the O'Neill School and the law school wanted to develop a dispute resolution curriculum and research on the IU campus. Ironically, until then, I did not think of what I did as "alternative dispute resolution" but as a way to stay in collective bargaining as a system.

I started as a tenure-track assistant professor at O'Neill in 1992, teaching new and different classes—two graduate and two undergraduate courses, one in constitutional and administrative law and the other a survey in negotiation and dispute resolution. Teaching forced me to learn; it broadened my understanding of how context shapes process and steered me further toward systems thinking, contrasting public justice in court and private justice in dispute resolution. The more I learned about how different systems produce varying outcomes, the more I became concerned about fairness and justice. What if there was no union? What if the system was undemocratic? This raised the question of how control over system design affected function, justice, and fairness. There was the potential for structural bias in dispute resolution systems.

Initially, I wrote articles about labor and employment that appeared in well-ranked law journals, which are not refereed. As a lawyer and not a social scientist, I was in the minority on this faculty. Most of my colleagues published work in scholarly journals with blind peer review. Adapting, I audited graduate statistics courses for a year. A colleague told me to research what I knew. I thought I knew arbitration and started attending conferences—the Society of Professionals in Dispute Resolution (SPIDR), the International Association for Conflict Management (IACM), the Industrial Relations Research Association (IRRA), and the Law and Society Association (LSA).

Arbitration Systems and the Repeat Player Effect

The US Supreme Court had recently decided *Gilmer v. Interstate/Johnson Lane Corp.* (500 US 20, [1991]), reinterpreting the Federal Arbitration Act to require a securities dealer claiming age discrimination in employment to arbitrate his claim pursuant to a mandatory, forced, or adhesive arbitration clause in his Securities and Exchange Commission registration form. As a labor arbitrator, I still thought arbitration was a fair system and a benefit for employees, whether or not there was a union. However, I wondered if it might be different without a union's institutional memory on specific arbitrators. I contacted the American Arbitration Association (AAA), and George Friedman gave me access to non-union employment arbitration case files. I began exploring employment arbitration decisions under the AAA Commercial Rules empirically, using multivariate regression, and comparing employees and employers as complainants. I did not control for repeat players. I presented it at the 1994 IACM conference, where most attendees had doctoral training in organizational behavior and social psychology and worked in business schools or psychology departments. I was an "other," but the IACM recognized the work as the best applied conference paper and made me feel at home.

At LSA conferences, I learned about Marc Galanter's "Why the Haves Come Out Ahead: Speculations on the Limits of Legal Change," about the civil justice system, game theory, and repeat players and one-shot players (Galanter, 1974). I began to suspect that non-union arbitration and labor arbitration were different animals because they exist in different systemic contexts. I applied Galanter's repeat play/one-shot play dichotomy to non-union arbitration. Taking a sample of non-union arbitration cases (under AAA Commercial and Employment rules), I defined repeat player as an employer that appeared in more than one case. Using simple frequencies and chi-square tests, I found that employers as repeat players won non-union employment arbitration cases statistically significantly more frequently than employers as one-shot players. In labor arbitration, where labor and management are both repeat players, the awards generally split 50/50 between labor and management. What I named "the repeat player effect" was a smoking gun, and it suggested the need for future research. I presented findings at the IRRA's 1997 and 1998 conferences, winning refereed conference paper competitions each year. I had found another empirical intellectual home.

In 1997, I published the repeat player article entitled "Employment Arbitration: The Repeat Player Effect" in the inaugural issue of a refereed journal, *Employee Rights and Employment Policy* (Bingham, 1997). This was the first-ever empirical study of the repeat player effect in non-union employment arbitration. The repeat player findings have been replicated by multiple other researchers with larger datasets and more sophisticated multivariate analyses. While scholars do not agree on an explanation for why it happens, I predicted correctly that mandatory, forced, or adhesive arbitration would come to pose a major public policy issue. It also triggered my interest in how a dispute system's design can shape justice—or the lack thereof.

I teach all my students about the mandatory, forced, or adhesive employment and consumer arbitration favored by corporate America. The vast majority of US voters have lost access to class actions and the courts more generally—even though they pay taxes to support courts to enforce the public laws that their democratically elected representatives in Congress passed. These arbitration clauses also can shift transaction costs, like attorney's fees, to the employee or consumer and thus deter and suppress claims and gut the enforcement of many public laws—e.g., the Fair Labor Standards Act, which mandates minimum wage, Title VII of the Civil Rights Act of 1964, which prohibits employment discrimination, and laws that provide consumer protection against defective cars or drugs.

The critical issue is control over dispute system design. While I did several additional analyses of AAA cases, in 2002 I lost access to the data. Others also took up the work, and my research priorities changed.

Research on Dispute System Design: Mediation at the US Postal Service

In 1994, I started parallel research on mediation. An O'Neill mentor, James Perry, had suggested I look at the Administrative Dispute Resolution Act of 1990, which authorized and encouraged federal agencies to use dispute resolution. Another mentor, then-Associate Dean Charles Wise, offered to collaborate on an interview study and teach me qualitative research. I was an assistant professor on the tenure track while my colleagues were training me in social science like a doctoral student—a cause for gratitude.

In 1994, I called the US Postal Service (USPS) Law Department to interview Cynthia Hallberlin, a litigator, shortly after she had settled a class-action race discrimination lawsuit by agreeing to establish a mediation program. Before I could finish the interview, she had asked for my CV and offered to take me to dinner wherever I was going to be the following week. Our serendipitous meeting in Dallas turned into an Indiana University-USPS collaboration that lasted from 1994 to 2006 and evaluated a workplace mediation program named REDRESS (which stands for Resolve Employment Disputes, Reach Equitable Solutions Swiftly). Using procedural justice literature, I designed an exit survey and data collection system that became a national program in every zip code. IU's evaluation employed dozens of students from 1994 to 2006.

The USPS goal was to move conflict management upstream, resolving cases early in the life of a dispute. In 1997, the USPS received about 28,000 equal employment opportunity (EEO) complaints a year, half of which proceeded to a formal administrative law judge hearing; however, the USPS ultimately prevailed in 95 percent of these complaints, as most employers do in EEO cases. By law, any federal agency EEO ADR program had to be voluntary.

I came to see mediation as an essential process step in any dispute system design, especially for conflicts between employees, or employees and their supervisors. However, I also saw how large institutions could use mediation to suppress conflict, depending upon the structure of the overall design. The USPS had control over how to design REDRESS; it selected mediators for the roster, trained them, assigned them to individual cases, and paid them. Mediators sometimes offer to assess a case's strengths and weaknesses or likely outcomes as a form of reality-testing. What would happen in caucus if these mediators told complainants they did not have a case? Even if the mediators were objectively correct, there might be the appearance of bias—employees might go back to the mail sorting floor and tell coworkers that the mediation program was a setup. Alternatively, it might cause employees to give up, discourage them from going forward to a formal hearing or litigation, and thereby suppress claims. ADR programs in EEO cases were not a mandatory subject of bargaining with USPS unions.

I had heard Robert A. Baruch Bush speak about transformative mediation at a 1996 LSA meeting and suggested to Cindy Hallberlin that she look at his book coauthored with Joseph Folger, *The Promise of Mediation* (Bush and Folger, 1994). The transformative model prohibited a mediator from evaluating the strengths and weakness of a case or expressing an opinion on the likely merits or outcome. This set of ethics precluded a mediator from pressuring or trying to persuade a complainant to accept a settlement; instead it focused on empowering disputants and helping them recognize each other's perspectives. Settlement was not a goal, although it might be a byproduct. From a dispute system design standpoint, I felt that this mediation model could reduce the risk of a mediator appearing biased in favor of the USPS.

We started in 1994 with pilots in three cities. In October 1997, it was surreal and exciting to have 30 minutes to present our pilot employee interview and procedural justice survey research on mediation in REDRESS before the postmaster general and his management committee. When we finished, there was a moment of silence. Then the postmaster general said to the general counsel and our law department team, "Sounds like a good program. I think we should go national. I want a plan on my desk Monday." The management committee was all male, with one Black man; the law department team was all female, with one Black woman.

Ultimately, the USPS adopted the transformative model for mediation and rolled REDRESS out nationwide over 18 months in 1998 and 1999. Ramping up nationwide data collection was hugely challenging, but I had an amazing team of graduate students who pulled it off and have gone on to become leaders in the dispute resolution field, including Gina Viola Brown, Susan Summers Raines, Tina Nabatchi, and Lisa-Marie Napoli.[1] To determine whether there was evidence that the EEO conflict management system changed after mediation was implemented, we collected five years of EEO complaint filing data before and after REDRESS, organized by zip code area (there were 85), month or accounting period, and date of implementation in each zip code area. We found the formal EEO complaint rate dropped by over 25%, a drop that correlated with implementing the mediation program in each zip code area in a given month or accounting period.

Over the 12-year evaluation in the exit surveys, there was no statistically significant difference between employee and supervisor satisfaction with the process (91-92% on average) or with the mediators (98%). The median settlement was $0, but in 30% of cases there were apologies or other actions such as reinstating leave, transfers, or temporary appointment to higher positions. Unions received copies of settlements to ensure they comported with collective bargaining agreements.

While a majority of employees and supervisors were satisfied or highly satisfied with their outcomes, there was a statistically significant difference. Supervisors were more satisfied than employees, a finding that replicated studies on grievance mediation in labor relations and on mediation in litigation—and a pattern also found in the tort litigation and labor-management contexts (Brett and Goldberg, 1983, and Lind, Kanfer, and Earley, 1990). Under expectancy theory, plaintiffs expect more and defendants less, so the former are disappointed and the latter relieved by settlement. In other research, we compared outside contractors versus USPS employees as mediators and found that employees were more satisfied with the outside independent contractor mediators.

We explored new models of organizational justice. Graduate student coauthors presented papers at conferences of the IACM. We determined that workplace mediation involved six factors in mediation, contrasted with the four-factor model for in-house grievance procedures (Nabatchi, Bingham, and Good, 2007). We found when disputants reported interpersonal justice with each other during mediation, they were more likely to reach a full resolution (Nesbit, Nabatchi, and Bingham, 2012). When they corroborated each other's reports of their communication behaviors during mediation, they were also more likely to settle. Lastly, those who received an apology from the other party were more likely to report a settlement. These findings supported the theory behind transformative mediation. Fostering disputants' communication with each other through empowerment and recognition in mediation might aid settlement, even if that is not a goal.

Indiana Conflict Resolution Institute

The O'Neill School hired me in 1992 to replace Rosemary O'Leary. However, Rosemary returned to IU in 1994 and I found a lifelong friend, research partner, and coauthor. In 1997, we co-founded the Indiana Conflict Resolution Institute (ICRI) at O'Neill with IU Strategic Initiatives funding. ICRI was a program evaluation research laboratory. It received funding from 1998 to 2006 from the William and Flora Hewlett Foundation Conflict Resolution Program as a special project. Hewlett ADR Theory Centers generally did not do applied program evaluation research, and we filled a gap. Together, Rosemary and I combined research on dispute resolution in public and private sector employment, administrative agencies, environmental conflict, and public policy. Rosemary had the environmental law expertise, and our co-edited book *The Promise and Performance of Environmental Conflict Resolution* (O'Leary and Bingham, 2003)[2] collected researchers' best thinking on program evaluation in that field.

In 2004, the Hewlett Foundation ended its Conflict Resolution program. My sons were approaching college and high school. My first husband and I mutually agreed to divorce.

The USPS funding for the IU REDRESS program evaluation ended in 2006. The REDRESS program lives on as of this writing, making it more than 25 years old. IU's USPS REDRESS research has been characterized as the most comprehensive evaluation of a workplace mediation program. Arguably, it was a positive force for change in how the USPS handled workplace conflict. In retrospect, Cindy Hallberlin and the USPS achieved my life goal of systems change. By taking research to scale, we created knowledge people can use to improve systems (Bingham, Hallberlin, Walker, and Chung, 2009). The USPS system was not perfect, but it gave employees voice they did not have before.

My research interests in systems continued to evolve. Elinor Ostrom's work drew me to look at the institutions and governance structures within which dispute resolution systems are embedded (Ostrom, 2005). In her Institutional Analysis and Development (IAD) framework, law and rules are important independent variables. My research on dispute resolution had long made me an "other" in the field of public administration; it was not mainstream. However, collaboration with Rosemary changed that. We argued that the federal Administrative Procedure Act and Administrative Dispute Resolution Act provide a legal framework for citizen and stakeholder voice in governance (Bingham, Nabatchi, and O'Leary, 2005).[3] An international rock star in public affairs, Rosemary invited me to co-edit special issues of two journals and two books (Bingham and O'Leary, 2008; O'Leary and Bingham, 2009) on collaborative public management and networks. She welcomed me into a field I knew little about when O'Neill hired me.

I retired from dispute resolution rosters 20 years ago and no longer practice mediation or arbitration. I teach it, research it, and write about the big picture—the systems. In 2007, Janet Martinez, Stephanie Smith, and I embarked on a 13-year adventure trying to write a comprehensive book about dispute system design. Our work culminated recently in the publication of *Dispute System Design: Preventing, Managing, and Resolving Conflict* (Amsler, Martinez, and Smith, 2020). The missing link in much of the mediation, arbitration, and dispute resolution literature is the context in which a process occurs. Dispute resolution professionals move from case to case, and from organization to organization. They might (or might not) understand or have access to information about the dispute system design in which they are working and who controls it. For dispute resolution to provide access to some form of justice, the dispute system design in which it occurs must reflect stakeholder participation and voice. If one powerful party controls system design, the result is more likely to be skewed in that party's favor or to serve its interests. The future use and institutionalization of dispute resolution requires systematic rigorous research on the relationships among system design, outcomes, and justice.

Through the field, I met my husband, Terry Amsler—we married in 2013. A steward of the field, he introduced me to public engagement and the importance of people's perspective on and in conflict over policy and governance. I am grateful for his generosity of spirit, compassion for the human condition, creativity, and continuing support. Together, we are working on how to strengthen democracy through people's voice in the local, state, and national governments in a project about engaging the public and underserved communities in dialogue about policy in public health. Starting with the legal and policy framework for public engagement, we hope to improve the system by scaling up a more inclusive model for the public's voice statewide in Indiana.

I am deeply grateful to all my colleagues, coauthors, students, and friends in the field of dispute resolution. Our collective and critically important work in this shared community has given my life meaning.

Notes

[1] Gina Viola Brown is now associate director of the American Bar Association's Section of Dispute Resolution and editor of its *Dispute Resolution Magazine*. Susan Summers Raines is professor at Kennesaw State and past editor-in-chief of *Conflict Resolution Quarterly*, Tina Nabatchi is now a chaired professor at the Maxwell School of Syracuse University, and Lisa-Marie Napoli is director of Indiana University's Political and Civic Engagement Program.

[2] This was cited as Best Book by the American Society for Public Administration Section on Environmental and Natural Resource Administration for 2005.

[3] This is in the top 1% of the most-cited articles in public administration in the past 30 years (St. Clair, et al., 2017).

References

Amsler, L., J. Martinez and S. E. Smith. 2020. *Dispute System Design: Preventing, Managing, and Resolving Conflict.* Palo Alto, CA: Stanford University Press.

Bingham, L. B. 1997. "Employment Arbitration: The Repeat Player Effect." *Employee Rights and Employment Policy Journal* 1(1): 189-220.

Bingham, L. B., C. J. Hallberlin, D. A. Walker and W. T. Chung. 2009. "Dispute System Design and Justice in Employment Dispute Resolution: Mediation at the Workplace." *Harvard Negotiation Law Review* 14(1): 1-50.

Bingham, L. B., T. Nabatchi and R. O'Leary. 2005. "The New Governance: Practices and Processes for Stakeholder and Citizen Participation in the Work of Government." *Public Administration Review* 65(5): 547-558.

Bingham, L. B. and R. O'Leary, eds. 2008. *Big Ideas in Collaborative Public Management.* Armonk, NY: M.E. Sharpe, Inc.

Brett, J. M. and S. B. Goldberg. 1983. "Grievance Mediation in the Coal Industry: A Field Experiment." *Industrial and Labor Relations Review* 37(1): 49-65.

Bush, R. A. B. and J. P. Folger 1994. *The Promise of Mediation: Responding to Conflict through Empowerment and Recognition.* San Francisco: Jossey-Bass.

Galanter, M. 1974. "Why the 'Haves' Come Out Ahead: Speculations on the Limits of Legal Change." *Law and Society Review* 9(1): 165-230.

Lind, E. A., R. Kanfer and P. C. Earley. 1990. "Voice, Control, and Procedural Justice: Instrumental and Non-instrumental Concerns in Fairness Judgments." *Journal of Personality and Social Psychology* 59: 952-959.

Nabatchi, T., L. B. Bingham and D. H. Good. 2007. "Organizational Justice and Workplace Mediation: A Six-Factor Model." *International Journal of Conflict Management* 18(2): 148-174.

Nesbit, R., T. Nabatchi and L. B. Bingham. 2012. "Employees, Supervisors, and Workplace Mediation: Experiences of Justice and Settlement." *Review of Public Personnel Administration* 32(3): 260-287.

O'Leary, R. and L. B. Bingham, eds. 2003. *The Promise and Performance of Environmental Conflict Resolution.* Washington, DC: Resources for the Future.

O'Leary, R. and L. B. Bingham, eds. 2009. *The Collaborative Public Manager.* Washington, DC: Georgetown University Press.

Ostrom, E. 2005. *Understanding Institutional Diversity.* Princeton, NJ: Princeton University Press.

St. Clair, R., D. Hicks and K.R. Isett. 2017. "An Investigation into the Characteristics of Papers with High Scholarly Citations in Public Administration: The Relativity of Theory and Method." *Review of Public Personnel Administration* 37(3): 323-350.

15

A Conflict Counter-Story: How a Puerto Rican Woman Ended Up in a Field Dominated by Anglo Men

By Jacqueline N. Font-Guzmán

◆

"That explains a lot!"

This was the response of a colleague when I told her where I had attended grade school. Her comment got me thinking: what, exactly, was being "explained?"

Jacqueline N. Font-Guzmán is professor of law and conflict studies and director of the Negotiation and Conflict Resolution Program in the Department of Interdisciplinary Studies at Creighton University. A Fulbright Scholar and recipient of the 2017 Nova Southeastern University Distinguished Alumni Achievement Award, she is a mediator and arbitrator certified by the Puerto Rico Supreme Court. Her book *Experiencing Puerto Rican Citizenship and Cultural Nationalism* was selected as the Puerto Rico Bar Association 2015 Juridical Book of the Year in the category of Essay Promoting Critical Thinking and Analysis of Juridical and Social Issues. Font-Guzmán's research focuses on health care disparities, law, citizenship, and conflict engagement—specifically, how people construct meaning at critical points in their lives to explore how meaning-making leads them to productively engage with conflict. She also explores how marginalized individuals create alternate stories and counter-narratives to address institutional/structural injustices. Font-Guzmán has a BA from Coe College in Cedar Rapids, Iowa, a MS in health care administration from Saint Louis University, a JD degree from the Interamericana University of Puerto Rico, and a PhD in conflict analysis and resolution from Nova Southeastern University in Fort Lauderdale, Florida.

That conversation reinforced what I have always felt to be true. Our past, our history, and the people we encounter in life matter. They matter because they shape our experiences, our stories, our identities, what we choose to do (or not do), our present, our future, and our ethical stance. This is my story of who I am as a conflict practitioner and scholar. This chapter is not a chronicle of my work in the conflict field. Those achievements can be found in my *curriculum vitae*; they are not who I am.

In the late 1960s and early 1970s, between the third and seventh grades, I went to a Montessori school in the Condado neighborhood in San Juan, Puerto Rico. My experiences in the Montessori school positively influenced my life. How I got there is memorable.

Through the start of third grade, I went to a private Christian school. My last day at that school began like every school day. My mother knocked on my bedroom door at the ungodly hour of 6:00 a.m. I struggled to wake up, dragged myself out of bed, took a shower, put on my uniform, ate something (reluctantly), and got in the car. This is where the routine ended. Instead of dropping me off, my mom walked me straight into the principal's office.

She looked at the principal and said, "I am curious. When I drop off my daughter at school every morning, does she stay in the classroom or does she wander off?"

"No!" said the principal. "Of course she does not wander off. We would never allow that to happen! We take security seriously."

"Then I need you to explain why every evening when I get home from work and check my daughter's notebook I read notes like, 'Jacqueline needs to learn how to count and subtract.' My daughter may not be a genius, but I am certain she is capable of counting numbers."

"We have many students in the classroom," the principal said, "so mothers come to help their children with the assignments and class participation."

My mother did not hesitate before responding. "I pay this school to teach my daughter," she said, "and since you cannot do it, I am withdrawing Jacqueline from this school right now."

The principal seemed stunned and told her she couldn't possibly do that.

"Yes, I can," my mother said. "Watch me."

My mom demanded to know the tuition balance, whipped out her checkbook, wrote a check, grabbed my hand, and just like that, we walked out of the principal's office. As we drove away in silence, I felt that something extraordinary had just happened. I also felt uneasy. What was next? Where would I go to school? What about my friends? After a few minutes of silence that felt like an eternity, I must have uttered my questions out loud because I heard my mother's reassuring voice.

"Don't worry," she said. "You will be in a new school with friends by the end of the week."

And I was. Within 48 hours I was in a Montessori school. No uniforms, learning at my own pace, small classes, and only minimum rules to facilitate learning. Creativity was encouraged, homework was done at school, and the playground was the beach. That day in the principal's office might have been my first lesson in how to engage with conflict at an uneven table (Kritek, 2002). I was not in a fair competition with my peers; I was competing with my peers' mothers. This dysfunctional power imbalance was unacceptable to my mother. Had my mother gone to my classroom as suggested by the principal, she would have been complicit in perpetuating institutional mediocrity and reinforcing unjust power structures. She chose to name the injustice—and find a better school.

At my new school I had a fair chance. There were no moms in the classroom, and I could deviate from conventional norms without being labeled a problematic child. I loved it. I could play kickball (which in my old school had been reserved for boys), and I could express my individuality by wearing trousers (also for boys only at the Christian school) instead of skirts.

But even at my new school, the table was not always even—it rarely is. For example, complaints I raised were not always given the same credibility given to those raised by boys. One boy in the class constantly pulled my ponytail, and when I mentioned this to a teacher, the boy denied it, and somehow his version of events became the controlling narrative. (The vicious cycle stopped when I socked him with my Samsonite briefcase when he was yanking my ponytail. He never pulled my ponytail again. I'm happy to say that I have significantly improved my conflict resolution skills since then.)

I did not know it back then, but the day my mother removed me from the Christian school, I learned two powerful lessons that shaped who I am today. First, not taking a side or not intervening can reinforce power imbalances, so you need to be aware of who benefits—and who gets hurt—by your decision to stand aside. Second, systems of domination matter. By systems of domination I mean social environments that sanction domination by the most powerful or privileged. Who is missing from the table or at risk of being effaced may be the result of systems of domination that disadvantage some and privilege others. At the Christian school, I was clearly at a disadvantage, and to this day, I am grateful that my mother took a stand.

These lessons were reinforced throughout my upbringing. As a child, when I was not at school (or being pulled from a school), I was in my grandfather's law office, which was located in his home. My mom and I lived next door.

I would spend hours at my grandfather's office at a desk (which was exclusively mine), drawing, doing homework, and listening to him prepare his clients for hearings and trials. My grandfather, an immigration lawyer, dedicated his life to taking stands and making invisible people visible. I was surrounded by a family of social justice advocates.

After completing my undergraduate degree in political science and my master's degree in health care administration and then working in health care for many years, I decided to go back to school to become a lawyer. As a health care administrator, I had seen my share of injustices and inequities; women and the poor usually received less than adequate treatment (Font-Guzmán, 2019). I wanted to use the legal system to advocate for the most vulnerable (Font-Guzmán, 2019).

Although I had earned my undergraduate and master's degrees in the United States, I returned home to Puerto Rico to study law and then litigated in Puerto Rico for more than 10 years. I enjoyed it. I certainly had frustrations with the legal system's lack of agility, and the inequities I saw in health care were also present in the legal system. The privileged and wealthy still had an upper hand. However, I found partnering with my clients—to help them get compensation and move from slum-like apartments to better housing, leave abusive relationships, get reinstated to jobs they had been unlawfully dismissed from because of their political affiliation, or make sure that people in prison received adequate medical treatment—especially gratifying. I treasured the relationships I developed with my clients. What a privilege to be with them in their space of desperation and see them slowly move out of it!

"Have you lived with a schizophrenic person?"

As an administrator working in health care institutions and the insurance industry, I was in settings where people were sick and desperately trying to access service. Many times their lives depended on it. I always chose the side of the patient and their families. I saw my role as making sure the system worked for them.

My legal practice was also centered around advocating for those who are often easily forgotten. More than half my legal practice focused on providing legal services of a noncriminal nature for persons involuntarily or voluntarily confined in custodial, correctional, or penal institutions and institutions for the mentally ill or mentally disabled. This was the population I chose to serve. It was my calling, and I have always felt joy in servicing those most in need.

If you are attentive to your surroundings and you work in health care and the legal system, you cannot help but be changed by what you see and learn. As an attorney and as an administrator, I usually entered the lives of those I served when they were at their lowest. They were angry, exhausted, confused, frustrated, fearful, vulnerable, and often desperate. They were entangled in a system where marginalization, unfairness, and structural violence (among many other types of violence) were normalized. By structural violence, I mean the processes and systems set up in our institutions that harm those who are supposed to be served or prevent them from accessing needed services (Galtung, 1990). Basically, if people were poor, minority, Black, LGBTQ+, or deemed different, their odds of successfully obtaining what they needed were significantly reduced.

I will always remember the day I met with the mother of a potential client in Puerto Rico. I was part of a team of lawyers working on a class action filed on behalf of patients who were institutionalized in a state psychiatric institution, and this woman represented a group of mothers who had organized to advocate for their mentally ill children. Her son was schizophrenic and institutionalized in the hospital.

We sat on a bench outside the hospital where I could feel the embrace of the hot Caribbean breeze. I asked fact-eliciting questions; she answered. After about a 20-minute exchange, I shared some possible plans of "attack" to expose the public hospital's substandard conditions. She looked into my eyes, placed her hand on my arm, and in a soft-spoken tone asked, "Have you lived with a schizophrenic person?"

I told her I had not.

She went on to share her experiences living with her son's schizophrenia and enlightened me about how my proposed legal strategies would lead to shutting down the hospital. "And then what?" she asked.

She had no other place where her son could receive treatment. I realized I had been listening to the facts—but not to her story. Facts told me what happened and when. Her story was richer. Her story painted a fuller picture of her situation: her context, her needs, the impact of schizophrenia on her life and her loved ones, her emotions, her relationships, who she was, and what she needed to heal and continue with her life. It was a humbling experience.

I thought the public psychiatric institution was reminiscent of Dante's circles of hell, but my potential client could not afford a private institution for her son. She was a poor working woman desperately trying to advocate for her son within health care and legal systems that had not been designed with her in mind and in many ways reinforced inequity. She could not spend months and even years meeting with attorneys, attending hearings, and waiting to have her day in court. She was not willing to have her soul crushed again, this time by the legal system.

I was struck by how the rules of engagement in the legal system were preventing this woman—and many other affected parties—from securing justice and a speedy solution to her legal problems and needs. I learned that day that listening to my clients' stories was just as important as fact-finding interviews. The fact-finding legal interview allowed me to build a better legal case. Listening to her story allowed me to establish a relationship and direct her toward places where some of her needs could be addressed.

The case lasted more than 20 years, and I had joined toward the end of the process. The leading and more senior lawyers changed their legal strategies, in part, as a result of the stories they were also hearing. From my perspective, three of the most significant changes were: 1) convincing the judge to hold status conference meetings at the psychiatric hospital instead of in court; 2) entering into a constructive dialogue with all the parties involved, especially government officials; and 3) considering system-wide issues in the health care state institutions, including those that were not part of the complaint, that needed to be addressed to provide redress to all the patients in the public psychiatric system. For example, overcrowding in the psychiatric hospital could not be solved unless outpatient psychiatric units were available to admit patients once they were discharged from the hospital. This was only possible thanks to the collaboration of all parties involved.

Like most things in life, my future client's predicament was not an "either-or" situation; it was a "yes, and" situation. She was on an uneven playing field. If I had known about conflict engagement processes at the time, I could have designed a process with my client to address some of her immediate needs while the legal system took its time vindicating her rights. Mediation is not a panacea. There would still be power imbalances between our client and government officials, but some of her needs could have been met sooner. We could have explored constructive ways of staying with those conflicts that could not be solved immediately (Mayer, 2008).

"You really should go. ADR is the future."

I crossed paths with ADR, specifically mediation, midway through my litigation years. A colleague told me about a mediation training in the Postal Service, which was launching its transformative mediation program in Puerto Rico. I was skeptical: how could we possibly achieve justice by "just talking?" But on the other hand, what if we could?

At the time the training started, in August 1998, I was swamped with legal work. Clients were back from their summer vacations and ready to reengage with their legal battles. My husband, a lawyer, suspecting I was going to bail out of the training, said, "You really should go. ADR is the future." He knew how busy my schedule was that week, but he also knew me well enough to know I would end up loving it. I did not know it then, but attending the workshop changed the course of my professional future. I also like to think it made me a better person, professional, friend, and colleague.

My introduction to mediation did not begin well. I knew about two-thirds of the trainees in the room. Most of them were lawyers. The trainers had set their agenda and structure for the next three days. Within the first two hours, we revolted. (I might have been one of the instigators.) We challenged the utility of the trainers' role plays, and we were adamant that their processes would not work. We had a visceral feeling that their model and the method of delivery needed to be adapted to our culture. We felt the agenda was constraining and culturally insensitive because it did not consider that as part of our learning process, we needed to spend time building and cultivating relationships among ourselves.

Our mini-insurgence had nothing to do with the trainers' experience and knowledge of the subject matter; they were impressive. And the trainers' reaction to our coup attempt was inspiring. They asked for feedback, called a break, met privately, and came back with a restructured agenda for the day and a promise to do the same for the next two days of the training. The trainers knew, like my mom way back when she decided to pull me out of school, that structures could be constraining and not conducive to learning. Unlike my mom, who did not expect the structure to change and therefore had to move me to a different school, the trainers viewed structure as much more malleable, something that could be modified to free us from our felt coercion.

My skepticism about mediation began to dwindle. I thought, "How cool is this! As a mediator I have the power to co-create with those in conflict a process that, while it may not guarantee a fair outcome, could allow for all voices to be heard in a fair way."

The workshop's lead trainer, Andrew Thomas, had a profound impact on my decision to get into the conflict engagement field. He modeled what he was teaching in a way I have seen few people do. Later, I had the privilege of co-leading a training with him.

Unlike the legal system, the mediation process provides opportunities to brainstorm, in a non-adversarial setting, about ways to improve clients' situation. In the case of the schizophrenic patient's mother, for example, mediation would have made thinking outside the box, and perhaps reaching an agreement that addressed system-wide challenges, possible. This possibility for systemic change becomes evident when we envision mediation as a social space embedded in a web of relationships that has the capacity to build and nurture relationships that have the potential for affecting societal change (Lederach, 2005).

And this change is possible when stories disrupt the *status quo* and create counter-narratives that eventually enter and transform the legal system to create systemic change (Font-Guzmán, 2019).

Such change was impossible for the patient's mother in the legal system not because she could not share her story—she had actually been voicing her concerns for a long time—but because others in positions to provide redress were not actually listening to that story. It suddenly struck me that advocating on someone's behalf at a trial was gratifying, but creating a safe space for someone to advocate for themselves and be listened to was exhilarating. As a mediator, the power to co-create a space that allows people to actually be heard and seen, to this day, is one of my main fascinations with mediation.

I went on to take many other workshops on diverse mediation models and dialogue processes and eventually obtained a PhD in conflict analysis and resolution from Nova Southeastern University. And that mother's story has accompanied me in every conflict intervention I have designed or led. Throughout my journey as a conflict specialist, I have never forgotten the importance of eliciting stories, understanding how they differ from facts, and being ready to listen.

I also strive to never let the conflict between parties distract me from the systemic power dynamics that negatively impact their situations outside the mediation. Like the mother of my potential client, they may be struggling with racism, misogyny, unfair housing regulations, poverty, or limited access to health care. Being aware of these dynamics allows me to have more empathy for the parties, consider the context in which their conflict is happening, effectively use the power of acknowledgment, and serve them better as they navigate through their conflict. At my mediation table, there is always time for these difficult conversations if parties wish to have them.

The Importance of Diverse Emerging Stories

When I joined the conflict resolution profession in the United States, however, I noticed that as an African American, Andrew Thomas, who had led my first training, was one of the few non-White professionals in the field. This saddened—and still saddens—me. The conflict field strives for openness, diverse ways of thinking, and social justice. Yet when I attend conferences and trainings, I see limited diversity among the scholars and practitioners in the conflict field. I fear that this lack of diversity and inclusion could lead our discipline toward a monolithic professional environment in which the discussion of different perspectives is stagnated, and I am hopeful that conflict practitioners and scholars will proactively seek more diversity. Slowly, but surely, I think, we are moving in the right direction.

My experiences in the Caribbean and Latin America showed me that the mediation models imported from the United States did not always fit those environments, a disconnect that flagged the lack of diversity in our field. Why would I expect US-centric processes, developed by people who were probably completely unaware of the cultural nuances of the Caribbean and Latin America, to be effective in those regions? Nonetheless, many of the US mediation models seemed to assume "universal truths" in terms of appropriate conflict intervention skills (Lederach, 1995).

One example of these "universal truths" in mediation training programs across the United States is the value of using "I statements," which are supposed to send a clear message of your needs in a non-threatening manner so that the other person will be more receptive to hearing what you are saying. In one training I co-led in Puerto Rico, a participant had great difficulty using "I statements," which she considered to be rude and confrontational, in addressing the person engaging in unwanted behavior. She experienced cognitive dissonance between what the statements were supposed to accomplish and what she was feeling. It turned out that within her cultural context, sharing a story was less confrontational and more effective. So we changed the exercise. We substituted "I statements" with storytelling. The trainee told about a time she had witnessed someone engaging in the unwanted behavior that she wanted the other person to change, and she talked about how the behavior had hurt the protagonist of her story. This took longer and was more indirect than any "I statement," but the trainee was heard, and the other person understood why changing the behavior was important.

As we debriefed about this trainee's experience, I remembered my own similar feelings in my first mediation training. My pushback, like hers, was not about the process itself or the trainers but about a clash of worldviews. My own view of how to interact in a conflict had made it difficult for me to consider new information and adapt, but from Andrew Thomas's modeling of careful consideration, improvisation, and the importance of recognizing and empowering trainees, I learned the importance of being flexible. We do not need to dismiss models that have been developed in other cultural contexts, I realized. We just need to adapt them.

Even with such understanding, however, I still experienced the potential effects of imperialistic Western models of conflict intervention years later, when I was invited by the US Department of State's Bureau of International Information Programs to offer a series of conflict engagement workshops in a Latin American country that was in political turmoil.

The atmosphere was highly polarized. The news media had reported that students on some university campuses were burning cars and throwing rocks, and I was asked to "mediate" among different student organizations. The program coordinator, an American who worked for a private US entity that was organizing the process, was my contact person but did not participate in the conflict intervention process.

Intercultural differences were evident before I even met the parties. From my perspective, the coordinator was excessively concerned with security and had inappropriately labeled the students as violent, volatile, and dangerous. The student leaders, the coordinator said, were "resisting" authority, and we needed to preserve "democracy" and "peace," terms I considered value-laden. The coordinator was afraid that if "order" were not "imposed" through strict guidelines, such as who was allowed to talk when, the mediation would be chaotic (as if there were any other kind).

In my frame, the students were being proactive and passionate about their interests. Through my cultural lens, the students' activist behavior was an integral part of being a university student. I had been there and done that. When problems arise, you discuss them in a passionate way, not taking turns to talk. Reflecting on my reaction and giving the coordinator the benefit of the doubt, perhaps she was not cold and emotionless; perhaps she was just operating from a worldview that was very different from mine. I suspect she meant well, but she had some deep misunderstandings about how to design a conflict intervention or process and assumed that I would set specific goals at the start, without first finding out what the parties wanted and needed.

My praxis was different. I knew that the context in which a conflict takes place matters. I did not endorse violence, but I decided to follow my intuition rather than the coordinator's suggestions for "keeping order" and her other rules, which felt controlling, dictatorial, and arrogant.

The meeting with the students took place in a house in the Andean mountains. We ate lasagna together and shared stories about who we were and where we came from. I talked about what growing up in Puerto Rico had been like, and about my culture and political challenges. The students talked about growing up in their country, their culture and their political challenges. We shared what mattered in our lives. We connected through our similarities and our differences.

Because I wanted to be in a mental space that would allow me to flex my conflict intervention style based on what the student leaders needed, I was especially interested in participants' interactions with each other. As it turned out, they did not need mediation; they needed a dialogue. This was not the type of conflict that would be resolved, but it could be de-escalated.

The disputes among the student organizations, I found, were not the root of the conflict; they were symptomatic of deeper problems. This was a socio-political intractable conflict that was riddled with decades of inequities, unfairness, injustices, physical and emotional violence, and hostilities. In fact, I remember thinking that only through constructive conflict would real change happen. I realized through our conversations that what they needed was not to problem-solve but to have a safe space to name the problems, regroup, and brainstorm ways of escalating conflict constructively and peacefully (Kriesberg, 2003). As a result of this conversation, relationships strengthened and new stories could emerge. Eventually, these conversations could lead to the systemic changes the students were demanding. Sometimes all you can do is support people so they can constructively stay with conflict—for the time being—and this is fine (Mayer, 2008). And that is what we did as we ate lasagna and enjoyed the local beer.

This experience taught me that mediation has its limits and every problem cannot (and should not) be solved in the moment. Sometimes our role as conflict practitioners is to support those who are navigating life's mysteries. This was also a reminder that I am at the service of those who ask for my help, not vice versa. I refused to use my conflict intervenor role to deprive the parties of self-determination.

As a Puerto Rican, I am intimately familiar with the painful reality of colonialism and how it can lead to erasing your agency (or self-determination) and sense of identity. I have experienced what it is like to have limited or no participation in the rules and laws that govern you (Font-Guzmán, 2015). I was not about to allow this to happen in my conflict intervention process. The student representatives would have meaningful participation in determining how they wished to proceed, be heard, and be listened to. We could then jointly agree on the design of the process or I could gracefully bow out if I found it was unacceptable. We did design a process, and although we didn't resolve all the students' concerns, we made a significant start.

"If I got the job, would you move to Omaha with me?"

It was Friday evening, and I was crossing out a few items on my to-do list before leaving the office when I received an email. A friend who was doing a one-year fellowship at Creighton University in Omaha, Nebraska, had sent a link to a job announcement for the position of associate director of the newly established Werner Institute for Negotiation and Dispute Resolution at the Creighton School of Law. I was not looking for a job. My husband and I were doing well in our litigation, mediation, facilitation, and training practice. Yet an inner voice said, why not?

I shared the email with my husband, prefacing it with: "This looks interesting. If I were to apply and get the job, would you move to Omaha with me?" After reading it, he said, "Yes, why not? Where is Omaha?"

And thus another journey began. I arrived at Creighton University in February 2006 eager to start my new job, although once again I found myself, a Puerto Rican woman, in a faculty where women and underrepresented groups were glaringly absent, on an uneven playing field.

From conversations with faculty administrators I learned that the School of Law was transitioning toward the twenty-first century and that the institute was a crucial element of this effort, intended to develop an innovative and interdisciplinary curriculum that would be available to graduate and law students.

What I saw as simple initiatives to advance the field and form better lawyers turned into insurmountable tasks. The law faculty consistently voted against cross-listing cutting-edge negotiation and conflict resolution (NCR) courses that addressed issues of culture, gender, power inequities, and social justice (Mirkay and Strand, 2019). Most law faculty saw conflict resolution skills and processes with a social justice focus as not "real law." The NCR courses were full, but not with law students.

I chose to focus on the good energy of the amazing colleagues I was collaborating with in the institute and the few allies I had among the School of Law faculty and the university at large. I had already learned to work around the system, within the system, and, when appropriate, leave the system. I eventually became the director of the institute and the NCR program. As director, with support from faculty and administrators outside the law school, I was able to sustain and expand our interdisciplinary master's and certificate program and to partner with other disciplines across campus that welcomed the expertise of the NCR faculty.

After 11 years in the School of Law, the provost moved the NCR program to the department of Interdisciplinary Studies in the Graduate School, where I continued to direct the program. It had turned out that the NCR program's progressive and interdisciplinary approach grounded in social justice were not a good fit for Creighton's School of Law; disrupting the *status quo* was terrifying for most members of the law faculty. Like that morning when my mother pulled me out of school, it was time to find another system and continue to do the work.

My experiences at Creighton reminded me that systems thinking and nurturing authentic relationships are essential to advancing our field. By listening, connecting, being curious, and exploring how the NCR program could fit and interconnect with other programs, departments, and schools at Creighton University, I found a way to move the program forward. But this could not have been done alone; relationships with faculty in the NCR program, across campus, and with the community were essential.

Like many other colleagues, I am concerned about the sustainability and development of innovative dispute resolution and conflict engagement programs in law schools and higher education. In the current political and social environment, academic institutions have a responsibility to change the world for the better. As I write this chapter, I often feel that we are failing law students by promoting a narrow view of the law. Law schools and academic institutions should increase conflict engagement courses in their curricula, provide tenured positions in dispute and conflict resolution, and hire more tenured faculty from underrepresented groups.

Looking Ahead

Our field has come far, but it can go much further. When I look ahead, many big questions come to mind, ones that I think can elicit new stories.

What if:
- We bring more underrepresented groups and more diversity into the field? (Expressed another way, what if we start seeing who is not in—and who *should* be in—our field? What if we look at who is in our field but feels under threat of becoming invisible? What if we reflect on the conditions that have led to repeatedly hearing the same voices?)
- We stop using disempowering language (such as "helping parties") and begin to use empowering language (such as "being of service" to parties)?
- We become less concerned with neutrality and more concerned with solidarity?
- We focus more on equity and less on equality?
- We more actively engage with socio-political conflicts?

For now, my story comes to an end. Or maybe it is more of a pause? As I think about all that our field can accomplish, I return to what I have learned, from my own mother, from the mother of the schizophrenic patient, from my first mediation trainer, and from many others: the playing field is rarely level, and taking a stand at the right time, especially when systems of domination are hurting people, is crucial.

Everyone has an important story, and if you really listen with understanding, curiosity, and creativity, you can design conflict engagement processes that allow people to navigate (and possibly disrupt) systems of domination so that they can find solutions that meet their needs and recognize their individual dignity. Perhaps most important:

we are all the sum of our own cultures, world views, and experiences.

References

Font-Guzmán, J. N. 2019. "'For Whom the Bell Tolls' in the Legal System: Access to Justice and Conflict Engagement." *Creighton Journal of Interdisciplinary Leadership* 5(1): 20-24.

Font-Guzmán, J. N. 2015. *Experiencing Puerto Rican Citizenship and Cultural Nationalism*. New York: Palgrave Macmillan.

Galtung, J. 1990. "Cultural Violence." *Journal of Peace Research* 27(3): 291-305.

Kriesberg, L. 2003. *Constructive Conflicts: From Escalation to Resolution*, 2nd ed. Baltimore, MD: Rowman & Littlefield Publishers, Inc.

Kritek, P. 2002. *Negotiating at an Uneven Table: Developing Moral Courage in Resolving Our Conflicts*. San Francisco, CA: Jossey-Bass Inc.

Lederach, J. P. 2005. *The Moral Imagination: The Art and Soul of Building Peace*. New York, NY: Oxford University Press.

Lederach, J. P. 1995. *Preparing for Peace: Conflict Transformation Across Cultures*. Syracuse, NY: Syracuse University Press.

Mayer, B. 2008. *Staying with Conflict: A Strategic Approach to Ongoing Disputes*. San Francisco, CA: Jossey-Bass Inc.

Mirkay, N. and P. J. Strand. 2019. "Disruptive Leadership in Legal Education." *Richmond Public Interest Law Review* 22(3): 364-378.

16

The Accidental Ombudsman

By Howard Gadlin

◆

"I want to free my music from my memory and taste and from my likes and dislikes so that my music, instead of saying something that I have to say or expresses me, changes me."
— *John Cage*

Howard Gadlin retired in 2015 after 17 years as ombudsman and director of the Center for Cooperative Resolution at the National Institutes of Health, where he developed new approaches to addressing and preventing conflicts among scientists. In establishing the Gadlin Lecture Series in his honor, NIH officials noted Gadlin's "big-picture approach" to ombuds work and said the lectures will "embody his ongoing commitment to scholarship, intellectual curiosity, creative problem-solving, and values of fairness and respect." From 1992 through 1998, he was university ombudsperson and adjunct professor of education at the University of California at Los Angeles, where he was also director of the UCLA Conflict Mediation Program and co-director of the Center for the Study and Resolution of Interethnic/Interracial Conflict. While in Los Angeles, he also served as consulting ombudsman to the Los Angeles County Museum of Art. Before moving to Los Angeles, Gadlin was ombuds and professor of psychology at the University of Massachusetts at Amherst. Gadlin is past president of the University and College Ombuds Association and of The Ombudsman Association and past chair of the Coalition of Federal Ombudsman. An experienced mediator, trainer, and consultant, he has many years' experience working with conflicts related to race, ethnicity, and gender, including sexual harassment, and is often called in as a consultant or mediator in "intractable" disputes. With colleagues he has written *Collaboration and Team Science: A Field Guide* (2nd ed., 2018), "The Welcome Letter: A Useful Tool for Laboratories and Teams," and "Mediating Among Scientists: A Mental Model of Expert Practice." He is the author of "Conflict Resolution, Cultural Differences, and the Culture of Racism," "Mediating Sexual Harassment," and "The Activist Ombudsman."

Accident and coincidence play a bigger role in our lives than we sometimes like to admit. I recently retired after 35 years as an ombudsman, first in universities and then at the National Institutes of Health.

I never intended to become an ombudsman.

In the fall of 1982, I was a professor of psychology at the University of Massachusetts at Amherst. I was an activist, more often involved in generating conflicts than resolving them. Being a professor had been my goal ever since my college days, even before I decided to major in psychology. It was my dream job, and I loved it. So when the chancellor asked me to take on the job of ombudsman, a two-thirds-time position, I was a little apprehensive. And I never expected it to be a life-transforming experience.

I grew up in a home that had only six books. My father, a salesman with a touch of Willy Loman (minus the infidelity) in him, grew up in the Depression. He dropped out of high school to help his family and never went back. Along with his two brothers, he made up the name Gadlin to replace Gadolowitz, which itself was an immigration officer's transliteration of Gedelowicz, to sound more American (read: less Jewish). My mother, who did not enter the world of work until my younger sister went to high school, had been abandoned as a child by her mother, who ran away with the milkman. At our apartment in Brooklyn and then Queens, she gave her children the attention and love she never received. She was very astute interpersonally, in the way only someone who has been hurt and insecure at the deepest level can be, so it was no surprise that I wound up in psychology.

I had a happy childhood, but I couldn't wait to leave home. My parents were somewhere between apolitical and vaguely liberal, but ever since Jackie Robinson joined my team, the Brooklyn Dodgers, I had followed stories about desegregation. A civil rights movement was underway.

Concern about the threat of nuclear war was growing. I wasn't content to be content. I wanted engagement and stimulation.

At Queens College, I leapt into my new life. In addition to taking classes, I worked on the student newspaper and was politically active. By the age of 26, I had my PhD and first job, as an assistant professor at the University of Illinois at Chicago Circle (now the University of Illinois at Chicago). In the late 1960s, Chicago was a great place to be an activist academic. Like many in my cohort, I was deeply involved in both teaching and turmoil. The turmoil even reached into my young family. With friends, we started a politically inspired commune where we wrestled with issues about money, child-rearing and discipline, sexuality and feminism. The friendships survived. The marriage did not.

In 1969, toward the end of my third year in Chicago, I was recruited to UMass. My start was not a quiet one.

In my first semester I helped organize and spearhead a challenge to Hubert Humphrey, who was scheduled to speak at the university. Hoping to undercut a possible disruption of his speech, Humphrey, who was preparing to run for president but was also teaching at a small college in Minnesota, had agreed in advance to answer questions about his political positions before delivering his prepared remarks. But by the time he walked onto the stage, the students were quite raucous, and many were shouting critical comments.

Trying to warm up the crowd, Humphrey remarked that he was a professor now and (condescendingly) reminded the audience that in the academic world, arguments are not settled by decibel level. After he quite successfully parried critical questions from three or four students, the energy in the small arena where he was talking subsided.

At that point, I took the microphone and said (self-righteously) with a smile, "Professor Humphrey, Professor Gadlin here."

Humphrey smiled back at me.

"I agree about the decibel level," I said, "but there is another level about which I am concerned, and that is the bullshit level." The audience went wild. Humphrey's smile disappeared.

I went on to give a brief but pointed critique of some of Hubert Humphrey's past political actions and positions. When a graduate student asked some other pointed questions, the audience erupted in cheers. Humphrey left the stage.

Those of us who had decided to challenge Humphrey had wanted to get him to answer questions about his political actions; we never intended to keep him from speaking. So I was surprised—and a bit scared—about the possible consequences for my job. The university administration was embarrassed and angry, a faculty senate committee was set up to investigate, and some state legislators called for me to be fired, but I was not punished. Although worried, in an odd way I felt that my credentials as a radical had been validated.

More was to come. The spring semester of 1970 was marked by increased protests against the war in Vietnam, and on April 30, after President Richard Nixon announced the invasion of Cambodia, student strikes erupted on more than 700 college campuses. Five days later, National Guard soldiers killed four protesting students at Kent State University in Ohio, and then, on May 15, police killed two students at Jackson State College in Mississippi. At UMass, the reaction was a volatile mixture of fear and anger. Some students and faculty wanted to cancel a strike we had planned, fearful that they, too, might be shot. Others thought we couldn't back down and had to proceed with the strike. Some students called for more militant actions. The university administration wanted the strike plans to dissolve. The student organizing committee, overwhelmed and unable to manage or resolve the competing factions, turned to the faculty advisory committee that I had organized with some colleagues.

I was asked to take over as chair of the strike committee. Together with the student leadership I developed a proposal designed to keep the strike going but also ensure that there would be no violence. At a massive outdoor rally, I asked for a pledge of nonviolence from the strikers and a commitment from the administration to restrain the campus police. The strike committee even asked that the administration let the strikers take responsibility for policing the campus.

The administration agreed, and we established a volunteer peace-keeping group. The pledge of non-violence was overwhelmingly supported, and the subset of students who had wanted to stop the strike continued their participation. Immediately after the rally, however, I learned that a small group of graduate students were planning to bomb the ROTC building—an action that surely would have been disastrous, both for the damage it would cause and its effect on the fragile agreements.

Through my contacts with other graduate students, two of the student strike leaders and I were able to meet with the group that was planning the bombing. At 2 am, after four hours of discussion and negotiation, they agreed not to go ahead. The strike continued through the end of the semester. There was no violence.

Sometime that year I was visited by Ellsworth "Dutch" Bernard, an English professor who had been appointed as the first ombudsman at UMass. I had never heard the term "ombudsman," and although I found Dutch quite engaging and well-intentioned, I remember being quite skeptical of the role, which I suspected was a way of coopting protest. I dismissed him as just another liberal academic and continued along my career path.

Twelve years later, in 1982, I was appointed ombudsman at UMass. I later learned that two factors had contributed significantly to making officials want me in the job: they believed that my history as an activist meant that I was not afraid to stand up to power and would not be intimidated by the university administration, and although I had never spoken with anyone other than the strike leaders about the 1970 negotiations with the would-be bombers, administrators had learned of my role. I might not have thought of myself as a conflict resolver, but others did. When I became ombuds, Dutch, who had retired in 1973, was one of the first people to visit me—not to ask for help but to offer support. We became good friends.

Serving as Ombudsman

Even though I had training in psychotherapy and experience in running T groups,[1] I was not really prepared for my new position.

I still recall the first time I met with an unhappy employee and his supervisor, hoping to help them resolve their differences regarding the supervisor's evaluation of the employee's performance. I felt as if I had been pulled into a giant industrial vacuum cleaner and then expelled, covered with dirt, through its exhaust.

Luckily the previous ombuds, my friend Janet Rifkin, referred me to Albie Davis, who was the queen of community mediation in Massachusetts at that time. I enrolled in one of her mediation training sessions and returned to campus a week later, warily ready to test my newly acquired skills. The following week I had my chance.

My first mediation was a student-faculty sexual harassment case. The hapless faculty member could not tell the difference between a student's enthused interest in her teacher's subject matter and his own infatuation with the young woman who actually paid attention to what he was saying. In a marathon session, we talked our way to an agreement in which, among other things, the faculty member apologized to the student and promised never to do again what he had denied having done in the first place. He even agreed to have a copy of the mediation agreement kept in a confidential file with the *proviso* that if he were ever again accused of sexual harassment, the file would be forwarded to his dean.

That mediation session was a pivotal experience for me. First off, I was excited about mediation. I sought out additional trainings and joined organizations that put me in contact with other practitioners and researchers in what was then known as alternative dispute resolution. After I got more experience, with lawyer colleague Nancy Braxton, I developed a divorce and family mediation practice. I wanted to work with as many different types of conflict as possible.

Attending meetings with mediators and ombuds was a revelation. Unlike status-conscious academics, with their barely hidden competitive undercurrents, people at ADR meetings were supportive and generous about sharing knowledge and techniques. These were cooperative competitors with a shared enthusiasm for the field they were building, brought together by the feeling that they were doing something valuable and new (or at least new to us). More enduring friendships emerged from those gatherings than I can enumerate.

In addition to introducing me to new colleagues, my entry into this field shook up my thinking; it forced me to rethink my ideas about how to bring about change. Until my appointment as ombudsman, I had kept up my activism, which still seemed to be the only way to produce significant change. Now that I was in the role of a neutral, I realized that I could also contribute to change. But it was more than that. As I met with a wide range of people, I was learning that for many folks, being treated respectfully and being heard were often even more important than getting the outcome they thought they wanted.

At the same time, that first mediation session was the beginning of an upheaval in my understanding of campus power dynamics and the role of faculty. As a faculty member, I had always taken it for granted that professors were widely respected and admired, but that assumption was quickly dismantled by those who came to talk with me. It was shocking to hear how many staff members felt insulted by the way faculty interacted with them; surprising to learn how many students felt mistreated by their teachers; dismaying to learn about the array of conflicts, from trivial to substantive, among faculty or faculty and administration. Like many academics, I had always valued scholarly intelligence and intellectual achievement, but now I was learning how often very smart people could be really dumb, not to mention cruel and insensitive.

By far the most dramatic change in my thinking came from listening to stories of sexual harassment from students, staff, and women faculty. Up until then I had an almost romanticized view of sexual relations among faculty and students. For me, such relationships were a logical extension of changing sexual mores, the loosening of restrictions on sexual expression and freedom, and an acknowledgment of sensuality as a part of human interaction. Now, hearing these stories of predation and exploitation, listening as (mostly) women described their deep disappointment when they realized that their mentor's interest in them was more sexual than intellectual, I was forced to rethink my own history over the previous decade.

If I could have, I would have sent out recall notices on many of my past relationships.

Mediating sexual harassment became an area of specialization, both as a way of making it safer for women to come forward at a time when most universities lacked effective or trusted policies or procedures and as a way of better understanding the dynamics of sexual harassment. I wrote papers and received invitations to give sexual harassment workshops around North America, including York University in Toronto, where I gave a two-day workshop and then, because of complications in my travel arrangements, stayed the weekend in Toronto and hung out with Brenda Hanning, one of the workshop organizers. One and a half years later, we were married.

My personal life wasn't the only thing that was changed by my focus on sexual harassment. Working with sexual harassment cases also forced me to appreciate more fully the second dimension of an organizational ombuds' responsibility—to identify problematic systemic factors in the organization. While mediators work from case to case, ombuds have to understand cases in the context of the larger organization in which they develop. This approach requires more than just keeping track of the frequency with which particular issues recur in an organization and reporting upward to leadership. Sexual harassment can't be reduced, or even eliminated, merely by identifying harassers and taking disciplinary or corrective actions. Fundamental aspects of an organization's climate and culture, as well as its procedures and processes for addressing grievances and conflicts, can create the conditions in which harassment occurs and is allowed to flourish, unchecked.

Trying to make sense of harassment, I began to realize that when working with people in conflict I had placed too much emphasis on personal traits and interpersonal dynamics. The dramatic nature of these dynamics in any particular mediation works mightily against viewing that conflict through a wider lens—one in which social forces give shape and meaning to these psychological factors. Although people experience and understand conflicts in personalized ways, they are often unaware of the contextual factors that elicit or exacerbate those conflicts. Now, in addition to attending to individual disputants, I was looking to understand how each dispute reflected systemic factors: features of the organizational culture, roles, policy, rules, or procedures that elicit, sustain, or exacerbate tensions, animosities, and miscommunications among the members of the organization.

An ombuds is well situated to see these systemic factors. Hearing many stories about certain recurring experiences in an organization—for example, bullying or sexual harassment—the ombuds can look beyond the idiosyncratic features of each instance and discern commonalities and patterns among these differences. With this information, the ombuds can help leaders understand the nature of a systemic problem and help them conceptualize the steps to be taken to ameliorate the problem. It is in this way that an ombuds can contribute to social change within an organization. Intellectually, this insight became the most exciting aspect of ombuds work for me.

Working from this vantage point and borrowing from my training in family therapy and systems theory, I listened in a different way to the stories people told me. I asked them different questions, questions that asked the disputants to reflect more on their interactions and the circumstances in which their conflict flared than on their individual perspectives.

I recall one situation in which IT management referred two high-level employees, team leaders in a division that had five highly interdependent teams, to me. These two employees argued regularly at team meetings, and because they differed in both gender and religion, management assumed that those differences were the basis of their recurring conflicts. But I noticed something interesting: although the two individuals did not seem to like each other, when we worked together, neither one ever mentioned gender or religion.

After hearing their accounts, I asked each one to describe the sorts of situations where they most often clashed. It turned out that at meetings, the woman was critical of the quality and timeliness of the division's output, and the man was defensive, both of the team and of his group's contributions. I then asked when and how often the five division leaders and their director met to evaluate their team's performance. The answer? Never. No time was set aside to reflect on their work process or output.

I noted that when a work group fails to establish norms for collective reflection and evaluation, that function is taken up along the fault lines of personal styles: one team lead was consistently critical, the other was consistently defensive. As we spoke, the two team leaders recognized that they had taken on themselves responsibilities that properly belonged to the division. They realized that each had interpreted in personal terms what was primarily a consequence of the dysfunction in their division. By the conclusion of our session, the two agreed to go together to the director and ask that the division establish processes for team self-reflection. The director, unprepared for the two of them cooperating on a proposal for how the division functioned, readily assented. This shift led to a new framework for communications and group self-assessment at division meetings. Not only were there fewer conflicts between the two with whom I had worked, but the division meetings were more energized and more productive.

Although I was not aware of it at the time, an interesting convergence between my ombuds musings about the functions of conflict and my scholarly work was developing. Over the years I had become interested in the social history of psychology—examining the role of psychological ideas and practices in terms of the social structures and processes in which they are embedded and to which they contribute. So at the same time that I was asking myself, the ombuds, "what purposes do conflicts play in organizations and the larger society?" I was asking myself, the psychology professor, "what purposes do psychological theories and practices play in the larger society?"

Ironically, putting conflict in a broader context by reflecting on the personal and social functions of conflict deepened and shifted my appreciation of the individual psychological needs that are served by conflict. Sigmund Freud once wrote:

> My emotional life has always insisted that I should have an intimate friend and a hated enemy. I have always been able to provide myself afresh with both, and it has not infrequently happened that the ideal situation of childhood has been so completely reproduced that friend and enemy have come together in a single individual—though not, of course, both at once or with constant oscillations, as may have been the case in early childhood. (Freud, 1966: 451)

In my early years as an ombuds and mediator I saw conflicts primarily as problems to be overcome, problems for the individuals who were caught up in them, and problems for the organizations in which conflicts occur. Later, I came to realize that conflicts often also satisfy peoples' needs. A mediator or ombuds can't "take away" people's conflicts without giving them, or helping them get, something else in exchange, something that in some way addresses the same needs that the dispute did. With the most intractable conflicts, a dispute taps into some aspect of the disputant's identity. When that happens, the possibility of resolving a conflict also threatens to alter the person's sense of who they are. In my divorce mediation practice, I noticed that often as a divorcing couple came closer to working out a mutually satisfactory settlement, one or the other of the partners would raise new issues. It was as if coming to agreement threatened their identity as people whose incompatibility could be resolved only by divorce.

Around this time, somewhere in the middle of my third two-year term as ombuds at UMass, I also realized that *my* identity had been changed by this work. Ombuds wasn't just a service I provided or a role I was playing; it provided levels of satisfaction that being a faculty member or even an activist did not. Being an ombuds required more than intellectual engagement—and required it with a wider range of people—than being a professor. And as ombuds, I was in a position to act on my commitments to fairness and equality.

Luckily, I had a sabbatical coming. I had encountered several people from the Hewlett Foundation-supported University of Hawaiʻi conflict resolution program at a meeting of the Society of Professionals in Dispute Resolution, and the prospect of learning from and working with them was more than enticing, so I set off for Honolulu. Although my mornings were spent working on a book, the rest of the time I was free to connect with Peter Adler, Neal Milner, David Chandler, John Barkai, and their colleagues. Participating in their network also established a framework of informal consultation essential to an ombuds, which is often a solitary role. That sabbatical reinforced my feeling that it was time to escape my life as a psychology professor.

It was also the beginning of another set of lasting friendships.

In 1991, toward the end of my fifth term as UMass ombudsman, I was offered the ombudsman position at UCLA, replacing Don Hartsock, who had established the office in 1969. I'm one of those New Yorkers who has always been drawn to California, and UCLA was appealing because it was both a public university and a first-rate school. But there was a catch: I was a tenured full professor at UMass, and at UCLA they believed that neutrality and independence required that the ombudsman not be a regular faculty member. I disagreed. I had always felt that the security of tenure protected my independence as an ombuds, but I knew that to accept the UCLA job, I would have to give up my professorship.

I gave up the golden handcuffs and moved to LA. There were many differences between life in a small western Massachusetts college town and a meandering city like Los Angeles. What most fascinated me were the demographic differences, both in the city and on campus. On the East Coast, Black-White relations and tensions shaped or permeated many of the major social issues. Not so in LA. Other ethnicities and communities—Asian and Latino—were equal partners with Blacks and Whites in defining the key parameters of inter-group politics and conflict. I found it fascinating and energizing. And of course, in addition to conflicts between individuals there was an abundance of inter-group conflict on campus and around the city, where some demographic aspect of identity itself was at the center.

One of the orienting principles of the ombuds role is to help people help themselves in addressing their problems and concerns. Since identity, directly or indirectly, was frequently identified as a key factor in many conflicts, I thought it would be helpful to develop a program in which participants would learn to better understand and resolve such disputes. Along with Vice Chancellor Raymund Paredes, then the highest-ranking Latino administrator at UCLA, I established a Campus Mediation Program oriented toward identity-based disputes. Each year we brought in a diverse group of 40 people: 30 students, undergrad and grad, and 10 staff and faculty (mostly staff). We held an initial three-day training in mediation basics (led by CDR Associates), followed by monthly sessions focused on specific aspects of mediation. In addition, students were required to take a full three-credit academic course on inter-group conflict. The course, which I taught along with guest lecturers from a large number of UCLA faculty with expertise in related areas, gave students an interdisciplinary perspective on identity and inter-group conflict. Staff and faculty members of the program were invited to sit in on the course as well.

The program clearly tapped into deeply felt needs of the participating students and many of the staff. The program office became a gathering place for the students, who took over governance of the program—planning programs, initiating additional trainings, inviting guest speakers, and most significantly, setting up a process for recruiting and selecting the next year's participants from the more than 100 applicants. The biggest impact on campus was the team of student and staff mediators who were available to mediate disputes on campus, with a particular interest in identity-based disputes, and to develop and present workshops in the residence halls. From my perspective, more noteworthy than their ability to mediate disputes was their increased ability to productively discuss and often mitigate identity-based differences, disagreements, conflicts, and tensions.

These discussions brought people closer together rather than driving them further apart, especially when we were called on to mediate a conflict. When I assigned a pair of mediators, I could confidently put together two students who in class had been engaged in a sort of grievance competition (whose identity group had it worse?) because I knew that having managed their own differences productively, they would be astute in working with disputing parties.

It's hard to describe how exciting our regular weekly case review discussions were. Making collective decisions and reviewing our cases, we felt as if we had moved into a level of honesty that was different from anything any of us had ever experienced. The program was one of the most satisfying experiences of my professional life.

As I had at UMass, I balanced my dispute resolution work with scholarly pursuits. With Carrie Menkel-Meadow, I established a Center for the Study and Resolution of Interethnic/Interracial Conflict, funded by the Hewlett Foundation. Working with colleagues both at UCLA and from around the country, we supported research and conferences related to identity-based conflicts.

In 1997, in my sixth year at UCLA, I was contacted by the National Institutes of Health and asked to participate in a speakers' series designed to help institute leaders compare mediation programs and ombuds offices, an effort spurred by a presidential order that all federal agencies should develop their own dispute resolution programs. As one of the speakers, I emphasized the ombuds' responsibility to identify and address systemic issues as well as handle individual cases. I guess I was persuasive because at the end of the process, I was invited to establish an ombudsman program at NIH.

The chance to create a new program, unencumbered by traditions and tailored to the specific needs of an enormous agency dedicated to conducting and supporting biomedical research, was enough to entice me and my wife to give up jobs we loved in a city we loved. We packed up again to embrace another period of personal and professional upheaval.

Starting an ombuds program from scratch is exciting, especially in an organization as vast and dynamic as the NIH was in those days. There are no precedents, no guidelines, and no former ombuds to tell you how they did it (or former users who tell you how *they* think the old ombuds did it). You are educating the organization about a role you have not yet created in an organization you do not yet understand. You want to help people explore and address the problems and conflicts that brought them to your office, but you do not yet have a deep feel for the issues they are confronting and the context that elicits and sustains those issues. Of course the profession has standards of practice and ethical guidelines, but these are usually too general and abstract to apply across the board to any one organization's idiosyncratic culture and dynamics.

Then there is the bureaucracy and the immense scale of the place. I have always worked at structured public universities, but that did little to prepare me for NIH, which comprises 27 separate institutes and centers of different biomedical disciplines, and for a bureaucracy as thick and challenging to navigate as the federal government's. Even more interesting is working in a research-based institution that is not also primarily an educational organization. As one NIH leader who had also just come from the academic world put it, "At least in the university, there is the civilizing influence of the responsibility for educating students." Not necessarily so at NIH.

As part of my efforts to make the office visible to the 20,000 people at NIH, I gave about 70 introductory talks in my first year, explaining the idea behind the ombuds function. When I was speaking to groups of scientists, who make up roughly half the population of NIH, I noticed mixed reactions when I spoke about mediation and related conflict resolution approaches. Although people were interested in techniques that might help resolve certain workplace disputes—such as dealing with poor performance or a problematic staff member, postdoc, or peer—achieving resolution was not especially relevant when it came to scientific disputes and disagreements. The more I worked with biomedical researchers and read the publications they willingly shared with me, the more I came to understand that researchers wanted help creating conditions in which disagreements could actually be productive.

Science progresses through conflict: contradictory research findings, competing theoretical perspectives, and different ideas about methodologies (in approaching a problem, applying statistics, or analyzing data) all inspire new research and advances. Differences were often the food that nurtured creativity.

The years that followed my arrival in 1998 were an amazing time to be at NIH. The institutes were in the early stages of a five-year period during which the budget was doubled, and the place buzzed with the excitement of scientists who had the resources to study the most important biomedical issues in their respective fields. For me, in addition to the contact high, there was the satisfaction of knowing that successfully mediating a dispute among scientists mattered to more than just the parties. If I was mediating conflicts within a vaccine development team, for example, resolution meant the team could focus on its work—and perhaps make a huge contribution to public health.

I was also fortunate because my early years at NIH coincided with a time when science itself was becoming increasingly collaborative and interdisciplinary. Scientists who had thrived on autonomy were gradually being required to learn about interdependence, joint ownership, and collective responsibility. They needed help in communicating across differences. Increasingly, my work with researchers involved engaging with scientific collaborators as they struggled to overcome barriers and challenges created by a wide range of conceptual, organizational, and personal differences.

Early on, I learned that scientists starting a research collaboration, carried away by their enthusiasm about the issues they were about to tackle, often failed to be explicit about what they expected from each other, especially in inter- or trans-disciplinary projects. They reminded me of the people I had worked with in divorce and family mediation who had fallen in love and tried to build a relationship around shared passion but hadn't been explicit about their expectations about marriage. Something similar happens with scientists who get excited about a research area and decide to work together: they spend lots of time thinking about the research but little about the vicissitudes of the research endeavor.

So I thought, why not create pre-nup agreements for scientists? I found a model in the partnering agreements that the Army Corps of Engineers was using in large-scale construction projects, which were getting a lot of attention at the time. Like those agreements, the pre-nups required clear statements about the goals of the project, decisions about who would do what, processes for determining authorship, delineation of domains of autonomy, and processes for resolving conflicts. My work on teams led me to L. Michelle Bennett, an NIH scientist who was promoting scientific teams and collaborations. Building on our shared interest, we wrote *Collaboration and Team Science: A Field Guide,* and soon we were writing papers and conducting workshops around North America.

My new-found appreciation of disagreement expanded my thinking about what we call the conflict resolution field. Before going to NIH, I was so accustomed to people asking for help resolving conflicts that I had taken to seeing conflict as an indicator that something was broken and needed to be fixed—rather than understood and even appreciated. But as Bernie Mayer pointed out in his wonderful book *Beyond Neutrality,* people in conflict don't necessarily want resolution.

That admonition, along with my understanding of the necessity of differing views in science, helped me see my work as helping people have better disagreements. It also helped me be more relaxed about resolution and more concerned about helping people understand how often they are so caught up in their conflict that they cannot understand how anyone could possibly see it in any way other than their own.

Early in my career, I thought I was working toward a conflict-free world. How wonderfully naïve. Now I find a certain pleasure in appreciating both the inevitability and desirability of conflict. When I was first learning about mediation, I remember being told that we, mediators, do not resolve disputes. The disputants do. I sort of understood that, but I had a hard time not seeing failure to reach agreement as a failure on my part. It took a career of more than 35 years to get to the point where I fully understood what I had been told at the outset: settlement is up to the parties. Unless people, at some level, actually want to settle, they can resist almost any techniques, or tricks, a mediator has to bring them together.

If we understand the circumstances in which differences lead to destructive and unproductive conflicts, we should be able to create circumstances in which those differences can be harnessed cooperatively. I am no longer naïve. I do not believe we will ever get to the point where differences will not be the basis for conflict. But we need not capitulate to destructive conflicts, and we can work toward expanding the sensibility needed for cooperative action.

This seems like a good project for retirement.

Notes

[1] A T-group or training group (sometimes also referred to as sensitivity-training group, human-relations training group, or encounter group) is a form of group training where participants, typically between eight and 15 people, learn about themselves and about small-group processes in general through their interaction with each other. They use feedback, problem-solving, and role-playing to gain insights into themselves, others, and groups.
See "T-groups," Wikipedia, last modified June 17, 2020, https://en.wikipedia.org/w/index.php?title=T-groups&action=history.

References

Freud, S. 1966. "The Interpretation of Dreams." In *The Basic Writings of Sigmund Freud*. Translated and edited by A. A. Brill, 181-468. New York: Random House.

17

A Mediator's Path

By David Hoffman

◆

Making My Way Toward Mediation

How, exactly, does one gets drawn into being a mediator—and why on earth would someone choose to be immersed in painful, messy, and sometimes intractable conflict as their day job?

David Hoffman is the founding member of Boston Law Collaborative, LLC, where he serves as a mediator, arbitrator, and Collaborative Law attorney. He also is the John H. Watson Jr. Lecturer on Law at Harvard Law School, where he teaches courses on mediation, Collaborative Law, legal ethics, and diversity. Hoffman was named Boston's "Lawyer of the Year" for 2020 in the field of mediation by the book *Best Lawyers in America* and *US News & World Report.* In 2014, the American College of Civil Trial Mediators gave Hoffman its Lifetime Achievement Award, and in 2015, the American Bar Association's Section of Dispute Resolution gave Hoffman its highest honor, the D'Alemberte-Raven Award. Hoffman's practice is focused on resolving conflict in business, family, and employment cases, and he has served as mediator and/or arbitrator in more than 2,000 commercial, family, employment, construction, personal injury, insurance, and other business cases. Hoffman has written or co-authored three books on the subject of dispute resolution: *Mediation: A Practice Guide for Mediators, Lawyers, and Other Professionals* (2013); *Bringing Peace into the Room: How the Personal Qualities of the Mediator Impact the Process of Conflict Resolution* (2003, with Daniel Bowling); and *Massachusetts Alternative Dispute Resolution* (1994, with David Matz). Hoffman is the past chair of the American Bar Association Section of Dispute Resolution, a founding member of the Massachusetts Collaborative Law Council, and a distinguished fellow of the International Academy of Mediators.

My first steps on the winding path to becoming a mediator began at the dinner table, in a comfortable upper-middle-class home in a mostly White, largely Jewish suburb of Baltimore, Maryland. Conflict at dinnertime bristled all around me. The quiet, not-so-subtle intensity of my father's criticism of my mother and everyone else at the table (including the maid who made our dinner and therefore made cameo appearances in the dining room) set my teeth on edge. Dad's habit—probably unconscious—of interrupting me and my brother made me feel unimportant, unworthy of adult attention. His criticism of our mother sometimes led to her retreating to their bedroom in tears. It was 1954, and I was 7—just becoming conscious of the negativity that filled the air after my father got home from work, often with a drink in hand.

As I think back to that time—and the way my father's stern demeanor and occasional anger-management problems sucked the oxygen out of our house from 5:30 p.m. until my bedtime—I can understand why I used to score high on "conflict avoidance" on the Thomas-Kilmann conflict mode test. More recently, I have asked other mediators about their scores on this test and found that a surprisingly high percentage of the people in our field have similar stories of family tensions that caused a part of them to recoil from conflict. Like moths drawn to the flame, however, those mediators and I found our way to a profession in which we plunge daily into the fire of conflict.

This no longer seems paradoxical or perverse to me. I think many people choose occupations that address core conflicts or traumas from their childhood. This is the narrative I hear, for example, from many psychotherapists. In my case, the conflicts were not always overt. There was simply an underlying thrum of unresolved tension in the house—the tension between my father's chronic irritability and incessant criticism on the one hand, and on the other, my mother's chronic sadness, which resulted in several psychiatric hospitalizations.

But those were not the only conflicts that surrounded me. The nightly TV news brought images of racial conflict: White police officers with dogs, billy clubs, and tear gas, trying to suppress the civil rights movement. My parents supported liberal causes, including racial integration, and yet I heard my father talk about people of color in derogatory Yiddish terms. My parents' espousing liberal views was not insincere. They sent my brother and me to public schools, which were integrated. As victims of anti-Semitism when they were growing up and with vivid memories of the Holocaust that was then only a decade behind us, my parents recognized that bigotry was both ubiquitous and dangerous. And yet we lived in a city that practiced apartheid. The African American maid who cooked and cleaned for us, Naomi Harris, lined up at the bus stop each evening—along with other African American women working in homes nearby—to return to the West Baltimore ghetto in which the residents were, as far as I could tell, exclusively Black.

Although I could not have given it a name then, I recognize in those early impressions of bigotry the beginnings of guilt and shame about the hypocrisy of growing up in a family that opposed race discrimination but enjoyed the material benefits that flowed from it. An important influence for me with regard to these tensions about race came from the rabbi in my synagogue, Abe Shusterman, who was one of the leaders of civil rights marches to desegregate Baltimore's public facilities. He became one of my heroes. In Sunday school he told us about the Holocaust and said we should tell our parents not to have Christmas trees, out of respect for our Jewish relatives who had died in Nazi concentration camps.

These two impulses—to honor the dead and fight for the living—set the tone at my synagogue, imprinting my friends and me with an indelible message: our highest purpose in life was *tikkun olam* (to heal the world). I found it unsurprising that a passionate commitment to healing the world was woven into the fabric of Judaism, since Jews are a tiny minority of the world's population that has generally been despised and persecuted throughout recorded history. My grandparents and their parents fled Eastern Europe because of pogroms, and I inherited from them the abiding fear (present more in the 1950s than now) that the Holocaust could happen again.

During my high school years, 1961 to 1965, my brother, my friends, and I marched in picket lines with CORE (the Congress of Racial Equality) on the streets on downtown Baltimore, trying to persuade department stores to hire African Americans. As we marched, we learned the songs of the civil rights movement from the Black people who led these protests. "We Shall Overcome," "We Shall Not Be Moved," and "Keep Your Eyes on the Prize" rocked my soul.

In 1965, as the Vietnam War heated up, I co-founded a small antiwar group, High School Students for Peace, and wrote editorials for my high school newspaper denouncing the war. As an undergraduate at Princeton in the late 1960s, I joined the radical group SDS (Students for a Democratic Society) and majored in political protest. I was motivated partly by idealism and partly by a rising tide of guilt over the comfort and privilege I had enjoyed my whole life. (I also minored in controlled substances, thinking that psychedelics would give me a direct experience of the divine, a spiritual yearning that was also a rising tide for me and many other hippies of that era.)

On graduation day 1970, I sat on the sidelines while my classmates got their diplomas. I, along with a handful of other Princeton students, had been disciplined for raucous heckling of a Nixon administration official, Walter Hickel, who had come to campus to speak, and therefore I had to wait an extra six months to officially graduate. But Cornell allowed me to begin doctoral studies in American Studies in the fall of 1970. I needed that degree to teach, which I had hoped to do at college campuses, which had become one of the epicenters of protest activities and the home of movements for peace, racial justice, and women's rights. Although my primary motivation was political, there was a part of me that felt drawn to teaching *per se*. But in 1973, when I completed my doctoral exams and started writing a dissertation that I never finished, the market for teachers in American Studies was nearly nonexistent. I put my academic career on hold because the only two entry-level teaching jobs in American Studies were in remote locations, my first marriage had ended, and I was co-parenting our daughter with my ex, who was not interested in leaving Ithaca, New York.

Instead I launched a woodworking business, using hand-me-down tools from my father, who was a dentist by day and skilled craftsman at night. For seven years, I grew my wood shop into a small cottage industry called "Knock on Wood," cranking out handmade toys, games, and kitchenwares while I waited for the market in American Studies to improve.

It never did, and so I toyed with the idea of making woodworking a lifetime career. I liked the authenticity of woodworking, but with each passing year I found myself yearning for an occupation that was both more political and more intellectual. Honest assessment also compelled me to admit that I was only a so-so woodworker—good enough to make a living, but not sufficiently skilled or passionate about it to feel that it was a calling, which is what I yearned for.

At this point, in the late 1970s, two paths beckoned: becoming a psychotherapist or going to law school. None of my studies to date pointed in either of these directions. But with the break-up of my first marriage, I became an avid consumer of psychotherapy, both individual and group, and I found it fascinating. And my interest in law was sparked by seeing the remarkable work of "movement" lawyers who were fighting for civil rights and civil liberties and challenging the authority of our courts to punish Vietnam protesters.

I wound up choosing law because it seemed to offer more opportunities to fight for social justice and a greater likelihood of making a decent living. I needed to make a financially sound choice because I had just remarried, and my second child (later followed by a third) was on his way. My wife, Beth Andrews, who (like me) grew up in an upper-middle-class home, was a potter, and we were both very committed to being financially independent of our parents. This was partly a matter of pride and partly an insecurity about money that Beth and I probably inherited from our parents, who grew up in the Great Depression.

Law lived up to its promise. After clerking for a year in 1984, I became a litigator at a downtown Boston law firm, Hill & Barlow, that paid me well and allowed me to do a lot of *pro bono* work. I represented an inmate on death row in Louisiana, and I handled ACLU cases involving free speech and privacy rights. But I became deeply disillusioned with the potential for litigation to make the world a better place. Courtroom battle was simply too blunt an instrument to remedy everyday injustices—too time-consuming, unnecessarily acrimonious, and too expensive for anyone but big corporations and wealthy individuals. One of my longest litigation cases, a nine-year court battle over the replacement of a six-acre roof at a gigantic grocery warehouse, pitted one huge company against another, and I could not help but notice how far afield such cases were from the impulse that had led me to law school.

So I called my law school advisor, Professor Frank Sander, for advice. I wanted to know how I might shift my practice from litigation to mediation and other forms of non-court dispute resolution. Frank was and still is widely known as one of the foremost leaders of the alternative dispute resolution movement, and he generously shared with me his views about how lawyers could gradually transition their practices from litigation toward ADR. He encouraged me to get trained as a mediator and arbitrator and form an ADR practice group within my firm, and I enthusiastically followed his advice. I joined every ADR referral panel that would have me: the American Arbitration Association, various federal and state court panels, and a community mediation program. I was lucky. The court panels were hungry for mediators, and, in the late 1980s and early 1990s, court dockets were more jammed than usual. I had an ever-increasing caseload of commercial and family mediations and a handful of arbitrations. I attended every ADR conference I could find. And I got trained in the practice of Collaborative Law, which essentially is representation of clients with a contractual commitment to negotiate in a cooperative manner and for the lawyers to withdraw from the case if it needs to go to court.

ADR provided me with something I had been missing for many years: a calling. Serving as a mediator, arbitrator, and Collaborative Law attorney was satisfying on so many levels. The pragmatic, problem-solving part of me found fertile ground for inventive, efficient solutions to vexing conflicts. The spiritual part of me found the practice of bringing peace into the room nourishing. The emotional, relational part of me (a valued inheritance from my mother) found the deep connection with people in mediation far more enriching than the intricacies of statutes, regulations, case law, and court rules.

Mediation and Social Justice

During my first few years as an ADR-focused lawyer, my main task was trying to become more proficient. I dove into the literature of negotiation and dispute resolution, seeking to understand the various theories that informed practice. I thought about the personal qualities that mediators can cultivate as an instrument for being peacemakers. I learned how to offer my clients a wide range of process options, following Frank Sander's famous recommendation of "fitting the forum to the fuss."

One of the connections for me between mediation and social justice was forged in the early 2000s. I had just returned to my old law firm from a six-month sabbatical hiking the Appalachian Trail end-to-end with my son (a wonderful adventure that provided much time for reflection), and I was considering the possibility of launching a new firm devoted to peacemaking. It took me a couple of years to find the courage to leave my role as a partner at Hill & Barlow, but I founded Boston Law Collaborative (BLC) in 2003 and never looked back. It was one the best decisions of my life.

Part of our mission at BLC is to influence the way the legal profession handles disputes by creating a practice model that empowers clients to resolve conflict more expeditiously and less expensively. By looking at our clients' problems in a more three-dimensional way—legal, financial, and emotional—we help them find solutions that are sometimes transformative, not only in emotionally complex family cases but also in dry business cases, where open communication and authentic connection often overcome seemingly intractable barriers to resolution.

However, even though practicing in a firm that was focused on peacemaking was fulfilling, something was missing—namely, getting more involved in addressing the persistent evils of discrimination that had drawn me to picket lines 40 years earlier. Then a door opened.

I had been teaching the mediation course at Harvard Law School—the same course that Frank Sander started in 1981 and taught until he retired in 2006. In November 2015, an anti-racism student group at HLS began putting black tape over the law school's shield because the shield's coat of arms was adopted from that of a slave-owning family, the Isaac Royall clan, that had donated the money for the first law professorship at Harvard. Then, in a move that shocked students, faculty, and staff at HLS, someone (or perhaps a group) removed the black tape from the shields all over campus and used it to deface the photographic portraits of all the African American professors at HLS. The tape was placed over their faces, which felt frightening—like a not-so-veiled threat. All this was taking place in the wake of increased police killings of Blacks such as Michael Brown in Ferguson, Missouri, in August 2014, and Freddie Gray in Baltimore in April 2015.

Students, particularly students of color, reacted to this assault by occupying the main classroom building at HLS for the next six months. My teaching assistant at that time, Rabiat Akande, a doctoral student from Nigeria, pointed out that we devoted a week of the mediation course each year to diversity issues and struggled to fit important material about race, class, gender, sexual orientation, and other matters into that one week, and she suggested that we expand the subject into its own separate course. I asked her to help me plan and teach the course, and she agreed. As a straight, White, cisgender male who is able-bodied and from an upper-middle-class background, I took this proposal for a new course, to be called Diversity and Dispute Resolution, to Dean Martha Minow with some trepidation. But the law school quickly approved the course.

Teaching this course, which I have been doing each January since 2017, has been one of the best learning experiences of my life. One reason it has been so valuable is that my students and I focus not just on understanding differences such as race, culture, class, gender, and sexual orientation, but also on the ways those differences affect the distribution of wealth and power in our society.

This focus on social justice informs the structure of the class itself. For example, my teaching assistant and I make sure that the voices of students with marginalized identities are heard at least as fully as everyone else. One technique for doing this is to ask the students to have preliminary discussions in small groups, with one student designated as the reporter to summarize the small group's views when the class reconvenes in a plenary session, and ask each small group to make sure that the reporter is someone who has had fewer reporting duties in previous classes than the others. This not only widens participation (by drawing out the introverts and moderating the participation of extroverts) but also creates a safer setting for students who are nervous about sharing their experiences and perspectives by allowing them to "test the waters" in a small-group setting.

Another tool that we use to create a safe space is an exercise on the first day of class called the "Social Identity Circle," in which the whole class stands in a large circle, facing each other. People take turns stepping into the middle of the circle and announcing some facet of their identity that is not obvious and inviting others to join them in the circle if they share that identity (for example, "please join me in the circle if you are an only child," or "please join me in the circle if you love to dance"). The purpose of this exercise is to get beyond the "single story" that we often have about each other initially based on our visible differences such as race, gender, age, and others. Chimamanda Ngozi Adichie's TED talk entitled "The Danger of a Single Story,"[1] which is assigned for the first day of the course, vividly illustrates this concept with her personal narratives.

The students who enroll in the Diversity and Dispute Resolution course come from a wide variety of backgrounds and bring many "intersectional" identities into the room, a term that refers to the various identities that any one person can have. I tell the students at the outset that, given all the privileges I have enjoyed (a friend once described me as having "won the intersectional lottery"), I come to the course as one of the learners. We put a lot of thought and effort into creating a supportive environment for all of us, myself included, to share our narratives and our experience of difference. And then we apply our insights about ourselves and others to the context of conflict, looking for strategies that enable us as dispute resolvers to work successfully with people who are different from us.

For me, one of the social justice dimensions of teaching this course stems from the idea that teaching and learning about diversity does not have to be the sole responsibility of people who already carry the extra burden of disparate treatment resulting from their identity, such as women, people of color, members of the LGBTQ community, and others. To be sure, an extra dose of humility and curiosity is needed when the professor has experienced few, if any, of the disadvantages that form the substance of the course.

In addition to teaching this course, I have recently teamed up with trainers—women, people of color, and members of the LGBTQ community—to bring workshops on diversity and implicit bias into the Boston community and beyond. (As I write this, COVID-19 has actually expanded the geographical reach of this work because of the increased use of video-conferencing.) I have discovered that the basic tools of mediation, such as active listening, eliciting people's narratives and underlying interests, and promoting understanding by distinguishing between intent and impact, can help people manage difficult conversations about difference.

I have always believed that we teach what we want to learn, and this maxim is certainly applicable to me in this area. One of the big lessons for me has been a deeper understanding that invidious distinctions based on difference—and the concept of difference itself—are a social construct. While certain kinds of difference may have a physical component—such as skin color or gender assigned at birth—the meaning we ascribe to those differences is socially constructed and therefore can be deconstructed. For example, students report being acutely aware of the hierarchies of power that exist within their own ethnic communities that look monolithic to outsiders (such as one Cambodian American student who reported on how she is often treated as "lower class" by Asian Americans whose ancestors come from Japan or Korea).

A second lesson is about privilege and intersectionality. The term "intersectionality" is generally used to describe the synergistic way that multiple disfavored identities (such as being both Black and a woman) substantially magnify the disadvantages faced by the people who have those identities. But the same phenomenon is true in reverse: being White, and a cisgender male, and upper-middle-class, and heterosexual substantially magnifies the privilege that any one of these characteristics provides.

A third lesson is that one of the most effective ways to counteract bias is to access the opposite feeling. There is a newly invented word to describe that feeling (i.e., positively inclined toward people who are different from us): "allophilia," coined by Professor Todd L. Pittinsky, in his excellent book *Us + Them: Tapping the Positive Power of Difference* (Pittinsky, 2012). Pittinsky was looking for a word that means the opposite of "discrimination," and such terms as "tolerance," "acceptance," even "fair treatment" didn't fit the bill. And so my goal, as a teacher—and also as a dispute resolver—is to help all of us access and deploy the allophilia that exists to one degree or another in all of us. In the classroom, one of our techniques has been to create opportunities for students to access and respectfully express their curiosity about each other's differences.

I believe there is enormous potential in fostering allophilia to help us all overcome the barriers of misunderstanding and mistrust in our society—barriers that stand in the way of achieving greater social justice. In addition, I believe that by training mediators and other dispute resolvers to work more skillfully with differences, we might expand the reach of mediation into communities, particularly communities of color and less affluent communities, where it is not widely used. In my view, one of the reasons that the ranks of mediators in the United States are predominately White and upper-middle-class is not lack of motivation to make our field more diverse but rather a lack of skill and clarity about how to build alliances across the gulfs of race, class, and other differences.

A few final words about teaching the Diversity and Dispute Resolution course: I don't think I would have found the courage to do it without the help of a small, longstanding support group of diverse mediators. We call ourselves the Three Guys, and I owe a huge debt of gratitude to the other two, Daniel Bowling and Homer La Rue, for educating me about my blind spots and expanding my experience of bridging differences with loving connection. We confer monthly, sometimes in person and sometimes by phone or video, to learn more about each other, ourselves, and our work. I have also learned a great deal from my adult children, whose political astuteness, passionate commitment to social justice, and willingness to show me where I am stuck in "old school" thinking has been a blessing. My wife, Leslie Warner, has also played a vital role in my education about diversity issues. I have been the beneficiary of her voracious reading about cultures other than our own and her keen attention to the news and social media sources of insight about injustices in our society.

Learning About What Makes People Tick

Although I chose law over psychotherapy as a profession, my interest in psychology, which stems in part from having family members who have struggled with mental health issues and from my own (ongoing) work with a psychotherapist, has been magnified by the practice of law. One of my first clients, who was going through a divorce, called me one day, upset about his bill. "Why are we litigating this divorce?" he asked. "We should just settle it." I told him I would be happy to hit the brakes on pretrial discovery and draft a settlement proposal. After I sent it to him, he called back: "Why are we being so reasonable?" he asked. "I want to fight this in court." The next week, he wanted to push for a settlement. I was baffled: why was he veering from guardrail to guardrail?

In my work as a mediator, I frequently encountered people experiencing deep ambivalence about settlement, and I wondered how I could help them reach an agreement that would not later be tainted by regret. I also encountered parties—and lawyers—who exhibited characteristics that psychotherapists would classify as pathological, such as narcissism, based on the diagnostic categories listed in the *Diagnostic and Statistical Manual of the American Psychiatric Association* (DSM).

As I thought about my docket of mediation cases, and how "difficult" many of the people in those cases were, I did some research and found that according to the National

Institute of Mental Health, 26.2 percent of the adult population of the United States has a diagnosable mental illness in any given calendar year. Why then, I wondered, am I seeing more than my share? If people with mental illness find themselves in conflicts more often than others (and one should not overlook the extent to which conflict exacerbates pre-existing vulnerability to mental illness), what do mediators need to know to help people feel empowered and safe in mediation?

I was married at the time to a therapist, Beth Andrews, who gave me an entry-level education about a new model of therapy called the Internal Family Systems (IFS) model. IFS was developed by a psychologist, Richard Schwartz, who noticed that his patients not only had different "parts" (e.g., a playful part and an industrious part) but that these various parts had family-like, and sometimes polarized, relationships with each other (Schwartz, 2001).

The IFS model was appealing for several reasons. First of all, it is intuitive: people often talk about having different parts ("a part of me wants to exercise, and another part wants more Netflix"). Second, it is non-pathologizing: there's nothing wrong with having multiple parts—we all do. It's also empowering: unlike the medical model, which relies on the power of the clinician to heal the patient, IFS teaches that patients already have the tools for their own healing, by bringing their parts into greater harmony and accessing curiosity about and compassion for all their parts.

When I began looking at my clients' various dysfunctions through the IFS lens, I began to see how IFS techniques could be useful not just for clinicians but also for mediators and lawyers. For example, the IFS model helps me understand my clients' ambivalence about settlement and their conflicting feelings about the people with whom they have disputes. With clients such as the man who vacillated between wanting to settle his divorce and wanting to fight, I now say something like the following: "It sounds like there's a part of you that wants to resolve this case and another part that wants to win." Such an intervention is not appropriate in every instance, but my experience has been that clients appreciate being seen fully, with all their complexity.

When I see parties in a mediation escalating their attacks and counterattacks, I now say something like: "I'm noticing that you each have a very forceful gladiator part that seems to be taking the lead in this discussion, which is feeling more and more like a battle. I wonder if you could each ask your respective gladiators to take a couple of steps back (they don't have to go away—they may want to keep an eye on what's happening here in case they're needed). You each also have some problem-solving parts. Perhaps you could each make some space for those parts at the table." In my experience, clients immediately understand the metaphor.

The IFS model posits that we not only have "parts" with their own complex internal relationships but we also have a core of energy called "Self," which is calm, curious, and compassionate. (In some religious traditions, this core is called "soul" or "spirit.") The goal of the IFS model is for people to be Self-led. Self energy is like the conductor in the orchestra. It does not play an instrument (the "parts" do that); instead, it coordinates the parts with the goal of playing harmoniously. For IFS clinicians, one of the most important techniques is helping clients "un-blend" from overactive parts (such as their inner "gladiators") so they can access their Self energy, which in turn can heal the wounded parts that the gladiators are trying to protect, by "witnessing" the pain of those wounded parts and giving them the experience of unconditional love and internal acceptance.

Using the IFS model has opened the door for me to have a deeper connection with my mediation and Collaborative Law clients, even the most difficult, because rather than "othering" them with a category (such as "narcissist"), I could recognize that they have "parts," just as I do. It was, and still is, a steep learning curve, but a highly useful one—a bit like learning to bat right-handed if you're a lefty. It requires using muscles that you already have but never used in that way before.

As I began to learn more about this model, Beth introduced me to Dick Schwartz, who graciously agreed to colead several workshops with me for mediators and lawyers. I have also added a discussion of IFS in all three of the courses that I teach at HLS, and my students have found the model to be tremendously useful in their understanding of how to resolve internal and external conflict.

I know there are many models of human psychology that mediators have found helpful, and I can make no larger claim for IFS than the fact that I have found it extraordinarily useful— not only in understanding, honoring, and helping clients manage their own complexity but in understanding, honoring, and managing my own. For example, in the past I have noticed a rising anger inside me when one of the parties in a mediation is being particularly stubborn or gratuitously adversarial. "Don't Mess Up My Mediation!" I hear an inner voice saying (I call this my DMMM part, for short), and I know that my irritation probably seeps out in various subtle ways that probably don't endear me to the "difficult" party. Now I can recognize my irritability as simply a part of me, one that we all have, and not a character flaw that would, if known to others, disqualify me from being a mediator. Also, the IFS model has helped me recognize that, when I find myself subtly—or not so subtly—"pushing" the parties in mediation toward a settlement, this impulse is just a part of me and that I also need to honor the part that wants those people to experience self-determination. And so, when I am feeling more Self-led, I try to help the parties access their own inner mediator (their Self energy) to guide them to a wise decision about resolution.

IFS has also helped me harmonize my professional work with a broader agenda of social justice. First, IFS is all about empowering people, which is a core component of a progressive social justice agenda. We can all be more effective in pursuing just goals when our parts are in alignment, and such alignment can help us overcome feelings of shame that may have been inflicted on us by bigoted assumptions and unjust treatment. Second, for those of us who experience guilt about the unearned privileges that we have enjoyed (e.g., simply by virtue of being White or male), the IFS model provides a means for healing the shame that those "parts" carry around with Self-led compassion and repurposing them to play a more constructive role in our internal system, such as being vigilant about the injustice in our society and more skillful in our attempts to redress it. Third, IFS provides valuable tools for understanding implicit bias—those unconscious attitudes and reactions based on race, gender, and other differences that have been instilled in us by messages we received as youngsters and cannot seem to shake, despite our conscious intention to be entirely unbiased. The IFS model helps us see that we all have bigoted "parts" that carry around these outdated and unwelcome images and stereotypes, and we also have idealistic parts that motivate us to pursue social justice.

Our Footprints in the Sand

As I enter my mid-70s, thoughts of mortality are increasingly unavoidable. For so many of us in the field of dispute resolution, myself included, our choice of vocation has been fortuitous. In part, this is because we can do this work, which is deeply rewarding, even at an advanced age. Our age and experience might even help us do our work better. We might not have as much wisdom as our clients ascribe to us (or hope we have), but if we've been paying attention all these years, we probably have more wisdom now than we did as youngsters. In addition, with each passing year, my insecurities about whether I am skilled enough or empathic enough to do this work fade into the rear-view mirror, not because I no longer care about those questions but because I have reached a place of greater acceptance of limitations that we all have.

Reflecting on our mortality also leads me to think more about what footprints I am leaving behind. What lessons have I imparted for my students? In what ways have I led my clients to have more capacity for resolving their conflicts in the future? In what ways have I opened the door for more people—of every kind—to pick up the dispute resolution baton that each of us will at some point be passing on?

Writing this essay has given me a welcome opportunity to consider these questions. For me, one of the answers lies in the famous statement by Mahatma Gandhi that "we must be the change that we want to see in the world." Being a peacemaker in the world outside us requires us to be a peacemaker in our internal world. And, the quest for greater self-understanding and self-acceptance, a quest I have tried to express in this essay, achieves its lasting impact when we can use those tools in our work as dispute resolvers to make the world a better place.

I conclude with an important lesson from my rabbi, Darby Leigh. At our High Holiday services a few years ago, he said: "The Talmud teaches us the importance of *tikkun olam* and that while it is not our responsibility to complete the work of healing the world, neither may we desist from it." Rabbi Darby went on: "And when you feel daunted by the enormity of the world's suffering, remember that there may be certain corners of the world (at home, at work, in our communities) where you are uniquely situated to do good." I try to bring that way of looking at life in these challenging times into each of my mediations, into my home, and out into the world each day.

Notes

[1] Adichie, C. N. "The Danger of a Single Story." Filmed 2009. TED video, 18:31. https://www.ted.com/talks/chimamanda_ngozi_adichie_the_danger_of_a_single_story?utm_campaign=tedspread&utm_medium=referral&utm_source=tedcomshare.

References

Pittinsky, T. L. 2012. *Us + Them: Tapping the Positive Power of Difference*. Boston: Harvard Business Press.

Schwartz, R. 2001. *Introduction to the Internal Family Systems Model*. Oak Park, IL: Trailheads Publications.

18

Finding Joy Through a Mediation Clinic and Asian American Identity

By Carol Izumi

◆

Straddling Two Cultures

Through choice or force, racial and cultural identity have colored every aspect of my existence due to three key influences: the Japanese American experience in the United States, racial and social inequality, and generational locus. My approach to conflict was formed from principles and qualities derived from these influential elements. Being *Sansei,* third-generation Japanese American (JA), ties me to both an immigrant and American-born sensibility.

Carol Izumi recently retired as a clinical professor of law at UC Hastings College of the Law, where she directed the Mediation Clinic and ADR Externship Program. A prominent dispute resolution teacher, scholar, trainer, and practitioner, she is an internationally known specialist in clinical legal education. Before joining Hastings' faculty, from 1986 to 2010 she was a faculty member at George Washington University Law School, where she still holds the title professor of clinical law emerita. At GW Law, she directed the Consumer Mediation Clinic and Community Dispute Resolution Center Project and served as associate dean for clinical affairs. In 1999, she co-founded the Community Dispute Resolution Center in Washington, DC, to provide free mediation services in adult misdemeanor cases, juvenile delinquency matters, and police-civilian disputes. A graduate of Georgetown University Law Center and Oberlin College, she was elected to membership in the American Law Institute in 2003 and shortly before her retirement from Hastings was awarded the 2019 Rutter Award for Teaching Excellence, which honors outstanding professors at California's top law schools.

Beginning with family history: my father, Shinsuke (*Issei*, first generation), the oldest son, left a well-to-do life in Japan at age 17 to emigrate to the United States and help his eldest sister, Shizuyo. (Recalling his comfortable upbringing, my dad quoted a friend, "Izumi, he's never lifted anything heavier than *hashi* [chopsticks].") He arrived in Los Angeles in 1922 with $3,000 and joined the household of Shizuyo, her husband, and three young sons in Boyle Heights, a neighborhood of JAs and Mexican Americans. Dad complained to me that "Old Man Hori," his brother-in-law, took his money, invested in Asahi Shoes in Little Tokyo, and made him "junior partner," a fancy term for salesman and stock clerk.

In contrast, my mother, Misao ("Misa") Oshima (*Nisei*, or second-generation, born in Sacramento), was pumping gas at age 11 at her father's one-room store that served Japanese farmers in the Sacramento Valley. "Uncle Coffee," her older brother, got his nickname from grinding beans for the customers. After Mom's mother died in the 1918 Spanish flu epidemic, her father returned to Nagasaki and brought back the "evil stepmother." (When I asked Mom why she thought so ill of her, all she said was, "Because she was so mean to us.") Mom called Sacramento a "one cow town"; as a young woman she fled to LA and landed a secretarial job at *The Rafu Shimpo,* the Japanese-English language newspaper founded in 1903.

Japanese of that era adopted or were assigned Christian names, often by Caucasian teachers. Dad chose Edwin, a nod to Prince Edward, duke of Windsor, and Mom became Iris. Ed and Misa married in LA in 1932. Their wedding photos, by noted JA photographer Toyo Miyatake, captured a Western-style reception with fashionable young JAs, abundant flowers and candelabra, the bride in an elegant traditional gown. Reaching for the "American Dream," my parents started a family and managed to attain a lifestyle not unlike other Angelenos of that era. That changed in 1941 after Japan attacked Pearl Harbor.

My parents and sister Nobuko Anne ("Neya" to me, derived from "big sister" in Japanese) were among the 120,000 Americans of Japanese descent who were incarcerated in internment camps because of race and residence; they lived in the West Coast military "exclusion zone." Because they were born in the United States, Mom and Neya were counted in the 80,000 US citizens, but Dad was an "alien ineligible for citizenship" due to the racial bar against Japanese. In 1942, pursuant to President Franklin D. Roosevelt's Executive Order 9066, our family was, in military euphemisms, "evacuated" from their home, "removed" to the Marysville "assembly center," and shipped to Tule Lake "relocation center" for indefinite detention.

With thousands of other "internees" behind Tule Lake's barbed wire, they shared partitioned barracks, communal dining halls, and public gender-separated bathrooms. Mom's friend Claire told me the women made toilet stall doors for privacy out of salvaged Oxydol detergent boxes. Tule Lake later became the segregation center for those arbitrarily deemed "disloyal" by the War Relocation Authority (WRA), including *Nisei* draft resisters who fought conscription to protest detention. My therapist once opined that incarceration "must have made your parents bitter." She did not understand that they survived adversity through Japanese cultural values of *gaman* (to endure hardship with patience and dignity) and *shikata ga nai* (it cannot be helped). Decades later, I absorbed these principles as "no whining allowed."

My family left Tule Lake within a year, qualifying under a highly restrictive WRA "Leave" program. Dad's translation skills were vital to the military; he secured the requisite sponsor, a military officer, and employment with the US Army Map Service (AMS) outside the exclusion zone.

As required, my family "resettled" to Cleveland and lived in the sponsor's home, Mom as housekeeper. Anti-Japanese sentiment hit immigrants and citizens alike, but my parents found a landlord who would rent them an apartment above a dry cleaner. Neya recalls that JA servicemen and others passing through Cleveland would drop in for Mom's home cooking or a brief stay, a welcoming way station. Growing up, I thought all JAs seemed to know each other personally or by one degree of separation. "Which camp was your family in?" was a common reference point.

In time, Dad became a cartographer and was transferred to AMS in Bethesda, Maryland; Mom got a secretarial job at the Library of Congress. They reunited with JAs they had known in LA or at Tule Lake, many of whom had resettled in Washington, DC, to fill federal government positions. Dad was finally granted US citizenship in 1952 with passage of the McCarren-Walter Act. I was born in 1954, when Neya was in high school. Hoping to inoculate me from the prejudice they faced, my parents did not teach me Japanese or give me a Japanese name, as they had with my sister.

Dad was transferred to St. Louis in 1959, and my folks bought a little rambler in Rock Hill, a suburb with a large African American population. I noticed that all my Black grade school chums lived on one side of Rock Hill Road, and we lived on the other side among White families. That was my first awareness of housing segregation and being situated between Black and White—an "in-between" status that foreshadowed an intermediary role for me.

At the time, St. Louis and other large Midwestern and Eastern cities had sizable numbers of JA families due to the WRA's resettlement policy, which decentralized JAs away from the West Coast. Our family socialized and engaged in civic life largely through the Japanese American Citizens League (JACL), a national civil rights organization founded in 1929. Through my local chapter, regional events, and an annual national convention, I connected with adult and youth members around identity, politics, civic engagement, public service, and social events. The JACL creed, "For Better Americans in a Greater America," and logo with "Security Through Unity" stressed patriotism and solidarity.

In 1960, Neya married an aerospace engineer, Bob Mitori, while getting her master's degree in social work at Washington University. Bob's family had resettled in St. Louis after being freed from Rohwer internment camp in Arkansas. As a 6-year-old flower girl in their wedding, I was surprised to hear that Ted, Bob's JA best man, had to go to Illinois to marry his White fiancée. I didn't know the word "miscegenation," but I understood "sticking with your own kind." I didn't see many interracial couples in St. Louis when I was growing up. While my public K-12 schools had a significant percentage of African Americans, there were only three other JA kids, 2 mixed-race sisters (half Chinese), one "Gonzalez," one Jewish student, and one self-identified gay male.

A typical *Sansei*, I was highly assimilated into majority American culture but also infused with Japanese customs, culture, and values. On New Year's Day, we ate traditional Japanese dishes with a half-dozen other JA families. *Shoyu* (soy sauce) and rice were on the table every night, even with turkey and yams on Thanksgiving. To this day, I take *koden* (money in an envelope) to funerals for the deceased's family. I was raised to respect elders, excel academically, and bring no shame to the family or the JA community, a sentiment captured in the phrase "The nail that sticks up gets hammered down." This philosophy infused a certain skill development: cautious listening, reading situational cues, and reflection before action.

At the same time, I was schooled in American principles of equality, freedom of speech and dissent, and individual choice. My behavior was either in harmony with the traditional Japanese values or in opposition to them. In grade school, I mortified my mom and sister by yelling at boys who taunted us in the mall, "Go home and ask your parents why you're racist!" While my folks silently suffered discrimination, I marched in protest, wrote letters to the editor, penned articles, and read *Rules for Radicals.* Yet, ever dutiful, I *bought* Abbie Hoffman's *Steal This Book.* Whereas my parents favored restraint, I valued the expression of divergent views. While internment remained an indelible marker for JAs, a broader "Asian American" identity formed in the late 1960s-early '70s around civil rights, Black Power, Third World student protests, and anti-Vietnam War activism. I devoured the new magazines, books, music, and poetry that came out of California and New York and embraced the distrust of the "Establishment."

It was a heady time for Baby Boomers to be coming of age. Conflict was everywhere, and I introduced it into our home. I still got straight As but defied "Oriental" and "Geisha" stereotypes, adopting an assertive, critical, risk-taking "hippie" persona. My behavior, appearance, and temper stirred arguments with my mother. (Dad avoided the scenes.) I'd yell and argue, but we also had many frank, rational discussions. In fact, I convinced my mother to let my pals smoke pot in our basement rec room by asking, "Isn't it better to know that we're safe here rather than out driving around?" Of course, we were still driving around smoking, but she was persuaded, her only complaint being "it smells up the drapes." In most cases, we could talk out or work around our differences.

Duality and marginalization, familiar to other racial and ethnic minorities, shaped my politics, choices, and relationships. Seeing firsthand the discrepancy between constitutional principles and the treatment of people of color fueled my passion for law and social justice. Facing conflict, I maneuvered between calmness and confrontation. My mother once warned my soon-to-be in-laws, "She's got a short fuse." I had to learn when to speak up or shut up, to vent anger or suppress it. During arguments, my husband, Frank, teases, "Where's the mediator?"

Lessons in Dispute Resolution

In high school, my favorite classes were "Dissent" and "American Problems," taught by talented teachers who nudged students to question authority and analyze issues from multiple angles. For my "American Problems" project, I examined community law enforcement from the officers' perspectives by joining a police ride-along program. I recall one night the officers were dispatched to a private home to help parents deal with their belligerent son and I saw that their job called for communication and conflict-defusing skills as well as the power to arrest. These classes attracted other students who were interested in societal change on causes such as environmental protection, civil rights, and gender equality. We learned about effective political strategies and celebrated the first Earth Day. As a volunteer with the United Front, a civil rights group fighting White supremacy in Cairo, Illinois, about two hours south of St. Louis, I rallied around economic boycott as a tactic. I banned grapes and lettuce from our house to support the United Farmworkers Union.

As a teen, I negotiated and had a trial. One negotiation was over prescription eyeglasses with sun-darkening lenses. When I discovered that the optician who made the glasses had ignored my eye doctor's order against such lenses, I demanded a refund, to Mom's embarrassment. The optician and I ultimately agreed that he would make replacement lenses at no charge. My trial involved contesting a speeding ticket for "doing 42 in a 30" in Dad's Chevy. I objected; the Malibu could not possibly accelerate that quickly after a full stop. My friend Kathryn drove me to the hearing and watched. I presented my evidence to the judge, cross-examined the officer, and walked out with the case dismissed and my driver's license in hand.

I didn't tell my parents, who neither celebrated nor condemned my contentious spirit, about the speeding ticket until after I had won my case. Their reactions ranged from resignation to bemusement to mild frustration. But even if they didn't understand me, they supported my choices. So when I told them I wanted to drive to San Francisco after graduation with two White high school pals, Nancy and Chas, and an older African American friend, Delbert, Mom considered Del's physique (he was 6 foot 3 and weighed 300 pounds) and nodded. "Good," she said. "With Delbert, no one will bother you." My parents funded my trip as a graduation gift.

I chose Oberlin College because of its history as the first college to admit Blacks and women. In a purposefully diverse student body, I learned practical lessons in facilitation, bridge-building, and problem-solving by serving as an elected student representative on the search committee for a new college president. By co-chairing the Asian American Alliance student organization and co-founding the Third World Women's group ALANA (an acronym for African, Latin, Asian, and Native American), I took part in campus conflicts over curricular, political, and social issues, such as creating a Third World dorm.

Japanese American redress efforts gained steam in my undergrad and law school years. In 1976, President Gerald Ford repealed Executive Order 9066 and acknowledged that the internment was wrong. Led by Asian American legislators, Congress created a bipartisan Commission on Wartime Relocation and Internment of Civilians (CWRIC) to review directives that had led to the incarceration. As a budding lawyer, I attended hearings on Capitol Hill with other JAs in a show of support to hear former internees, historians, academics, and others testify. The CWRIC found that no military necessity justified the internment and recommended monetary reparations, a formal apology, and creation of a fund for research and public education projects. Against long odds, legislation passed. Mom and Dad received a presidential letter of apology and $20,000 each in reparations. To them, the apology held more value than the money. The redress movement and my experiences with various groups and alliances at Oberlin showed me that with political alliances and activism, bipartisan legislative clout and strategies, litigation, negotiation, and grass-roots community involvement, monumental justice goals can be achieved. I appreciated—and still appreciate—an assortment of problem-solving methods.

I plunged into legal dispute resolution as a 3L at Georgetown University Law Center in 1979 and 1980 through a litigation/mediation clinic. I had applied only to law schools that offered opportunities for hands-on lawyering, and Georgetown's clinical program was the largest in the country. In the clinic's civil division, we alternated roles and assignments weekly in DC Superior Court, representing low-income tenants in the Landlord-Tenant Court and mediating cases in the Small Claims and Conciliation Branch.

One of my clinic clients, Mrs. M, was sued for nonpayment of rent, and we filed an affirmative defense based on housing code violations. Unfortunately, awaiting our trial date, Mrs. M assaulted the property manager and was institutionalized at a psychiatric hospital. In those pre-cell phone days, Mrs. M would call me at home late at night and say, "Izumi, you gotta get me outta here!" Working with Mrs. M and many others taught me about the important connection between advocates and those we aim to serve, individuals who are often in difficult straits as well as in conflict. My legal clinic experience was transformative.

Although I mediated and negotiated through the law school's clinic, "alternative dispute resolution" was not a common phrase at the time. The curriculum was litigation-centric, so I took Trial Advocacy, Evidence, and Civil and Criminal Procedure and learned how to interview and cross-examine witnesses, make an opening and closing statement, enter photos and documents into evidence, and devise a trial strategy. Minority law students formed affinity groups, and I was elected president of the Asian American Law Students Association. In 1980, a career in mediation never dawned on me, but I thought I might like civil litigation.

Building a Career

After law school, my mother feared I couldn't hold a job. In a six-year period, I clerked for a judge, was an associate at a small firm, and held two public interest positions. For the DC Bar, one of the public interest jobs, I staffed the Landlord-Tenant Information Service and mediated cases referred by the Landlord-Tenant Court. At the law firm, I represented clients in negotiation, mediation, and litigation. I soured on the "hired gun," billable-hours model of private practice and sought a public interest career that would check these boxes: expand access to justice, serve disadvantaged members of the community, be intellectually challenging, allow for self-direction and autonomy, be fun and rewarding, and pay enough to reduce my law school debt.

I found my calling in 1986, when I was hired by George Washington University Law School to direct its Consumer Litigation Clinic and separate Consumer Mediation Clinic. I applied for the "supervising attorney" position because I had managed student interns competently in prior jobs and the job would mean that I could invest more professionally in mediation, a process I valued from my legal clinic and private practice days.

When I began teaching, my mother asked, "Do you know what you're doing?"

I told her the truth: "I'm one day ahead of the students."

I had no training as a clinical teacher, but savvy and supportive colleagues tutored me in pedagogy, faculty politics, and the quirks of academia. Most law schools had only one or two professors teaching ADR courses; at GW, Charles Craver was, and still is, a most valued colleague. Back then, GW clinical teachers lacked faculty status and were on one-year renewable contracts, and faculty perquisites were not conferred until the 1992 MacCrate Report[1] criticized legal education and pressed for upgrades in experiential programs.

I became GW Law School's first Asian American female faculty member. Throughout my life and my career, I have often been the first or the only Asian American female doing something or serving in a specific role, a distinction that comes with burdens and benefits. There's the weight of unwillingly representing an entire race and having people's expectations of me limited by stereotypes. On the plus side, I was a resource for Asian American law students as the faculty advisor to their student organization and a role model for achieving professional goals. Like other faculty of color, I brought a different perspective and set of experiences to campus. At GW, I sometimes felt marginalized more from faculty hierarchy than racial exclusion. In my 18th year as a clinical professor on a long-term contract, I complained as a panelist at a faculty retreat that I would always be junior to the most recent tenure-track hire. Thereafter, GW created a clinical tenure system, and I was awarded tenure.

Each clinic had a seminar and fieldwork component. My Litigation Clinic students represented low-income consumers who had filed complaints in the DC Department of Consumer and Regulatory Affairs, alleging unlawful business practices such as defective products, fraud or misrepresentation, and unlicensed contractors. We routinely filed in DC Superior Court and bypassed the administrative forum. Students and their clients learned a hard lesson about winning a civil judgment: defendants rarely hand over the money, and post-judgment procedures are burdensome and often fruitless. A court victory could be unfulfilling.

The Consumer Mediation Clinic (CMC) provided free telephone mediation for DC-MD-VA consumers who had disputes with businesses over used and new cars, defective products, service contracts, and credit card billing, among other things. Consumers came to us from agency referrals and directly through an intake "hotline." Fortunately, I forged a relationship with consumer reporter Liz Crenshaw at the local NBC-TV affiliate, and for years she ran an evening news story on the CMC each semester that prompted more inquiries than we could handle. Under this relatively novel process, student-mediators fielded calls, entered intakes in our computer system, and sent letters of introduction inviting the parties to participate in the free and voluntary process. Students then conducted "joint" and "individual sessions" (i.e., conference calls and one-party calls) until the parties reached a resolution or hit an impasse.

Students favored the Consumer Mediation Clinic; they liked the subject matter variety, the facilitative process, and the potential for happy endings. I was in my element running the Mediation Clinic; I loved the fervent students, the types of disputes, and the academic environment. I never tracked settlement rates because I didn't want the students to feel, or exert, settlement pressure or measure their performance by that metric. Instead, a good mediation was one in which the student used her best efforts and skills to provide an even-handed, structured process, attended to ethical responsibilities, and learned from her experience.

To gain credibility and confidence, I took hundreds of hours of mediation training from pioneering teacher-trainer-mediators Linda Singer and Michael Lewis and their Center for Dispute Settlement (CDS) colleague Edna Povich and mediated for various community and government programs that were ongoing or starting up, such as the Equal Employment Opportunity Commission, the DC Office of Human Rights, and the DC Citizens Complaint Center (CCC). Linda and Michael were at the forefront of dispute resolution program innovation and administration, and as adjunct professors at GW's and Georgetown's law schools, they influenced generations of lawyers. The Citizens Complaint Center, a '60s-era community justice center, needed an army of trained volunteers to co-mediate community disputes. For years, I relished going to the Complaint Center after work to mediate and apprentice new mediators, and I appreciated the connection to such experienced trainers. I co-authored my first ADR article with Michael, "Dispute Resolution Alternatives: A Growing Option for Businesses" (Lewis and Izumi, 1990), joined the CDS Board of Directors in 2002, and chaired it from 2007 to 2010.

In 1993, consumer cases were folded into the GW Civil Litigation Clinic, and my Consumer Litigation Clinic was closed. What a godsend: I could concentrate solely on mediation teaching, training, supervision, and practice.

Coincidentally, a fiscal crisis shuttered the Citizens Complaint Center, creating a vacuum in the city's conflict resolution landscape. The CCC's demise gave me the opportunity to join forces with Steve Dinkin at CDS, who aimed to fill the void left by the center. We met with civic leaders, judges, city and federal officials, prosecutors, public defenders, police, community activists, mediators, and funders, and held conflict resolution trainings to generate support. In 1999, we launched the DC Community Dispute Resolution Center (CDRC), overseen by Steve, to provide free mediation of adult misdemeanor cases, juvenile delinquency matters, and police-civilian complaints, focusing on these cases to meet the needs and interests of our community partners: the US Attorney's office for misdemeanor cases, the DC Office of Corporation Counsel (now the Office of the Attorney General for DC) for juvenile delinquency matters, and the Citizen Complaint Review Board (now the Office of Police Complaints) for police-civilian mediations.[2]

Best of all, this new enterprise meant I could design a new clinical course called the CDRC Project so my George Washington Law School clinic students could conduct CDRC mediations. To my knowledge, this was the only clinic at the time mediating criminal cases. Steve (and his successors) and I co-taught the requisite seminar, supervised the mediations, and co-mediated ourselves when students were unavailable.

CDRC mediations were scheduled in two- or three-hour blocks in the late afternoon and evening hours at institutional locations with security check-ins. Mediating criminal cases presented distinct challenges: respondents had a right to counsel but complainants did not; the court proceedings, stayed pending mediation, loomed in the background; and ethical issues surfaced around voluntariness, mediator neutrality, and confidentiality. Yet I found CDRC mediations especially rewarding. Most important, CDRC party evaluations showed a high rate of satisfaction with the process and high completion rate for agreements.

Around this time ADR started spreading to many sectors. Law schools expanded ADR classes beyond the basics, started graduate programs and dispute resolution centers, and founded specialty law journals. In the early 1990s, a group of us initiated a new Section on Alternative Dispute Resolution within the Association of American Law Schools (AALS). As a member of the section's executive committee and its chair, I participated in two AALS conference events that signaled the acceptance of ADR within the legal profession and academy: a program on "Standards of Professional Conduct in ADR" (Feerick, Izumi, Kovach, and Love, 1995) and a 1996 mini-workshop on ADR. To my colleagues and me, these programs heralded ADR as a distinct field and validated the work we were doing, often in isolation, at our law schools.

As a rookie teacher, I became active in the AALS Section on Clinical Legal Education and chaired the section in 2002. When I began teaching, mediation clinics were so rare that the Clinical Section did not even have an ADR practice group, so at annual conferences, I was stuck in the Civil Litigation group, where, frankly, I felt an attitude of litigation superiority, or elitism, that might be summed up as "real lawyers go to trial." In fact, mediation clinics continue the fight for legitimacy and recognition. Just a few years ago, we opposed the ABA's proposed redefinition of "law clinic" that included only advocacy clinics. We prevailed, and the definition now covers mediation clinics.

Moving West

In 2010, after 24 years as a clinical professor, including four years as associate dean for clinical affairs, I retired from GW as emerita professor of clinical law. One month later, I began my new position as clinical professor of law at the University of California Hastings College of the Law in San Francisco, becoming director of the Mediation Clinic and acting associate director of Hastings' Center for Negotiation and Dispute Resolution (CNDR). Concurrently, my husband became the chancellor and dean of Hastings. I was thrilled to join CNDR and Hastings, where the programs in ADR and experiential education were much larger than those at GW. However, I resented the implication that I was simply the "trailing spouse," since I secured a faculty appointment on my own merits.

At Hastings, I directed the ADR Externship and the Mediation Clinic, co-teaching the latter both semesters. In the externship, I supervised advanced ADR students placed at court, agency or nonprofit dispute resolution programs. Clinic students co-mediated small claims cases in San Francisco Superior Court, attending court once or twice each week to offer mediation during court sessions.

I also supervised clinic students in mediation of discrimination complaints in housing, employment, and public accommodations for the San Francisco Human Rights Commission and the California Department of Fair Employment and Housing, cases that excited students because the mediations lasted longer and involved more complex substantive issues. These cases often posed challenges for students and professors alike; offensive language or behavior by a party and power imbalances tested our ethical mettle. It was easier to empathize with human complainants than with institutional or corporate respondents.

On July 1, 2020, I retired from Hastings after 34 years as a clinical professor and mediation clinic director at two different law schools. To help keep the clinic at full capacity, I've agreed to be "recalled to service" at Hastings to teach the Mediation Clinic in the spring semester for three years. I am grateful to have retired on a high note, having received the 2019 Rutter Award for Teaching Excellence.

Reflections on the Past and Future

As I look back on my career, I feel very lucky. My values, interests, and identity steered my career to the intersection of three movements: ADR, clinical legal education, and Asian American activism. This inextricable combination has given me purpose and satisfaction, and these three movements' shared goals have matched my own: make all voices heard, expand avenues to recourse, afford agency over decision-making, redistribute resources, decentralize power, and recognize each person's humanity.

Being in DC, an early adopter of all things ADR, I had opportunities galore, from mediating and arbitrating for multiple organizations to chairing the DC Bar Attorney-Client Arbitration Board and creating its mediation component. This hot spot united individuals from diverse backgrounds and occupations who had an appetite for informal dispute resolution, and I met, collaborated with, and leaned on many wonderful individuals. The ABA Dispute Resolution Section, the National Association for Community Mediation, and the Society of Professionals in Dispute Resolution were all based there. My favorite DC "ADR people" connection was the Culture and Conflict Resolution book group organized by Carrie Menkel-Meadow, with Howard Gadlin, Homer La Rue, Kevin Avruch, Wallace Warfield, Donna Stienstra, and Melanie Greenberg. Co-authorship with Homer was my motivation to write "Prohibiting 'Good Faith' Reports under the Uniform Mediation Act: Keeping the Adjudication Camel Out of the Mediation Tent" (Izumi and La Rue, 2003). The people in ADR sparked my joy. Group generalizations are often inapt, but I've found my ADR colleagues to be an inquiring, reflective, moral, and unfailingly supportive bunch.

I identify deeply as a clinical professor of law. The practice of mediation, not merely the theoretical, animates my academic work. Educating and supervising students to serve the community through their mediations has been especially rewarding. I found my tribe in the AALS Clinical Section, a sanctuary of like-minded lawyers dedicated to *praxis*. We have pushed new policies and standards that afforded greater job security (tenure and long-term contracts), perquisites (research budgets, sabbaticals), and governance rights. One of my proudest moments was receiving the section's 2018 William Pincus Award for Outstanding Service and Commitment to Clinical Legal Education, the first ADR professor to do so.

As I've noted, throughout my career I have often been the first or the only Asian American female in a workplace or role, so I've been delighted to see the number of Asian American law teachers skyrocket since my first year. Pan-Asian demand for empowerment and recognition imbued my commitment to AAPI (Asian American/Pacific Islander) issues. Two such endeavors included a team of Asian American conspirators: a nonprofit and a book. In 1993, five friends and I formed the Asian Pacific American Bar Association Educational Fund (AEF) to award summer fellowships that placed law students in public interest jobs to benefit the AAPI community. More than 25 years later, AEF's impact and capacity have ballooned tenfold. My co-authored casebook, *Race, Rights and Reparations: Law and the Japanese American Internment* (Yamamoto, Chon, Izumi, Kang, and Wu, 2001), was produced with a grant from the Civil Liberties Public Education Fund, which was established by Congress as part of the larger redress effort.

Implicit bias and its effect on mediator neutrality have become a central interest (Izumi, 2010 and 2017), sparked by Jerry Kang's presentation at the 2005 Conference of Asian Pacific American Law Faculty. Jerry's talk made me want to apply implicit bias research to mediation ethics using Asian stereotypes and examples drawn from the Mediation Clinic. Since then, I have given dozens of implicit bias presentations to lawyers, mediators, arbitrators, students, teachers, and others.

In the big tent of dispute resolution, I have inhabited one nook—mediation education—these 30-odd years. Like other disciplines, the vastness of our field, with innumerable roles, activities, and processes, creates specializations. I admire our colleagues who work on the front lines of seemingly endless racial, ethnic, religious, and political clashes around our country and the world. I sometimes wonder if humans are doomed to repeat the same injustices and atrocities in shifting locations, failing to learn lessons from history, but perhaps with Pollyanna positivity, I have faith that dispute resolution, and mediation specifically, *can* make the world a better place.

I cite three reasons for my belief that the key values and the state of mediation are more solid than ever. First, the field adapts to a shifting environment and modern needs. The role of the mediator, or dispute resolution neutral, has expanded to encompass more functions and facets. Process models and practices have morphed as research, empirical evidence, and human conduct require. Social science, behavioral science, and neuroscience are now commonly discussed; interdisciplinary projects gather diverse orientations; international programs open cultural perspectives. Core mediation tenets remain timely and relevant, yet challenges pivot with the times.

Second, I have been attending ABA and AALS dispute resolution programs from their inception, and every year I am more impressed by a new generation of teachers, scholars, and practitioners who are contemplating and writing about our field. These "young lions" question, prod, and cajole us to look anew at how dispute resolution matters (or not). Appropriately, there is less romanticism about dispute resolution and more criticism from inside the field. The 30th anniversary of Richard Delgado's seminal critique, "Fairness and Formality: Minimizing the Risk of Prejudice in Alternative Dispute Resolution" (Delgado, Dunn, Brown, Lee, and Hubbert, 1985), was an occasion to re-evaluate ADR against social justice goals (ADR Symposium, 2017). ADR *should* be evaluated from critical race, feminist legal theory, LGBTQ, and other analytical viewpoints.

Of course, there are shortcomings. One failure is the continuing lack of diversity within mediator and arbitrator ranks. Despite years of lip service and committees, statistics show that people of color continue to lag in representation, from eligible pools to ultimate selection. At a 2015 presentation to the International Academy of Mediators, Claudia Viera and I revealed statistics on mediators of color within seven service providers: the range was 3 percent to 14 percent. The good news is there is action beyond complaining. For instance, Homer La Rue has proposed a rubric, the Ray Corollary Initiative, to push the numbers up, transferring rules from sports and law firms.

I saved for last the third, and biggest, reason for my confidence in ADR's future: my Mediation Clinic students. Each semester, they have shown up, earnest and primed to learn theories and techniques to apply in their mediations. Many have been students of color from immigrant families who have faced and overcome adversity. Given the intensity of hands-on learning in the clinic, I have had deep and frequent interactions with them in my office, the classroom, the courtroom, and the mediation room. They have struggled, tackled obstacles, and come out better for it. With an altruistic spirit, they have supported their peers and committed to public service. They have been demanding of me and the world in the right ways. Their passion, aspirations, growth, and resilience inspire me. They are the future, and it is good.

Notes

[1] Robert MacCrate was an American lawyer who served as president of the New York State Bar Association and the American Bar Association. With the backing of the ABA Task Force on Law Schools and the Profession, the 1992 MacCrate Report criticized the state of American legal education and called for a practice-oriented, rather than theory-oriented, approach to legal education.

[2] The CDRC undertaking led to my book chapter, "ADR Processes in Criminal and Delinquency Cases," in the American Bar Association's *ADR Handbook for Judges*, which was published in 2004.

References

ADR Symposium. 2017. *SMU Law Review* 70(3-4): 595-913.

Delgado, R., C. Dunn, P. Brown, H. Lee and D. Hubbert. 1985. "Fairness and Formality: Minimizing the Risk of Prejudice in Alternative Dispute Resolution." *Wisconsin Law Review* 1985(6): 1359-1404.

Feerick, J. D., C. Izumi, K. Kovach, L. Love, R. Moberly, L. Riskin and E. Sherman. 1995. "Standards of Professional Conduct in Alternative Dispute Resolution Symposium." *Journal of Dispute Resolution* 1995(1): 95-128.

Izumi, C. and H. C. La Rue. 2003. "Prohibiting 'Good Faith' Reports Under the Uniform Mediation Act: Keeping the Adjudication Camel Out of the Mediation Tent." *Journal of Dispute Resolution* 2003(1): 67-98.

Izumi, C. 2010. "Implicit Bias and the Illusion of Mediator Neutrality," *Washington University Journal of Law & Policy* 34(3): 71-155.

Izumi, C. 2017. "Implicit Bias and Prejudice in Mediation." *SMU Law Review* 70: 681-693.

Lewis, M. and C. Izumi. 1990. "Dispute Resolution Alternatives: A Growing Option for Businesses." *Board of Trade News*. April, 1990.

Yamamoto, E. K., M. Chon, C. Izumi, J. Kang and F. H. Wu. 2001. *Race, Rights and Reparations: Law and the Japanese American Internment*. New York: Aspen Publishers, Inc.

19

From the Portal to the Path: Finding the "Me" in Mediator

By Marvin E. Johnson

◆

The environment we start out in has a significant impact on us. Where we live, who else lives within our space, our personal experiences, our accomplishments, our failures, our extracurricular activities, and the opportunities that exist in our community influence who we are and who we become.

> "No one is free until we all are free."
> — Martin Luther King, Jr.

I was born and lived the formative years of my life in Rochester, a mid-size city with a progressive history, locat-

---

Marvin E. Johnson is a nationally recognized mediator, arbitrator, and trainer with more than 27 years of dispute resolution experience. He has worked for the Department of Labor, the Federal Labor Relations Authority, the Federal Mediation and Conciliation Service, the National Treasury Employees Union, the National Football League Players' Association, and the National Academy of Conciliators and was a professor of labor relations, law, and dispute resolution at Bowie State University. Johnson serves as a mediator, arbitrator, fact-finder, and facilitator in public and private disputes. He provides diversity and dispute resolution training and lectures extensively on the subject of conflict management. Johnson is the founder and editor of the journal *Practical Dispute Resolution* and has written widely on dispute resolution and diversity.

ed on the shores of Lake Ontario in the northwestern part of the state of New York. In the early 1800s, Rochester was one of the last stops on the Underground Railroad before Canada. The Rochester community was active in the women's suffrage movement as well as the abolition movement, and Susan B. Anthony spoke in the area a number of times. Because of the area's progressivism, the noted abolitionist and civil rights activist Frederick Douglass made Rochester his home in 1847.

As a conductor of the Underground Railroad, Douglass opened his home and utilized the Rochester African Methodist Episcopal (AME) Zion Church to help abolitionists such as Harriet Tubman transport slaves to Canada. He also used the church as a temporary office for his newspaper, *The North Star*. The AME Zion Church was and still is my family's church.

> "The spiritual is stronger than any material force..."
> — *Ralph Waldo Emerson*

My family played an important role in the church. Plaques on the walls honor members of my family, and church buildings bear family members' names. My mother, a very spiritual woman, was in the church every Sunday, singing in the choir during the service and performing her other duties thereafter. At least a couple of evenings during the week, she attended meetings and choir rehearsal. As the youngest child, I was not allowed to stay home alone, and I spent many an evening entertaining myself in the back of the church. I remember seeing the likenesses of Frederick Douglass, Susan B. Anthony, and Harriet Tubman etched in the stained-glass windows.

The important history of my church was also part of sermons from the pulpit, and even though I wasn't old enough to participate in family discussions when we gathered for special events and holidays, I overheard the talk of the significant role our church had played in the abolitionist and women's rights movements and the impact it had on the Rochester community. Family members also talked about the impact that race had on the life of everyday Blacks in matters such as housing, employment, and health care and the extra effort Blacks had to apply to get ahead. Hearing these stories as a child helped me understand the history of my church, my community, and my people. It helped me understand my background—what I was a part of and how it shaped who I was.

Knowing who you are is very important in understanding others and the issues they have to deal with. You cannot help others unless you know yourself. The many lessons I learned in church helped me, as a person and as a mediator, to have faith in the human race and the individuals within. There is some goodness in each person and redemption for those who need it.

> "Increased community participation enhances the benefits received by the entire community."
> — Merlin[1]

African Americans settled on either the west or the northeast side of Rochester. Initially, my family lived in the Hanover Housing Projects on the northeast side of town, where I attended elementary school through third grade. After my family moved to the west side of town, I attended a different elementary school and graduated from Madison High School, also on the west side of town.

The Montgomery Neighborhood Center was a social and cultural community focal point for the African American residents of the west side of Rochester. There I received drama instruction and had roles in plays, took archery and gardening classes, and even won an award for my gardening efforts. I learned how to ice skate, canoe, cook, and bake. I went on trips to museums, played basketball, attended day camp, joined the Cub Scouts, and participated in the glee club. These educational and cultural activities helped with my self-discovery and my self-expression and shaped my character and personality. The center also brought the larger neighborhood together, by allowing church groups and community organizations to use the building for fundraisers, gatherings, and galas. The center fulfilled a variety of needs and in doing so fostered both individual and community pride.

The center's staff, who were either attending or had graduated from college, got a lot of respect from community members, and there was little conflict at the center. When there were disagreements, they were resolved in the office of the director, a woman who was not a "mediator type" but had enough street smarts to keep the peace. I was never called into the director's office. I believe the ultimate threat of suspending access to the center may have been a major deterrent to misbehavior and a large settlement factor. My entire center experience was the foundation of my belief in community.

> "A dream doesn't become a reality without sweat, determination, and hard work."
> — *Colin Powell*

Along with the Montgomery Neighborhood Center, Black businesses were the anchors of the neighborhood. Clarissa Street, sometimes called Rochester's Broadway, was lined with Black-owned grocery stores, restaurants, benevolent and fraternal clubs such as the Elks, barbershops, doctors' offices, and, on adjacent streets, churches. In fact, a number of Black businesses on Clarissa Street were listed in the 1954 edition of the *Green Book*, the annual guidebook for

African American travelers that inspired the movie of the same name. Rochester's Black-owned businesses instilled pride in the community. They also inspired a transformational moment in my youth.

Looking and acting "cool" was and still is a big thing for young people. I remember peers teasing me about certain clothes I wore to school, and as soon as I was old enough to get a work permit, I became a newspaper carrier. I made enough money to buy my own clothing and most of the other things I wanted, from my first new bicycle to my first car. Clothes were never a problem again.

I delivered papers for the *Democrat & Chronicle*, Rochester's morning newspaper. School started at 8 a.m. and my route took two hours to complete, so I had to get up very early to deliver the papers. Because I played sports, I had to collect money from my customers after I got home from practice and before I did my homework. I maintained this routine for seven or eight years. There were thousands of carriers in the Rochester area, and near the end of my senior year, I was one of four carriers—and only the second Black carrier—to receive the $12,000 Gannett Newspaper Boy College Scholarship, an award based on school record, ability as a carrier, and community activities.

> "Keep track of your expenses or you'll end up losing money."
> — *International organizational change consultant Richard Moran*

For me, delivering papers was like being one of the Black business owners on Clarissa Street. I bought the newspapers from the D&C at a wholesale rate and sold them at a retail rate fixed by the company. Because I had no customer complaints and always paid for my papers on time, I was asked to take over the routes of other carriers, and my route grew from 80 to well over 200, at which point my parents stepped in to curtail my expanded business because it was taking time away from my studies.

Delivering papers taught me the fundamentals of business at a very young age. I learned how to interact with and manage the expectations of existing customers while meeting and soliciting new ones. I learned about profits and losses, having a reserve fund, managing and saving money, customer service, record-keeping, and time management. It instilled confidence and a sense of independence and responsibility and prepared me for handling business responsibilities later in life.

Many people today want to be mediators and have their own practice. They see mediation as a noble profession, and they want to help people resolve disputes. Many do not think of mediation as a business. They think that after they receive their 40-hour mediation certificate, clients will beat down their door. But mediation *is* a business. If you are going to develop a mediation practice, you must understand the business side of the practice.

> "Great relationships are about understanding similarities and respecting differences."
> — *Unknown*

James Madison High School included grades seven through 12. During the years I attended, Madison had a very diverse multicultural student body with a respected honor society and powerhouse teams in football, wrestling, and basketball. I followed in my brother's athletic footsteps, starting on the varsity basketball team and serving as its co-captain. Wanting to be my own person, though, I also started on the varsity football team and ran track in my senior year and received the All Sports Trophy for my efforts.

I did very well academically. From personal experience, I learned that scholars and accomplished athletes are rewarded for their accomplishments and receive certain implicit benefits, not only trophies, plaques, and student government leadership positions but access to influential people and opportunities unavailable to others.

But in high school I also experienced the disadvantages of being placed in certain categories. I had good friendships with all segments of my high school community, including students ranked in the top and lowest percentiles of my class (I was in the top 11 percent), a fact I was proud of. My inner circle of friends, though, all played sports and were above-average students. We all wanted to attend college.

That almost didn't happen. My 10th-grade high school counselor, who was White, discouraged me from going to college and told me that I should instead get a job "working with my hands." He said the same thing to most of the Black male students who were not ranked in the top 10 percent of the class.

If I had listened to him, I would not have gone to college. But in my junior year, Josh Lofton, the city's first Black high school counselor, came to my school. That year, more Black students than ever before applied to, were accepted by, and attended college. And at Lofton's urging, Rochester's Black community organizations and a few of the White foundations provided the much-needed scholarships that made college possible for me and my classmates.

My experiences as a child and young adult—at home, in the community, at work, and at school—enabled me to understand who I was as a person and how important community can be. These experiences also allowed me to develop an implicit skill set that ultimately helped me accept and connect with a wide variety of people and be a good mediator.

> "Don't fight forces, use them."
> — R. Buckminster Fuller

My father died the summer before my sophomore year in high school, and my mother, a domestic worker, could not afford to pay for my college education. The newspaper scholarship and the numerous other scholarships I received from community organizations enabled me to go to Bowling Green State University, where I was excited about trying out for a large university's basketball team. Unfortunately, I was not selected. Disappointed and lacking a basketball scholarship to help pay my expenses, I decided not to return to BGSU the following fall.

Leaving BGSU turned out to be a difficult and significant decision point on my path to becoming a mediator. In my Rochester community and many working-class communities in this country, sports and academics often intersect. I had to decide to prioritize educational achievement over athletics, a lesson I have shared with other persons of color in my role as a mentor and diversity leader in the conflict resolution field. I didn't give up sports, but they no longer provided my main identity.

> "In the middle of difficulty lies opportunity."
> — Albert Einstein

After I accepted that basketball was not going to fulfill my hopes and dreams, I decided to enroll as a sophomore at Kent State University, where I quickly had to choose an academic major. My father was my inspiration. One of the first Black letter carriers in Rochester, he had been a member of the Letter Carrier's Union. One of the days that my father took me to his job, I listened to him and other carriers as they were sorting the mail they were about to deliver. I heard the story of a fellow carrier's termination, grievance, and successful return to work with back pay. Still feeling the power of that story, I selected industrial relations as my major.

> "If you are neutral in situations of injustice, you have chosen the side of the oppressor."
> — *Desmond Tutu*

I arrived at Kent State University in January 1969. Martin Luther King Jr. had been assassinated the year before, and protests against the Vietnam War were rampant. Campus racial tension at Kent State was high. Black students were concerned about many things: the lack of minority faculty, administrators, and student scholarships, the absence of a Black Studies Program, the failure to recruit minority student athletes to the university, the lack of on-campus entertainment that appealed to Black students, and the lack of funding for the Black United Students organization for Black History Month and homecoming. I ran for and won a seat on the Student Senate. I was appointed chair of the Major Events Committee, and we dramatically increased the number of campus events that appealed to Black as well as White students with performances and appearances by Sly and the Family Stone, Roberta Flack, the Fifth Dimension, Nancy Wilson, Smokey Robinson, and Julian Bond. That year, the Student Senate allocated the largest increase ever in funding to the Black United Students for minority activities.

At the same time, I was a member of the intramural Brothers Together Basketball Team. We went undefeated, winning the University Championship twice and the Ohio State Intramural Championship in 1970, a feat that in a time of great racial tension was a cause for celebration in the Black community—and a source of great pride for me. I still have the letter from the highest Black ranking member of the administration emphasizing what the Championship meant to the University's entire Black community. Later, the wider university indirectly acknowledged this and my other achievements at Kent State by presenting me with awards for leadership and service to the students and the university.

After Kent State, I wanted to attend law school or get a master's degree in labor relations but could not afford to do either—until a scholarship from the Industrial and Labor Relations program at the University of Wisconsin allowed me to pursue the master's degree. I found out two years later that the UW fellowship had been established by someone from Rochester who learned of my financial straits. Once again, the Rochester community had come to my aid.

At UW, where my specialization was in unions and collective bargaining, I studied the dignity and the significance of work, the people who performed the work and the impact it had upon them, how the work and the workers were managed, and the tensions that flowed from these intersecting needs in the workplace. Collective bargaining between the union and the company, I learned, is the vehicle for managing these tensions. If the parties reach a bargaining impasse, they can call in a mediator to help them resolve the matter before turning to an adversarial process. I saw impasse and the need for mediation not as a failure but an interesting space to resolve the natural conflict between workers and management. I also continued to see a perfect connection between social justice and mediation, and after I graduated with a master's degree in 1974, this heightened my passion to be a mediator.

> "The choices you make . . . affect what you will have, be, or do in the tomorrow of your life."
> — *American author and speaker Zig Ziglar*

After graduating from UW, I moved to Washington, DC, and began working as a federal labor relations specialist in the Office of Federal Labor Management Relations, which is now the Federal Labor Relations Authority, or FLRA, an independent agency that governs labor relations between the federal government and its employees. There I acquired a working knowledge of the legal process as it related to labor relations in the federal sector, including decision-writing, labor law research, oral case presentation, and reading and analyzing briefs, court transcripts, and exhibits. But I still wanted to attend law school.

In the fall of 1977, I finally realized this dream and started my first year at Catholic University Law School. My class included the smallest number of minority students in several years, a fact that greatly concerned second- and third-year Black law students. Wanting to take some action, in the second semester of my first year I volunteered to help the admissions office recruit more minority students, which helped the school admit almost three times as many minority students as the year before. This then led to leadership positions in the school's Black American Law Students Association (BALSA) chapter and the board of the CU Law School's student bar as well as graduation-day honors that included the Student of the Year award from BALSA and the Corpus Juris Secundum award from the law school for outstanding civic achievement among students.

After graduating, I took a job as assistant counsel for the National Treasury Employees Union (NTEU), providing legal counsel to the NTEU Pennsylvania and Delaware local chapters and representing them in all phases of labor relations. Being assistant counsel for a union was excellent training for becoming an employment or a labor management attorney, and I won most of my cases and received high praise for my work. However, I was miserable. My passion to be a mediator, which had intensified during my studies in Wisconsin, was still strong. I knew there was another way to resolve differences, one that did not take such a destructive toll on the parties. Being a mediator, I believed, would be more satisfying and more consistent with what was important to me.

My personal and professional experience has confirmed that. Resolving disputes is a complicated process, one with many latent layers and barriers that are not the focus of the conflict. Mediators doing the work at the highest level know this—and know that they must deal with mutually exclusive elements, what each side sees as its own resolution of the dispute. I embrace the skill and creativity that are required to deal with this paradox and find the cooperative space between the parties' articulated resolutions. If the dispute cannot be resolved through mediation, litigation is always an option, and the attorneys can take over. But before they do, mediation provides a fair process and a safe place to explore other possible options.

Friends and acquaintances—and a chance meeting—helped me move into the mediation field. One afternoon, on a train from Philadelphia to Washington, I ran into Harold Davis, who was a mediator with the Federal Mediation and Conciliation Service, then the nation's largest public agency for labor/management dispute resolution and conflict management, and I told him about my disappointment with representing employees and my desire to be a mediator. With his blessing, the National Academy of Conciliators (NAC), a small nonprofit that used mediation techniques to resolve homeowner warranty disputes, hired me as director of legal programs. (This move required me to take a pay cut, but I figured it was a price worth paying.) At the NAC, I learned a lot about mediation but did more mediation training than mediating. Edna Johnson, whom I had met at the University of Wisconsin and who was then chair of the business department at Bowie State University, was looking for someone to teach business law and help with other business courses, and I accepted the job in hopes it would move me closer to my goal of becoming a full-time mediator. Although I had to take another pay cut, in my non-teaching days I was able to write and speak about mediation and start to build a mediation practice.

"Stand up for what you believe in, even if it means standing alone."
— *Singer Andy Biersack*

During this time, I became involved with several leading organizations that focused on what was then called alternative dispute resolution, or ADR. Typically, these organizations ascribe to the core values of the conflict resolution field, including transparency, fairness, inclusion, and collaboration. However, human beings run organizations, and they are concerned, as they should be, with their responsibility for the efficient and effective running of the entity. This overarching factor, and the fact that the leadership of conflict resolution organizations often changes after each annual election, foster continual blind spots regarding social justice issues within the conflict resolution community and profession. These blind spots militate against advancing and sustaining progressive social justice policies.

Ever since my days at Kent State and Catholic University Law School, I have been involved in leading social justice and diversity initiatives. In the 1980s, I was one of the people of color in the Society of Professionals in Dispute Resolution (SPIDR) who met secretly during the organization's conferences because of the lack of diversity in the membership and leadership and the lack of support for diversity policies. I later got involved in the collaboration between the People of Color Caucus and the Environmental/Public Policy Section of SPIDR, which led to convening important dialogues about diversity at SPIDR Annual Conferences between 1994 and 1997. The recurring themes and issues raised during these dialogues pushed SPIDR's leaders to change the organization's policies and bylaws. These changes, which included a diversity policy statement; a diversity environmental impact statement requirement for conference proposals; a bylaw about appointing a person of color to the board; a diversity representative for each section, chapter, and task force; a diversity conference track; board diversity training; and adding youth as a membership category, were all adopted by the Association for Conflict Resolution (ACR), the organization into which SPIDR was merged. But because organizations' focuses change with their leaders, these historic commitments were not sustained. Designing and advocating for diversity initiatives weren't enough. I had to become involved in arguing for them all over again.

A similar dynamic occurred with the American Bar Association's (ABA) Section of Dispute Resolution. For some time, the ABA had a Standing Committee on Dispute Resolution, of which I was a member, and its diverse leaders were sensitive to diversity issues. In 1993, when the ABA created the Section of Dispute Resolution, the section reflected this sensitivity in its bylaws and policies. (I served as the chair or co-chair of the Diversity Committee for the first six years of the section's existence.) Working with the leadership at that time, the section received awards from the ABA's Commission on Racial and Ethnic Diversity for its various diversity initiatives, which included a Minority and Women Resource Bank, a requirement that a diversity impact statement be included in each conference workshop proposal, and a pre-conference Forum for Women and Minorities in Dispute Resolution before the section's annual conference. These notable initiatives began to unravel around 2006, however, and the cycle of promoting diversity had to be started again.

I was asked to run for president or chair of SPIDR, ACR, and the International Academy of Mediators (IAM) several times, but I declined each request, believing that as the leader of a predominantly White organization, I could not continue to be a voice for social justice. Former IAM president Eric Galton, however, eventually convinced me that being president of the IAM would be an important platform for advocating for diversity in general and increasing the diversity of the IAM membership in particular. Making those changes was not easy, but with the assistance of a few close friends, we achieved more than a 500% increase in the number of people of color who became members of IAM during my time as president. When I stepped down, I left it up to the new members of color and the other IAM members to continue the work. The cycle continues, as I am now helping IAM with the development of its first Diversity and Inclusion Committee.

Throughout my life, I have received knowledge, strength, and support from communities of various kinds. I see the mediation field as a community. As a relatively new field, it consists of mediators from different professions of origin, people with varied backgrounds and dispute resolution exposure and experience. The portal through which mediators entered the field, the decade they joined the field, the training they received, and the venue in which they practice all form lenses through which they understand and practice mediation. Such demographic and professional diversity should be a good thing for the mediation community. Why is this so? Because diversity fosters many of the same positive features that mediation provides: increased creativity and problem-solving, better understanding of others, appreciation and respect of different views, and efficient and productive decision-making.

But diversity also means differences in perspectives as well as disagreements about what constitutes good practice, which inadvertently has spawned dissension within and between some groups in the mediation community. These disagreements include, among other things, setting goals for the process and choosing tools appropriate for achieving those goals; determining who is qualified to be a mediator and to manage the process; deciding whether certification should be granted according to specialized subsections of the field; and determining which subsections of the field are better than others. This last challenge has caused practitioners from different subgroups to criticize each other—commercial mediation versus family mediation, environmental mediation versus community mediation, etc.—or one profession to argue superiority over another (law versus psychology). A 2011 ACR Diversity of Practice Report revealed this internal incivility and tribal mentality in one member's comment to a colleague from another subgroup. The member essentially said, if you don't agree with me, you're not a competent mediator.

Demographic differences are especially noteworthy because discussions of them are typically confounded by differences in power and access. Frequently, those with more power and access are not directly impacted by such differences and are less conscious of them. At the same time, many people with power are tired of hearing about demographic differences, a stance that helps undermine the efforts of demographic minorities to participate fully in the mediation community, to be leaders, and to be considered and selected for all sorts of cases.

"Those affected by the problem are the ones that can best solve it."
— Merlin

As a Black man, I have found the obstacles to becoming a respected mediator with a successful private practice are numerous, varied, complicated, and often indescribable. When someone from a traditionally underrepresented group overcomes these barriers, that person develops many skills that are common among many successful mediators—patience, persistence, creativity, likeability, a willingness to voice unfavorable concerns, influence, emotional intelligence, truthfulness, trustworthiness, an ability to ask difficult questions, good listening skills, strong analysis, problem-solving skills, and many more.

To me, it feels as if those in power have turned a blind eye to the impact that demographic differences have upon many people's ability to become full members of the mediation community. They do not want to address the problem. I have heard some say, "We've had numerous discussions about these issues. It is time to move on." As with many important issues, however, putting our heads in the sand is not going to make the problem go away (e.g., see race, gender, sexual orientation, gun control). If disagreements about how to address demographic differences remain in the shadows of the mediation community, they will continue to reappear until they are finally addressed. If the mediation field is going to flourish as a community, we must resolve our internal disagreements.

The ACR Diversity of Practice Report found a need for more dialogue among the specialized mediator subgroups with different viewpoints. If the ADR field were a community similar to the one I was a part of in my youth and the one I believe I have embraced in my professional career, all stakeholders would come together and do for ourselves what we do for others. As we know from our practices, dialogue can produce greater understanding and creative, unanticipated solutions that could enhance the field and benefit everyone involved—the practitioners, the parties, the representatives, and the public.

> "You make a living from your work, but you make a life by what you give."
> — *Unknown*

All my work with conflict resolution organizations has involved giving back to the community, but my most important contribution has involved the Center for Alternative Dispute Resolution. As a professor at Bowie State University, a historically black university (HBCU), I recognized the lack of diversity in the ADR field and created the Center for Alternative Dispute Resolution, the first such organization in the University of Maryland system and the first at an HBCU. The center produced the first biweekly cable TV program that addressed dispute resolution issues and established the Mediators of Color Alliance, a website-based network to support and advance the interests of mediators of color in the dispute resolution field. In 2017, the center, recognized and respected nationally and internationally, celebrated 30 years of providing dispute resolution education and training to diverse audiences.

Writing this chapter has made me see strong threads and continuity, all connected to community and commitment. I realize that what was instilled in me by my family, in the AME Zion Church and at the Montgomery Neighborhood Center in Rochester became a force that fueled me to create the Center for Alternative Dispute Resolution. The social justice stories I heard at home and in church and the mentorship I received at the Montgomery Center, in high school from Josh Lofton, at Kent State from business professor Tom Reuschling, at Wisconsin from labor economist Jack Barbash, and in the ADR field from arbitrator and mediator Jerry Ross and arbitrator Herb Fishgold all instilled in me the passion to pay it forward. I know that some experienced mediators see mentoring as training their competition. But for me, sharing my experience, providing information, and answering questions about joining the field are the least that I can do to help establish a pipeline of new mediators.

> "If you are a part of a community, the community is a part of you."
> — *Merlin*

Who I am and my passion for conflict resolution and social justice derive from the education, understanding, and support I received from my community in Rochester. There are some who think that anyone who advocates for social justice issues should not be a mediator, but I strongly disagree. For me, being an advocate for social justice means standing up for what is fair regarding diversity, equality, inclusion, and human rights in general. After all, attorneys and other advocates, knowing that adversarial processes (litigation and arbitration) are not the only ways to create change, maintain their advocacy practices while also mediating disputes. Bringing diverse communities or subsections of a community together to create change using conflict resolution skills surely is a valuable contribution to society and the field of conflict resolution. So, why can't social justice advocates practice the same way that attorneys and other advocates do?

An advocate for social justice can also be a good mediator—as long as the mediator is not advocating for social justice while in the role of mediator. To do this, one has to: 1) have the knowledge, skills, and understanding to recognize when latent fairness issues are present in a mediation; 2) have the ability to allow the parties to discover such issues from their own perspectives; and 3) foster the parties' self-determination to resolve the issue based on their collective understanding of fairness. I practice and train others in this approach to social justice in mediation.

Several years ago, I was invited to return to Rochester for a community event honoring me and my conflict resolution work. In attendance were my family, my grade school and high school friends, my high school football coach, and a number of community leaders, including the former mayor. I received a proclamation from the new mayor establishing August 9, 2014, as Marvin E. Johnson Day in the city of Rochester. This recognition came from my hometown community, the one that taught me, supported me, and made me who I am today. I was overwhelmed with emotion when Toni Watkins Duhart, a childhood friend who envisioned the event, said "You are one of us and your success is our success—we are proud of you." Of all the honors I have ever received, including two US presidential appointments, this is the one I cherish the most.

Notes

[1] Merlin is the pen name that I have used for decades when writing poetry and inspiring quotations.

References

Merlin [Johnson, M. E.]. 1976. *Different Strokes for Different Folks.*

20

The Road to Becoming a Neutral: Working in the Interest of Human Needs

By Homer C. La Rue

---◆---

I have been invited to write an autobiography like this several times but have been unable to identify why I should. My CV shows considerable accomplishments, and I think that a White person might well wonder why I have not considered my story worth telling.

The answer is rooted in history. For centuries, people of color and women have been told, through the spoken and unspoken words and behavior of every person of authority

---

Homer C. La Rue is professor of law at Howard University School of Law, where he founded the law school's first Alternative Dispute Resolution Clinic and was the first director of the law school's Clinical Law Center. He also is the founder and director of the Howard Law ADR Program. He also serves as an independent arbitrator and mediator in a variety of industries involving a wide range of issues. He has held numerous leadership positions, including serving as chair of the Section of Dispute Resolution of the American Bar Association, a current vice-president and member of the board of governors of the National Academy of Arbitrators, a past member of the board of governors of the International Academy of Mediators, and president of the Society of Professionals in Dispute Resolution (which merged with two other organizations to become the Association for Conflict Resolution). La Rue, who has devoted a significant portion of his time and experience to helping increase diversity in arbitration and mediation, frequently gives lectures and presentations to law faculty, law students, and various other groups on issues concerning racial and ethnic diversity in the conflict resolution field.

who touched their lives, that we are not even on the scale of "worthiness." Why then, would my story be worth telling?

This past spring, the American Bar Association's Dispute Resolution Section honored me with the D'Alemberte-Raven Award, the section's highest tribute, for outstanding service in dispute resolution. Being so honored has allowed me to trust that I am safe to speak on my behalf and on behalf of those unrecognized who came before me, that there may be value in telling the story of an African American who had the audacity to dream that he might make a difference by learning how to help others resolve their disputes.

The theme of my story is that I am (and have always been) in search of community and that this search has led me to work to understand and address human needs. Community, beyond my family, was unavailable for me as a child, especially during my formal education, and I longed to understand how to generate connection in a world filled with explicit and implicit messages that no one was interested in connection with me, a Black man—and that because of the explicit and pervasive cultural messaging about Black men, most people were actually afraid of me, my height at 5' 6" notwithstanding. My separateness somehow inspired me to trust that our vast human diversity would be a source of learning and growth that can arise only from a deeper, truer understanding—and ultimately, a reconciliation—of our outrageously, wonderfully diverse views, behaviors, cultures, beliefs, and interests.

Ultimately, I came to appreciate that understanding the resolution of conflict is an integral part of our search for true community. Community means for me, in part, the resolution of differences toward understanding and finding a better way of being. This better way of being, however, is not static. Inherent in it are the seeds for the next conflict, the next competition of seemingly different interests. That threat, however, also provides an opportunity for the next finding of a better way of being. To me, this dialectical process is the way to understand the world and how to act in it.

The Beginning of the Search

My journey began in a small Midwestern town that was approximately 80 percent White and 15 percent Black and near no major city. My family was working-class, but as those who know the history of labor from World War II through the 1960s understand, in those decades America's working class became its middle class. And even working-class African Americans, who did not share equally in the gains of that period, had the opportunity to raise a family that did not live on the edge of poverty. People like my parents worked hard in the factory, in health care, or similar jobs, sent their kids to college, and retired after years of labor and sacrifice with relative economic security and dignity.[1]

In my little town in the Midwest, my family was my father, who was a GM factory worker and UAW member for 38 years. My mother, who was a registered nurse, was the first African American nurse supervisor in the local hospital. I was the middle child with two sisters. This was the first community that I knew.

As a result of the Great Migration of Blacks from the rural South to cities in the North and West,[2] my hometown consisted of a relatively large number of African Americans. As in most Midwest cities and towns of the time, we lived and worshipped in communities separate from Whites.[3]

My paternal great-grandfather had moved to my hometown ahead of the Great Migration, settling there sometime around the early 1900s. The family story is that my great-grandfather, who was never without a pistol in his belt and Bowie knife in the side of his boot, signed up to fight in the Spanish American War. After leaving the service, he worked in a mining camp in Georgia where he got into a fight with a White supervisor and had to flee. As the story is told, he wanted to get as far from Georgia as possible and was determined to cross the Ohio River to be out of reach of the racist justice of the South. He settled in Anderson, Indiana, marrying and raising one of the first Black families.

My mother, born and raised in Louisville, Kentucky, was a devout Catholic. Her ancestors, still enslaved at the time, had been brought to Louisville by White Catholic slave owners, many from Maryland. The archbishop of Baltimore ordered the organization of a parish for Black Catholics in Louisville in 1868, five years after the Emancipation Proclamation.

The Louisville connection remained a strong one for my mother. Every year, my parents loaded up the Buick, packed us three kids into the back seat, and drove nonstop from Anderson to Louisville for my mother's family reunion. We could never figure out why our father refused to stop for bathroom breaks or snacks once we crossed the Ohio River and headed south, and it was only years later that we understood that this was his way of protecting his family from racism that could end in tragedy—and the pain and degradation that he must have felt being powerless to alter this system. On the Sunday of the reunion, Louisville's St. Augustine church was filled with Black Catholics, many of whom were my mother's family and extended family members. I understood then that my mother had found more than religion in St. Augustine. She had found community, and perhaps for me, it was the birthplace of my own quest.

My mother pushed my father to agree to rear us kids as Catholic. This might not have been a heavy lift for my mother. My father was not particularly religious when

I was growing up, although as he aged he became more Catholic than those born into the faith. Over the almost 50 years of his marriage to my mother, I think that my mother's devotion simply won him over, that he saw the comfort that belief and ritual brought her.

My sisters and I were the only African American kids in an all-White Irish-Catholic school. School was not always a pitched battle, but each day had the potential for emphasizing the differences between us and our classmates.

Black children learn quickly, from everything said (and implied), that the world outside their home is not safe and that they must be cautious not to call undue attention to themselves. To some extent, this was reinforced by some of the teachings of the Catholic Church. "Pride goes before destruction," Proverbs 16:18 warns. "And a haughty spirit before stumbling." Combine this with the family caution, and a young Black child learned the lesson of unwarranted meekness, a lesson that battles with the desire to speak one's worth and to take joy in that worth and in speaking it. I understood early on that I was smart, worked hard, and had a "way with people." I did not want to be meek, however, because I had something to contribute, so early on I began to learn to listen deeply, to "read the room" carefully and accurately. But I still understood that stepping up and speaking out carried the real risk of being rejected—or perhaps even worse, of being treated as if I were invisible. My sisters and I knew that we were different and perceived as lesser than the White children. We knew we had to work harder, and I knew I had to protect my sisters. Thus, without recognizing it, I began my mediation training.

The irony of my early story is that by all accounts, I was quite successful at managing all of this. I got very good grades. I was president of my class from my sophomore year to my senior year, when I also was the student council president. I learned to wear what author Frantz Fanon calls the "White mask" (Fanon, 1952).[4] But I struggled to understand the implicit and explicit bias generated by my sisters' and my skin color and the contradictions fostered by these differences. As I look back, I recognize that I had no concepts, no words, to articulate those differences.

The social justice component of some segments of Catholicism was not part of my Catholic school teaching, where the emphasis was on following the rules. There was little discussion of the need for Catholics to seek to right the injustices being highlighted by the civil rights movement. Some did name them: I recall that one teacher in my high school, a sister of the Holy Cross who was younger than her cohort, did raise in class from time to time the ideas that dogs should not be let loose on peaceful demonstrators and that all children should be safe in their church. But I also recall the unchallenged response of one of my classmates: if "those people" were not in the streets demonstrating, there would be no need to use the dogs.

The textbooks of the day made no mention of the many achievements and contributions of Black Americans. If these were included at all, they were in passing comments about slavery at some point in America's past and about Black people being slaves who were freed by Abraham Lincoln. Sometimes I tried to point out that someone was trying to make my difference a liability, an example of something "less." At other times, I quickly grasped the absurdity of the contradiction and chose not to engage.

As I reflect back, I understand that I was beginning to develop one of the skills required of every mediator—discerning what is not being said and understanding how that silence impacts the resolution of the conflict. Without a doubt, I did not always then (maybe do not always now) make the correct choice about how the conflict could or should be resolved. I think now, however, that I was on the road to recognizing how much we can learn from our life experiences—if only we are open to learning, not being "one who already knows."

The Other Community—Learning about Social Justice

Growing up, I was acutely aware of the post-*Brown v. Board of Education* segregation of the communities and most of the schools in my hometown, an awareness that became even more poignant when my family was the first to buy a house in an all-White area of my hometown. I will always recall, with admiration and fondness, the couple who lived next door to my family's new house. "Good people are good people," one of them told my mother and father. "We're staying." In a little less than a year, my block and several others in the area became nearly all-Black. The folks next door remained.

The local union that represented workers in the car plants, which employed almost everyone in my hometown and surrounding areas, also attempted to build community by holding picnics in the summers, on holidays and sometimes just to get union members' families together. "Together" meant that African American and White families would gather at the local state park, which had been rented for the day by the local union, but the African American families stayed in one part of the park, while the White families assembled their picnics in an adjacent but separate area. What is now termed "Midwest nice,"[5] the idea that Midwesterners are generally agreeable but tend to avoid discussing differences, was most assuredly at work during those gatherings. People would wave, even smile, and wish one another well, but Black and White stayed separate. These limitations notwithstanding, the gatherings struck me, as a young person, as an attempt, however flawed, to create a community.

When their working lives were threatened, however, the union members were definitely ready to form a real community. My father, who had a high school education, was a member of the local union for his entire working life. For a short time he was a committeeman, a shop steward whom fellow workers turned to when they had a problem in the workplace, and in that role helped fellow workers decide whether to file a grievance. For most of his time in the factory, however, he was a rank-and-file bargaining unit member who went to work every day, walked the picket line when called upon, and voted to ratify a new contract when it was put to the bargaining unit for a vote.

The local union went on strike three times during my years in junior high and high school. These strikes were over issues affecting the local company and union, since the master agreement between the UAW and GM had been agreed upon. My father understood how collective action impacted his personal ability to work and earn a living wage, and no matter how much he complained about what the union was not doing, he understood the need for solidarity on the picket line once the union called for a strike. Black and White workers literally stood side-by-side on cold days and nights or huddled together around makeshift fires to keep warm against Indiana's cold winter winds. I do not know whether deep friendships were formed on those picket lines, but I remember my father occasionally saying that this or that "White guy" he met on the picket line turned out to be a "pretty good fella." I do know that none of those relationships resulted in any invitations to other people's homes.

The Path to Community in College

My college years began in 1966 at Purdue University. As a resident of Indiana, I was able to attend this land-grant university at a cost that was a challenge for a working-class family but doable. My first choice would have been Antioch College in Yellow Springs, Ohio, because I was fascinated by its progressive programs, but its cost was far beyond my family's reach. So to Purdue I went.

To say that Purdue was not a welcoming environment in 1966 is an understatement. I later learned of the story of A. Leon Higginbotham Jr., the African American civil rights advocate, author, and federal court judge [6] who attended Purdue for a short time in 1944, and I was surprised to find how little had changed between his college days and mine.

Higginbotham enrolled in Purdue in West Lafayette, Indiana, in 1944 at the age of 16. Purdue was (and is) known as an engineering school, Higginbotham wanted to be an engineer, and the school offered tuition discounts for good academic performance. At the time, the student body included approximately 6,000 White and 12 Black students. Black students were not permitted to live in the dormitories, so Higginbotham and the other 11 Black students were placed in a building called International House, the only building where Blacks could live in West Lafayette and where they slept in an unheated attic. When Higginbotham met with the university president, Edward C. Elliott, and asked whether the students could sleep in a section of one of the heated dormitories, Higginbotham later recalled, Elliott said, "Higginbotham, the law doesn't require us to let colored students in the dorm, and we will never do it," and he told him to accept things as they were or leave the university that day. Higginbotham transferred to Antioch College in 1945 but later said this encounter led him to abandon engineering and turn to the study of law (Lewis, 1991).

My strong sense in 1966 was that the university's approximately 130 African American students—out of the total student population of approximately 20,000—still were not being treated fairly or equitably. As a sophomore,

I teamed up with a brilliant young Black woman, Linda Jo Mitchel, a junior who was majoring in English Literature. Together, during February, Black History Month, under the name the Negro History Study Group, Linda and I organized Purdue's first Black Student Organization and arranged the first student demonstration for equitable treatment ever held at the West Lafayette campus.[7]

In a 2009 ceremony marking the 40th anniversary of the Black Students Organization's founding,[8] I described the protest.

> . . .[We] knew that a takeover of a building, which had been done at Columbia University, would end in disaster for Black students at Purdue. In an article in the *[New York] Times Magazine*, which covered the takeover of the Columbia University campus by student activists, Purdue, by way of contrast, was noted as a "Hotbed of Rest."
>
> Linda and I concocted a scheme to bring attention to the issues that Black students faced at Purdue and to do so in a way that would minimize the negative impact on the participants. We knew that many of the 130 Black students on Purdue's campus were on scholarship or were working to put themselves through school. . . .
>
> . . .Each student was instructed to find a brick and to appear in front of the student union the next morning with that brick. They also were told to conceal the brick until they got to the steps of the student union. Many carried their bricks in brown paper bags. We agreed that once assembled in front of the student union, no Black stu-

dent would speak to anyone—not one word. At a signal from Linda and me, everyone revealed their brick and began to march to the administration building. At the steps of the building, the students formed orderly rows brandishing their bricks but speaking not a word.

There was a brief meeting between Linda, me, and a third leader of the march with the dean of students for the university. A set of nine demands were given to him . . .[9]

At the end of the meeting, we went outside to the steps of the administration building where the Black students were still standing in absolute silence. By this time, a crowd had gathered at the administration building, including a number of police, both from the campus and from Lafayette, Indiana. At my signal, the Black students stacked their bricks into two columns on the steps of the administration building. Once all of the bricks were stacked, two of the students unfurled a banner which had been prepared the night before . . . It read "THE FIRE NEXT TIME." The students then dispersed . . . in silence.

In the weeks and months that followed, the administration began to make changes but never acknowledged that the changes were the result of 130 Black students demonstrating at the steps of the administration building. (La Rue, 2009)

Not long ago, Purdue University's Development Office asked me for a financial contribution. In declining to send money, I tried to explain the continuing dissonance between my wanting an apology from the university and realizing that I had moved on. "After all of these years," I wrote, "I do not recall my time at Purdue with a great deal of fondness. I was 18 years of age, and I took on the responsibility to persuade the university to embrace that which it should have, in my opinion, come to embrace through its own reflection as an institution of higher education. . . . I graduated on time, and I have had a good life, in part because of the education that I received at Purdue. During the time that I attended Purdue, however, the institution was not certain that I belonged there, nor did it recognize my sacrifices while I was there."

The Study of Law—and Interest in Arbitration

As I moved toward graduation, I was possessed with an intense interest to understand politics and social movements. I also had a burning desire to do more than understand the world; I wanted to have an impact on it. I began my graduate education in 1970 in the PhD program in political theory at Cornell. Before the year was out, however, I was convinced that law provided a better path.

Upon starting to study law, I was certain of only one thing. I was most satisfied professionally and personally if I could help solve problems by bringing people together. Working together meant trying to understand the underlying interests of those involved in conflict, even when I disagreed with someone's position.

Near the end of the second semester of my first year of my Contracts course, we were given an arbitration decision to read. The professor noted that the contract dispute that was the subject of the arbitration had arisen out of a collective bargaining agreement. A collective bargaining agreement, he explained, is a contract. Unlike the contract disputes that we had studied all year, the professor said, disputes between the parties about a collective bargaining agreement were not resolved in court but in arbitration. He explained the role of the arbitrator and the rules of the process, including the fact that both parties agreed that the arbitrator's decision would be final and binding. There was no right to appeal.

I was intrigued to imagine that I could reach a position in which people would trust me to make a decision about a matter of such significance to them, and I decided right then that I wanted to work as an arbitrator. I began to understand that the role of an arbitrator, unlike that of a public court judge, is dependent upon two primary factors. An effective arbitrator must be able to provide a fair and efficient hearing of the issues—and must be able to render a well-reasoned decision and award.

Before working as an arbitrator, however, I spent a number of years working as a mediator in public-sector labor disputes in the New York metropolitan area, where I learned, in the trenches, about the possibilities and limitations of being a mediator. One of the principal advantages of mediation is the possibility of helping disputing parties find a solution to their problem that meets both their interests, at least in part. The parties learn, in the moment, to think beyond their positions and identify their own and then their mutual interests—which creates the possibility of community, even if it's only temporary.

By the time I started teaching in 1983 as one of the founding faculty at the City University of New York's law school, I was thoroughly committed to building community by trying to address our disparate human needs. As a teacher of civil procedure, I began to incorporate the growing body of literature about what became known as alternative dispute resolution while teaching law students the rules for formal litigation. In my practice as a mediator and before then as a union-side attorney, I had seen the injuries done to effective problem-solving when the only tool the lawyers had was a hammer, so with various experiential exercises in classes and discussions, I learned to ask students a fundamental question: "What might have been an alternative way to attempt to solve the client's problem?"

Professor Howard Lesnick, then academic dean at CUNY Law School, was an inspiration as a law teacher and a shining example of how creative lawyering can serve human needs. More than any other person, he influenced me to explore alternative ways to think about the incorporation of ADR in the teaching of civil procedure. Howard, who died in April 2020, is the person who taught me how to become a lawyer, a law teacher, and a better human being. He helped me start on my journey of discovering what it means to always be "becoming." It is a journey—not easy and certainly not a path with a straight line.

A common theme for Howard, and I believe for me as well, is in the Talmudic saying: "Do not be daunted by the enormity of the world's grief. Do justly now, love mercy now, walk humbly now. You are not obligated to complete the work, but neither are you free to abandon it." Like Howard, I struggle to understand and accept my own obligation, to further, rather than to complete, the work of addressing and relieving, to some extent, humanity's grief. Far too often, I am overwhelmed with the frustration that I will not complete the work.

In 1983, I also began to incorporate arbitration into my neutral practice. Much of my arbitration practice has been in labor and employment, with a few commercial cases. In the years since, I have continued to explore ways to make the practice of arbitration and mediation serve the interest of fair and efficient ways to resolve disputes. In this era of arbitration-bashing (often for good reason), linking arbitration with notions of fairness in the resolution of disputes might seem strange. But as an active member of the dispute resolution legal community, I have challenged the use of arbitration in individual employment cases in the non-union sector and in consumer disputes. The courts have been too quick to determine that the arbitral forum is suitable for virtually all disputes. There has been a judicial mis-reliance on the principles set forth in the Steelworkers Trilogy[10] to argue that arbitration simply means a change of forum rather than a very fundamental access-to-justice issue.

Working for Diversity

People in conflict are willing to accept the outcome as fair if they believe they have been truly heard, and in both arbitration and mediation, that in part means that the neutral is someone whom the parties believe has a connection to their own life experiences. The dispute resolution field has for too long ignored the importance of diversity based on race, gender, and ethnicity, and a big focus of my work has been aimed at changing that.

For many years, I have focused on what I call the "front-end" issues of diversity and inclusion. How do we increase the number of people of color and women who are arbitrators, mediators, and in other neutral dispute-resolution roles? There have been modest gains on the "front end," at least with regard to gender diversity. More recently, I have focused on the "back-end" problem, the fact that those who select arbitrators and mediators, particularly for high-stakes disputes, do not select people of color. The "gatekeepers,"[11] who are almost always White lawyers, select neutrals whom they know—and who look like them. As a result, the final slates of candidates seldom include people of color (La Rue and Symonette, 2020).

I recently developed a program called the Ray Corollary Initiative™ (RCI™) that seeks to change the way arbitrators and mediators are selected. This initiative is named for Charlotte Ray, the first Black female lawyer (Howard Law) in the United States. The RCI seeks a demonstrable commitment from all areas of the conflict resolution community that every final group of candidates for an arbitration or a mediation will include 30 percent people of color, both female and male. (Empirical studies have shown that the 30 percent metric significantly increases the probability that a person of color will be selected (La Rue and Symonette, 2020).) The RCI, modeled after the Rooney Rule in professional football and the Mansfield Rule in "Big Law"[12] is designed to increase the selection of neutrals of color in arbitration and mediation.

The brief history of the Rooney Rule is that after decades of criticism of National Football League teams' minority hiring practices, data in 2002 showed that while more than 60 percent of players were Black, only 6 percent of head coaches were. The rule, named after then-Pittsburgh Steelers Chairman Dan Rooney and adopted in 2003, requires teams to interview at least one minority candidate for each head coach vacancy (La Rue and Symonette, 2020). The Mansfield Rule, named for Arabella Mansfield, who became the first female attorney in the United States in 1869, is an outgrowth of the Rooney Rule and is aimed at increasing diversity in Big Law. The work began with 102 law firms becoming "Mansfield Certified," which required each firm to demonstrate, with data, that the firm considered at least 30 percent diverse lawyers—women, people of color, LGBTQ+, and lawyers with disabilities—for all governance and leadership roles. The RCI has been adopted by the National Academy of Arbitrators as a nationwide initiative. While much work remains, the adoption of the RCI by a major conflict resolution organization is a source of great satisfaction and pride. I have not abandoned the good work, even if I might not see its completion.

One of my great pleasures in recent decades has been a new kind of community with The Guys, Daniel Bowling and David Hoffman, longtime friends and journey mates on the path to enlightenment who have helped me understand the beauty of how our human diversity nurtures our souls. Our relationships began with attempting to understand how our different experiences had brought us to pursue a life in conflict resolution. In the beginning, we went on weekend trips, retreats of a sort, with ever-deepening conversations about race and its role in all our lives. Those conversations continue today. The relationship is as close as I have ever come to reaching true community, one where difference has become the source of deeper understanding and greater self-enlightenment. I'm befuddled that I have found one kind of community with two White men, one a Jew and the other a Buddhist.

My community with "the guys" complements the fundamental importance of my relationship with my wife of more than 35 years. The fact that we have shared values has deepened our love and respect for each other over the years. We certainly don't agree on everything: she, too, is a labor neutral, now retired, who can be quite articulate and forceful in presenting her viewpoint. But our differences are always underpinned with the full confidence that each of us will use the present difference as a path to a deeper understanding of the other, of ourselves, and of what it means to be in a relationship.

My understanding of my pursuit of community has been deepened by learning to communicate skillfully with my adult children. One of my sons, for example, has a view about Blacks and guns that is firmly grounded in his well-studied understanding of the history of the tenuous state of Black life in America and is very different from my own pertaining to guns in America today. Neither of us has convinced the other to switch his view of the Second Amendment, but our discussions always bring us closer as father and son.

My other son, a gay Black man, has taught me much about my own limitations about gender identity and sexuality. My ability to learn what he has had to teach me began when he was in college and came out to his mother and me. My embrace of him as my son, whom I love and respect, has allowed me to appreciate our difference and the power of diversity as a means to enlightenment.

Another family member reminds me that my work of understanding, accepting, and appreciating difference is incomplete. My wife and I live with our adult daughter, whom we adopted when she was very young and who is schizophrenic. Schizophrenia affects the way a person thinks, acts, expresses emotions, and relates to others, and I continue to struggle to act, with any semblance of skill, on my belief that difference can lead to a deepening of relationship with another. My daughter's inability to relate to me in a way that assures me of some connection to me as her father forces me to struggle mightily.

I end this story with a tribute to my loving family. The COVID-19 pandemic made an in-person ceremony for the D'Alemberte-Raven Award last April impossible, so my wife and the rest of my family held a surprise Zoom celebration for me, which touched me deeply. In the virtual award ceremony itself, I closed my statement with a picture of my family and the video-recorded congratulatory words of our two grandsons, Tommy and Jackie. Thank you to you all.

Notes

[1] This story of America's postwar working class is brilliantly told by Steven Greenhouse in his book *Beaten Down, Worked Up: The Past, Present, and Future of American Labor* (Greenhouse, 2019).

[2] This was the widespread migration of African Americans in the 20th century from rural communities in the South to large cities in the North and West. At the turn of the 20th century, the vast majority of Black Americans lived in the Southern states. From 1916 to 1970, during this Great Migration, it is estimated that some six million Black Southerners relocated to urban areas in the North and West. Isabel Wilkerson has described the Great Migration thoroughly and thoughtfully in her book *The Warmth of Other Suns: The Epic Story of America's Great Migration* (Wilkerson, 2010).

[3] I do not recall any mosques or synagogues in my hometown when I was growing up.

[4] French writer Frantz Fanon, combines autobiography, case study, philosophy, and psychoanalytic theory to describe and analyze the experience of Black men and women in white-controlled societies. Of the many books I read in college, this was the most revealing in helping me understand the development of my self-identity. Fanon F., *Black Skin, White Masks*. trans. Philcox, R. (New York: Grove Press. 1994).

[5] "Midwest nice" has been the subject of many discussions, including one on National Public Radio by Andrew Meriwether. Meriwether, A. "What's the Deal with 'Midwest Nice?'" Recorded January 11, 2020. WBEZ NPR, 8:25. https://www.wbez.org/stories/whats-the-deal-with-midwest-nice/601c44f7-643b-4075-a1a9-9605bbcd66a6.

[6] Aloyisus Leon Higginbotham Jr. (February 25, 1928 – December 14, 1998) was a prominent African American civil rights advocate, author, and federal court judge. Higginbotham was the seventh African American Article III judge appointed in the United States and the first African American United States District Judge of the United States District Court for the Eastern District of Pennsylvania.

[7] The University's version of that history is told in a short film clip entitled Black Purdue University, https://www.youtube.com/watch?v=lMaQyMyQpDc.

[8] In 2009, Purdue University's Black Cultural Center, a department within the Division of Diversity and Inclusion, celebrated the 40th anniversary of its founding. The center is described on Purdue's webpage as follows: "Purdue University's Black Cultural Center is a vibrant element of University life, offering a wealth of programs and services for the entire campus community. We bring together the wonderful diversity of the Purdue family by nurturing and presenting the rich heritage of the African American experience through art, history, and cultural understanding. The center sponsors outstanding student performing arts ensembles in dance drama, choral music, and creative writing. We also house a special collections library, a computer lab, and student organization office and meeting space."

[9] I still have an original version of the demands, written on a typewriter. The document, in all capital letters, reads:

LIST OF DEMANDS TO THE UNIVERSITY

WE DEMAND THAT THE UNIVERSITY PRESSURE ITS DEPARTMENTS TO RECRUIT QUALIFIED BLACK PROFESSORS FOR THE 1968-1969 SCHOOL YEAR.

WE DEMAND THAT THE PROFESSORS OF THE HISTORY DEPARTMENT INTEGRATE THEIR SEGREGATED, BIGOTED, AND INSULTING U.S. HISTORY COURSES.

WE DEMAND IMMEDIATE INTEGRATION OF STUDENT ORGANIZATIONS.

WE DEMAND COURSES DEALING WITH BLACK CULTURE.

WE DEMAND THAT BLACK ARTS BE INCORPORATED INTO THE MUSIC AND ART APPRECIATION COURSES.

WE DEMAND THAT THE UNIVERSITY COMPILE A LIST OF DISCRIMINATORY HOUSING AND MAKE THIS LIST PUBLIC

WE DEMAND MORE THAN A TOKEN INTEGRATION OF THE ADMINISTRATION.

WE DEMAND THAT THE UNIVERSITY SEE TO IT THAT BLACK PROFESSORS DO NOT MEET DISCRIMINATION IN PROCURING HOUSING.

WE DEMAND THAT A COURSE DEALING WITH DISTORTION BE INSTITUTED AS A GENERAL CORE REQUIREMENT FOR ALL STUDENTS.

OR

.... THE FIRE NEXT TIME ....

james baldwin

[10] These are three US Supreme Court cases decided in 1960 that defined the nature of collective bargaining and the role of arbitration under US labor law: United Steelworkers v. Warrior & Gulf Navigation Co., 363 U.S. 574 (1960); United Steelworkers v. Warrior & Gulf Navigation Co., 363 U.S. 574 (1960); and United Steelworkers of America v. Warrior & Gulf Navigation Co., 363 U.S. 574 (1960).

[11] Johnson, M. E. and H. C. La Rue. "The Gated Community: Risk Aversion, Race, and the Lack of Diversity in the Top Ranks," *Dispute Resolution Magazine* 15 (Spring 2009): 17.

[12] This is the nickname for the world's biggest law firms, most of which have headquarters in cities such as New York, Los Angeles, Dallas, Chicago, and Boston.

References

Fanon F. 1952. *Black Skin, White Masks.* Translated by R. Philcox New York: Grove Press.

Greenhouse, S. 2019. *Beaten Down, Worked Up: The Past, Present, and Future of American Labor.* New York: Alfred A. Knopf.

La Rue, H. C. "Student Activism Statement." Presented at the Pioneer Award Ceremony, West Layfette, Indiana, August 10, 2009.

La Rue, H. C. and A. A. Symonette. 2020. "The Ray Corollary Initiative: How to Achieve Diversity and Inclusion in Arbitrator Selection." *Howard Law Journal* 63(2) 215-247.

Law Shelf Educational Media. "The Mansfield Rule and 'Big Law's' Embrace of Diversity Hiring." 2019. https://lawshelf.com/blog/post/the-mansfield-rule-and-big-laws-embrace-of-diversity-hiring.

Lewis, N. A. 1991. "Black Judge's Success Story Begins in Cold Attic." *The New York Times*, July 19, 1991.

Maiese, M. 2005. "Neutrality." Beyond Intractability, June 2005. https://www.beyondintractability.org/essay/neutrality/

Wilkerson, I. 2010. *The Warmth of Other Suns: The Epic Story of America's Great Migration.* New York: Random House.

21

My Life in Community

By Bernie Mayer

◆

Why I answered the phone is beyond me. My parents were both out. Tom, my 15-year-old brother, was in his room, and I was in mine. The phone was by my parents' bed. I probably wanted a bit of excitement, and in those days answering the heavy black rotary dial phone was often an adventure. Maybe the voice on the other end was a family friend, a relative, or someone calling my father about a work emergency. But what I got was not the sort of excitement I was looking for.

Mrs. M (more than 65 years later, I still feel constrained to maintain confidentiality) would often call and rant at my parents. In retrospect, I can understand why. Four of her children had been taken away from her and placed at Bellefaire, a residential treatment center located in a suburb of Cleveland. My father was the director, and Bellefaire was where we lived. My parents would never hang up on her,

---

Bernie Mayer has provided conflict intervention for families, communities, NGOs, unions, corporations, and governmental agencies throughout North America and internationally for more than 35 years. He recently retired as professor of conflict studies in the Program on Negotiation and Conflict Resolution at Creighton University and is a founding partner of CDR Associates, a conflict intervention firm headquartered in Boulder, Colorado. His most recent book is *The Conflict Paradox: Seven Dilemmas at the Core of Disputes* (2015). Earlier books include *The Dynamics of Conflict* (2012), *Staying with Conflict* (2009), and *Beyond Neutrality* (2004).

despite the fact that she could go on for what seemed like hours. They would just listen, try to get a word in edgewise, and be rational in the face of her diatribes about how awful they were. Sometimes they would put the handset down, return periodically to say "uh, huh," and then put it down again. Why was it better to do that than say, "I have to go. Sorry, I can't talk any longer. Bye," and hang up? Perhaps they were honoring the pain that lay within the craziness—or maybe they were afraid of aggravating her further.

I don't know the circumstances that led to her losing custody of her children, but I can imagine. A depressed and mentally ill mother, many children, neglect, perhaps even abuse. In those days, the system was not geared toward supporting the family so the children could stay at home or toward moving quickly to find a new permanent home for them. Supposedly we do this better now. Maybe. Of course, Mrs. M was angry—but unable to use that anger effectively. So she ranted, reinforcing everyone's beliefs about just how crazy and unfit a parent she was.

This time she got me. I was an obedient, conflict-averse, sometimes anxious but even-tempered 7-year-old. I adored my father and thought he was beyond doubt the most amazing man in the world (this was long before adolescent rebellion set in). A concentration camp survivor, quick-witted, funny, charismatic, and a great storyteller, he always seemed sure of himself. Plus he was the ruler of this little world in which we lived.

When she discovered who had answered the phone, Mrs. M must have thought she had a chance for payback. "Your parents are immigrants," she yelled. (I had no idea what the word meant.) "They don't belong here. I am going to have you taken away from them like they took my children away. They are going to be sent back to Germany. You won't ever see them again." It went on like this for maybe 15 minutes—but it seemed like hours.

I was devastated and ran sobbing to my brother's room. He had no idea about what had been going on. He tried his best to comfort me. He told me that nothing Mrs. M had said was true. We were not going back to Germany. She couldn't take me away, nor could anyone else. She was crazy. Or something like that. It helped. When my mother came home, she basically reiterated my brother's message about my security, although with a bit more empathy for Mrs. M. She told me that even though Mrs. M was an adult, I did not have to listen to her. I could just hang up. I never got a chance to do that, though. I did occasionally see Mrs. M on campus, but only from a distance, and I never had another word with her. Surely a good thing.

Why, when I think back to my childhood at Bellefaire—a happy place for me, filled with kind, caring people—is this the event most seared into my memory? I wonder whether this points to something essential about both the nature of community and of conflict. The paradox of community is that what is good about it—the magic of love, safety, and space for growth—is inescapably connected to the sacrifice it demands, the pain it can inflict, and the challenges it presents. I have come to believe that this paradox offers a microcosm of how conflict plays out. All conflict is to some extent about relationships and boundaries—boundaries among individuals, families, groups, and communities.

What does anti-Black racism look like viewed through the paradox of community and autonomy? When we struggle to deal with racism, we are grappling with which communities we are part of, which we do (and do not) accept, which we feel welcomed into, and whom we welcome into our community. Black Lives Matter is a call by Black Americans to be fully accepted as equal members in the larger community of America, but at the same time a desire to be recognized as a group with a rich culture, an important history, and a particular knowledge and lived experience inside that larger community. And, of course, it is also a call to change the lethally skewed distribution of power and benefits among the communities that make up our society.

This is too complex a lesson for a 7-year-old to draw from a 15-minute conversation with an angry adult. What I clearly knew at the time was that the good work that my parents did was somehow involved with pain, that the effort to make a difference was not a smooth ride. No pain, no gain. If you don't want conflict, don't try to make things better.

A further—yet to be understood—message was that part of my specialness and therefore my identity derived from my belonging to a community that was defined by a purpose: to help children and families. Such belonging is a gift, but one that at times requires standing up for that purpose in the face of anger, pain, and hopelessness.

My childhood home was the director's house on the Bellefaire campus. Bellefaire was (and is) located on 32 acres of land, most of which in those days were woods, fields, and meadows. The buildings were solid yet elegant brick-and-mortar structures with slate roofs built around a walkway that wound around a hexagonal brick chapel with stained-glass windows. The walkway ran between a double ring of oak trees. At one end was the administration building, where my father had his office. But in that building there was also a woodshop, a library (where Miss Sugar read stories to us every Saturday morning), a printing press, a sewing and clothing room, a food storage center, and a colonnade. Shim Cohen, the Bellefaire School principal, supervised the use of the woodshop one evening every week where I would regularly go to make things—birdhouses, stools, lamps, toy boats, and more.

In summers, we would gather every morning on the steps of the administration building for flag raisings. All the children and staff would gather there, sing songs, sometimes there would be a skit, the flag would be raised up what then seemed to me a gigantic flagpole, we would say the pledge of allegiance and then go about our day. Often Jack Emmer, a house parent and social worker, would lead us in singing "My Hat, It Has Three Corners" or "If I Had a Hammer." Sometimes we would put on skits. (Once when my brother Tom was working as a summer counselor, I got to throw a lemon meringue pie in his face in front of the whole community!)

The walkway connected the eight "cottages" where the youth lived and a school building. On the outer edges of the campus were several other buildings—our house, a gym and swimming pool, an infirmary, some staff housing, an equipment shop, and a laundry. There were meadows, a pond, a wild strawberry patch, baseball fields, and tennis courts, but most wonderful to me were the woods. Bellefaire itself contained no more than 10 acres of woods, but they backed up onto woods that were part of John Carroll University, and to me they seemed enormous. They were filled with maple, elm, oak, hawthorn, and chestnut trees but also with grapevines, berry bushes, and a lot of poison ivy. Great adventures happened there.

I was aware that my life was in some ways strange and different from those of my friends who lived in typical middle-income postwar suburban homes on pleasantly shaded streets in the surrounding community. But it seemed normal to me—Bellefaire was the only home I knew. I was proud of the ways in which I was different, the son of Holocaust survivors, a resident of a treatment center, not wealthy—in fact, poorer than most of my friends but living as if wealthy, with access to so much land and so many resources. And of course, my father was the impresario of the whole show. I did not want to be too different. I wanted to be part of the larger community, but at the same time I wanted to be special and apart. This desire to both belong and yet be special seems pretty universal.

Bellefaire provided an intense experience in community. It was fertile soil out of which my interest and commitment to both social activism and constructive conflict engagement grew. But it was just the first of many communities that were formative for me. I have been part of college living cooperatives, political collectives, intentional living communities, and a business partnership that lasted 30 years, and I now live in a small town that is, in its own way, a very distinctive community.

I am not unique in this regard. All of us live a life in community, and the communities we are part of and the dance we do between our need for both affiliation and individuality are a defining element of our identity, no matter what our vocational or professional focus. This is not a new concept. Developmental psychologists from a broad variety of perspectives have described this tension (focusing most often on the parent child relationship—the pull toward separation and individuation versus the need for belonging and attachment) as central to our growth (see, for example, Erikson, 1950; Mahler, 1969; Kerr and Bowen, 1988; Sayers, 1999; and Freud, 2002).

But those of us who work on conflict have a particular vantage point on this dance. Almost all important conflicts are based in part on identity needs, with the tension between community and autonomy an important dimension (Mayer, 2012, and Rothman, 1997). Our formative experiences with communities not only help define who we are but how we understand and intervene in conflict. I certainly cannot imagine my life as a conflict professional independently of the communities that formed me and sustained me and at times have also confined me.

What impact has my life in communities had on me? How have these experiences been formative to my life's work—especially my understanding of the complexity and paradox that underlie conflict and conflict intervention? Exploring these questions requires digging a bit deeper into my life in several of these communities.

Bellefaire: Life Has Purpose

Bellefaire was founded in 1868 as the Jewish Orphan Home. Its original purpose was to provide a home for Jewish war orphans from the North after the Civil War (a similar facility for Southern war orphans was established at the same time in New Orleans), and it became Bellefaire when it relocated to its present location in 1926. By around 1940, the need for orphanages had diminished, and Bellefaire was gradually transformed into a treatment center for emotionally disturbed youth (the term of art at the time). My father was brought in to guide the transition in 1945, the year before I was born.

Living in this setting involved me in the institutional life of Bellefaire. I played with Bellefaire kids, went to religious services and programs, and in many other ways participated in Bellefaire's communal life. When I was older, I worked there as a childcare worker and camp director.

The sense of purpose and commitment in the face of adversity pervaded the Bellefaire milieu, but it also was part of my family's own culture. In the years after World War II, a significant percentage of Bellefaire's staff, including my parents, and many of the youth there were Holocaust survivors. My father was arrested on Krystallnacht, the "Night of Broken Glass," November 9 and November 10, 1938, and transported to the Buchenwald concentration camp in Germany, where he came very close to perishing. How he survived is a story in itself, but not for this chapter.

Before his arrest, my father had joined an underground movement to oppose the Nazis. The movement was largely ineffective, but he showed great courage in participating. Many of his compatriots from that time did not survive. Fortunately, the Nazis never discovered his membership; if they had, he would have been immediately executed,

My father had been a committed leftist in Germany, and I grew up as a "red diaper baby." The threat of McCarthyism loomed large in our lives, and a number of my friends' parents were hauled in front of the House Un-American Activities Committee. Several served time in jail. Politics of a distinctly leftist nature were the source of ongoing discussions, arguments, and bonds in my parents' friendship circle and at our dinner table.

So I was surrounded by an unspoken but very powerful message: life is about service, about trying to make the world a better place, and about helping people, especially children. This meant putting yourself out, taking chances, and sometimes putting yourself in harm's way. Service, however, was not at heart an individual undertaking. For us to be effective, to be sustained in what is often a draining and difficult effort, and to find joy in the process, requires community.

The impetus toward service is complicated, however. Lurking over everything for Holocaust survivors and their children is a sense of guilt—why did we survive when so many did not? We must give meaning to our survival—or what good are we? But there is an even more powerful optimistic message, as well, an often-unacknowledged lesson of the Holocaust, which is that with courage and conviction and the support of a loving community, goodness will prevail. Anne Frank was right! Despite unimaginable tragedy, our world and our lives can get better—and frequently do. I grew up with this message all around me, and it has informed every step of my life.

We are desperately in need of that outlook now.

From Activist to Mediator and Back Again

My path took me through years of activism in the peace, civil rights, student, labor, environmental, and anti-imperialist movements. And yet my professional journey led me to mediation and conflict resolution, where the defining characteristics seemed to be neutrality, impartiality, and process focus. Mediation seemed like a way to empower people to take control over their own lives, to bring the 1960s ideal of participatory democracy closer to fruition and address individual problems and social change at the same time.

A pivotal moment came as a result of my involvement in organizing demonstrations against the Rocky Flats Plant (a nuclear weapons manufacturing facility that is now closed) several miles south of Boulder. As part of these efforts, I attended a training in nonviolent social change conducted by Christopher Moore. I found the training fascinating, in large part because of the experiential approach that he used. There were almost no lectures or didactic presentations. Instead we learned by doing, role-playing, reflecting, and group engagement. Nonviolence training is in many respects about creating a community for action and support in preparation for intense and often dangerous interactions. (We are currently seeing the creation of such communities of change throughout the United States in support of Black Lives Matter.)

Chris and I became close friends and co-trainers in nonviolence and civil disobedience. I continued to offer nonviolence training and help organize the peacekeeping efforts at a series of mass protests. Chris and I also offered training in consensus decision-making and conflict resolution for activists as well as in other settings (for example, for inmates and guards at the Boulder County Jail). When

Chris became interested in mediation, I followed in his footsteps and thus began our 30-year collaboration (along with Mary Margaret Golten and Susan Wildau) as partners at CDR Associates (originally the Center for Dispute Resolution) in Boulder, Colorado.

From the beginning, I felt that I had found my vocation. Mediation and related conflict intervention roles seemed natural to me. I found this work challenging, fascinating, worthwhile, and I could even make a living at it. In the years when I identified myself primarily as an activist, I often found myself in the roles of consensus builder (within a community struggling for change) or negotiator (when dealing with those in authority—police, university administrators, management). During numerous protests at Oberlin College, where I had been president of the Student Senate, I had frequently been designated to negotiate with the administration. So this new vocation seemed to harness an important part of my personality and values. I believed in trying to communicate with people I disagreed with, focusing on underlying values and concerns, and speaking forcefully but constructively. Of course, sometimes I was terrible at this, as we all are. I saw myself not only as part of a community of activists but as a member of a larger community that included those I disagreed with, often fervently. I believed that it was through my participation in this larger community that real change would occur.

But I was never completely comfortable with the neutrality part. That was less natural. I believed in being fair, respectful, empowering of parties, mistrustful of my capacity to judge the right path for others to take, and committed to the power of consensus when making difficult decisions. But neutrality was another story. There was this problem of coercive power and social injustice that I felt demanded something other than neutrality. In the absence of some affirmative effort to deal with power differentials, whether between police and minority communities, men and women, employers and employees, a purely neutral stance could easily contribute to the perpetuation of an oppressive relationship.

This tension was rooted in my identity and value system, and over the years it became the foundation of my thinking, my teaching, my practice, and my writing. It can be seen in some of my earliest published work on power dynamics in mediation (e.g., Mayer, 1987), and in virtually all my books but especially in *Beyond Neutrality: Confronting the Crisis in Conflict Resolution* (Mayer, 2004). I want to empower disputants to make their own decisions, but I also am committed to recognizing how power differentials, structural and personal, affect conflict. This perhaps paradoxically has often made me more credible as an intermediary. But I have also come to see the ally role (e.g., advocate, consultant, coach, organizer) as an essential conflict intervention role.

The Juniper Street Collective: Community Requires Autonomy

The most powerful communal experience of my adult life, one that overlapped the first 25-plus years of my work as a conflict specialist, was in an intentional community in Boulder, Colorado, the Juniper Street Collective. I was a member of the JSC from 1973 until about 2002.

I moved to Boulder in 1972, intending to be there only for the summer, knowing I was ready to leave New York City, where I had gone to graduate school and started my professional life as a social worker, but not sure where I was heading. I wanted to experience Colorado and to work on a farm or in some other outdoor setting. My brother was on the faculty of the University of Colorado, and some of his colleagues had started The Community on Nelson Road, a communal farm with about 20 members. So a friend and I signed on for the summer. In the end, I remained in Boulder for more than 30 years and at the Nelson Road community for 18 months. I loved the setting and proved to be a terribly inept but avid farmer (I drove a school bus to make some actual money). There I made some lifelong friends and met my first wife, Reggie Gray, and her 2-year-old son, Ethan.

The farm was an incredible but complicated place. Its efforts at building a community ran smack up against two related problems: how to handle what was at times intense conflict in accordance with the values of community, and how to contend with the individualistic nature of our socialization, which was reinforced by the cultural norms and structure of the world in which we grew up.

The ethos of the time supported alternatives to the nuclear family structure, but the liberation values of the '60s also promoted intense individualism. Efforts to suppress this individualism were at best ineffective and often destructive. This tension emerged around issues big and small. How thoroughly did the garden need to be cleared of rocks? How should parents (or others) respond to children who were being "disrespectful" or "disruptive"—and was that even a thing? How should community finances reflect the different economic circumstances of members? While we tried to resolve the tensions between our individual needs and those of the group, Reggie and I began to feel that some of our essential concerns were being overrun by the demands of the group.

So when a house on Juniper Avenue in Boulder, next door to my brother and sister-in-law's home, became available, Reggie and I grabbed it. It became our home for 30 years. Together, our two homes (which each couple owned separately) became the Juniper Street Collective. For most of the 30 years we lived there, one or both of our houses had additional residents who were not family members but who were important members of the community (they were also what defined us as a community, not just an extended family).

For 15 years, we ate together five times a week, bought groceries as a group, took turns providing childcare to the children in the collective, tended a joint garden, went on camping and skiing trips, celebrated holidays, and met once a week to talk about whatever needed discussion. What most often demanded attention was how to integrate our needs for autonomy with our commitment to the collective. We seldom defined it in these terms, but in retrospect, that was what our most intense discussions were about. And the structural arrangements we created reflected this. We lived in two separate houses that provided significant private space for each of us. The collective grew out of that structure, but it is also what allowed us to endure. Our cooking arrangements also reflected the need to be both individuals and a group. We took turns taking primary responsibility for dinner, for cooking and cleaning up. Others might help with serving and clearing the table, but the bottom-line responsibility was one person's. In part this was for practical reasons of childcare and work responsibilities, but it also was in recognition that we each had different approaches to cooking that maybe did not need to be continually renegotiated with others. For example, some of us (guilty) were messier cooks than others.

The most ferocious argument I remember having as a group was about chickens. Early on in the collective experience, several of us thought it would be a good idea to raise chickens. One person was adamantly against this idea, and we had quite a heated interchange that culminated in the rest of us being pronounced guilty of "bucolic romanticism" (a terrible accusation, coming from a leftist). Fair enough, actually. In an outcome that is not uncommon in group conflict, we finally agreed to go ahead with the plan, but it never happened. The discord sapped our energy to execute the project.

Why was this seemingly peripheral issue so intense? For most of us, raising chickens seemed an interesting, useful, and, above all, unifying group project. But for the dissenter, this plan was dragging him into something that he did not want to do and did not reflect his vision of what the group's collective identity and focus should be. He felt that the collective energy of the group ought to be expressed more around political action and interaction.

A chapter in *The Conflict Paradox: Seven Dilemmas at the Core of Disputes* (Mayer, 2015) called "Community and Autonomy" suggests that each are necessary aspects of the other and that almost all conflicts are in part a reflection of the interaction between these polarities. The JSC flourished best when we could maintain our sense of groupness without undermining our need to follow an autonomous, individual path through our lives—when in fact these two elements of our identity supported and nurtured one another. When our capacity to fully experience both our autonomy and our collectivity began to diminish, the collective became a less defining part of our lives.

This was a very gradual process that perhaps began with the birth of our younger son, Mark (the older three JSC youth were then in their teens), when we came to the conclusion that we needed to redraw some boundaries to reflect the different developmental needs of our children. We began to eat together less frequently and put some limits on unannounced entry into each other's homes. These changes reflected our changing needs as we moved into a new stage in our personal, parental, and professional lives. But they did not take place easily. Feelings were hurt, and tensions, which we generally succeeded in working our way through, arose.

In retrospect, some of the ideas we had about how this community would work were naïve, but the arrangement nevertheless proved to be remarkably durable and powerful. I carried two important lessons from this experience into my parallel life as a conflict engagement practitioner. One was that communities are powerful. They enable us to live fuller lives, are an essential part of our identity, are the places where we work out who we are and what we believe in, and exercise important constraints on our development. The second was that constructive communities must allow our individualism to flourish. The pull between these two realities requires that communities of all kinds learn to handle conflict effectively. And the lessons we have all drawn from our lives in communities is what informs our approach to conflict throughout our lives.

Community and Autonomy at CDR

The interaction between community and autonomy has been a major theme of my professional life as well, as a partner at CDR Associates in Boulder, Colorado, a professor of conflict studies at Creighton University, and more generally as a conflict intervener.

CDR was a bit of an organizational anomaly. Its structure appeared similar to a law firm, with partners and a staff of associates, assistants, and consultants. But CDR was a nonprofit corporation. The partners reported to a board of directors (who formally appointed the partners and a managing partner). In practice, during the years I was at CDR, the board operated primarily in an advisory, supportive capacity, although ultimate fiduciary responsibility rested with its members.

The partners were the hub of the CDR community, operated by consensus, and as long as we were able to work together effectively, it all worked pretty well. But of course we did not always function in an optimal way. We supported each other, but we also fought. We respected each other, but we sometimes became irritated with each other. We walked our talk about conflict, communication, and collaboration most of the time, but on occasion we also exhibited some distinctly sub-optimal behaviors. In other words, we were like any other human community.

Some of our differences were pretty trivial (for example, about how to fill out time sheets or what music to play in our lobby). Others were more significant (how we should calculate compensation, what our parental leave policies should be, which projects we should undertake, and what staff we should hire). When we were at our best, which I like to think was most of the time, we were a creative, innovative, and effective organization. We pioneered the use of collaborative approaches to conflict in many arenas, developed internationally recognized training programs, contributed to the growth of the conflict field, and helped many communities, organizations, families, and individuals along the way. We worked with societies in transition from war to peace and dictatorship to democracy around the world. Some of the people we trained and collaborated with went on to become major leaders in the field (including the editors of this volume).

But CDR was not always an easy organization to function in, and along the way, we lost some very skilled practitioners (and friends). At our worst, each of us demanded too much commitment to the collectivity from others while demanding too much autonomy for ourselves. This is a struggle all organizations face, and we were no different, despite our values and professional focus. I believe that one reason we were as effective as we were at a critical time in the growth of our field was because we were mostly able to reconcile a commitment to the CDR community with a respect for individual skills and needs. We were very successful in coming together to develop a common approach to training and to intervention—but one that accommodated our very different styles, personalities, and ways of thinking.

From time to time, our differences became more heated, particularly when we had to make major decisions about the future direction and structure of CDR. On several occasions we brought in third parties to help facilitate our process and mediate specific disputes. Sometimes we resisted asking for help, sometimes we resisted the help itself, but on those occasions when we fully committed and engaged with a conflict intervention process—surprise, surprise—it really helped.

CDR was my most important and meaningful professional home. My colleagues and partners there were and still are close friends, teachers, and collaborators. But there, too, the time came when the business model of CDR had evolved (because it had to) to one that seemed to leave me less room to pursue my own path. I needed more autonomy than the collective could constructively accommodate. For example, although I could take a leave of absence to write a book, CDR would then be deprived of the income that I might otherwise produce, and this put a significant burden on everyone else. Not coincidentally, about the time I was coming to terms with the need to move on professionally, I relocated to Canada to be with my life partner (and wife), Julie Macfarlane.

The Negotiation and Conflict Resolution Program at Creighton University (originally called the Werner Institute) provided me an opportunity to enter into a new community that accommodated the kind of autonomy I needed at this point in my career. I have just retired after 14 years as a professor of conflict studies at Creighton. The NCR program has been a nurturing professional community for me, and here, too, I developed important professional and personal friendships. I feel very fortunate that these two wonderful communities, CDR and NCR, have been an essential part of my life as a conflict practitioner for more than 40 years.

In almost every conflict I have worked on, a central dynamic has been one of boundaries, the need to commit to a common approach while protecting the space for personal growth and freedom. This is a basic facet of the human experience. Unless we can help people both connect and remain separate, we will be able to arrive at only superficial or short-term solutions to our most serious problems. Perhaps the essential lesson I have taken from my own experiences in community is to pay close attention to this dynamic. Often our efforts to find common ground can be overly weighted on one element of this dynamic and thus create unintended problems. In divorce mediation, we might, for example, push for too great a level of commonality in parenting—or too rigid a separation of responsibilities. As always, we need to pay constant attention to how our own experiences with community affects how we guide conflict interactions.

Our Global Community

As I write this, in the spring and summer of 2020, we are in the middle of the COVID-19 crisis, one of the most intense challenges we have ever faced as a global community. The choices we make about addressing our individual needs while making sacrifices for the common good are literally matters of life and death. So, too, are the decisions we make about which communities we identify most strongly with. We are constantly challenged to think of ourselves as part of a world community, a national community, and a range of local communities and to act as responsible members of each. And for the most part we seem to be doing just that. It's truly amazing that so many people have been willing to upend their lives to try to address the coronavirus threat.

My family and I have been self-isolating in our home on the north shore of Lake Erie. Perhaps paradoxically, while we are more physically separated from the larger community around us than ever, we are also more connected and involved in it. Because we can't physically engage with the range of communities we normally identify with, we virtually engage with them—and we do so more frequently, more intentionally, and often more effectively than ever. This crisis will reset the individual-community system for all of us, and it will no doubt affect the nature of the conflicts that we work on as well.

COVID-19 is also showing us that there are many communities that do not have the choice or ability to isolate and are suffering a disproportionate share of the worst consequences of the pandemic. The sense of betrayal and abandonment that people of color in particular experience by the larger communities within which they exist has exploded into massive public protests since the murder of George Floyd. This, too, is a story of community—and privilege. We are being challenged to change the fundamental structure and flow of power among the different elements of our national and local communities. This is no simple matter, but it is vital to our future. We can't fix this problem by simply redefining community, promising to be better, or focusing on immediate policy changes in policing practices. Systemic change requires system disruption, and that always involves pain.

Our capacity and commitment as global and national societies to protect and to own our least powerful and most marginalized communities and to honor their autonomous and equal place within our larger community will say a great deal about our moral future. Our history on this front is not encouraging, but I continue to hope and believe that progress is possible. Constructive conflict engagement is more necessary now than ever.

References

Erikson, E. 1950. *Childhood and Society.* New York: W. W. Norton and Company.

Freud, S. 2002. *Civilization and Its Discontents.* London: Penguin.

Kerr, M. E. and M. Bowen. 1988. *Family Evaluation: An Approach Based on Bowen Theory.* New York: Norton.

Mahler, M. 1969. *On Human Symbiosis and the Vicissitudes of Individuation.* New York: International Universities Press.

Mayer, B. 1987. "The Dynamics of Power in Mediation and Conflict Resolution." *Mediation Quarterly,* Summer, 1987 (16): 75-85.

Mayer, B. 2004. *Beyond Neutrality: Confronting the Crisis in Conflict Resolution.* San Francisco: Jossey-Bass/Wiley.

Mayer, B. 2012. *The Dynamics of Conflict: A Guide to Engagement and Intervention.* 2nd ed. San Francisco: Jossey-Bass/Wiley.

Mayer, B. 2015. *The Conflict Paradox: Seven Dilemmas at the Core of Disputes.* San Francisco: Jossey-Bass/Wiley and the American Bar Association.

Moore, C. 2014. *The Mediation Process: Practical Strategies for Resolving Conflict.* 4th ed. San Francisco: Jossey-Bass/Wiley.

Rothman, J. 1997. *Resolving Identity Based Conflict in Nations, Organizations, and Communities.* San Francisco: Jossey-Bass/Wiley.

Sayers, S. 1999. "Identity and Community." *Journal of Social Philosophy* 30(1): 147-160.

22

When Should I Be in the Middle? I've Looked at Life from Both Sides Now

By Carrie Menkel-Meadow

◆

"Be yourself. Everybody else is taken."
—Oscar Wilde

Carrie Menkel-Meadow is Distinguished Professor of Law (and Political Science) at the University of California, Irvine. Before moving to UCI, she taught at Georgetown University Law Center where she was the A.B. Chettle Professor of Law, Dispute Resolution and Civil Procedure (now Emerita) and director of the Georgetown-Hewlett Program in Conflict Resolution and Legal Problem Solving. Menkel-Meadow was previously a professor at UCLA for 20 years (Law and Women's Studies) and was Acting Director of the UCLA Center for the Study of Women and Co-Director of UCLA's Center on Conflict Resolution. A Fulbright scholar, Menkel-Meadow taught and conducted research in Chile, Argentina, and China, and has taught conflict resolution in 25 countries. She is the author of over 20 books and 200 articles, including among others, *Dispute Resolution: Beyond the Adversarial Model* (3rd ed. 2019), *Negotiation: Processes for Problem Solving* (3rd ed. 2020); *Mediation: Practice, Policy and Ethics* (3rd ed. 2020) (all of these with Andrea Kupfer Schneider and Lela Love, also in this volume); *Mediation and Its Applications for Good Decision Making* (2016), *What's Fair: Ethics for Negotiators* (with Michael Wheeler, 2004) and *Very Short Introduction to Negotiation* (2021), as well as the three-volume edited series, *Complex Dispute Resolution* (2012). She received (the first) ABA Award for Excellence in Dispute Resolution Scholarship (2011) and the 2019 American Bar Foundation Award for Distinguished Scholarship. She has been a mediator and arbitrator for more than 30 years.

Early Personal History: Origin Stories

Anyone who is a mediator has an "in the middle" story. Perhaps one is the middle child, or one got into the middle of a scrape in the school yard, or is an only child who sits between two parents with "issues." I often date my motivations to be a mediator to a political "in the middle story" that sets the tone for the issues I have grappled with during my career—helping resolve other people's disputes yet working toward social justice, often from a "non-neutral" stance, which can be both a professional and personal conflict of interest. This essay explores my personal history as a mediator and the larger policy and political issues that I see affecting the evolution of our field. I think that today we seem to be "in the middle" of our own more lofty aspirations and the costs and challenges that have come from great institutionalization of our field.

In 1968 at Columbia University I was a student activist in the protest and shutdown of the university to demand an end of the Vietnam War; a halt to the military-industrial establishment's research on campus; the cessation of plans for a new "racist" gymnasium that would have built a fortress excluding the local community in Harlem; release, without disciplinary charges, for anyone arrested during our protest; removal of any Columbia trustees who had ties to the military-industrial complex, the major banks, and the complicit press; and a host of other demands (Cronin, 2018). I described myself as an advocate for social justice, bordering on the radical, from the comfortable political liberal left of New York (think anti-nuclear activity, the civil rights movement, the consumer movement, and just the cusp of the modern feminist movement at my women's college, Barnard). From my Holocaust refugee family (one parent Jewish, the other Catholic, with a politically active anti-Nazi and pacifist grandfather), and our membership in the Ethical Culture Society of New York, a secular humanist religion in which I was raised and later married, I learned political activism as well as aspirations for world peace. At the Columbia protest I joined those who occupied a building.

Alas, my then-boyfriend (now husband of close to 50 years) was a member of the Navy ROTC at another Ivy League campus and asked me to come to the Military Ball, which was a black-tie affair. Can you imagine the cognitive dissonance? So, being the dutiful, soon-to-be-raging-feminist-girl-in-love that I was, I left my building, went home, grabbed my high school senior prom dress, and went to the Military Ball in Philadelphia. In that very cataclysmic year, 1968 (which saw the assassinations of Bobby Kennedy, Martin Luther King, Jr., and riots all over the United States), racial tensions were building and riots broke out in Philadelphia, and we were told to leave the ball. I waved my hand in a peace sign and headed back to New York, where I discovered that I had been banished from my occupied building on the Columbia campus because I was now a "traitor" to the cause. What side was I on?

The next day we learned that the university was planning to call in the police to arrest the hundreds of students who had occupied buildings, and we feared police brutality would ensue. So I helped organize a group who took their sleeping bags to camp out in front of the occupied buildings because, we believed, if we interposed our human bodies "in the middle," the university would certainly not trample on its own "innocent" and peace-seeking "neutral" students. We were wrong. The police were called in and the occupiers were trampled on, some beaten (documented in photographs on the cover of *Life* magazine and in the *New York Times*), and many were arrested. In the ensuing fracas of billy clubs, tear gas, and riot gear, I was convinced the United States revolution of '68 was about to begin. I narrowly avoided physical harm and arrest and then helped organize a citywide solidarity march of students and workers from all over the city who confronted the university and the New York Police Department.

So how is this a mediation story? During the march I tried to engage the NYPD, who were guarding us, and tried to explain that we were protesting "for them"—for higher pay, for unions, for social justice for all. Why were they beating us? Why were they following the orders of the ruling class? I found myself at the head of the march, confronting a professor from Columbia Law School (Mike Sovern, a labor law professor and mediator and arbitrator who later became dean of the law school and Columbia University's president) and asked him why we couldn't just all sit down and talk about it all. To his credit, Sovern actually did try to mediate the student strike. Twenty-two years later, when I sat opposite him as a law school accreditation examiner in the university president's office, he said, "Don't I know you from someplace?" When I explained where we had "met" before, he said, "Well, now you have joined the Establishment, too." Was I looking at both sides then?

In a recent speech at Barnard College on the 50th anniversary of the Columbia '68 student strike, I recalled how I often visit "my steps," the brick ones on the Columbia campus where I slept for several days, reminders of my first efforts to put my body "in the middle" to prevent violence and later to try to use words to persuade those on the "other side" to see the justness of our cause. But, though my body was "in the middle," I remained committed to the causes we were fighting for in the student strike.

After law school I became a poverty lawyer who sued governmental and private entities for discrimination, tenant and welfare rights, bad prison conditions, special education rights, due process, and other legal claims of social justice. Then came my real mediative "epiphany": we often won lawsuits on the evidence, constitutional, statutory, or technical grounds, but the underlying problems would not go away. Sympathetic government officials (social workers, prison managers) wanted to do better but did not have sufficient funds. In particular, having sued several Pennsylvania prisons on institutional and individual civil rights violations grounds, I worked with a special master appointed to monitor class-action settlements. Together, the former plaintiffs and defendants in the lawsuit joined forces to lobby for greater legislative appropriations to meet the requirements of the court-approved settlement, in an early attempt to "expand the pie" of available resources. My favorite case, which was very controversial at the time, was one in which I settled a race discrimination case against a trucking company by getting my client what he really wanted—a truck of his own to begin his own independent trucking operation. A negotiated settlement was forward-facing and tailored to his needs, more than a litigated and more backward-facing judgment would have been (if we had won!). We both had concerns, at the time, about the tensions between individual satisfaction (his and mine) and the possible costs to larger justice issues in maintaining the class action.

And so, as a new law teacher, while still litigating as a clinical professor, I began to look for ways to "solve the problem," rather than "win" the case (Menkel-Meadow, 1984). I began to teach negotiation and mediation, first at the University of Pennsylvania, later at the University of California at Los Angeles and Georgetown, and then at the University of California Irvine law schools, trying to change the legal culture and teach students to listen to both sides, examine needs and interests (my take was a little different from Fisher & Ury's *Getting to Yes* focus on instrumental interests), and look for creative, value-enhancing, integrative solutions to legal and social problems that were both tailored to parties' particular needs and circumstances—but also to consider social justice outcomes and effects on third parties (thank you to Mary Parker Follet, 1995, conceptually and Gary Friedman for behavioral mediation training (Friedman and Himmelstein, 2008)).

In the early 1980s I worked with Jack Himmelstein and Gary Friedman of the Program for the Study and Application of Humanistic Psychology in Law, based at Columbia Law School, in a series of summer seminars in Colorado to teach law professors how to teach experientially and focus on legal problem-solving with more intense personal interaction and attention to human needs. Though Gary's training was incredibly valuable to me and others, I grew impatient with people trying to mimic Gary, trying to twist themselves into what they were not. (I call this the "charismatic" school of mediation, most often, but not exclusively, practiced by men.) People had to find their own way, just as I have done, and as I counsel my students to do.

I moved west (from the more conventional East) to more creative California and trained at Esalen and other new institutions to learn a totally new way to teach, practice, train, and be. Since I was already using these methods, experiential role plays, in my law teaching, it was not as strange as it would be for others. Work at Esalen sought to combine the "psychosocial" (internal processes) of individuals with larger social causes, using more direct communication methods (e.g., encounter groups and workshops that combined cognitive work with other dimensions—e.g., meditation, dance, drawing, etc.). These multiple modalities of accessing conflict, consciousness, and group action were great influences on my teaching and mediation practice. The early days of the modern ADR movement were about new and more interactive processes as well as the search for more creative outcomes and solutions.

I also chose at this time to challenge conventional legal scholarship by developing some of the theoretical and practical (from my clinical experience) concepts that would help form the alternative dispute resolution movement—problem-solving rather than winning cases, exploring mutual needs, not legal endowments, and non-legal approaches to creativity (Menkel-Meadow, 2001). My scholarly work in the 1980s won recognition three times by the Center for Public Resources for Best Articles in ADR, and I soon became one of the first female mediators and arbitrators in some major American and international disputes, particularly in mass torts (such as asbestos, Dalkon Shield) and class actions (discrimination in brokerage industry and elsewhere). I founded a mediation clinic at UCLA Law School in the mid 1980s, and my students and I mediated landlord-tenant cases, civil lawsuits under $50,000, university disputes, employment, and community matters. I continued to do family, employment, environmental, commercial, and institutional cases as a private practitioner. I am proud to say that a good part of my work (since I have a day job as a professor and can choose my cases) has been repeat-player referral from lawyers and parties who were pleased with what I had accomplished for them. (Full disclosure—like all of us, I have had many failed cases.)

I am honored to know that significant elements of our field's canons, ethics, principles, teloi, and techniques have emerged from my engagement with the theories animating dispute resolution and other fields, my experiences as a neutral and as a teacher, and my integration of theory and lived research. Therefore, the remainder of my chapter will not dwell on my idiosyncratic biography, detailing the path that only I can and will take, but will focus instead on the issues and matters I have been privileged to work on during the course of my career thus far and their relationship to the directions I have taken (and continue to take) in my scholarship and teaching. This exploration may help to explain why so many have told me that they view me as a "mother" of this field. My chapter also will try to explain how I have reconciled myself, a committed political activist and poverty and civil rights lawyer, to the mediation canons of neutrality, confidentiality, and self-determination of the parties. I also hope it will address whether tailored creative problem-solving by the parties, in private, always satisfies the claims and demands of social justice with which I started my career.

Practice and Teaching

I began mediating in the early 1980s after teaching negotiation in various clinical and non-clinical settings in law schools and after training with Gary Friedman with his "understanding" (no caucus) model of mediation. This model suited my own theoretical approach to mediation, as "facilitating or teaching negotiation to the parties" based on the empowerment models of mediation and my problem-solving model of negotiation (meaning that parties arrive at their own "tailored" solutions to their problems). My cases involved family and domestic disputes, educational, and institutional disputes within my own university and then, through the mediation clinic at UCLA, working with students as co-mediators, all matters in civil litigation, landlord-tenant, consumer disputes, and other *ad hoc* requests we had for mediation. After I mediated a number of disputes within my university I grew sensitive to conflicts of interest (e.g., students mediating disputes involving students and professors, and administrators who tried to avoid or sabotage mediated outcomes), and I began to focus as a scholar, as well as a practitioner, on ethical issues in alternative dispute resolution. I began to experience conflicts of interest in my large case work, too, with repeat players and more heavily resourced parties, and was one of the first to begin writing about these issues (Menkel-Meadow, 2017). I was especially privileged in my professional life to be able to view ethical and practice issues from my actual work in the field and then reflect on them in a more deliberative fashion as a scholar.

As a result of my work with the Center for Public Resources and its founder, James Henry, three major involvements grew my mediation practice. First, I was listed on several CPR distinguished neutrals panels, and I began mediating larger cases: major asbestos insurance disputes through the Wellington facility, employment disputes at higher corporate levels, intellectual property disputes, class actions, commercial disputes, health care, and other mass torts disputes. I encountered many lawyers, managers, and corporate officials who were intrigued by new ways of solving problems, and over the years I developed many long-term relationships with leaders in major companies and the legal profession. They continue to choose me as a mediator, even knowing that I had been a plaintiff's lawyer and a political activist. Sometimes being perceived as being "on the other side" of a dispute or claim gave me enhanced credibility.

Second, I became part of the CPR training corps and began training others in mediation and dispute resolution in major corporations, major law firms, and for many federal and state court systems. With Margaret Shaw, I trained and evaluated mediators in various federal court programs, and together we also conducted master classes to demonstrate different models of mediation in a variety of professional training venues. Training venues were especially useful places to test out different models of mediation with both lawyer-representatives and would-be mediators. It also gave me an early window into the administrative needs of courts and corporations to institutionalize, internalize, and regularize the use of mediation. Creativity and innovation often began to give way to efficiency and cost reduction—a conflict of values that continues.

Third, James Henry asked me to chair, and the Hewlett Foundation funded, a project to develop mediation and arbitration ethical standards for both individual and institutional providers (now codified in the *Georgetown-CPR Ethical Standards for Use of ADR and Principles for Providers of ADR services*). I headed (with Elizabeth Plapinger of CPR) a large commission of lawyers, judges, consumer advocates, and dispute resolution professionals as we dealt with issues including fees, conflicts of interest, voluntariness, confidentiality, and accountability of providers for outcomes. With the assistance and guidance of Geoffrey Hazard, then director of the American Law Institute and professor of law from both Yale and Penn, I had a great mentor in the complexity of drafting rules and standards for a very complex profession, requiring judgment, flexibility, and discipline. I later tried, vainly, to get the American Bar Association to include some ethical standards for ADR professionals in the lawyers' Model Rules of Professional Conduct.[1]

Through this work I began lifelong friendships and substantive discussions with other ADR founders such as Ken Feinberg, Frances McGovern, Eric Green, Stephanie Smith, Larry Susskind, Mary Rowe, and others who developed the first practices of dispute system design. At about this time I also became the first arbitrator in the Dalkon Shield ADR process, in which I handled hundreds of cases, where the women victims were often amazed (and usually pleased) that they had a woman as a hearing officer or arbitrator. The question of whether arbitration and formulaic "grid" case settlement (think Feinberg's September 11 Victim's Compensation Fund) or a more cathartic mediation process was appropriate for such cases (Elie, 2019) has remained both a practical and scholarly interest for me (Menkel-Meadow, 1998). I began teaching dispute system design, both in the United States and abroad. From my

CPR work I was engaged in more than dyadic and individual disputes, and I became interested in multiparty dispute resolution, which I then began teaching regularly in several law schools. As a former class-action plaintiffs' attorney, this was a natural outgrowth of my efforts to practice and study "good" aggregative settlements (Menkel-Meadow, 1995) as other legal scholars, including those more critical (e.g., Owen Fiss and Judith Resnik) decried the "privatization" of justice through class action and other aggregative settlement devices. For me, class-action settlements often provided faster relief to plaintiffs and more forward-looking remedies (such as medical monitoring) and other creative solutions that judges might not have been able to order in formal litigation.

At UCLA I met and worked with Howard Gadlin, who became the university ombuds, and together we received a Hewlett Conflict Resolution Center university grant to develop a program using mediation and conflict resolution theories and practices to study and understand inter-ethnic and racial conflicts. In the middle of this period, the 1992 Rodney King riots broke out in Los Angeles, and both of us were involved in a variety of both university- and community-based projects to see whether we could use mediative and other conflict resolution practices to "heal" or at least deal with the city's and the university's complex multi-racial/ethnic conflicts. Although we and many others were not able to heal all the wounds of this conflict, our work opened up the processes of mediation to be used in many similar situations, which continues today in modern civil rights struggles such as Black Lives Matter (see Levine & Lum, 2020; Pfund, 2013).

At about this time I had several conversations with Margaret Shaw, Frank Sander, and Howard Gadlin about the origins of so many of us as mediators—children of (or children of victims of) the Holocaust, growing up in conflictual, dysfunctional, or alcoholic families—wondering whether we were a generation that wanted to "heal the world" (Menkel-Meadow, 2005). This work has remained important to me, as I now work not only nationally but internationally in multi-racial and multi-ethnic settings, and the question of how differences can be mediated is very real at every level of individual and national existence.

In 1992, when I moved to Washington, DC, to teach at Georgetown at the same time the Clintons came to town, I was privileged to be involved in high-level policy discussions about the uses of mediation in the public sphere. I was asked, along with DC mediator John Bickerman, to train Attorney General Janet Reno and her senior staff in mediation skills (which failed miserably in the Elian Gonzalez dispute with Cuba). Reno's interest in the field led to the development of an ADR office in the Department of Justice, which attempted to change negotiation and settlement policies in a variety of federal agencies. I became a mediator in the federal Court of Appeals for the District of Columbia, where I saw how clever lawyers could manipulate the process for their own or a client's gain. I was also a repeat player for some large-firm lawyers who employed me for both mediation and arbitration of a variety of large disputes. I also served as a trainer, adviser, and sometimes outside mediator for a variety of federal agencies (EPA, Energy, Labor) and the Federal Judicial Center (trainer and adviser to federal judges) and a member of the federal ADR Committee of the Administrative Conference of the United States (ACUS), an interagency consortium of ADR professionals in the federal executive branch. This experience of working in so many settings at the same time allowed me to see how mediation was a very "plastic" process, usefully employed for creative problem-solving and more party engagement but also often coopted to privatize disputes or have them settle quickly. I was definitely seeing mediation itself from both sides then.

As a scholar, since I had participated in some of them, I became involved in assessing the validity of class-action settlements under Rule 23 of the federal rules of Civil Procedure, wrote articles, and participated in the American Law Institute's law restatement projects on aggregative litigation, lawyer's ethics, and a variety of substantive law reform projects. As a university professor and mediator I also began to mediate both individual (tenure cases) and institutional issues for many universities (after having served as a trainer for United Educators, one of the first insurance companies specializing in educational disputes). I also did dispute system design and evaluation work for the World Bank, the United Nations, the International Red Cross, and the Smithsonian Institution. (More both sides now?—working for establishment institutions while trying to develop internal justice systems?) As I saw the ethical challenges of working in dispute system design where the clients are organizations but the users are individuals, I sometimes resigned from such work when it seemed contrary to my personal or social justice values (Menkel-Meadow, 2009).

Around this time, I was privileged to work in two relatively major disputes of very different characters, which I'll relate while honoring confidentiality of those involved. As a result of some of my class-action work, Frances McGovern, a noted mediator and dispute resolution system designer, assisted federal Judge Sam Pointer in attempting to use creative dispute resolution techniques in the national class-action silicon breast implant litigation. As that litigation was nearing a nationwide settlement (later dismissed when a panel of experts found no epidemiological proof of causation), I was contacted to assist in the development of a mediational process of client counseling for class members who wanted to be counseled confidentially about their legal options. Though the dismissal of the national class-action obviated the need for programmatic implementation, the process of planning a truly unique class-action counseling process, using mediative norms and skills, was a perfect illustration of how our justice system could be reconfigured to provide both individual and more aggregative justice, with more flexible and party-tailored processes.

As other system designers have noted, when it needs to, our legal system can be used to deliver more individualized justice, with both future-facing (mediative) and backward-judging (adjudication) values, which is useful in times when must we remember the past (such as the Holocaust) before we can move on (Menkel-Meadow, 2004). My current scholarly and practical work is concerned with these important questions of the delivery of justice, as well as peace, in a variety of different settings: transitional and restorative justice, as well as dispute system design issues. This is the "macro" justice question of use of ADR or mediation. Can systems, institutions, and processes be intentionally designed to deliver a *qualitatively* different form of justice (tailored, sensitive, needs-satisfying solutions), both in tandem with, or separate from, the *quantitative* justification of mediation and ADR (settling more cases and reducing caseloads, or "efficiency")? For me, the issue has always been the qualitative rationale for mediation as a problem-solving process.

In a very different matter, I mediated a dispute between a major donor to a university art museum in which the donor's family was not happy (and threatening major litigation) about how the bequest was being managed. In that case, working in a highly emotionally charged matter, the creativity of the parties, lawyers, and the process we used saved the museum, the donor's art and financial gifts, and utilized a one-of-a-kind solution (which I cannot reveal here). This matter illustrated to me that, in proper circumstances, away from brittle, winner-take-all results in court, tailor-made solutions could resolve disputes, heal relationships, and demonstrate that contingent and creative solutions can work.

My mediation practice has spanned, over more than 30 years, matters involving family, contracts, commercial, employment, health, educational, insurance, civil rights, landlord-tenant, art, corporate management, consumer, environmental, general civil litigation, class action, mass tort, intellectual property, and international disputes, in both private and public conflicts. I was fortunate enough to be at the founding of uses of modern mediation and thus have been lucky enough to be a generalist. I fear that more modern mediation (Menkel-Meadow, 2018) seems to be requiring not only sophisticated process skills but substantive expertise, which I worry about. Creative solutions, in my view, come from the cross-pollination of ideas from different realms that good mediation provides. Yet for all that mediation promises us, it also presents some issues of concern (Menkel-Meadow, 1991).

What Values in Mediation? Whose Justice (Just-Us)?[2]

Mediation, as a practice and as a profession, is motivated by several key values: self-determination of the parties; a promise of confidentiality in information-sharing in service to problem-solving for the parties in their own matter; neutrality; non-bias and non-judgmentalness from the mediator; and, increasingly, concern about the ethics and integrity of the mediator. As mediation was "rediscovered" (from more ancient forms of dispute resolution in Africa and Asia) in the 1970s in the United States in civil litigation (having been around a bit earlier in labor relations, where I first encountered it as a labor lawyer), it was used primarily in family law, small claims matters, and then more generally in all forms of disputes, both legal and social.

I was around for the modern reemergence of this process as I was criticizing the brittleness of legal decision-making—winners and losers and monetization of most outcomes in formal courts, with attention to past wrongs rather than future solutions. Mediation offered a way to do things differently—to be creative in solutions and involving the parties directly in processes that could be tailored to their own needs.

However, from the beginning there were also tensions for me in the work—which was individual, deep, psychological, and healing—and the need for more politically engaged group, organizational, and institutional change.

Mediation of individual, family, employment, educational, and relationship disputes can be enormously rewarding as one guides the "magic" or the "sacredness" of human understanding. We witness people learning to empathize with others, understand (if not agree with) others, and frame (and reframe) situations to be made, ideally much better, or sometimes only "livable," but better than other alternatives. We try to make lemonade out of lemons and often succeed. For this work I am fulfilled and proud and happy to teach new generations to practice and expand our craft.

Yet given my political and social concerns, it has never been enough for me to heal, solve, or reframe people's disputes as they come on an *ad hoc* basis. Like many of us searching for social justice through problem-solving, I want more. I want the world to develop what Howard Gadlin has called a certain "sensibility" about mediation and joint problem-solving—an approach to others that treats all people as ends, not means, and that seeks to empower the disempowered, to be fair, and, where possible, to correct, not just to ameliorate wrongdoing, inequalities, pain, and suffering—to look for real, authentic, and better solutions and understandings than those currently offered up by our institutions and our alienated interactions with each other. Some, like Howard Gadlin (Gadlin, 2007) and me, want conflict resolution tools to be used for systemic as well as individual change and social justice.

Like others, I worry that too much mediation has been distorted by co-optation and assimilation to other forms of dispute resolution (notably, its use in mandated court programs) and what Margaret Shaw dubbed "mediation lite"—the use of mediation forms to reduce case backlogs, with little attention to the deeper engagement of the people it is intended to serve. Another concern is the growing practice, in private mediation, for more evaluative, no-joint-session, shuttle-diplomacy forms of mediation. Major litigation, commercial, employment, and divorce mediation have now become professionalized, organized, and institutionalized as well as commercialized, so that in my home town of Los Angeles, the norm is now closer to dispute management by a mediator who shuttles back and forth between the parties, "selling" solutions or settlements, without any or much quality face-to-face time.

In efforts to become acceptable as offering a go-to form of dispute resolution, modern mediation practitioners market themselves and compete for cases (including pitching their different approaches in large-case beauty contests) in a way that has the feel, for me, of crass commercialization and loss of the founding spirit. But, some might ask, were we any different in our own evangelical pitches to urge people to try another way?

Of continuing related concern is whether a process based on "voluntariness" should be mandated in any or all settings, as is now common in some court systems and growing in practice in other parts of the world. When we think that mediation, as an approach to problem-solving, is a good thing, can everyone be required to use it always? The challenges of the current polarization of our polity have caused me to question that if we simply dialogue long enough, we will all be able to "get along" (Menkel-Meadow, 2018b). There are lines I will not cross and compromises I will not make about some basic values. My culture, or "religion," is feminism—in the humanist sense of equality for all people, so there are limits in where I think mediation is appropriate (Menkel-Meadow, 2011).

So one question I have about our field is, what is (or is not) "mediateable?" When are dialogue, creative solution-seeking, even empathy, hard or impossible to achieve? When does justice require rulings of right and wrong—calling out what is simply unacceptable behavior (hate speech, KKK, Nazis, bullying, etc.) and yes, even punishing it? As the recent criminal trial of Harvey Weinstein for sexual assault has revealed, some things may not be mediatable when an important part of the public wants to "view" justice and punishment.

My German pacifist grandfather was an activist in the Esperanto movement in the early 20th century. In my work around the world, I have thought of mediation as the new Esperanto, hoping that a common core of language and practices would encourage curious inquiry, reframing, creative problem-solving, empathetic listening, and an increase in human understanding across all cultures. Yet my international work has also caused me to question whether this is possible. Is mediation an "ethnocentric" discipline of a "talking cure" that privileges articulation, talking and listening, and pragmatic and equalized problem-solving, most common in more equal and direct cultures that value "just getting on with it"? Mediation has been put to dangerous uses in the locations of its founders (including Maoist distortions of Confucian "harmony" principles in China and "wise elder" mediation in many

African communities) with deference to hierarchy (whether wealth-, family-, religion-, or gender-inspired) that in many cultures diminishes any real "autonomy" some parties can have in participating in the process. So I continue to teach mediation all over the world, with pride and with worry, that when one launches, teaches, or supports new ideas or practices (or older ideas repackaged), one can never be sure of what the "uptake" or opportunistic use of that practice (or theory) will be. I don't want to be "in the middle" of a process that imposes agreements or solutions to enforce peace or harmony or particular political outcomes just to enforce someone else's ideas of what that peace or harmony should be.

While some applaud how mediation is moving into the modern world of technology with online dispute resolution, I remain committed to face-to-face human encounters, even though I recognize that some access to justice goals can be achieved in some matters by permitting asynchronic computer-assisted dispute resolution (e.g., consumer, smaller value, or some international matters) (Menkel-Meadow, 2016). Yet as we try to "Get to Yelp," using online reputational complaining as a modern form of direct class action for consumer redress, I worry about access to techno-justice, as I have always worried about access to any justice institutions. Will the elderly, disabled, or those without access to smartphones or computers need more help, rather than less, to directly resolve their problems? And with the diminishment of face-to-face human encounters, aren't we more likely to increase polarization than create community?

As mediation becomes a process of confidential and private decision-making, many criticize the "privatization of justice." A host of related macro or jurisprudential issues keep me up at night. What is the relationship of mediation to the rule of law and larger societal justice? Is mediation "just" for the parties in agreement in the bubble of the mediation process? Should we be concerned about the extent to which mediation agreements "track" or conform to the law? Should parties know their "rights" as well as their responsibilities to each other and to others affected by what they do inside mediation? Should the law be the determining principle in reaching solutions, as some have suggested, and if not, what other governing principles should we apply, such as fairness and consent? Should mediators be accountable to the parties, to the larger society, for the outcomes they "preside" over? What is the relation of individualized, *ad hoc*, if consensual, decision-making to the justice of a fair and equitable society? What should a mediator do if parties want to use confidentiality and non-disclosure agreements (NDA) to resolve individual problems but shield the rest of the world from knowing about past injustices (Menkel-Meadow, 2020)? When should we facilitate "amnesty" or reduced or confidential responsibility to "move forward"?

I find my current inspiration in my teaching in many different venues where a new generation is eager to learn how to solve problems with different tropes and skill sets and where disciplinary authority (e.g., legal rules) may mean less than actually and pragmatically looking for good solutions to many intractable problems (e.g., ethnic and political conflict, environmental survival, and international migration). As a mediator sitting "in the middle" of time, starting as a "founder" to "hand off" to the new parties practicing mediation, I look forward to seeing what a new generation will make of what some of us have tried to do. One can only hope that they can create less adversarial ways of dealing with differences to try to create a better world, both for individuals and for larger groups of people in pain or need of justice and fairness.

When I speak, two of the questions I hear often are "How can I become you? What did you do to get here?" The answer is that I bucked conventional legal scholarship demands with the help of a very supportive faculty at UCLA, which was especially important since I was working in more than one field—including legal ethics, socio-legal studies, interdisciplinary work with my (committed and feminist) husband, and empirical research supported by the National Science Foundation. I won the first-ever CPR award for ADR scholarship and as a result wound up being chosen as a mediator in some pretty big cases, as described here, and on the CPR Board which led to many other things, also described here. To young women—and anyone else who wants to get into this field today—I say, "Be creative. Be a founder of something. Don't accept things as they are. Make your own way."

Notes

Author's Note: Thank you to Joni Mitchell, composer, and Judy Collins, who recorded my favorite version of "Both Sides Now" on the 1967 album *Wildflowers*.

[1] Eventually, the ABA Model Rules of Professional Conduct (for lawyers) "recognized" ADR in two ways: Those who are third-party neutrals, including both mediators and arbitrators, are recognized (Rule 2.4 "Lawyer as Third Party Neutral") but told only that they must inform clients they are not acting as their legal representatives. And the definitional section 1.0 (m) defines "tribunals" (which must be told "the truth," Rule 3.3) as including arbitration, but not mediation, thereby eliding the many ethical issues involved in the practice of mediation (conflicts of interest, disclosures, fees, accountability, malpractice, etc.). Now ethical standards in mediation exist as precatory, not mandatory, rules in a set of principles jointly developed by the American Bar Association, the Association for Conflict Resolution, and the American Bar Association—Model Standards of Conduct for Mediators.

[2] Thanks to my friend and former colleague in mediation training, law professoring, and life, Charles Lawrence III. See Lawrence III, C., "'Justice' or 'Just Us': Racism and the Role of Ideology," *Stanford Law Review*, 35, no. 4 (1983): 831.

References

Cronin, P., ed. 2018. *A Time to Stir: Columbia '68.* New York: Columbia University Press.

Elie, P. 2019. "What Do The Church's Victims Deserve?" *The New Yorker*, April 15, 2019.

Fisher, R. and W. Ury. 1981. *Getting to YES: Negotiating Agreement Without Giving In*. 1st ed. Edited by B. Patton. New York: Houghton Mifflin.

Fisher, R., W. Ury and B. Patton. 2011. *Getting to YES: Negotiating Agreement Without Giving In*. Rev. ed. New York: Houghton Mifflin.

Follet, M. P. 1995. "Constructive Conflict." In *Mary Parker Follet—Prophet of Management: A Celebration of Writings from the 1920s*. Edited by P. Graham. Boston: Harvard Business School Press.

Friedman, G. and J. Himmelstein. 2008. *Challenging Conflict: Mediation Through Understanding*. Washington DC: American Bar Association Press.

Gadlin, H. and S. Sturm. 2007. "Conflict Resolution and Systemic Change." *Journal of Dispute Resolution* 2007(1): 1-64.

CPR-Georgetown Commission on Ethics and Standards of Practice in ADR. "Principles for ADR Provider Organizations." International Institute for Conflict Prevention & Resolution. May 1, 2002. https://www.cpradr.org/news-publications/articles/2010-07-06-principles-for-adr-provider-organizations.

Lawrence III, C. 1983. "'Justice' or 'Just Us': Racism and the Role of Ideology." *Stanford Law Review* 35(4): 831-856.

Levine, B. and G. Lum. 2020. *America's Peacemaker: The Community Relations Service and Civil Rights 1964-2014*. Columbia, MO: University of Missouri Press.

Menkel-Meadow, C. 1980. "The Legacy of Clinical Legal Education: Theories About Lawyering." *Cleveland State Law Review* 29(3): 555-575.

Menkel-Meadow, C. 1984. "Toward Another View of Legal Negotiation: The Structure of Problem-Solving." *UCLA Law Review* 31(4): 754-842.

Menkel-Meadow, C. 1985. "Portia In A Different Voice: Speculations on a Women's Lawyering Process." *Berkeley Women's Law Journal* 1(1): 39-63.

Menkel-Meadow, C. 1991. "The Co-Optation of Innovation: Pursuing Settlement in an Adversary Culture: The Law of ADR." *Florida State Law Review* 19(1): 1-46.

Menkel-Meadow, C. 1995. "The Ethics of Mass Torts Settlements: When the Rules Meet the Road." *Cornell Law Review* 80(4): 1159-1221.

Menkel-Meadow, C. 1998. "Taking the Mass Out of Mass Torts: Reflections of a Dalkon Shield Arbitrator on Alternative Dispute Resolution, Judging, Neutrality, Gender and Process." *Loyola of Los Angeles Law Review* 31(2): 513-550.

Menkel-Meadow, C. 2001. "Aha? Is Creativity Possible in Legal Problem Solving and Teachable in Legal Education?" *Harvard Negotiation Law Review* 6(2001): 97-144.

Menkel-Meadow, C. 2004. "Remembrance of Things Past? The Relationship of Past to Future in Pursuing Justice in Mediation." *Cardozo Journal of Conflict Resolution* 5(2): 97-115.

Menkel-Meadow, C. 2005a. "Roots and Inspirations: The Intellectual History of ADR." In *Handbook of Dispute Resolution*. Edited by R. Bordone and M. Moffitt. San Francisco: Jossey-Bass.

Menkel-Meadow, C. 2005b. "The Lawyer's Role(s) in Deliberative Democracy." *Nevada Law Review* 5(2): 347-369.

Menkel-Meadow, C. 2006. "Peace and Justice: Notes on the Evolution and Purposes of Plural Legal Processes." Paper presented at the Inaugural Lecture of the A. B. Chettle, Jr. Chair in Dispute Resolution and Civil Procedure, Georgetown University Law Center, Washington, D.C., April 25, 2005. Published in *Georgetown Law Journal* 94: 553-580.

Menkel-Meadow, C. 2009. "Are There Systemic Ethics Issues in Dispute System Design? And What We Should (Not) Do About It: Lessons From International and Domestic Fronts." *Harvard Negotiation Law Review* 14(1): 195-231.

Menkel-Meadow, C. 2011a. "Mediating Multi-Culturally." In *Mediation Ethics*. Edited by E. Waldman. San Francisco: Jossey-Bass.

Menkel-Meadow, C. 2011b. "Scaling Up Deliberative Democracy as Dispute Resolution in Health Care Reform: A Work in Progress." *Law and Contemporary Problems* 74(3): 1-30.

Menkel-Meadow, C. 2016. "Is ODR ADR? Reflections of an ADR Founder from 15th ODR Conference, The Hague." *International Journal of Online Dispute Resolution* 3(1): 4-7.

Menkel-Meadow, C. 2017. "The Evolving Complexity of Dispute Resolution Ethics." *Georgetown Journal of Legal Ethics* 30(3): 389-414.

Menkel-Meadow, C. 2018a. "Mediation 3.0: Merging the Old and the New." *Asian Journal of Mediation.* 1(7): 1-20.

Menkel-Meadow, C. 2018b. "Why We Can't 'Just All Get Along': Dysfunction in the Polity and Conflict Resolution and What We Might Do About It." *Journal of Dispute Resolution* 2018(1): 5-25.

Menkel-Meadow, C. Forthcoming, 2020. "What is an Appropriate Measure of Litigation? Quantification, Qualification and Differentiation of Dispute Resolution." *Oñati Socio-Legal Series*.

Pfund, A., ed. 2013. *From Conflict Resolution to Social Justice: The Work and Legacy of Wallace Warfield*. New York, London: Bloomsbury Press.

23

Becoming a Peacemaker

By Christopher W. Moore

━━━━━◆━━━━━

At the age of 3, when I first met my new neighbor of the same age, I socked him in the jaw. This behavior, however, was not my norm. Whether because of my size (3½ pounds at birth and small for my age as I got older), athletic prowess and ability to fight physically (low to nonexistent), aversion to harming anything (insects, lizards, mice, dogs, people ... even inanimate objects), or superior communication skills (listening, engaging in conversation, and solving

---

Christopher W. Moore is a partner in CDR Associates, a 44-year-old collaborative problem-solving and conflict management firm. An internationally recognized mediator, facilitator, dispute resolution systems designer, and trainer, he has engaged in the resolution of complex multiparty cases since the early 1980s. In the United States, he helps diverse governmental, private sector, and nongovernmental organizations at national, interstate, and state levels resolve a wide range of public, environmental, and organizational dilemmas. Internationally, Moore consults in more than 50 countries, working with international governmental organizations, national governments, the private sector, and civil society to implement peace accords, resolve ethnic/religious disputes, design dispute resolution systems, and promote sustainable development. A major focus over the past several years has been developing dispute resolution systems to facilitate returns of internally displaced persons and refugees and settle related housing, land, and property disputes, work that has taken him to Afghanistan, Liberia, Myanmar, South Sudan, Sri Lanka, and Timor-Leste. Moore, who holds a PhD in political sociology and development from Rutgers University, is the author of *The Mediation Process: Practical Strategies for Resolving Conflict* (2014) and is a co-author of *The Handbook of Global and Multicultural Negotiation* (2010).

problems), I seemed almost destined to become a peacemaker.

Family Roots and Early Years

My story begins with my grandparents and parents. My father's father, at different times during his life, served as a Presbyterian minister and ran a chicken farm. Grandmother raised three children. Both, for a time, were White faculty members at a historically Black college. Their values regarding racial equality strongly influenced my father and ultimately me—and my future activities advocating for civil rights.

My mother's parents lived in Pennsylvania, where my grandfather and his three brothers owned the largest Ford dealership in the area. My maternal grandparents were adventurers, taking trips to Nova Scotia in a Model T and owning a biplane piloted by a barnstormer. I learned from them the value of an effective business partnership, entrepreneurship, and love of travel, which would help me build effective work teams, encourage me to learn how to sell my skills, and take me to many faraway places.

I owe much to my parents as well. My mother was a loving and gifted elementary schoolteacher who gave me an appreciation for art, song, and drama—and taught me, a child with dyslexia, to read. I'm forever indebted to her for how she changed my life.

My father was a big brain. He went to high school at 15, graduated at 17, and earned a PhD in nuclear physics at 23. During World War II, he worked on the Manhattan Project to develop the atom bomb and afterward as associate director of the Nuclear Weapons Division of Los Alamos Scientific Laboratory in New Mexico. We strongly loved and respected each other's shared values concerning the importance of peace, but our approaches to achieve it were dramatically different. His was nuclear deterrence; mine would be nonviolent action and negotiated dispute resolution.

My parents were sticklers for equal treatment, whether in their own relationship, with my sister and me, or others from different backgrounds. They also made sure my sister and I knew something about the world, organizing family trips to Europe and most states in the United States.

In high school, I fell in love with the social sciences, especially political science and sociology. I also joined the debate team and learned how to analyze issues, speak in a clear and organized manner, and effectively advocate points of view on diverse topics of the day.

College Years

The 1960s changed us as a country and changed me personally. Leaving the closed world of Los Alamos, a company town that was a cross between a high-powered university and a military base, and going "East" to Juniata College in rural Pennsylvania, where my mother had been a student, was a shock. Freshman year was difficult. I was a Westerner, occasionally wearing cowboy boots, and very liberal in comparison to most of my fellow students. I was a misfit.

With a small group of classmates, I became involved in the civil rights movement at its zenith, advocating for the recruitment of more Black faculty and students of color, tutoring African American children in a nearby conservative Appalachian community that had been a Klan capital in the 1920s, and sharpening my consciousness about attitudinal, behavioral, and structural racism.

At the same time, the Vietnam War was escalating. Many of my friends began shifting their focus from civil rights to opposing the war. After seeing the horrors of the conflict on the nightly news, reading Gandhi and King, and engaging in many long nights of heated discussions, in my senior year I decided I was opposed to the war and applied for conscientious objector (CO) status.

During the mid-'60s, being opposed to the war at my college was not a popular position. I had many arguments with fellow students. Classmates spat on me, threatened to beat me up, burned antiwar posters I'd placed around campus, and deposited the ashes on my desk. But I stood my ground. Ironically, some of these same students came to me for draft counseling when they became seniors and eligible for the draft.

In 1968, I became actively involved in politics. I campaigned for Eugene McCarthy, an antiwar candidate running against President Lyndon Johnson, and later Hubert Humphrey. My friends and I cut our long hair, got "Clean for Gene," and canvassed door-to-door in communities hostile to our antiwar views.

That summer, several of us bought a Volkswagen bus—which we named Rocinante, after Don Quixote's horse—and drove to Chicago, the site of the Democratic Convention and massive antiwar demonstrations. By this time, I had decided that simply writing letters and campaigning for a presidential candidate were not going to stop the war. I needed to engage in nonviolent protest and join the demonstrations. They seemed necessary and, in my mind, the only way to bring about peace.

Chicago and the demonstrations there were eye-openers for me, not only because of the number of people advocating for peace but because of the level of violence perpetrated by the police. After days of participating in peaceful demonstrations, being teargassed, and witnessing beatings of protestors by the police, I realized how hard changing public policy about the war was going to be. My faith in the existing political process was seriously shaken. I was ready to become a full-time activist and work for change.

Becoming an Activist

Upon my graduation from college in 1969, the American Friends Service Committee (AFSC) hired me to be a counselor for a work camp whose participants were studying institutional racism in the ghetto of Wilmington, Delaware.[1] During this period I became a member of the Religious Society of Friends, known as Quakers, and, after multiple appeals and the involvement of my junior high school math teacher, a German immigrant who came to the United States in the 1930s and fought for this country during World War II, the draft board granted my request to be a CO.

Ironically, my lottery number for the draft was high, and I was never drafted. Nevertheless, I performed two years of equivalent voluntary service at a government approved agency, the Friends Peace Committee (FPC) in Philadelphia, where I worked on ending the Vietnam War. I helped organize large peace demonstrations in Washington, trained others to be nonviolent peacekeepers, served as one myself, provided draft counseling, and conducted workshops in high schools and universities on nonviolent social change.

Paradoxically, it was as an activist that I landed in the "middle" of multiple significant conflicts. I monitored nonviolent peacekeepers during demonstrations in New Haven protesting the murder trial of Bobby Seale, who was a leader of the Black Panthers, a radical African American political group. I was also a member of a Quaker crisis intervention team that worked among the city of Philadelphia, its police department, and the Black Panthers prior to the latter's Revolutionary People's Constitutional Convention (RPCC) to reach agreements for how peace could be maintained in the city. The team provided a cadre of more than 200 nonviolent peacekeepers that enabled thousands of convention participants and members of the Black community to exercise their constitutional rights of free speech and assembly and helped prevent outbreaks of violence between demonstrators and police.

During my last year at FPC, I met Norm Wilson, the director of the Antioch-Putney Graduate School of Education and a fellow Quaker. Norm, who had served in the US Army of occupation of Japan and as a former representative in the country for the AFSC, urged me to pursue a master's degree in teaching social change, as he believed that an advanced degree would increase my credibility as an advocate. Norm became an important mentor and role model for how to live one's life guided by strong values and working for peace.

After graduate school, I joined some friends who were building a new nonviolent social change movement: the Movement for a New Society (MNS), a graduate school for organizers, and an intentional living community, the Philadelphia Life Center. Several friends (Susanne Terry, Steve Parker, Berit Lakey, Peter Woodrow, Chuck Esser, and Stephanie Judson) and I formed the Training Action Affinity Group (TAAG), a work group that provided training in nonviolent social change. My experiences with TAAG deepened my thinking about how to create effective horizontal organizations and strategies for making nonviolent change and shaped my contribution to *The Resource Manual for a Living Revolution* (Coover, Deacon, Esser, and Moore, 1977), a guide for community organizers. During this time, I enrolled in a PhD program at Rutgers University in political sociology and development because I wanted to learn more about social change theory.

It was at the Life Center that I first learned about formal mediation. The TAAG brought Bill Lincoln and Josh Stulberg from the American Arbitration Association to teach us new methods to resolve community disputes. I later applied these approaches when intervening to help address a violent conflict between Black and White youth at a high school in New Jersey. The training was a critical incident that would launch me in a new life direction as a mediator. But not just yet.

Joining the Mediation Movement and Growing Up to Be a Mediator

In the late 1970s, I left the Life Center for several consultancies in Colorado with the AFSC. This time, my work was coordinating direct action and nonviolent peacekeepers for a nuclear disarmament campaign to close the Rocky Flats Plant, a facility that manufactured triggers for nuclear weapons. (Several years later, in part due to our local and national protest efforts, nuclear accords were reached between the United States and the Soviet Union, and the plant was decommissioned.)

After my last consultancy with AFSC, I was ready for a change.

I decided to stay in Colorado and try my hand at becoming a mediator, full time, to make the world a better place. Idealistic? Yes ... so what! But I had doubts. Would I be able to step back from being an activist on issues I deeply cared about? Would I be able to recognize that diverse parties had legitimate interests they were striving to achieve and avoid passing judgment? Could I trust the parties to be their own advocates rather than taking on that role myself? Would I be mindful enough to say "no" to cases that were too close to my heart for me to serve as an effective, impartial intermediary—or would my hubris get in the way? Above all, I feared that I would miss living in the mainstream of history, engaged in addressing the big issues of the day—civil rights, the draft, ending the Vietnam War, closing Rocky Flats.

Two lucky breaks propelled me toward my goal: meeting Susan Carpenter and John Kennedy, the principals of Accord, one of the first environmental conflict management firms in the United States, and meeting Mary Margaret Golten, the assistant director of the Denver Conciliation Service (DCS), a neighborhood justice center. Because of my experience working to address highly controversial conflicts, Susan and John invited me to consult with them on a book they were writing on environmental and public dispute resolution (Carpenter and Kennedy, 2001). They later asked me to become Accord's director of training, a job in which I designed and presented seminars across the country on natural resource conflict management. After working for Accord for several years, I moved to DCS because it handled more diverse cases. I became its director of training and helped establish and build the capacities of a number of community mediation centers in Colorado and several other states. I also began to mediate community disputes.

Internally, I played a key role in reshaping DCS's management structure from a hierarchical organization to an association of equal partners—Mary Margaret Golten, Susan Wildau, Bernie Mayer, and me. We rotated the managing partner function and made decisions by consensus. These friends would be my business partners for more than 40 years. Susan and I also became life partners, enjoying a relationship that has been wonderful and tremendously enriching for both of us.

While at DCS I completed my PhD with a dissertation that became the basis for my book *The Mediation Process: Practical Strategies for Resolving Conflict* (Moore, 2003), which has now been translated into multiple languages. One of my major contributions to the field, it lines up well with my core belief that being a mediator and acquiring these skills shoulders us with a higher responsibility to share what we know to improve society.

From Barking Dogs and Divorces to Regulatory Negotiations, Policy Dialogues, and Interstate Disputes

Initially, most of my cases at DCS focused on community or "barking dog" disputes. But community disputes alone could not financially support DCS. Our organization, like other community dispute resolution centers across the country, struggled to find enough clients who could afford to pay adequate fees for services and attract the kinds of disputes that could generate significant income. Serendipity struck when the organization applied for and received a grant from the William and Flora Hewlett Foundation to conduct an experiment to see whether, with the foundation's financial help, DCS could become a fully fee-for-service nonprofit. (At this time, most dispute resolution organizations relied exclusively on grants or funding from governments to support their operations.) We were fortunate to have Bob Barrett as our grant officer. He was passionate about dispute resolution and instrumental in building the field through support for theory centers and sustainable practitioner organizations. And he believed in us.

With Hewlett's funding, we were able to make the transition to a predominantly fee-for-service nonprofit and establish a national practice. We changed our name to the Center for Dispute Resolution (CDR) to reflect our provision of services beyond the Denver area. Several years later, we changed it again to CDR Associates (which stood for Collaborative Decision Resources), highlighting the broader range of problem-solving services we provided beyond mediation.

To become financially sustainable, we needed to find and serve fee-paying markets. One was the provision of conflict management training. We developed a wide range of public training programs, including meeting facilitation, negotiation, general mediation, and specialized applications of mediation. Our programs became nationally and internationally known and drew participants from around the world. They helped build our reputation and enhanced our becoming reflective practitioners who could integrate theory and practice and make tangible for others the concepts, skills, and theories we applied in our own dispute resolution practice.

Our public programs also served as the foundation and launching pad for customized conflict management seminars provided to all levels of government and the private sector. Concurrently, we expanded our mediation practice, focusing on the resolution of family disputes, multiparty conflicts in organizations, and public controversies. We selected the latter two foci because of their potential to help larger numbers of people.

One of my early multiparty cases was the Wolf Summit, a meeting convened by the governor of Alaska to develop a new policy to control wolves by culling them as a method to prevent the decline of caribou and moose ("ungulate") herds due to predation. The issue was highly controversial: state officials and diverse hunters supported culling, and most environmentalists and animal rights activists opposed the idea. The proposed policy led to a boycott of the state, which hurt Alaska's tourist industry.

The governor brought 120 stakeholders together in the Fairbanks ice arena to develop proposals for the new policy. Bernie and I were hired to design and facilitate the multi-day policy dialogue. Close to 1,400 people took part in the negotiations as formal parties, by providing research results or testimony or attending as observers. Many proponents of wolf control dressed in hunting outfits or wolf furs, both inside the arena and outside, where they demonstrated and displayed carcasses of wolves and partly eaten prey.

We reframed the issue beyond control of wolves to include "other predators," principally recreational and trophy hunters. The reframed goal for the summit read, "How can the population of ungulates be protected from decline due to wolves *and* other predators?" Those three additional words made the difference between a deadlock over killing wolves and the development by summit participants of a number of broadly supported recommendations to the governor for diverse ways to safeguard ungulate herds from predation.

Cases such as the Wolf Summit gradually helped build my reputation as a facilitator and mediator of highly complex public disputes. I began to provide intermediary assistance in a number of local, state, regional, and national disputes related to environmental issues, growth management planning, government regulations, and water. These included both policy dialogues and regulatory negotiations. I was thrilled that I could now be involved in helping address important public issues.

Living in the western United States, where the scarcity of water creates many conflicts over its use, I began to focus on resolving water and (often-related) natural resource issues. A particularly interesting case involved the states of Colorado, Nebraska, and Kansas over allocation of the water of the Republican River. Although the states had an interstate compact, Kansas authorities felt continuously shorted by those in upstream states, and they took a lawsuit to the US Supreme Court. Under the supervision of the court, CDR staff member Mike Hardy and I mediated a settlement of the highly contested trans-boundary water issues that the court approved.

Since the Republican River case, I've had the opportunity to mediate many other water issues, such as flows for the Platte River Cooperative Agreement among the states of Colorado, Wyoming, and Nebraska to protect endangered species and provide water for agricultural and power needs; flows on Colorado's Gunnison River to meet the interests of power generators, natural resource management agencies, and agriculturalists; and the operation of the Truman Dam in Missouri and the Green Mountain Dam in Colorado.

Although parties reached agreements in these cases, a small number of my interventions do not settle. When this happens, I often come down with a strong case of "mediator doubt." Like many of my colleagues, I wonder, "If I had just been a more skilled mediator, could an agreement have been achieved?"

One such case was the Missouri River spring rise negotiations to protect an endangered species, the pallid sturgeon. By replicating historic flows, the plan was to create new habitat for the fish and potentially encourage spawning. More than 50 parties participated in the talks: multiple federal agencies (including the Army Corps of Engineers), 27 Indian tribes, eight states, and representatives of agricultural, municipal, and conservation interests. I was the lead mediator and worked with a team of three colleagues. After six months of talks, negotiations broke down. Several factors contributed to this outcome. The first was structural: the negotiations involved a large number of parties with very diverse and competing interests. Second were conflicting values among the parties about the Endangered Species Act, which some strongly supported and others opposed. Value differences made it difficult to find compromises. A third factor was the parties' differing goals for the negotiation, which I refer to as the "whether versus how" question. Representatives of federal agencies, conservation groups, and upstream states believed the result should address "how" to conduct a rise. Other parties, primarily those representing agriculture, navigation, downstream states, and some tribes, believed the outcome should determine "whether" a rise should be conducted at all. Finally, the operating protocol developed by the parties included a *proviso* that no agreements would be considered final until there was a consensus on all issues. Consequently, any party could object to a component of an agreement and block approval of a total package. A small number of parties could not agree on elements to be included in the total package. Negotiations stopped without a consensus on recommendations to the involved federal agencies.

The case demonstrates, however, that achieving settlement is not the only indicator of success or the mediators' skill. At the conclusion of the negotiations, a lead negotiator for the Corps remarked that the agency had obtained 95 percent of what it needed from the talks. Extensive sharing of information, exploration of parties' interests, and generation of potential options to satisfy them enabled the agency to craft a plan to conduct spring rises that was satisfactory for most of the parties. For this controversial public issue, mediation served an important purpose.

Going International

By the late 1980s, I decided to expand my practice to include international work. To do so, however, I needed to answer several questions: What arenas did I want to work in? What assistance would be useful to international parties? Would collaborative decision-making and dispute resolution approaches developed in the United States work in different cultures?

The first question was easy. I wanted to work in the areas of social justice, development, the environment, and peace within and between countries, and I wanted to help introduce and build sustainable institutions and procedures to achieve them. On the question of what help would be useful, my US experience indicated that training would be the most marketable service. Direct mediation assistance would take more time to develop. Whether dispute resolution approaches developed in North America were applicable in other cultures was the most complex question. At the time, few publications offered detailed information on intercultural dispute resolution and mediation procedures, so my partners and I had to learn through experience, research, and experimentation. We had to learn how people from different cultures viewed and engaged in conflict and its resolution and how their knowledge, "knowledge from here," would relate to our "knowledge from away" (Adler and Burkhoff, 2002). To accomplish this, we developed methods of our own and built on those of a relatively small group of other practitioners to figure out how to share information so that the knowledge and skills of the people we worked with and our own could be coordinated, integrated, and mutually enhanced (Moore and Woodrow, 2010).

Two projects illustrate some of my learning in the international area. In the late 1980s, I was asked by the Asia Foundation (TAF) and the Sri Lankan Ministry of Justice to help implement a new dispute resolution system for community disputes. The project involved designing and implementing Mediation Boards with multiple panels of local people from across the country. While legislation had created the boards, their actual structure, functioning, and resolution procedures had not been not firmly established.

With no opportunity to conduct a situation assessment prior to our consultancy, Susan and I undertook extensive research, corresponding with our TAF and ministry partners and interviewing Sri Lankans living in the United States about cultural norms and dispute resolution practices. Upon our arrival in Sri Lanka, we met with P.B. Herat, the secretary of the ministry, a visionary, and a major champion of the project. (Having a strong champion is one of the most important factors for the success of any dispute system design initiative.) We worked with P.B. and his colleagues to design the new system. We then conducted a prototype 40-hour training program for a group of experienced family court counselors who had been tapped to serve as trainers for the system.

One dilemma of working interculturally is whether to be prescriptive, providing information and advice on mediation exclusively from the trainers' culture, or to elicit information from participants about their cultural values, norms and procedures (Lederach, 1996). Because we strongly believe that dispute resolution mechanisms and procedures cannot be effectively designed and implemented without considering the local cultural context in which they will be operating, we decided to explore ways that participants' "knowledge from here" and our "knowledge from away" could be integrated into the redesign of the training program.

Following the workshop, we asked participants to help us redesign the training program for new board mediators so that it would be more culturally appropriate and acceptable. Using small groups because cultural norms in Sri Lanka made it difficult for individuals to give direct feedback publicly to people in authority—in this case, the "foreign trainers"—we asked trainees to critically examine the content, procedures, simulations, and teaching methods in the introductory program. We posed four questions: 1) what was culturally acceptable that they could *adopt* "as is" as part of their dispute resolution process; 2) where would it be important to *adhere* to their current cultural practices; 3) what could be *adapted* to make the program more culturally congruent, acceptable and effective; and 4) what was totally new that could be *advanced* and incorporated into their process (Moore and Woodrow, 2010). We believed that the approaches integrated into the boards' process—the use of mediation panels as opposed to individual intermediaries, the division of labor among panel members, opportunities for parties to choose their intermediaries, implementation of interest-based negotiation (IBN), increased emphasis on restoration of disputants' relationships, application of human rights standards, use of witnesses, et cetera—would be very effective and culturally appropriate for the Sri Lankan context.

Our work with the Mediation Boards, which has continued for the past 20 years, has been one of our most fruitful initiatives. We helped co-design and build capacity for one of the most successful mediation programs in Asia, and as of 2016, the ministry and its trainers have established more than 300 Mediation Boards, trained thousands of mediators, and settled more than 100,000 disputes (Gunawardana, 2011).

Working with the People's Mediation Committees in the People's Republic of China's Xinjiang-Uyghur Autonomous Region proved to be another fascinating experience full of lessons and insights. Unlike Sri Lanka, China had a well-established mediation system with standardized procedures and more than 100,000 locally elected volunteer mediators in the region who provide dispute resolution services for diverse ethnic communities. CDR was asked by TAF and the Regional People's Mediation Committees to present a training program on best mediation practices from other countries that could potentially be incorporated into the Chinese system.

As a first step, I assembled a male-female team of mediators from Sri Lanka and the Philippines to conduct an on-site situation assessment. Our interviews with members of multiple Mediation Committees revealed that:

- When committee mediators hear about a dispute, they initiate contact with the disputants.

- Committee mediators investigate, visiting the site of the dispute, questioning all parties and neighbors, and gathering evidence.
- Committee mediators give little attention to opening statements or building rapport.
- Committee mediators utilize and facilitate positional negotiation, commonly starting sessions by asking disputants, "What are your requirements?" (e.g., positions), not by exploring parties' interests.
- Committee mediators give advice and offer settlement recommendations or nonbinding decisions.

Based on information from the assessment, we prepared a training program that demonstrated respect for the committees' current approaches while introducing procedures and methods from other places that might be incorporated into their current practices. We utilized a culture-contrast approach. First, we talked generally about the mediation process and common tasks to be accomplished at each stage regardless of the culture in which they were practiced. We then asked an experienced Chinese mediator to conduct a mediation demonstration using a real case to show "common" committee practice. We followed this demonstration with one of our own, together with a presentation on how different cultures handled the stages of mediation and associated tasks.

We then asked participants to identify similarities and differences in cultural approaches and consider what might be adopted, adapted, or advanced in their procedures. This approach emphasized that there was no one right way to resolve disputes as long as parties accepted that the process and outcomes were reasonable and fair, that both complied with relevant and just laws, and that no party's human rights were ignored or violated. Ultimately, participants identified and adopted a number of new approaches for committee mediators.

Direct Involvement in Resolving International Conflicts

Working on international disputes has required me to operate in an environment of significant complexity and uncertainty and rely on my wits and instincts as well as mediation theory, extensive research, and practical experience. My involvement has been in three areas: conducting "training-as-an-intervention" to prepare disputing parties (either separately or together) to effectively engage in negotiations; training parties in conflict resolution procedures followed by my facilitation or mediation; or serving directly as an intermediary.

A training-as-intervention for only one party began with a phone call at the time the Oslo Peace Accords were secretly being negotiated. The caller, from the United Nation's Development Programme (UNDP), wanted negotiation training for participants in its Programme of Assistance to the Palestinian People. Upon further exploration, I learned that the training would be at an undisclosed location for some members of the Palestinian Liberation Organization to prepare them to engage in water negotiations with the Israeli Government.[2]

Officials from the UNDP requested a customized training program with one caveat—the focus could not be on actual Palestinian-Israeli water issues. They were concerned that if trainees focused on real issues, they would become so engaged in discussing substance they would never learn effective negotiation procedures. To address this constraint, Susan and I developed a simulation that incorporated many of the issues Palestinians might encounter in their negotiations over water, but we located the conflict in two fictional Latin American countries with all place names in Spanish.

The simulation worked well. Participants learned effective negotiation procedures and reached agreements. One of the most interesting comments during the debriefing of the exercise came from the leader of the Palestinian team. He said, "Isn't it remarkable that the people (the parties in the simulation) have issues that are so similar to ours, and they are able to reach agreements? What is blocking us (the Palestinians and Israelis) from doing the same?" During the follow-up discussion, they concluded that history, absence of trust, and lack of effective procedures to develop integrative agreements were the major barriers for their real negotiations to be successful.

Another "training as intervention" occurred in 1989 when several South African organizations invited CDR and partners to present a series of seminars on negotiation and mediation to prepare diverse parties to negotiate various issues to end apartheid. Among other things, we presented a month-long series of seminars for representatives from governmental and opposition political groups that were not banned and leaders of major Black trade unions and employers' councils.

The second kind of intervention, which includes both training and intermediary assistance, is illustrated by my work with the Okavango River Basin Commission (OKACOM), an international body of senior government officials from Angola, Botswana, and Namibia, to help them better manage transboundary river disputes. The beginning of the intervention was a situation assessment conducted by Mary Margaret and me in each country. We used the information collected to co-design a series of workshops with the commissioners that they could attend with representatives from the private and non-governmental sectors. Topics covered included procedures for effective communications, conflict analysis, interest-based negotiation, and facilitation. During the workshops, participants had an opportunity to get to know each other as individuals, work together, build more effective working relationships, and learn practical problem-solving skills. After the training programs, we facilitated talks between representatives of the three countries to design issue and dispute resolution procedures and a mechanism to resolve transboundary river concerns. These are now in place and being used to address a range of issues concerning conservation, tourism, and water use.

An example of direct intervention as an intermediary in an international negotiation that did not include training was my facilitation/mediation for the Middle East Desalination Research Center (MEDRC), an entity established in 1996 as part of the Middle East peace process. MEDRC provides a forum for principal parties in the Middle East conflict and others in the region to discuss issues where there is a potential for cooperation. My work involved designing and facilitating a series of meetings of MEDRC's Executive Board and several working committees composed of high level representatives of the governments of Israel, Jordan, the Palestinian Authority, and international donors to develop a strategic plan for cooperation, information exchange and development of projects for desalination of water—a project whose effects could be far-reaching, because increasing the supply of fresh water is expected to lower conflict in this water-scarce area. Since the consultancy, MEDRC, among other initiatives, has conducted numerous workshops and dialogues on climate change, water diplomacy, and public administration and provided training programs and consultations on desalination and water reuse.

Retirement?

Over the last eight years, much of my international practice has focused on internally displaced persons and refugees from wars and the global crisis related to their returns or resettlement.[3] To address problems of displacement, I've developed a significant practice in dispute systems design and capacity building for the resolution of housing, land, and property disputes for the Norwegian Refugee Council, UN Habitat, UNDP, and various ministries of justice. This work has taken me to Afghanistan, the Democratic Republic of Congo, Jordan, Lebanon (for work in Syria), Liberia, Myanmar, South Sudan, Sri Lanka, and Timor-Leste. Collaborative dispute resolution systems implemented in these countries have been found to be highly effective in facilitating many refugee returns or resettlement in other communities when returns are not possible. This focus has been especially satisfying for me because it merges two of my greatest passions—peace and social justice—and has enabled me to live out and practice some of my deepest values.

Retirement? Well, as my grandson used to say when he was quite young and not ready to change what he was doing, "No, not yet." I've now reached my 73rd year and am still going strong. I believe I have a number of good years left to help people build peace, achieve social justice, and make the world a better place.

Notes

[1] At that time, after the assassination of Martin Luther King, Jr. and subsequent riots, Wilmington was under military marshal law.

[2] We later learned that the vagueness about the participants and the location of the seminar came from the fact that some prospective participants might not have Israeli government approval to travel and attend a program in Jerusalem and that phone lines to discuss this matter were not secure. (We also learned that the Israelis had engaged in similar negotiation programs as the one proposed for Palestinians.)

[3] United Nations High Commissioner for Refugees, "Worldwide Displacement Hits All-Time High as War and Persecution Increase," June 18, 2015, https://www.unhcr.org/558193896.html.

References

Adler, P. and J. E. Birkhoff. 2002. *Building Trust: When Knowledge from 'Here' Meets Knowledge from 'Away.'* Portland, OR: National Policy Consensus Center.

Carpenter, S. and W. J. D. Kennedy. 2001. *Managing Public Disputes: A Practical Guide for Professionals in Government, Business and Citizen's Groups.* San Francisco: Jossey-Bass.

Coover, V., E. Deacon, C. Essert and C. Moore. 1977. *Resource Manual for a Living Revolution.* Philadelphia, PA: New Society Press.

Gunawardana, M. 2011. *A Just Alternative: Providing Access to Justice through Two Decades of Community Mediation Boards in Sri Lanka.* Colombo, Sri Lanka: The Asia Foundation.

Lederach, J. P. 1996. *Preparing for Peace: Conflict Transformation Across Cultures.* Syracuse, NY: Syracuse University Press.

Moore, C. W. 2014. *The Mediation Process: Practical Strategies for Resolving Conflict.* 4th ed. San Francisco: Jossey-Bass.

Moore, C. W and P. J. Woodrow. 2010. *The Handbook of Global and Multicultural Negotiation.* San Francisco: Jossey-Bass.

24

Seeking Justice in the Shadow of the Law

By Ellen Waldman

◆

Family Background

The handwritten inscription on the title page of the autobiography *Labor Lawyer* reads, "To Dearest Ellen, my lovely granddaughter, with hope for a brilliant and happy life in a world of peace and justice."

The book's author, my father's father, gifted it to me in 1971. I was nearly 10 years old.

Ellen Waldman is professor of law at Thomas Jefferson School of Law in San Diego, California, where she founded and supervises the school's Mediation Program, which gives students an opportunity to mediate disputes in small claims court. She also teaches mediation and negotiation, aiming to introduce broader concepts and help students understand that mediation and negotiation skills are important in a wide variety of contexts and endeavors. She has taught mediation-related courses nationally and internationally and has published more than 25 articles and book chapters in the areas of alternative dispute resolution and bioethics. She has also edited *Mediation Ethics: Cases and Commentaries* (2011), an in-depth treatment of the difficult issues that can arise in mediation practice. Before joining Thomas Jefferson, Waldman clerked for the Hon. Myron Bright of the Eighth Circuit in Fargo, North Dakota, and practiced with a litigation firm in Washington, DC, specializing in insurance defense. While pursuing her LLM degree in Washington, Waldman was a fellow at the Institute of Law, Psychiatry, and Public Policy in Charlottesville, Virginia. Her current research focuses on mediation and social inequality, in particular on the increasing gap between the haves and have-nots in society and the effect of this on mediation practice.

Any story of how I came to mediation—and my particular slant on the craft—must begin with my family, and most particularly my grandfather. He was a larger-than-life character who left his imprint on the national political scene as well as the Waldman generations to follow.

I did not learn about his early life and career directly from him, but rather from his autobiographies and other historical sources. He makes a brief cameo in Philip Roth's counter-factual novel, *The Plot Against America*, as one of a group of prominent Jewish leftists taken into custody when the anti-Semite Charles Lindbergh ascends to power. In real life, my grandfather's activities were tracked and monitored in bulky FBI files, and his role protecting organized labor's right to strike is memorialized in Supreme Court briefs and white papers.

My grandfather's life is the tale of an immigrant who never quite lost his infatuation with the promise of America, in particular its commitment to democracy, social and economic opportunity, and the rule of law. My grandfather's tenacity was fueled by his optimism that the ideals embedded in the Constitution could be operationalized to advance the plight of the otherwise powerless. His fight was always a fight for the underdog, waged in the courtroom or on a political soapbox, but always according to the norms that he felt embodied the best of American society. An escapee from the land of pogroms, tsarist authoritarianism, and Bolshevik revolution, he was profoundly grateful for the opportunity to live in a country guided by social democratic ideals.

A short sketch of his life explains my abiding confidence that legal norms embody a rough form of justice, just as the details of my own life reveal a growing discomfort with the mechanisms by which those norms find expression.

The Roots of My Family Tree

My grandfather, an innkeeper's son, grew up in a small Ukrainian village. His family was poor but literate, and even at a young age, he nurtured the dream of becoming a lawyer. He left his village for America in 1909 at the age of 17. Upon arriving in New York, he followed the path of countless immigrants: by day he worked on the floor of a chandelier factory, while at night he studied English.

His interest in workers' rights was piqued by an early experience at the factory manning a metal stamping press. The work was arduous and unforgiving. Workers fed metal strips into a clattering machine at an ever-increasing pace. The workers had no control over how quickly the metal came at them, and the machines had no safety guards. The day started at 7 a.m. and ended at 6 p.m., with a half-hour break for lunch. When the nimble-fingered young girl working the adjacent machine lost her hand to the machine, the foreman came by to demand that all witnesses sign a paper certifying that it was the girl's fault. My grandfather refused, saying he did not believe his skillful machine-mate had done anything wrong. He was promptly fired. In his own words, he notes, "I had received my first lesson in labor relations" (Waldman, 1944: 25).

Moved by that experience, my grandfather became a cutter in the garment industry, joined the union, and took on the role of ensuring adherence to the collective bargaining agreement on the shop floor. He was further radicalized when 146 garment workers in a nearby non-union shop were incinerated in the Triangle Shirtwaist Factory fire of 1911. He was part of the horrified crowd who watched as girls stood atop the blazing building and jumped to their deaths below. The factory did not contain an on-site toilet, and "to prevent work interruptions," the doors to the hall and stairway were kept locked.

Joining other workers at a gathering to consider the fire and what should come next, my grandfather was introduced to the leading lights of the Socialist Party. He swiftly became a convert, was elected to the New York Assembly in 1917 on the Socialist ticket, and was to play a prominent role in the party for the next 20 years. He became one of the most prominent labor lawyers in the country, representing the International Longshoremen, the Transport Workers Union, and the Amalgamated Clothing Workers of America. Improving the lot of workers, both through legislative reform and legal advocacy, was to become the driving force of his professional life.

My grandmother, Belle Bernstein, was a woman with similar passions. When she and my grandfather met in 1924, she had been out of law school three years and was working as a trial lawyer for the National Desertion Bureau of New York City, an organization founded for the protection of indigent women who had been deserted by their husbands (Waldman, 1944: 162). Like my grandfather, she was a political animal whose sympathies lay far to the left. She was a skilled political hostess, campaign partner, and professional helpmate—and she brought her charm, poise, and encyclopedic knowledge of current affairs to the many gatherings staged at their town house in Brooklyn Heights.

My father went into the family business, joining my grandfather's practice. My earliest memory is of him sitting at the living room table, sharpened pencils and yellow legal pad arrayed before him. He was a talented and effective lawyer, dedicated to his craft and well-liked by colleagues and adversaries alike. What I remember best about my father was his capacity to put his own self-interest and personal emotions to the side and recognize the validity of opposing viewpoints. Even if he were being treated unfairly (as labor lawyers often were by hostile, business-oriented judges), he was able to tick off the legal reasons why the other side might have prevailed. The same was true in his personal life. I never saw him lose his temper; never saw him behave in other than a generous and fair-minded fashion. He was, as I have written elsewhere, Aristotle's "man of virtue" and my idea of what a litigator was and did.

My mother also had a bent for law and public service. In 1947, she was one of approximately 10 women enrolled in Columbia Law School, spending long hours along with my father in the close confines of the law review staff cubicles. Family lore has it that my father—tall, handsome, and a ravishing tennis player—dated all the other women on the law review before taking out my mother. But seeing them together in law school photos, that bit of apocrypha seems unlikely. After graduation, my mother went to Washington, DC, and wrote Supreme Court briefs for the National Labor Relations Board. Within two years, she had married my father, moved back to New York, and begun work at Harlem Legal Services. While raising four children, she spent the bulk of her career heading up the Commission on Law and Social Action at the American Jewish Congress, where she worked on cases involving separation of church and state, discrimination, affirmative action, women's reproductive rights, and genetic testing.

The astute reader will note that this is a lot of lawyers crammed onto one bough of a family tree. I used to joke that chromosomal abnormalities stifled the creativity of those with Waldman DNA, making it impossible to contemplate a career outside of law. But sociology, not biology, was likely the root cause. In my family culture, the law was viewed as a mechanism for progressive social change, and lawyering was celebrated as a noble calling. Of course, as a kid, I knew that not every legal job worked toward the eradication of poverty, discrimination, and suffering. Still, from what I could see, lawyers were working on the positive side of the ledger, improving rather than degrading our individual lives and collective fortunes.

My Path

I don't know if this is true in other families, but in mine a subtle form of typecasting began early. My eldest brother, avid consumer of histories and biographies, became "The Intellectual." The second brother, a physically graceful and talented tennis player, was "The Athlete," and the third, a high-achieving utility player on the twin scholastic and athletic fronts, was "The Competitor." And me—well, I was the youngest and much-coveted "Only Girl."

Although I was held to the same high standards as my brothers, I felt free to craft a slightly different persona—more ethereal, less moored to the practical. Whereas my brother read histories, I read novels and imagined how characters plucked from my favorite books might interact if they found themselves at the same dinner party. I was interested in the prismatic power of literature; how events assume different contours when refracted through a character's idiosyncratic point of view. Narrators proved unreliable, protagonists displayed only partial insight, and relationships formed, strained, tore, and reconfigured in endless variety. Maybe it was this early attraction to the rich, layered, and multitudinous worlds conjured by the authorial imagination that propelled me toward immersion in literature and psychology and not the relentless logic of the law.

I chose to attend Brown University, which at that time was known for its academic rigor, lack of core requirements, and co-ed bathrooms. I thought that its easy embrace of diversity, not just racial and ethnic but intellectual and stylistic, would be a good fit for someone relatively unformed. Brown's campus made room for all types: econ bros, semiotics enthusiasts, aesthetes, engineering nerds, Timothy

Leary-type drug experimentalists, disciplined athlete-scholars and beautiful people like John-John Kennedy and his pre-Raphaelite girlfriends. And though it might have been simpler for like personalities to stick with like, most didn't, and it was possible to move seamlessly from group to group. It made for a stimulating and joyful four years.

I enjoyed my college adventure, but at the end, I wasn't sure of the next step. Maybe teaching. I had worked as a teaching assistant and found it rewarding. But would that be enough? I wanted to do serious work in the world, like my grandfather, grandmother, father, and mother. And though I knew a lot about literature, I didn't really know much about how our government, including the judiciary, was supposed to work and the corresponding obligations of citizenship. And what if teaching wasn't the answer? I needed options. So I applied to law school as a sort of finishing school—a way to gain a more in-depth understanding of the rules that govern our social interactions—and as a possible plan B.

I didn't intend to practice—at least not in any traditional sense. But in my family, to be a lawyer is to be a litigator, so I thought I needed to at least see what litigation was all about. I ended up at a small "boutique" litigation firm that heavily advertised its *pro bono* First Amendment practice but focused mainly on insurance defense work.

My first day at the firm presaged my date-stamped stay there. I arrived at 8:00 a.m. and was told I was being put on a "big case." At 8:01, the file room clerks began bringing Redweld expandable binders into my office, one dolly at a time. By lunchtime, half of my office floor was covered. By 5 p.m., only a tiny bit of carpet around my desk was visible. The rest of the office floor was obscured by the red tide of binders. It was my job, with the Dictaphone that was given to me by my secretary, to read the contents of these

Redwelds, record the "highlights" into the Dictaphone, and capture the status of the case.

As it turned out, the case was a modern-day Jarndyce v. Jarndyce, the long-running inheritance case in Charles Dickens's *Bleak House*.[1] Four other firms had been actively litigating portions of the dispute in three separate jurisdictions over the course of the prior two years. My firm was only the latest celebrant to the party.

Apparently, our client had issued an excess casualty insurance policy to a company that had already been the subject of a number of product liability claims. When, unsurprisingly, the company made a claim on the policy, we responded with a battery of defenses, including fraud in the inducement, as well as the usual contractual exclusion arguments. I worked on this case for nearly two years, and it never seemed that we got any closer to a resolution. At our firm alone, several partners and associates were being kept busy almost full-time on the case. The bills must have been enormous. It seemed to me, as a matter of simple math, that the amounts our client was paying its manifold defense counsel had to exceed the amount the client would have paid out on the policy, but simple math was not all that was involved. As I came to learn, our client did not want to garner a reputation as an "easy touch," and so the reflex was to deny first and research legal grounds later.

Although as a young associate, relegated to relatively mundane tasks such as propounding discovery and writing research memos, I couldn't begin to see the "big picture" strategy for this case, I began to wonder whether that picture was perhaps even worse than the one I could see through my tiny, micro-focus lens. Decisions regarding whether to settle and for how much seemed to be made by division heads who were more interested in the budgetary health of their own particular silo than the larger welfare of the company. I also began to wonder whether the entire litigation project had taken on some sort of propulsive life of its own. No one among the phalanx of lawyers, claims adjusters, or corporate decision-makers involved in the case seemed to question whether this litigation constituted a sensible expenditure of time or money. What really was the end game here?

My befuddlement over this adversarial quicksand led me to think more deeply about conflict, how it arises and escalates, and what to do about it. Surely, if the insurance company and its policyholder had been visited, like Ebenezer Scrooge, by the ghost of Christmas future, replete with eve-of-holiday sanctions motions, discovery requests, and exorbitant sunk costs, they would have found some alternative solution. In my off-hours (say, midnight to 6 a.m.), I started to research alternative approaches to conflict and came to learn that the city in which I was working had an evening training program for those wishing to learn more about mediation. The Center for Dispute Settlement, founded by mediation pioneer Linda Singer, offered citizens of all professional (and non-professional) backgrounds training in exchange for a commitment to provide *pro bono* mediation services to the court for a year following completion of the training. My initial inquiries to the center were rebuffed because, in the words of the intake person, "we already have too many lawyers." Although from my vantage point, I could hardly imagine that was the case, I vowed to take a battering-ram approach to the problem and simply called the center every week thereafter until they agreed to let me in.

I'd like to say that the training I took was transformative and that I was a natural. But it wasn't, and I wasn't. It wasn't transformative because I had already come to many of the course's conclusions about conflict and human nature through my litigation activities at the law firm. And I wasn't a natural because I had already, as a young associate, taken on many of the characteristics that impede lawyers' capacities to mediate. I was better at speaking than listening, at formulating judgment than facilitating conversation, and at identifying the "sensible solution" than letting the parties come to their own conclusions at their own pace. It took a while to break those habits.

After the training concluded, I happily began fulfilling my "debt" to the center by mediating court-referred cases in the evenings. Almost without exception, the people who came to the center left more peaceful and satisfied than when they entered. Neighbors, consumers, ex-lovers, and estranged business partners all had an opportunity to explain their grievances, attain a broader perspective of "the problem," and collaborate on solutions that would help heal old wounds and prevent the emergence of new ones. For one starved as I was for some assurance that my actions, if not by day in the law firm then at night at the center, were improving people's lives, the immediacy of those positive impacts was intoxicating. And the more cases I did, the more obvious became the need for delicacy and nimbleness of thought to truly excel at the craft.

In addition to appreciating the simple joy of feeling useful, I liked the fact that mediation practice seemed to inhabit the psychologically lush universe of the literary imagination. Mediation made vivid the contradictory, protean, and endlessly surprising aspect of human nature. Individuals who come to mediation are not flattened into one-dimensional stick-figures, rendered bland and indistinct by the labels of "plaintiff" and "defendant." Disputant appetites—their rage, lust, hubris, regret, and grace—are on full display, and mediation makes a place for them in the process. Narrative lines and fragments flow, intersect, and diverge, and while the mediator works to ensure that all the threads remain visible, like any clever reader, she does not regard any one voice as authoritative. Mediation invites its participants to exchange the arid factual staccato of the legal brief for a subtler, more raucous tale of adventure and misadventure. Perhaps in mediation, I found not just a more sensible way of approaching disputes but a "legal tool" that at the same time embraced the psychological and narrative complexity of human conflict.

Within two years or so of the training, I had left the law firm and was studying mediation full-time. Part of my study involved an internship at the Community Mediation Center (now the Fairfield Center) in Harrisburg, Virginia, servicing the Shenandoah Valley, a rural corner of Virginia. The Mediation Center was just beginning to fold divorce mediation into its stable of services and struggling with how to treat couples with a history of domestic violence. Should they be offered mediation, or should they be excluded? If they were included, what sorts of modifications to the process should be made to ensure that the process did not inflict harm on the vulnerable spouse?

At that time, domestic violence experts were beginning to note that violence in families did not take just one form and that different patterns of violence probably called for different interventions. At the same time, mediation theorists were partnering with psychologists to devise sophisticated screening devices designed to ascertain whether victims of marital violence nonetheless retained sufficient capacity for self-assertion to participate effectively and safely in the mediation process.

The Mediation Center's solution to the conundrum of what to do with couples who were seeking a mediated divorce but reported past relationship violence was to hand off those cases to the only volunteer lawyer in the vicinity: me. Most of the women I dealt with had left the marital home. They were living in shelters and working with counselors. Most, however, did not have the resources to hire an attorney. What they wanted from me, beyond a safe space to negotiate with their spouse, was information. They wanted to avoid court and to resolve their dispute informally. But they were desperate to learn the general outlines of what divorcing spouses in Virginia were entitled to. They wanted to know what the Virginia legislature had determined was a fair child support award, what constituted marital property, how spousal support is calculated and debts divvied up. With information, most of the women I dealt with proved capable, indeed formidable, negotiators. Moreover, the process of negotiating their post-marital relationship with their former abuser did appear to be empowering. But this was only because, in the first phase of the process, I laid out in joint session my understanding of how judges in the couple's jurisdiction, following legislative mandates, would divide their property and determine child and spousal support had they chosen to have the terms of their divorce entirely determined by the court.

So my experiences on the ground were teaching me that information about the legal landscape was an important backdrop to successful mediation—at least in the divorce context. And these same experiences highlighted how many disputants were going into mediation (and court) unrepresented—and counting on mediation providers to fill that informational gap. At the same time, my dive into the divorce mediation literature indicated that mediation scholars and theoreticians were moving away—not toward—the notion of mediator as information provider. Indeed, the field as a whole seemed to be adopting an "anti-law" bias that struck me as unhelpful and potentially destructive (Marlow, 1985).

For my LLM thesis, I began writing a long paper (ultimately published as a law review article) entitled "The Role of Legal Norms in Divorce Mediation: An Argument for Inclusion" in which I argued that mediators—and mediation theory—were heading in the wrong direction. Whereas early family mediation pioneers assumed that educating parties regarding the legal norms implicated by their dispute would be part of the mediator's task, second-generation thinkers were arguing that mediators should limit their involvement with the law and urge disputants to seek the advice and input of outside counsel. If disputants chose to disregard that advice, that was none of the mediator's affair.

To my mind, this was irresponsible. Even early in the 1990s—when I wrote the paper—the number of self-represented litigants was huge and growing. Existing data at the time revealed that between 25 percent and 50 percent of couples entering into mediation were doing so without the benefit of counsel. And yet the emergent "best practices" would have mediators eschew all discussion of legal norms, delegating that function to a chimera. The first iteration of the Model Standards for Mediators, published one year after my paper, cautioned that although self-determination was a foundational principle, mediators "could not assure informed consent" but should advise parties of the importance of consulting outside professionals. Along the same lines, the standards warned that "mixing the role of mediator and other professional providing advice was problematic" and that mediators who, "upon the request of parties, assume other dispute resolution roles" will be held to have undertaken additional responsibilities and obligations and will be held to the standards of other professions (Joint Committee of Delegates from the American Arbitration Association, the American Bar Association, and the Society of Professionals in Dispute Resolution, 1994: Standard VI). If lawyer-mediators were found to have acted like lawyers in providing legal information, then they would, the Model Standards proclaimed, be subject to the tort standards applicable to practicing attorneys.

In other words, the Model Standards cautioned against straying into an advisory role. In doing so, they sent a chilling message to those who might wish simply to provide information and offered support for those who would circumscribe the mediator's task to facilitating negotiations, removing from the mediator's role any educational or protective element. Certainly, there was nothing in the standards that would justify providing information about relevant legal norms and serving as a backstop against grossly unfair or unconscionable agreements. I became more and more worried that the field was closing its eyes to a real and growing problem.

But why, one might ask, was my romance with informal dispute resolution so quickly complicated by worry that the mediation field was not sufficiently attuned to what disputants knew or did not know about their legal rights? Was this some atavistic pull, some reversion to the Waldman lawyerly mean?

Unlike many in the mediation field, my move into mediation did not entail a rejection of legal norms. Whereas many of my colleagues see legal rules as rigid, formalistic impediments to a more individually responsive, organic version of justice, I see something more sheltering and redemptive. Like Thomas More in Richard Bolt's *A Man for All Seasons*, I would not "cut a great road through the law to get after the Devil? ... for when the law was down, and the Devil turned round ... where would [we] hide, the laws all being flat?" (Bolt, 1990: 66).

My father and grandfather faced More's dilemma head-on. Their push for labor's rights often faced overt judicial hostility. Injunctive relief, derived from the medieval chancellor's powers of equity to right existing wrongs, was frequently used to stymie labor's quest for safer working conditions and fairer wages. And yet they both had an abiding faith in the essential fairness of the larger system in which they functioned. They would not cut the laws flat, despite their imperfections—and neither, it turns out, would I.

Into Academia

When I left my LLM program, I was offered a teaching job out in San Diego. Part of my job was to reinvigorate the law school's anemic mediation clinic, pulling the students out of clerical roles at a local mediation center and into the role of mediator at small claims court. To maintain my skills, I signed up to serve on the Superior Court's mediation roster. Two of my early cases made an impression because they reinforced for me how class and education matter, even in the supposedly egalitarian mediation environment, and how the mediator has more power than our rhetoric sometimes suggests.

My first case involved a personal injury claim brought by a gardener against a golf course. The details of the plaintiff's injury and the numbers discussed have long since faded. But what I remember was the scene that greeted me when I arrived to introduce myself to both parties and their attorney. The plaintiff and his wife were huddled close together on one waiting-room sofa, staring off into space. Across the room, the defendant golf course owner, his attorney, *and the plaintiff's counsel* were discussing their favorite holes on the golf course in question, their strengths and weaknesses as golfers, and their preferred time of day to play. The plaintiff clearly did not play golf, did not have his weekends free for recreational sports, and probably could not have afforded the greens fee even if he did.

I did my best in those initial few minutes to tend to the plaintiffs, offering them coffee and making small talk, but I'm sure they must have felt as if they had entered into a members-only clubhouse where they didn't belong.

Throughout the mediation, the plaintiff's attorney urged them to settle for numbers that I thought seriously undervalued the claim. What was my role in this dynamic, when I couldn't help but conclude that the gardener's lawyer would rather have been putting with a nine iron than trying to make his client whole? I endeavored to "sow seeds of doubt" as we mediators are trained to do, but the seeds didn't sprout and the defendant, no doubt influenced by the plaintiffs' uncertainty and the plaintiff counsel's disinterest, held firm. In this case, as with others to follow, I experienced the strictures imposed by the neutral role as a constraint on my impulse to provide coaching to the weaker party.

The second case stays with me for different reasons. It was a breach of contract claim, and although the liability claim had some merit, the damages were speculative. Messy, messy facts. The plaintiffs, a husband and wife, published a magazine with racy content. As a result of the defendant's actions, the magazine failed, the plaintiffs suffered significant losses, and, according to the wife, the stress of the failing business led to a medically complicated miscarriage.

The defendants emphasized both in joint session and caucus that the sexually provocative nature of the magazine would not play well in front of a conservative San Diego jury. They also planned to bring as much of the plaintiffs' bohemian lifestyle into the courtroom as possible. The plaintiffs were unrepresented at the mediation, and the wife was still distraught about the miscarriage. There was no way the defendants would be held legally responsible for the wife's emotional distress or medical bills, but the wife could not take in that information without feeling that her suffering was being diminished and dismissed.

The defendants were reasonable and sympathetic, and there were limits to what they would pay. After several hours of discussion, they asked point-blank what number I thought the case should settle at. I had no idea. There were so many imponderables, including the unconventional nature of the magazine and the possibility that a finder of fact would conclude that the plaintiffs' livelihood made them morally unsympathetic and thus legally unworthy of relief. Today, I would have dodged the question or at least limited my guesswork to a range. Back then, I thought for a minute and made up a number. The discussions continued for another hour or two and then ... they settled at that number.

Why that number? There was no reason other than that it was the number that had come out of my mouth. Our words have a weight that often is diminished or downplayed in policy discussions. When it is suggested that a mediator's duty to avoid conflicts of interest should mirror those of an arbitrator or judge, many counter that such duties are excessive, given that the mediator has no power of decision. Indeed, mediator qualities that might suggest an inability to maintain impartiality are waved away with the reminder that "mediators don't decide anything." This may be technically true, but my experience was a discomfiting reminder that while disputants may maintain decisional authority in a formal sense, they are likely to be enormously influenced by mediator assessments, not to mention proposals for settlement. What follows is that mediators should not enter into such assessments flippantly or in an ill-informed fashion. We influence decision-making more than we might like to acknowledge.

Looking Backward and Forward

Mediation has changed enormously since the late 1980s, when I first became intrigued with the idea of litigation alternatives. What began as a social movement has morphed into a hybrid craft/profession and then into (for some) a lucrative business. What began as an antipode to the adversary system has now been institutionalized within that system and functions as a routine part of many courts' and government agencies' dispute processes. I don't see this as necessarily bad.

But just as the field has changed, I find my relationship to it shifting over time. I find myself often in the critic's role, seeking to temper what I perceive as overblown claims or breezy endorsements. Mediation has the potential to be a therapeutic intervention, delivering both procedural and substantive justice. But like any tool in human hands, it has the potential to harm. When we become enthralled with the notion of "party-driven outcomes" without adequately interrogating party capacity in choosing those outcomes, we do harm. When we ignore the role financial incentives play in mediator behavior and the repeat player effect in David-Goliath face-offs, we do harm. When we assume that merely providing access to dispute resolution solves the "access to justice" problem, we do harm.

Mediation's novelistic elements retain their attraction. I love how the process opens the door to the full scope and variety of the human condition and how the story line proceeds on multiple levels. But, as the philosopher Martha Nussbaum reminds us, the best novels are more than mere entertainment; they are paradigms of moral activity (Nussbaum, 1990). They expand our moral imagination to encompass situations far beyond the limits of our own experience and seed empathic connection with the imperfect inner lives of others. Mediation, like literature, plunges us—the neutral reader—into the acute particulars of human life, into its "context-embeddedness" (Nussbaum, 1990: 38), inviting us to explore ethically demanding scenarios from a place of safety. But in that exploration, how can we avoid thinking deeply about what is required of us, the safe and neutral spectator? For me, that thinking led me back to the centrality of the norms that guide our social interaction and the certainty that people should be educated about those norms when facing decisions of import.

My grandfather, after a half-century serving as "the champion of unpopular causes," continued to believe that "the courts, with regrettable lapses, still serve as the primary bulwark of our liberties" (Waldman, 1975). I inherited his respect for the common law, for the gradual evolution of legal norms as ancient principles bump up against new social facts and problems, and for the democratic ideal of impartial, transparent, judicial, and legislative decision-making. My own experience with litigation tarnished my view of many aspects of the adjudicatory process, but not for the rule of law.

I find myself, then, in the curious position of being both an enthusiast for mediation and an admirer of legal norms—not necessarily because disputants should always end up adopting them as the basis of their agreement but rather for use as a benchmark, as some measure of what society deems fair in any particular circumstance. And, unsurprisingly, as an academic and the product of a family culture where nothing was valued quite so highly as education and the power that knowledge brings, I continue to push for mediation models and ethical cannons that focus attention on the knowledge base available to disputants when they are called upon to forge their own solutions—and on the mediator's responsibility for avoiding unconscionable outcomes. I value party autonomy and the liberation that party choice brings—but that choice must be educated and considered. And, as mediators take their place amid a long and storied group of professionals devoted to managing societal disruption, I hope we keep our eyes on those twin goals my grandfather wished for me—a world of peace *and* justice.

Notes

[1] Charles Dickens's discussion of Jarndyce v. Jarndyce in *Bleak House* makes clear that the litigation is mired in adversarial inertia. It has gone on for many years and will probably continue long into the future, enriching advocates and depleting litigants' spirit and resources—a plague on society generally.

References

Bolt, R. 1990. *A Man for All Seasons: A Play in Two Acts*. First Vintage International Edition. NY: Vintage International

Joint Committee of Delegates from the American Arbitration Association, American Bar Association, and Society of Professionals in Dispute Resolution. 1994. *The Model Standards of Conduct for Mediators*. Washington, D.C.: American Bar Association; New York: American Arbitration Association; Washington, D.C.: Society of Professionals in Dispute Regulation.

Marlow, L. 1985. "The Rule of Law in Divorce Mediation." *Mediation Quarterly* 9(1): 5-13.

Nussbaum, M. 1990. *Love's Knowledge*. New York: Oxford University Press.

Waldman, L. 1944. *Labor Lawyer*. New York: Dutton and Co., Inc.

Waldman, L. 1975. *The Good Fight: A Quest for Social Progress*. New York: Dorrance.

Alternative Frames for Evolution of a Field

◆

ADR Processes

Facilitation and mediation of environmental, public policy, and aggregate conflicts

- Peter S. Adler
- Howard Bellman
- Bernie Mayer
- Carrie Menkel-Meadow
- Christopher W. Moore
- Lucy Moore

Mediation and negotiation of individual (often legal) disputes

- Lisa Blomgren Amsler
- Jacqueline N. Font-Guzmán
- Howard Gadlin
- David Hoffman
- Chris Honeyman
- Carol Izumi
- Marvin E. Johnson
- Lela Porter Love
- Ian Macduff
- Bernie Mayer
- Carrie Menkel-Meadow
- Andrea Kupfer Schneider
- Ellen Waldman
- Nancy A. Welsh

Mediation of international and cross-cultural disputes

- Peter S. Adler

- Johnston Barkat
- Jacqueline N. Font-Guzmán
- Howard Gadlin
- Carrie Menkel-Meadow
- Christopher W. Moore
- Thomas J. Stipanowich

Arbitration of business and employment disputes
- Lisa Blomgren Amsler
- Chris Honeyman
- Homer C. La Rue
- Carrie Menkel-Meadow
- Thomas J. Stipanowich
- Nancy Welsh

Internal conflict resolution (e.g., ombuds, internal mediation, conflict coaching, dispute system design)
- Lisa Bloomgren Amsler
- Johnston Barkat
- Howard Gadlin
- Carrie Menkel-Meadow
- Christopher W. Moore
- Geetha Ravindra
- Colin Rule

Online dispute resolution (ODR)
- Colin Rule

◆

Career Development*

Neutral

- Peter S. Adler
- Johnston Barkat
- Howard Bellman
- Howard Gadlin
- David Hoffman
- Marvin E. Johnson
- Christopher W. Moore
- Lucy Moore

Academic, researcher

- Lisa Blomgren Amsler
- Jacqueline N. Font-Guzmán
- Chris Honeyman
- Carol Izumi
- Homer C. La Rue
- Lela Porter Love
- Ian Macduff
- Bernie Mayer
- Carrie Menkel-Meadow
- Andrea Kupfer Schneider
- Thomas J. Stipanowich
- Ellen Waldman
- Nancy A. Welsh

---

* This categorization reflects the authors' primary roles at the time they wrote their chapters. Many authors who are now primarily neutrals also serve, or have served, as professors and have led dispute resolution organizations or programs. Similarly, most of the authors who are now academics or researchers also serve, or have served, as neutrals on a regular basis. Finally, those who are now primarily administrators serve, or have served, as neutrals, academics and researchers.

Program administrator
- Geetha Ravindra
- Colin Rule

Culture
Bicultural US experience
- Johnston Barkat (Indian/Pakistani American)
- Jacqueline N. Font-Guzmán (Caribbean, Latin American)
- Carol Izumi (Japanese American)
- Marvin E. Johnson (African American)
- Homer C. La Rue (African American)
- Geetha Ravindra (Indian-American)

Immersion in another culture
- Peter S. Adler (Peace Corps, India)
- Lucy Moore (Justice of the Peace, Navajo Nation)
- Colin Rule (Peace Corps, Eritrea)

Gateways to the Field
Labor-management
- Lisa Blomgren Amsler
- Howard Bellman
- Chris Honeyman
- Marvin E. Johnson
- Homer C. La Rue

Law
- Lisa Blomgren Amsler

- Howard Bellman
- Jacqueline N. Font-Guzmán
- David Hoffman
- Carol Izumi
- Marvin E. Johnson
- Homer C. La Rue
- Lela Porter Love
- Ian Macduff
- Carrie Menkel-Meadow
- Geetha Ravindra
- Andrea Kupfer Schneider
- Thomas J. Stipanowich
- Ellen Waldman
- Nancy A. Welsh

Psychology, sociology
- Peter S. Adler
- Johnston Barkat
- Howard Gadlin
- Ian Macduff
- Bernie Mayer

Social activism, community organizing
- Howard Gadlin
- Carol Izumi
- Bernie Mayer
- Carrie Menkel-Meadow
- Christopher W. Moore
- Lucy Moore

Generations
First wave – founders, early entrants

- Peter S. Adler
- Howard Bellman
- Howard Gadlin
- Marvin E. Johnson
- Ian Macduff
- Bernie Mayer
- Carrie Menkel-Meadow
- Christopher W. Moore
- Lucy Moore
- Thomas J. Stipanowich

Second wave – institutionalizers, reformers, researchers

- Lisa Blomgren Amsler
- Johnston Barkat
- David Hoffman
- Chris Honeyman
- Carol Izumi
- Homer C. La Rue
- Lela Porter Love
- Geetha Ravindra
- Ellen Waldman
- Nancy A. Welsh

New generation

- Jacqueline N. Font-Guzmán
- Colin Rule
- Andrea Kupfer Schneider

Institutional Contexts for Conflict Resolution

- Lisa Blomgren Amsler (USPS)

- Johnston Barkat (higher education, international agencies)
- Howard Bellman (state agencies)
- Howard Gadlin (higher education, NIH)
- Chris Honeyman (NLRB, WERC)
- Lela Porter Love (courts)
- Carrie Menkel-Meadow (courts, international agencies)
- Geetha Ravindra (courts, international agencies)
- Ellen Waldman (courts)
- Nancy A. Welsh (courts)

About the Editors

Howard Gadlin retired in 2015 after 17 years as ombudsman and director of the Center for Cooperative Resolution at the National Institutes of Health. From 1992 through 1998, he was university ombudsperson and adjunct professor of education at the University of California at Los Angeles, where he was also director of the UCLA Conflict Mediation Program and co-director of the Center for the Study and Resolution of Interethnic/Interracial Conflict. Before moving to Los Angeles, Gadlin was ombuds and professor of psychology at the University of Massachusetts at Amherst. Gadlin is past president of the University and College Ombuds Association and of The Ombudsman Association and past chair of the Coalition of Federal Ombudsman. With colleagues, he has written *Collaboration and Team Science: A Field Guide* (2nd ed., 2018) and *The Minimal Family* (1992). He has authored articles and chapters on scientific teams, mediation among scientists, mediation of harassment and discrimination in the workplace, the ombuds role, and cultural dynamics in conflict resolution.

Nancy A. Welsh is professor of law and director of the Dispute Resolution Program of Texas A&M University School of Law. She was previously the William Trickett Faculty Scholar and professor of law at Penn State University, Dickinson School of Law. Welsh has written more than 60 articles and chapters that have appeared in law reviews, professional publications, and books. Welsh is also co-author of the fourth, fifth, and sixth editions of *Dispute Resolution and Lawyers* (2009, 2014, and 2019). She succeeded Harvard Law Professor Frank Sander as co-chair of the Editorial Board of the *Dispute Resolution Magazine*, conducted research as a Fulbright Scholar in the Netherlands, and served as chair of both the ABA Section of Dispute Resolution and the AALS Alternative Dispute Resolution Section. Before joining the legal academy, she was the executive director of Mediation Center in Minnesota and practiced law with Leonard, Street and Deinard.

www.ingramcontent.com/pod-product-compliance
Lightning Source LLC
Chambersburg PA
CBHW060512230426
43665CB00013B/1491